Network Troubleshooting Tools

Network Troubleshooting Tools

Joseph D. Sloan

O'REILLY®

Beijing · Cambridge · Farnham · Köln · Paris · Sebastopol · Taipei · Tokyo

Network Troubleshooting Tools
by Joseph D. Sloan

Published by O'Reilly & Associates, Inc., 101 Morris Street, Sebastopol, CA 95472.

Editors: Robert Denn and Mike Loukides

Production Editor: Catherine Morris

Cover Designer: Emma Colby

Printing History:

August 2001: First Edition.

Library of Congress Cataloging-in-Publication Data

Sloan, Joe.
   Network Troubleshooting Tools / Joe Sloan.--1st ed. p. cm.
   Includes bibliographical references and index.
   ISBN 0-596-00186-X
   1. Computer networks--Maintenance and repair 2. Computer networks--Management.
   I. Title.

TK5105.5 .S557 2001
004.6--dc21   2001035422

Table of Contents

Preface

This book is not a general introduction to network troubleshooting. Rather, it is about one aspect of troubleshooting—information collection. This book is a tutorial introduction to tools and techniques for collecting information about computer networks. It should be particularly useful when dealing with network problems, but the tools and techniques it describes are not limited to troubleshooting. Many can and should be used on a regular basis regardless of whether you are having problems.

Some of the tools I have selected may be a bit surprising to many. I strongly believe that the best approach to troubleshooting is to be proactive, and the tools I discuss reflect this belief. Basically, if you don't understand how your network works before you have problems, you will find it very difficult to diagnose problems when they occur. Many of the tools described here should be used before you have problems. As such, these tools could just as easily be classified as network management or network performance analysis tools.

This book does not attempt to catalog every possible tool. There are simply too many tools already available, and the number is growing too rapidly. Rather, this book focuses on the tools that I believe are the most useful, a collection that should help in dealing with almost any problem you see. I have tried to include pointers to other relevant tools when there wasn't space to discuss them. In many cases, I have described more than one tool for a particular job. It is extremely rare for two tools to have exactly the same features. One tool may be more useful than another, depending on circumstances. And, because of the differences in operating systems, a specific tool may not be available on every system. It is worth knowing the alternatives.

The book is about freely available Unix tools. Many are open source tools covered by GNU- or BSD-style licenses. In selecting tools, my first concern has been availability. I have given the highest priority to the standard Unix utilities. Next in priority are tools available as packages or ports for FreeBSD or Linux. Tools requiring separate compilation or available only as binaries were given a lower priority since these may be available on fewer systems. In some cases, PC-only tools and commercial tools are noted but are not discussed in detail. The bulk of the book is specific to Ethernet and TCP/IP, but the general approach and many of the tools can be used with other technologies.

While this is a book about Unix tools, at the end of most of the chapters I have included a brief section for Microsoft Windows users. These sections are included since even small networks usually include a few computers running Windows. These sections are not, even in the wildest of fantasies, meant to be definitive. They are provided simply as starting points—a quick overview of what is available.

Finally, this book describes a wide range of tools. Many of these tools are designed to do one thing and are often overlooked because of their simplicity. Others are extremely complex tools or sets of tools. I have not attempted to provide a comprehensive treatment for each tool discussed. Some of these tools can be extremely complex when used to their fullest. Some have manuals and other documentation that easily exceed the size of this book. Most have additional documentation that you will want to retrieve once you begin using them.

My goal is to make you aware of the tools and to provide you with enough information that you can decide which ones may be the most useful to you and in what context so that you can get started using the tools. Each chapter centers on a collection of related tasks or problems and tools useful for dealing with these tasks. The discussion is limited to features that are relevant to the problem being discussed. Consequently, the same tool may be discussed in several places throughout the book.

Please be warned: the suitability or behavior of these tools on your system cannot be guaranteed. While the material in this book is presented in good faith, neither the author nor O'Reilly & Associates makes any explicit or implied warranty as to the behavior or suitability of these tools. We strongly urge you to assess and evaluate these tool as appropriate for your circumstances.

Audience

This book is written primarily for individuals new to network administration. It should also be useful to those of you who have inherited responsibility for existing systems and networks set up by others. This book is designed to help you acquire the additional information you need to do your job.

Unfortunately, the book may also appeal to crackers. I truly regret this and wish there were a way to present this material to limit its worth to crackers. I never met a system manager or network administrator who wasn't overworked. Time devoted to security is time stolen from providing new services to users or improving existing services. There simply is no valid justification for cracking. I can only hope that the positive uses for the information I provide will outweigh the inevitable malicious uses to which it may be put. I would feel much better if crackers would forego buying this book.

In writing this book, I attempted to write the sort of book I often wished I had when I was learning. Certainly, there are others who are more knowledgeable and better prepared to write this book. But they never seemed to get around to it. They have written pieces of this book, a chapter here or a tutorial there, for which I am both immensely thankful and greatly indebted.

I see this book as a work in progress. I hope that the response to it will make future expanded editions possible. You can help by sending me your comments and corrections. I would particularly like to hear about new tools and about how you have used the tools described here to solve your problems. Perhaps some of the experts who should have written this book will share their wisdom! While I can't promise to respond to your email, I will read it. You can contact me through O'Reilly Book Support at *booktech@oreilly.com*.

Organization

There are 12 chapters and 2 appendixes in this book. The book begins with individual network hosts, discusses network connections next, and then considers networks as a whole.

It is unlikely that every chapter in the book will be of equal interest to you. The following outline will give you an overview of the book so you can select the chapters of greatest interest and either skim or skip over the rest.

Chapter 1, *Network Management and Troubleshooting*

> This chapter attempts to describe network management and troubleshooting in an administrative context. It discusses the need for network analysis and probing tools, their appropriate and inappropriate uses, professionalism in general, documentation practices, and the economic ramifications of troubleshooting. If you are familiar with the general aspects of network administration, you may want to skip this chapter.

Chapter 2, *Host Configurations*

> Chapter 2 is a review of tools and techniques used to configure or determine the configuration of a networked host. The primary focus is on built-in

utilities. If you are well versed in Unix system administration, you can safely skip this chapter.

Chapter 3, *Connectivity Testing*

Chapter 3 describes tools and techniques to test basic point-to-point and end-to-end network connectivity. It begins with a brief discussion of cabling. A discussion of *ping*, *ping* variants, and problems with *ping* follows. Even if you are very familiar with *ping*, you may want to skim over the discussion of the *ping* variants.

Chapter 4, *Path Characteristics*

This chapter focuses on assessing the nature and quality of end-to-end connections. After a discussion of *traceroute*, a tool for decomposing a path into individual links, the primary focus is on tools that measure link performance. This chapter covers some lesser known tools, so even a seasoned network administrator may find a few useful tools and tricks.

Chapter 5, *Packet Capture*

This chapter describes tools and techniques for capturing traffic on a network, primarily *tcpdump* and *ethereal*, although a number of other utilities are briefly mentioned. Using this chapter requires the greatest understanding of Internet protocols. But, in my opinion, this is the most important chapter in the book. Skip it at your own risk.

Chapter 6, *Device Discovery and Mapping*

This chapter begins with a general discussion of management tools. It then focuses on a few tools, such as *nmap* and *arpwatch*, that are useful in piecing together information about a network. After a brief discussion of network management extensions provided for Perl and Tcl/Tk, it concludes with a discussion of route and network discovery using *tkined*.

Chapter 7, *Device Monitoring with SNMP*

Chapter 7 focuses on device monitoring. It begins with a brief review of SNMP. Next, a discussion of NET SNMP (formerly UCD SNMP) demonstrates the basics of SNMP. The chapter continues with a brief description of using *scotty* to collect SNMP information. Finally, it describes additional features of *tkined*, including network monitoring. In one sense, this chapter is a hands-on tutorial for using SNMP. If you are not familiar with SNMP, you will definitely want to read this chapter.

Chapter 8, *Performance Measurement Tools*

This chapter is concerned with monitoring and measuring network behavior over time. The stars of this chapter are *ntop* and *mrtg*. I also briefly describe using SNMP tools to retrieve RMON data. This chapter assumes that you have a thorough knowledge of SNMP. If you don't, go back and read Chapter 7.

Chapter 9, *Testing Connectivity Protocols*
   This chapter describes several types of tools for examining the behavior of low-level connectivity protocols, protocols at the data link and network levels, including tools for custom packet generation and load testing. The chapter concludes with a brief discussion of emulation and simulation tools. You probably will not use these tools frequently and can safely skim this chapter the first time through.

Chapter 10, *Application-Level Tools*
   Chapter 10 looks at several of the more common application-level protocols and describes tools that may be useful when you are faced with a problem with one of these protocols. Unless you currently face an application-level problem, you can skim this chapter for now.

Chapter 11, *Miscellaneous Tools*
   This chapter describes a number of different tools that are not really network troubleshooting or management tools but rather are tools that can ease your life as a network administrator. You'll want to read the sections in this chapter that discuss tools you aren't already familiar with.

Chapter 12, *Troubleshooting Strategies*
   When dealing with a complex problem, no single tool is likely to meet all your needs. This last chapter attempts to show how the different tools can be used together to troubleshoot and analyze performance. No new tools are introduced in this chapter.

   Arguably, this chapter should have come at the beginning of the book. I included it at the end so that I could name specific tools without too many forward references. If you are familiar with general troubleshooting techniques, you can safely skip this chapter. Alternately, if you need a quick review of troubleshooting techniques and don't mind references to tools you aren't familiar with, you might jump ahead to this chapter.

Appendix A, *Software Sources*
   This appendix begins with a brief discussion of installing software and general software sources. This discussion is followed by an alphabetical listing of those tools mentioned in this book, with Internet addresses when feasible. Beware, many of the URLs in this section will be out of date by the time you read this. Nonetheless, these URLs will at least give you a starting point on where to begin looking.

Appendix B, *Resources and References*
   This appendix begins with a discussion of different sources of information. Next, it discusses books by topic, followed by an alphabetical listing of those books mentioned in this book.

Conventions

This book uses the following typographical conventions:

Italics

> For program names, filenames, system names, email addresses, and URLs and for emphasizing new terms when first defined

`Constant width`

> In examples showing the output from programs, the contents of files, or literal information

`Constant-width italics`

> General syntax and items that should be replaced in expressions

---

Indicates a tip, suggestion, or general note.

Indicates a warning or caution.

Acknowledgments

This book would not have been possible without the help of many people. First on the list are the toolsmiths who created the tools described here. The number and quality of the tools that are available is truly remarkable. We all owe a considerable debt to the people who selflessly develop these tools.

I have been very fortunate that many of my normal duties have overlapped significantly with tasks related to writing this book. These duties have included setting up and operating Lander University's networking laboratory and evaluating tools for use in teaching. For their help with the laboratory, I gratefully acknowledge Lander's Department of Computing Services, particularly Anthony Aven, Mike Henderson, and Bill Screws. This laboratory was funded in part by a National Science Foundation grant, DUE–9980366. I gratefully acknowledge the support the National Science Foundation has given to Lander. I have also benefited from conversations with the students and faculty at Lander, particularly Jim Crabtree. I would never have gotten started on this project without the help and encouragement of Jerry Wilson. Jerry, I owe you lunch (and a lot more).

This book has benefited from the help of numerous people within the O'Reilly organization. In particular, the support given by Robert Denn, Mike Loukides, and Rob Romano, to name only a few, has been exceptional. After talking with authors working with other publishers, I consider myself very fortunate in working with technically astute people from the start. If you are thinking about writing a technical book, O'Reilly is a publisher to consider.

The reviewers for this book have done an outstanding job. Thanks go to John Archie, Anthony Aven, Jon Forrest, and Kevin and Diana Mullet. They cannot be faulted for not turning a sow's ear into a silk purse.

It seems every author always acknowledges his or her family. It has almost become a cliché, but that doesn't make it any less true. This book would not have been possible without the support and patience of my family, who have endured more that I should have ever asked them to endure. Thank you.

1

Network Management and Troubleshooting

The first step in diagnosing a network problem is to collect information. This includes collecting information from your users as to the nature of the problems they are having, and it includes collecting data from your network. Your success will depend, in large part, on your efficiency in collecting this information and on the quality of the information you collect. This book is about tools you can use and techniques and strategies to optimize their use. Rather than trying to cover all aspects of troubleshooting, this book focuses on this first crucial step, data collection.

There is an extraordinary variety of tools available for this purpose, and more become available daily. Very capable people are selflessly devoting enormous amounts of time and effort to developing these tools. We all owe a tremendous debt to these individuals. But with the variety of tools available, it is easy to be overwhelmed. Fortunately, while the number of tools is large, data collection need not be overwhelming. A small number of tools can be used to solve most problems. This book centers on a core set of freely available tools, with pointers to additional tools that might be needed in some circumstances.

This first chapter has two goals. Although general troubleshooting is not the focus of the book, it seems worthwhile to quickly review troubleshooting techniques. This review is followed by an examination of troubleshooting from a broader administrative context—using troubleshooting tools in an effective, productive, and responsible manner. This part of the chapter includes a discussion of documentation practices, personnel management and professionalism, legal and ethical concerns, and economic considerations. General troubleshooting is revisited in Chapter 12, once we have discussed available tools. If you are already familiar with these topics, you may want to skim or even skip this chapter.

General Approaches to Troubleshooting

Troubleshooting is a complex process that is best learned through experience. This section looks briefly at how troubleshooting is done in order to see how these tools fit into the process. But while every problem is different, a key step is collecting information.

Clearly, the best way to approach troubleshooting is to avoid it. If you never have problems, you will have nothing to correct. Sound engineering practices, redundancy, documentation, and training can help. But regardless of how well engineered your system is, things break. You can avoid troubleshooting, but you can't escape it.

It may seem unnecessary to say, but go for the quick fixes first. As long as you don't fixate on them, they won't take long. Often the first thing to try is resetting the system. Many problems can be resolved in this way. Bit rot, cosmic rays, or the alignment of the planets may result in the system entering some strange state from which it can't exit. If the problem really is a fluke, resetting the system may resolve the problem, and you may never see it again. This may not seem very satisfying, but you can take your satisfaction in going home on time instead.

Keep in mind that there are several different levels in resetting a system. For software, you can simply restart the program, or you may be able to send a signal to the program so that it reloads its initialization file. From your users' perspective, this is the least disruptive approach. Alternately, you might restart the operating system but without cycling the power, i.e., do a *warm reboot*. Finally, you might try a *cold reboot* by cycling the power.

You should be aware, however, that there can be some dangers in resetting a system. For example, it is possible to inadvertently make changes to a system so that it can't reboot. If you realize you have done this in time, you can correct the problem. Once you have shut down the system, it may be too late. If you don't have a backup boot disk, you will have to rebuild the system. These are, fortunately, rare circumstances and usually happen only when you have been making major changes to a system.

When making changes to a system, remember that scheduled maintenance may involve restarting a system. You may want to test changes you have made, including their impact on a system reset, prior to such maintenance to ensure that there are no problems. Otherwise, the system may fail when restarted during the scheduled maintenance. If this happens, you will be faced with the difficult task of deciding which of several different changes are causing problems.

Resetting the system is certainly worth trying once. Doing it more than once is a different matter. With some systems, this becomes a way of life. An operating system that doesn't provide adequate memory protection will frequently become wedged so that rebooting is the only option.* Sometimes you may want to limp along resetting the system occasionally rather than dealing with the problem. In a university setting, this might get you through exam week to a time when you can be more relaxed in your efforts to correct the underlying problem. Or, if the system is to be replaced in the near future, the effort may not be justified. Usually, however, when rebooting becomes a way of life, it is time for more decisive action.

Swapping components and reinstalling software is often the next thing to try. If you have the spare components, this can often resolve problems immediately. Even if you don't have spares, switching components to see if the problem follows the equipment can be a simple first test. Reinstalling software can be much more problematic. This can often result in configuration errors that will worsen problems. The old, installed version of the software can make getting a new, clean installation impossible. But if the install is simple or you have a clear understanding of exactly how to configure the software, this can be a relatively quick fix.

While these approaches often work, they aren't what we usually think of as troubleshooting. You certainly don't need the tools described in this book to do them. Once you have exhausted the quick solutions, it is time to get serious. First, you must understand the problem, if possible. Problems that are not understood are usually not fixed, just postponed.

One standard admonition is to ask the question "has anything changed recently?" Overwhelmingly, most problems relate to changes to a working system. If you can temporarily change things back and the problem goes away, you have confirmed your diagnosis.

Admittedly, this may not help with an installation where everything is new. But even a new installation can and should be grown. Pieces can be installed and tested. New pieces of equipment can then be added incrementally. When this approach is taken, the question of what has changed once again makes sense.

Another admonition is to change only one thing at a time and then to test thoroughly after each change. This is certainly good advice when dealing with routine failures. But this approach will not apply if you are dealing with a system failure. (See the upcoming sidebar on system failures.) Also, if you do find something that you know is wrong but fixing it doesn't fix your problem, do you really want to change it back? In this case, it is often better to make a note of the additional changes you have made and then proceed with your troubleshooting.

A key element to successful debugging is to control the focus of your investigation so that you are really dealing with the problem. You can usually focus better

---

* Do you know what operating system I'm tactfully not naming?

if you can break the problem into pieces. Swapping components, as mentioned previously, is an example of this approach. This technique is known by several names—problem decomposition, divide and conquer, binary search, and so on. This approach is applicable to all kinds of troubleshooting. For example, when your car won't start, first decide whether you have an electrical or fuel supply problem. Then proceed accordingly. Chapter 12 outlines a series of specific steps you might want to consider.

System Failures

The troubleshooting I have described so far can be seen roughly as dealing with *normal failures* (although there may be nothing terribly normal about them). A second general class of problems is known as *system failures*. System failures are problems that stem from the interaction of the parts of a complex system in unexpected ways. They are most often seen when two or more subsystems fail at about the same time and in ways that interact. However, system failures can result through interaction of subsystems without any ostensible failure in any of the subsystems.

A classic example of a system failure can be seen in the movie *China Syndrome*. In one scene the reactor scrams, the pumps shut down, and the water-level indicator on a strip-chart recorder sticks. The water level in the reactor becomes dangerously low due to the pump shutdown, but the problem is not recognized because the indicator gives misleading information. These two near-simultaneous failures conceal the true state of the reactor.

System failures are most pernicious in systems with tight coupling between subsystems and subsystems that are linked in nonlinear or nonobvious ways. Debugging a system failure can be extremely difficult. Many of the more standard approaches simply don't work. The strategy of decomposing the system into subsystems becomes difficult, because the symptoms misdirect your efforts. Moreover, in extreme cases, each subsystem may be operating correctly—the problem stems entirely from the unexpected interactions.

If you suspect you have a system failure, the best approach, when feasible, is to substitute entire subsystems. Your goal should not be to look for a restored functioning system, but to look for *changes* in the symptoms. Such changes indicate that you may have found one of the subsystems involved. (Conversely, if you are working with a problem and the symptoms change when a subsystem is replaced, this is strong indication of a system failure.)

Unfortunately, if the problem stems from unexpected interaction of nonfailing systems, even this approach will not work. These are extremely difficult problems to diagnose. Each problem must be treated as a unique, special problem. But again, an important first step is collecting information.

Need for Troubleshooting Tools

The best time to prepare for problems is before you have them. It may sound trite, but if you don't understand the normal behavior of your network, you will not be able to identify anomalous behavior. For the proper management of your system, you must have a clear understanding of the current behavior and performance of your system. If you don't know the kinds of traffic, the bottlenecks, or the growth patterns for your network, then you will not be able to develop sensible plans. If you don't know the normal behavior, you will not be able to recognize a problem's symptoms when you see them. Unless you have made a conscious, aggressive effort to understand your system, you probably don't understand it. All networks contain surprises, even for the experienced administrator. You only have to look a little harder.

It might seem strange to some that a network administrator would need some of the tools described in this book, and that he wouldn't already know the details that some of these tools provide. But there are a number of reasons why an administrator may be quite ignorant of his network.

With the rapid growth of the Internet, turnkey systems seem to have grown in popularity. A fundamental assumption of these systems is that they are managed by an inexperienced administrator or an administrator who doesn't want to be bothered by the details of the system. Documentation is almost always minimal. For example, early versions of Sun Microsystems' Netra Internet servers, by default, did not install the Unix manpages and came with only a few small manuals. Print services were disabled by default.

This is not a condemnation of turnkey systems. They can be a real blessing to someone who needs to go online quickly, someone who never wants to be bothered by such details, or someone who can outsource the management of her system. But if at some later time she wants to know what her turnkey system is doing, it may be up to her to discover that for herself. This is particularly likely if she ever wants to go beyond the basic services provided by the system or if she starts having problems.

Other nonturnkey systems may be customized, often heavily. Of course, all these changes should be carefully documented. However, an administrator may inherit a poorly documented system. (And, of course, sometimes we do this to ourselves.) If you find yourself in this situation, you will need to discover (or rediscover) your system for yourself.

In many organizations, responsibilities may be highly partitioned. One group may be responsible for infrastructure such as wiring, another for network hardware, and yet another for software. In some environments, particularly universities, networks may be a distributed responsibility. You may have very little control, if any, over what is connected to the network. This isn't necessarily bad—it's the way universities work. But rogue systems on your network can have annoying consequences. In this situation, probably the best approach is to talk to the system administrator or user responsible for the system. Often he will be only too happy to discuss his configuration. The implications of what he is doing may have completely escaped him. Developing a good relationship with power users may give you an extra set of eyes on your network. And, it is easier to rely on the system administrator to tell you what he is doing than to repeatedly probe the network to discover changes. But if this fails, as it sometimes does, you may have to resort to collecting the data yourself.

Sometimes there may be some unexpected, unauthorized, or even covert changes to your network. Well-meaning individuals can create problems when they try to help you out by installing equipment themselves. For example, someone might try installing a new computer on the network by copying the network configuration from another machine, including its IP address. At other times, some "volunteer administrator" simply has her own plans for your network.

Finally, almost to a person, network administrators must teach themselves as they go. Consequently, for most administrators, these tools have an educational value as well as an administrative value. They provide a way for administrators to learn more about their networks. For example, protocol analyzers like *ethereal* provide an excellent way to learn the inner workings of a protocol like TCP/IP. Often, more than one of these reasons may apply. Whatever the reason, it is not unusual to find yourself reading your configuration files and probing your systems.

Troubleshooting and Management

Troubleshooting does not exist in isolation from network management. How you manage your network will determine in large part how you deal with problems. A proactive approach to management can greatly simplify problem resolution. The remainder of this chapter describes several important management issues. Coming to terms with these issues should, in the long run, make your life easier.

Documentation

As a new administrator, your first step is to assess your existing resources and begin creating new resources. Software sources, including the tools discussed in this book, are described and listed in Appendix A. Other sources of information are described in Appendix B.

The most important source of information is the local documentation created by you or your predecessor. In a properly maintained network, there should be some kind of log about the network, preferably with sections for each device. In many networks, this will be in an abysmal state. Almost no one likes documenting or thinks he has the time required to do it. It will be full of errors, out of date, and incomplete. Local documentation should always be read with a healthy degree of skepticism. But even incomplete, erroneous documentation, if treated as such, may be of value. There are probably no intentional errors, just careless mistakes and errors of omission. Even flawed documentation can give you some sense of the history of the system. Problems frequently occur due to multiple conflicting changes to a system. Software that may have been only partially removed can have lingering effects. Homegrown documentation may be the quickest way to discover what may have been on the system.

While the creation and maintenance of documentation may once have been someone else's responsibility, it is now your responsibility. If you are not happy with the current state of your documentation, it is up to you to update it and adopt policies so the next administrator will not be muttering about you the way you are muttering about your predecessors.

There are a couple of sets of standard documentation that, at a minimum, you will always want to keep. One is purchase information, the other a change log. Purchase information includes sales information, licenses, warranties, service contracts, and related information such as serial numbers. An inventory of equipment, software, and documentation can be very helpful. When you unpack a system, you might keep a list of everything you receive and date all documentation and software. (A changeable rubber date stamp and ink pad can help with this last task.) Manufacturers can do a poor job of distinguishing one version of software and its documentation from the next. Dates can be helpful in deciding which version of the documentation applies when you have multiple systems or upgrades. Documentation has a way of ending up in someone's personal library, never to be seen again, so a list of what you should have can be very helpful at times.

Keep in mind, there are a number of ways software can enter your system other than through purchase orders. Some software comes through CD-ROM subscription services, some comes in over the Internet, some is bundled with the operating system, some comes in on a CD-ROM in the back of a book, some is brought from home, and so forth. Ideally, you should have some mechanism to track software. For example, for downloads from the Internet, be sure to keep a log including a list identifying filenames, dates, and sources.

You should also keep a change log for each major system. Record every significant change or problem you have with the system. Each entry should be dated. Even if some entries no longer seem relevant, you should keep them in your log.

For instance, if you have installed and later removed a piece of software on a server, there may be lingering configuration changes that you are not aware of that may come to haunt you years later. This is particularly true if you try to reinstall the program but could even be true for a new program as well.

Beyond these two basic sets of documentation, you can divide the documentation you need to keep into two general categories—configuration documentation and process documentation. Configuration documentation statically describes a system. It assumes that the steps involved in setting up the system are well understood and need no further comments, i.e., that configuration information is sufficient to reconfigure or reconstruct the system. This kind of information can usually be collected at any time. Ironically, for that reason, it can become so easy to put off that it is never done.

Process documentation describes the steps involved in setting up a device, installing software, or resolving a problem. As such, it is best written while you are doing the task. This creates a different set of collection problems. Here the stress from the task at hand often prevents you from documenting the process.

The first question you must ask is what you want to keep. This may depend on the circumstances and which tools you are using. Static configuration information might include lists of IP addresses and Ethernet addresses, network maps, copies of server configuration files, switch configuration settings such as VLAN partitioning by ports, and so on.

When dealing with a single device, the best approach is probably just a simple copy of the configuration. This can be either printed or saved as a disk file. This will be a personal choice based on which you think is easiest to manage. You don't need to waste time prettying this up, but be sure you label and date it.

When the information spans multiple systems, such as a list of IP addresses, management of the data becomes more difficult. Fortunately, much of this information can be collected automatically. Several tools that ease the process are described in subsequent chapters, particularly in Chapter 6.

For process documentation, the best approach is to log and annotate the changes as you make them and then reconstruct the process at a later time. Chapter 11 describes some of the common Unix utilities you can use to automate documentation. You might refer to this chapter if you aren't familiar with utilities like *tee*, *script*, and *xwd*.*

---

* Admittedly these guidelines are ideals. Does anyone actually do all of this documenting? Yes, while most administrators probably don't, some do. But just because many administrators don't succeed in meeting the ideal doesn't diminish the importance of trying.

Management Practices

A fundamental assumption of this book is that troubleshooting should be proactive. It is preferable to avoid a problem than have to correct it. Proper management practices can help. While some of this section may, at first glance, seem unrelated to troubleshooting, there are fundamental connections. Management practices will determine what you can do and how you do it. This is true both for avoiding problems and for dealing with problems that can't be avoided. The remainder of this chapter reviews some of the more important management issues.

Professionalism

To effectively administer a system requires a high degree of professionalism. This includes personal honesty and ethical behavior. You should learn to evaluate yourself in an honest, objective manner. (See the later sidebar "The Peter Principle Revisited.") It also requires that you conform to the organization's mission and culture. Your network serves some higher purpose within your organization. It does not exist strictly for your benefit. You should manage the network with this in mind. This means that everything you do should be done from the perspective of a cost-benefit trade-off. It is too easy to get caught in the trap of doing something "the right way" at a higher cost than the benefits justify. Performance analysis is the key element.

The organization's mind-set or culture will have a tremendous impact on how you approach problems in general and the use of tools in particular. It will determine which tools you can use, how you can use the tools, and, most important, what you can do with the information you obtain. Within organizations, there is often a battle between openness and secrecy. The secrecy advocate believes that details of the network should be available only on a need-to-know basis, if then. She believes, not without justification, that this enhances security. The openness advocate believes that the details of a system should be open and available. This allows users to adapt and make optimal use of the system and provides a review process, giving users more input into the operation of the network.

Taken to an extreme, the secrecy advocate will suppress information that is needed by the user, making a system or network virtually unusable. Openness, taken to an extreme, will leave a network vulnerable to attack. Most people's views fall somewhere between these two extremes but often favor one position over the other. I advocate prudent openness. In most situations, it makes no sense to shut down a system because it *might* be attacked. And it is asinine not to provide users with the information they need to protect themselves. Openness among those responsible for the different systems within an organization is absolutely essential.

Ego management

We would all like to think that we are irreplaceable, and that no one else could do our jobs as well as we do. This is human nature. Unfortunately, some people take steps to make sure this is true. The most obvious way an administrator may do this is hide what he actually does and how his system works.

This can be done many ways. Failing to document the system is one approach—leaving comments out of code or configuration files is common. The goal of such an administrator is to make sure he is the only one who truly understands the system. He may try to limit others access to a system by restricting accounts or access to passwords. (This can be done to hide other types of unprofessional activities as well. If an administrator occasionally reads other users' email, he may not want anyone else to have standard accounts on the email server. If he is over-spending on equipment to gain experience with new technologies, he will not want any technically literate people knowing what equipment he is buying.)

This behavior is usually well disguised, but it is extremely common. For example, a technician may insist on doing tasks that users could or should be doing. The problem is that this keeps users dependent on the technician when it isn't necessary. This can seem very helpful or friendly on the surface. But, if you repeatedly ask for details and don't get them, there may be more to it than meets the eye.

Common justifications are security and privacy. Unless you are in a management position, there is often little you can do other than accept the explanations given. But if you are in a management position, are technically competent, and still hear these excuses from your employees, beware! You have a serious problem.

No one knows everything. Whenever information is suppressed, you lose input from individuals who don't have the information. If an employee can't control her ego, she should not be turned loose on your network with the tools described in this book. She will not share what she learns. She will only use it to further entrench herself.

The problem is basically a personnel problem and must be dealt with as such. Individuals in technical areas seem particularly prone to these problems. It may stem from enlarged egos or from insecurity. Many people are drawn to technical areas as a way to seem special. Alternately, an administrator may see information as a source of power or even a weapon. He may feel that if he shares the information, he will lose his leverage. Often individuals may not even recognize the behavior in themselves. It is just the way they have always done things and it is the way that feels right.

If you are a manager, you should deal with this problem immediately. If you can't correct the problem in short order, you should probably replace the employee. An irreplaceable employee today will be even more irreplaceable tomorrow. Sooner or later, everyone leaves—finds a better job, retires, or runs off to Poughkeepsie with an exotic dancer. In the meantime, such a person only becomes more entrenched making the eventual departure more painful. It will be better to deal with the problem now rather than later.

Legal and ethical considerations

From the perspective of tools, you must ensure that you use tools in a manner that conforms not just to the policies of your organization, but to all applicable laws as well. The tools I describe in this book can be abused, particularly in the realm of privacy. Before using them, you should make certain that your use is consistent with the policies of your organization and all applicable laws. Do you have the appropriate permission to use the tools? This will depend greatly on your role within the organization. Do not assume that just because you have access to tools that you are authorized to use them. Nor should you assume that any authorization you have is unlimited.

Packet capture software is a prime example. It allows you to examine every packet that travels across a link, including applications data and each and every header. Unless data is encrypted, it can be decoded. This means that passwords can be captured and email can be read. For this reason alone, you should be very circumspect in how you use such tools.

A key consideration is the legality of collecting such information. Unfortunately, there is a constantly changing legal morass with respect to privacy in particular and technology in general. Collecting some data may be legitimate in some circumstances but illegal in others.* This depends on factors such as the nature of your operations, what published policies you have, what assurances you have given your users, new and existing laws, and what interpretations the courts give to these laws.

It is impossible for a book like this to provide a definitive answer to the questions such considerations raise. I can, however, offer four pieces of advice:

* First, if the information you are collecting can be tied to the activities of an individual, you should consider the information highly confidential and should collect only the information that you really need. Be aware that even seemingly innocent information may be sensitive in some contexts. For example,

---

* As an example, see the CERT Advisory CA-92.19 Topic: Keystroke Logging Banner at *http://www.cert. org/advisories/CA-1992-19.html* for a discussion on keystroke logging and its legal implications.

source/destination address pairs may reveal communications between individuals that they would prefer not be made public.

- Second, place your users on notice. Let them know that you collect such information, why it is necessary, and how you use the information. Remember, however, if you give your users assurances as to how the information is used, you are then constrained by those assurances. If your management policies permit, make their prior acceptance of these policies a requirement for using the system.

- Third, you must realize that with monitoring comes obligations. In many instances, your legal culpability may be less if you don't monitor.

- Finally, don't rely on this book or what your colleagues say. Get legal advice from a lawyer who specializes in this area. Beware: many lawyers will not like to admit that they don't know everything about the law, but many aren't current with the new laws relating to technology. Also, keep in mind that even if what you are doing is strictly legal and you have appropriate authority, your actions may still not be ethical.

Economic considerations

Solutions to problems have economic consequences, so you must understand the economic implications of what you do. Knowing how to balance the cost of the time used to repair a system against the cost of replacing a system is an obvious example. Cost management is a more general issue that has important implications when dealing with failures.

One particularly difficult task for many system administrators is to come to terms with the economics of networking. As long as everything is running smoothly, the next biggest issue to upper management will be how cost effectively you are doing your job. Unless you have unlimited resources, when you overspend in one area, you take resources from another area. One definition of an engineer that I particularly like is that "an engineer is someone who can do for a dime what a fool can do for a dollar." My best guess is that overspending and buying needlessly complex systems is the single most common engineering mistake made when novice network administrators purchase network equipment.

One problem is that some traditional economic models do not apply in networking. In most engineering projects, incremental costs are less than the initial per-unit cost. For example, if a 10,000-square-foot building costs $1 million, a 15,000-square-foot building will cost somewhat less than $1.5 million. It may make sense to buy additional footage even if you don't need it right away. This is justified as "buying for the future."

The Peter Principle Revisited

In 1969, Laurence Peter and Raymond Hull published the satirical book, *The Peter Principle*. The premise of the book was that people rise to their level of incompetence. For example, a talented high school teacher might be promoted to principal, a job requiring a quite different set of skills. Even if ill suited for the job, once she has this job, she will probably remain with it. She just won't earn any new promotions. However, if she is adept at the job, she may be promoted to district superintendent, a job requiring yet another set of skills. The process of promotions will continue until she reaches her level of incompetence. At that point, she will spend the remainder of her career at that level.

While hardly a rigorous sociological principle, the book was well received because it contained a strong element of truth. In my humble opinion, the Peter Principle usually fails miserably when applied to technical areas such as networking and telecommunications. The problem is the difficulty in recognizing incompetence. If incompetence is not recognized, then an individual may rise well beyond his level of incompetence. This often happens in technical areas because there is no one in management who can judge an individual's technical competence.

Arguably, unrecognized incompetence is usually overengineering. Networking, a field of engineering, is always concerned with trade-offs between costs and benefits. An underengineered network that fails will not go unnoticed. But an overengineered network will rarely be recognizable as such. Such networks may cost many times what they should, drawing resources from other needs. But to the uninitiated, it appears as a normal, functioning network.

If a network engineer really wants the latest in new equipment when it isn't needed, who, outside of the technical personnel, will know? If this is a one-person department, or if all the members of the department can agree on what they want, no one else may ever know. It is too easy to come up with some technical mumbo jumbo if they are ever questioned.

If this seems far-fetched, I once attended a meeting where a young engineer was arguing that a particular router needed to be replaced before it became a bottleneck. He had picked out the ideal replacement, a hot new box that had just hit the market. The problem with all this was that I had recently taken measurements on the router and knew the average utilization of that "bottleneck" was less than 5% with peaks that rarely hit 40%.

This is an extreme example of why collecting information is the essential first step in network management and troubleshooting. Without accurate measurements, you can easily spend money fixing imaginary problems.

This kind of reasoning, when applied to computers and networking, leads to waste. Almost no one would go ahead and buy a computer now if they won't need it until next year. You'll be able to buy a better computer for less if you wait until you need it. Unfortunately, this same reasoning isn't applied when buying network equipment. People will often buy higher-bandwidth equipment than they need, arguing that they are preparing for the future, when it would be much more economical to buy only what is needed now and buy again in the future as needed.

Moore's Law lies at the heart of the matter. Around 1965, Gordon Moore, one of the founders of Intel, made the empirical observation that the density of integrated circuits was doubling about every 12 months, which he later revised to 24 months. Since the cost of manufacturing integrated circuits is relatively flat, this implies that, in two years, a circuit can be built with twice the functionality with no increase in cost. And, because distances are halved, the circuit runs at twice the speed—a fourfold improvement. Since the doubling applies to previous doublings, we have exponential growth.

It is generally estimated that this exponential growth with chips will go on for another 15 to 20 years. In fact, this growth is nothing new. Raymond Kurzweil, in *The Age of Spiritual Machines: When Computers Exceed Human Intelligence*, collected information on computing speeds and functionality from the beginning of the twentieth century to the present. This covers mechanical, electromechanical (relay), vacuum tube, discrete transistor, and integrated circuit technologies. Kurzweil found that exponential growth has been the norm for the last hundred years. He believes that new technologies will be developed that will extend this rate of growth well beyond the next 20 years. It is certainly true that we have seen even faster growth in disk densities and fiber-optic capacity in recent years, neither of which can be attributed to semiconductor technology.

What does this mean economically? Clearly, if you wait, you can buy more for less. But usually, waiting isn't an option. The real question is how far into the future should you invest? If the price is coming down, should you repeatedly buy for the short term or should you "invest" in the long term?

The general answer is easy to see if we look at a few numbers. Suppose that $100,000 will provide you with network equipment that will meet your anticipated bandwidth needs for the next four years. A simpleminded application of Moore's Law would say that you could wait and buy similar equipment for $25,000 in two years. Of course, such a system would have a useful life of only two additional years, not the original four. So, how much would it cost to buy just enough equipment to make it through the next two years? Following the same reasoning, about $25,000. If your growth is tracking the growth of technology,* then two years ago it would have cost $100,000 to buy four years' worth of technology. That will have fallen to about $25,000 today. Your choice: $100,000 now or $25,000 now and $25,000 in two years. This is something of a no-brainer. It is summarized in the first two lines of Table 1-1.

Table 1-1. Cost estimates

	Year 1	Year 2	Year 3	Year 4	Total
Four-year plan	$100,000	$0	$0	$0	$100,000
Two-year plan	$25,000	$0	$25,000	$0	$50,000
Four-year plan with maintenance	$112,000	$12,000	$12,000	$12,000	$148,000
Two-year plan with maintenance	$28,000	$3,000	$28,000	$3,000	$62,000
Four-year plan with maintenance and 20% MARR	$112,000	$10,000	$8,300	$6,900	$137, 200
Two-year plan with maintenance and 20% MARR	$28,000	$2,500	$19,500	$1,700	$51,700

If this argument isn't compelling enough, there is the issue of maintenance. As a general rule of thumb, service contracts on equipment cost about 1% of the purchase price per month. For $100,000, that is $12,000 a year. For $25,000, this is $3,000 per year. Moore's Law doesn't apply to maintenance for several reasons:

- A major part of maintenance is labor costs and these, if anything, will go up.

- The replacement parts will be based on older technology and older (and higher) prices.

- The mechanical parts of older systems, e.g., fans, connectors, and so on, are all more likely to fail.

- There is more money to be made selling new equipment so there is no incentive to lower maintenance prices.

Thus, the $12,000 a year for maintenance on a $100,000 system will cost $12,000 a year for all four years. The third and fourth lines of Table 1-1 summarize these numbers.

---

* This is a pretty big if, but it's reasonable for most users and organizations. Most users and organizations have selected a point in the scheme of things that seems right for them—usually the latest technology they can reasonably afford. This is why that new computer you buy always seems to cost $2500. You are buying the latest in technology, and you are trying to reach about the same distance into the future.

Yet another consideration is the time value of money. If you don't need the $25,000 until two years from now, you can invest a smaller amount now and expect to have enough to cover the costs later. So the $25,000 needed in two years is really somewhat less in terms of today's dollars. How much less depends on the rate of return you can expect on investments. For most organizations, this number is called the *minimal acceptable rate of return* (MARR). The last two lines of Table 1-1 use a MARR of 20%. This may seem high, but it is not an unusual number. As you can see, buying for the future is more than two and a half times as expensive as going for the quick fix.

Of course, all this is a gross simplification. There are a number of other important considerations even if you believe these numbers. First and foremost, Moore's Law doesn't always apply. The most important exception is infrastructure. It is not going to get any cheaper to pull cable. You should take the time to do infrastructure well; that's where you really should invest in the future.

Most of the other considerations seem to favor short-term investing. First, with short-term purchasing, you are less likely to invest in dead-end technology since you are buying later in the life cycle and will have a clearer picture of where the industry is going. For example, think about the difference two years might have made in choosing between Fast Ethernet and ATM for some organizations. For the same reason, the cost of training should be lower. You will be dealing with more familiar technology, and there will be more resources available. You will have to purchase and install equipment more often, but the equipment you replace can be reused in your network's periphery, providing additional savings.

On the downside, the equipment you buy won't have a lot of excess capacity or a very long, useful lifetime. It can be very disconcerting to nontechnical management when you keep replacing equipment. And, if you experience sudden unexpected growth, this is exactly what you will need to do. Take the time to educate upper management. If frequent changes to your equipment are particularly disruptive or if you have funding now, you may need to consider long-term purchases even if they are more expensive. Finally, don't take the two-year time frame presented here too literally. You'll discover the appropriate time frame for your network only with experience.

Other problems come when comparing plans. You must consider the total economic picture. Don't look just at the initial costs, but consider ongoing costs such as maintenance and the cost of periodic replacement. As an example, consider the following plans. Plan A has an estimated initial cost of $400,000, all for equipment. Plan B requires $150,000 for equipment and $450,000 for infrastructure upgrades. If you consider only initial costs, Plan A seems to be $200,000 cheaper. But equipment needs to be maintained and, periodically, replaced. At 1% per month, the equipment for Plan A would cost $48,000 a year to maintain, compared to $18,000 per year with Plan B. If you replace equipment a couple of times in the next decade, that will be an additional $800,000 for Plan A but only $300,000 for Plan B. As this quick, back-of-the-envelope calculation shows, the 10-year cost for Plan A was $1.68 million, while only $1.08 million for Plan B. What appeared to be $200,000 cheaper was really $600,000 more expensive. Of course, this was a very crude example, but it should convey the idea.

You shouldn't take this example too literally either. Every situation is different. In particular, you may not be comfortable deciding what is adequate surplus capacity in your network. In general, however, you are probably much better off thinking in terms of scalability than raw capacity. If you want to hedge your bets, you can make sure that high-speed interfaces are available for the router you are considering without actually buying those high-speed interfaces until needed.

How does this relate to troubleshooting? First, don't buy overly complex systems you don't really need. They will be much harder to maintain, as you can expect the complexity of troubleshooting to grow with the complexity of the systems you buy. Second, don't spend all your money on the system and forget ongoing maintenance costs. If you don't anticipate operational costs, you may not have the funds you need.

2

Host Configurations

The goal of this chapter is to review system administration from the perspective of the individual hosts on a network. This chapter presumes that you have a basic understanding of system administration. Consequently, many of the more basic issues are presented in a very cursory manner. The intent is more to jog your memory, or to fill an occasional gap, than to teach the fundamentals of system administration. If you are new to system administration, a number of the books listed in Appendix B provide excellent introductions. If, on the other hand, you are a knowledgeable system administrator, you will probably want to skim or even skip this chapter.

Chapter 1 lists several reasons why you might not know the details of your network and the computers on it. This chapter assumes that you are faced with a networked computer and need to determine or reconstruct its configuration. It should be obvious that if you don't understand how a system is configured, you will not be able to change its configuration or correct misconfigurations. The tools described in this chapter can be used to discover or change a host's configuration.

As discussed in Chapter 1, if you have documentation for the system, begin with it. The assumption here is that such documentation does not exist or that it is incomplete. The primary focus is network configuration, but many of the techniques can easily be generalized.

If you have inherited a multiuser system that has been in service for several years with many undocumented customizations, reconstructing its configuration can be an extremely involved and extended process. If your system has been compromised, the intruder has taken steps to hide her activity, and you aren't running an integrity checker like *tripwire*, it may be virtually impossible to discover all her customizations. (*tripwire* is discussed briefly in Chapter 11.) While it may not be feasible, you should at least consider reinstalling the system from scratch. While this may seem draconian, it may ultimately be much less work than fighting the same battles over and over, as often happens with compromised systems. The best way to do this is to set up a replacement system in parallel and then move everyone over. This, of course, requires a second system.

If rebuilding the system is not feasible, or if your situation isn't as extreme as that just described, then you can use the techniques described in this chapter to reconstruct the system's configuration.

Whatever your original motivation, you should examine your system's configuration on a regular basis. If for no other reason, this will help you remember how your system is configured. But there are other reasons as well. As you learn more, you will undoubtedly want to revisit your configuration to correct problems, improve security, and optimize performance. Reviewing configurations is a necessary step to ensure that your system hasn't been compromised. And, if you share management of a system, you may be forced to examine the configuration whenever communications falter.

Keep a set of notes for each system, giving both the configuration and directions for changing the configuration. Usually the best place to start is by constructing a list of what can be found where in the vendor documentation you have. This may seem pointless since this information is in the documentation. But the information you need will be spread throughout this documentation. You won't want to plow through everything every time you need to check or change something. You must create your own list. I frequently write key page numbers inside the front covers of manuals and specifics in the margins throughout the manual. For example, I'll add device names to the manpages for the *mount* command, something I always seem to need but often can't remember. (Be warned that this has the disadvantage of tying manuals to specific hardware, which could create other problems.)

When reconstructing a host's configuration, there are two basic approaches. One is to examine the system's configuration files. This can be a very protracted approach. It works well when you know what you are looking for and when you are looking for a specific detail. But it can be difficult to impossible to find all the details of the system, particularly if someone has taken steps to hide them. And some parameters are set dynamically and simply can't be discovered just from configuration files.

The alternative is to use utilities designed to give snapshots of the current state of the system. Typically, these focus on one aspect of the system, for example, listing all open files. Collectively, these utilities can give you a fairly complete picture. They tend to be easy to use and give answers quickly. But, because they may focus on only one aspect of the system, they may not provide all the information you need if used in isolation.

Clearly, by itself, neither approach is totally adequate. Where you start will depend in part on how quickly you must be up to speed and what specific problems you are facing. Each approach will be described in turn.

Utilities

Reviewing system configuration files is a necessary step that you will have to address before you can claim mastery of a system. But this can be a very time-consuming step. It is very easy to overlook one or more key files. If you are under time pressure to resolve a problem, configuration files are not the best place to start.

Even if you plan to jump into the configuration files, you will probably want a quick overview of the current state of the system before you begin. For this reason, we will examine status and configuration utilities first. This approach has the advantage of being pretty much the same from one version of Unix to the next. With configuration files, the differences among the various flavors of Unix can be staggering. Even when the files have the same functionality and syntax, they can go by different names or be in different directories. Certainly, using these utilities is much simpler than looking at kernel configuration files.

 The output provided by these utilities may vary considerably from system to system and will depend heavily on which options are used. In practice, this should present no real problem. Don't be alarmed if the output on your system is formatted differently.

---

ps

The first thing any system administrator should do on a new system is run the *ps* command. You are probably already familiar with *ps* so I won't spend much time on it. The *ps* command lists which processes are running on the system. Here is an example:

```
bsd4# ps -aux
USER      PID %CPU %MEM   VSZ  RSS  TT  STAT STARTED      TIME COMMAND
root     6590 22.0  2.1   924  616  ??  R    11:14AM   0:09.80 inetd: chargen [2
root        1  0.0  0.6   496  168  ??  Ss   Fri09AM   0:00.03 /sbin/init --
root        2  0.0  0.0     0    0  ??  DL   Fri09AM   0:00.52 (pagedaemon)
root        3  0.0  0.0     0    0  ??  DL   Fri09AM   0:00.00 (vmdaemon)
root        4  0.0  0.0     0    0  ??  DL   Fri09AM   0:44.05 (syncer)
root      100  0.0  1.7   820  484  ??  Ss   Fri09AM   0:02.14 syslogd
daemon    109  0.0  1.5   828  436  ??  Is   Fri09AM   0:00.02 /usr/sbin/portmap
root      141  0.0  2.1   924  616  ??  Ss   Fri09AM   0:00.51 inetd
root      144  0.0  1.7   980  500  ??  Is   Fri09AM   0:03.14 cron
```

```
root      150  0.0  2.8  1304   804  ??   Is    Fri09AM   0:02.59  sendmail: accepti
root      173  0.0  1.3   788   368  ??   Is    Fri09AM   0:01.84  moused -p /dev/ps
root      213  0.0  1.8   824   508  v1   Is+   Fri09AM   0:00.02  /usr/libexec/gett
root      214  0.0  1.8   824   508  v2   Is+   Fri09AM   0:00.02  /usr/libexec/gett
root      457  0.0  1.8   824   516  v0   Is+   Fri10AM   0:00.02  /usr/libexec/gett
root     6167  0.0  2.4  1108   712  ??   Ss    4:10AM    0:00.48  telnetd
jsloan   6168  0.0  0.9   504   252  p0   Is    4:10AM    0:00.09  -sh (sh)
root     6171  0.0  1.1   464   320  p0   S     4:10AM    0:00.14  -su (csh)
root        0  0.0  0.0     0     0  ??   DLs   Fri09AM   0:00.17  (swapper)
root     6597  0.0  0.8   388   232  p0   R+    11:15AM   0:00.00  ps -aux
```

In this example, the first and last columns are the most interesting since they give the owners and the processes, along with their arguments. In this example, the lines, and consequently the arguments, have been truncated, but this is easily avoided. Running processes of interest include *portmap, inetd, sendmail, telnetd,* and *chargen.*

There are a number of options available to *ps,* although they vary from implementation to implementation. In this example, run under FreeBSD, the parameters used were *-aux.* This combination shows all users' processes (*-a*), including those without controlling terminals (*-x*), in considerable detail (*-u*). The options *-ax* will provide fewer details but show more of the command-line arguments. Alternately, you can use the *-w* option to extend the displayed information to 132 columns. With AT&T-derived systems, the options *-ef* do pretty much the same thing. Interestingly, Linux supports both sets of options. You will need to precede AT&T-style options with a hyphen. This isn't required for BSD options. You can do it either way with Solaris. */usr/bin/ps* follows the AT&T conventions, while */usr/ucb/ps* supports the BSD options.

While *ps* quickly reveals individual processes, it gives a somewhat incomplete picture if interpreted naively. For example, the *inetd* daemon is one source of confusion. *inetd* is used to automatically start services on a system as they are needed. Rather than start a separate process for each service that might eventually be run, the *inetd* daemon runs on their behalf. When a connection request arrives, *inetd* will start the requested service. Since some network services like *ftp, telnet,* and *finger* are usually started this way, *ps* will show processes for them only when they are currently running. If *ps* doesn't list them, it doesn't mean they aren't available; they just aren't currently running.

For example, in the previous listing, *chargen* was started by *inetd.* We can see *chargen* in this instance because it was a running process when *ps* was run. But, this particular test system was configured to run a number of additional services via *inetd* (as determined by the */etc/inetd.conf* configuration file). None of these other services show up under *ps* because, technically, they aren't currently running. Yet, these other services will be started automatically by *inetd,* so they are available services.

In addition to showing what is running, *ps* is a useful diagnostic tool. It quickly reveals defunct processes or multiple instances of the same process, thereby pointing out configuration problems and similar issues. %MEM and %CPU can tell you a lot about resource usage and can provide crucial information if you have resource starvation. Or you can use *ps* to identify rogue processes that are spawning other processes by looking at processes that share a common PPID. Once you are comfortable with the usual uses, it is certainly worth revisiting *ps* periodically to learn more about its other capabilities, as this brief discussion just scratches the surface of *ps*.

top

Although less ubiquitous, the *top* command, a useful alternative to *ps*, is available on many systems. It was written by William LeFebvre. When running, *top* gives a periodically updated listing of processes ranked in order of CPU usage. Typically, only the top 10 processes are given, but this is implementation dependent, and your implementation may let you select other values. Here is a single instance from our test system:

```
15 processes:  2 running, 13 sleeping
CPU states:  0.8% user,  0.0% nice,  7.4% system,  7.8% interrupt, 84.0% idle
Mem: 6676K Active, 12M Inact, 7120K Wired, 2568K Cache, 3395K Buf, 1228K Free
Swap: 100M Total, 100M Free

  PID USERNAME PRI NICE   SIZE    RES STATE   TIME   WCPU    CPU COMMAND
 6590 root      35    0   924K   616K RUN     0:15 21.20% 20.75% inetd
  144 root      10    0   980K   500K nanslp  0:03  0.00%  0.00% cron
  150 root       2    0  1304K   804K select  0:03  0.00%  0.00% sendmail
  100 root       2    0   820K   484K select  0:02  0.00%  0.00% syslogd
  173 root       2    0   788K   368K select  0:02  0.00%  0.00% moused
  141 root       2    0   924K   616K select  0:01  0.00%  0.00% inetd
 6167 root       2    0  1108K   712K select  0:00  0.00%  0.00% telnetd
 6171 root      18    0   464K   320K pause   0:00  0.00%  0.00% csh
 6168 jsloan    10    0   504K   252K wait    0:00  0.00%  0.00% sh
 6598 root      28    0  1556K   844K RUN     0:00  0.00%  0.00% top
    1 root      10    0   496K   168K wait    0:00  0.00%  0.00% init
  457 root       3    0   824K   516K ttyin   0:00  0.00%  0.00% getty
  214 root       3    0   824K   508K ttyin   0:00  0.00%  0.00% getty
  213 root       3    0   824K   508K ttyin   0:00  0.00%  0.00% getty
  109 daemon     2    0   828K   436K select  0:00  0.00%  0.00% portmap
```

Output is interrupted with a *q* or a Ctrl-C. Sometimes system administrators will leave *top* running on the console when the console is not otherwise in use. Of course, this should be done only in a physically secure setting.

In a sense, *ps* is a more general *top* since it gives you all running processes. The advantage to *top* is that it focuses your attention on resource hogs, and it provides a repetitive update. *top* has a large number of options and can provide a wide range of information. For more information, consult its Unix manpage.*

netstat

One of the most useful and diverse utilities is *netstat*. This program reports the contents of kernel data structures related to networking. Because of the diversity in networking data structures, many of *netstat*'s uses may seem somewhat unrelated, so we will be revisiting *netstat* at several points in this book.

One use of *netstat* is to display the connections and services available on a host. For example, this is the output for the system we just looked at:

```
bsd4# netstat -a
Active Internet connections (including servers)
Proto Recv-Q Send-Q  Local Address          Foreign Address        (state)
tcp       0      0  bsd4.telnet            205.153.60.247.3473    TIME_WAIT
tcp       0  17458  bsd4.chargen           sloan.1244             ESTABLISHED
tcp       0      0  *.chargen              *.*                    LISTEN
tcp       0      0  *.discard              *.*                    LISTEN
tcp       0      0  *.echo                 *.*                    LISTEN
tcp       0      0  *.time                 *.*                    LISTEN
tcp       0      0  *.daytime              *.*                    LISTEN
tcp       0      0  *.finger               *.*                    LISTEN
tcp       0      2  bsd4.telnet            sloan.1082             ESTABLISHED
tcp       0      0  *.smtp                 *.*                    LISTEN
tcp       0      0  *.login                *.*                    LISTEN
tcp       0      0  *.shell                *.*                    LISTEN
tcp       0      0  *.telnet               *.*                    LISTEN
tcp       0      0  *.ftp                  *.*                    LISTEN
tcp       0      0  *.sunrpc               *.*                    LISTEN
udp       0      0  *.1075                 *.*
udp       0      0  *.1074                 *.*
udp       0      0  *.1073                 *.*
udp       0      0  *.1072                 *.*
udp       0      0  *.1071                 *.*
udp       0      0  *.1070                 *.*
udp       0      0  *.chargen              *.*
udp       0      0  *.discard              *.*
udp       0      0  *.echo                 *.*
udp       0      0  *.time                 *.*
udp       0      0  *.daytime              *.*
udp       0      0  *.sunrpc               *.*
udp       0      0  *.syslog               *.*
Active UNIX domain sockets
Address   Type   Recv-Q Send-Q   Inode    Conn    Refs  Nextref Addr
c3378e80 dgram        0      0        0 c336efc0       0 c3378f80
c3378f80 dgram        0      0        0 c336efc0       0 c3378fc0
c3378fc0 dgram        0      0        0 c336efc0       0        0
c336efc0 dgram        0      0 c336db00       0 c3378e80       0 /var/run/log
```

---

* Solaris users may want to look at process management utilities included in */usr/proc/bin*.

The first column gives the protocol. The next two columns give the sizes of the send and receive queues. These should be 0 or near 0. Otherwise, you may have a problem with that particular service. The next two columns give the socket or IP address and port number for each end of a connection. This socket pair uniquely identifies one connection. The socket is presented in the form *hostname.service*. Finally, the state of the connection is given in the last column for TCP services. This is blank for UDP since it is connectionless. The most common states are `ESTABLISHED` for current connections, `LISTEN` for services awaiting a connection, and `TIME_WAIT` for recently terminated connections. Any of the TCP states could show up, but you should rarely see the others. An excessive number of `SYN_RECEIVED`, for example, is an indication of a problem (possibly a denial-of-service attack). You can safely ignore the last few lines of this listing.

A couple of examples should clarify this output. The following line shows a Telnet connection between *bsd4* and *sloan* using port *1082* on *sloan*:

```
tcp      0    2  bsd4.telnet          sloan.1082              ESTABLISHED
```

The next line shows that there was a second connection to *sloan* that was recently terminated:

```
tcp      0    0  bsd4.telnet          205.153.60.247.3473     TIME_WAIT
```

Terminated connections remain in this state for a couple of minutes, during which time the socket pair cannot be reused.

Name resolution can be suppressed with the *-n* option if you would rather see numeric entries. There are a couple of reasons you might want to do this. Typically, *netstat* will run much faster without name resolution. This is particularly true if you are having name resolution problems and have to wait for requests to time out. This option can help you avoid confusion if your */etc/services* or */etc/hosts* files are inaccurate.

The remaining TCP entries in the `LISTEN` state are services waiting for a connection request. Since a request could come over any available interface, its IP address is not known in advance. The * in the entry `*.echo` acts as a placeholder for the unknown IP address. (Since multiple addresses may be associated with a host, the local address is unknown until a connection is actually made.) The `*.*` entries indicate that both the remote address and port are unknown. As you can see, this shows a number of additional services that *ps* was not designed to display. In particular, all the services that are under the control of *inetd* are shown.

Another use of *netstat* is to list the routing table. This may be essential information in resolving routing problems, e.g., when you discover that a host or a network is unreachable. Although it may be too long or volatile on many systems to be very helpful, the routing table is sometimes useful in getting a quick idea of what networks are communicating with yours. Displaying the routing table requires the *-r* option.

There are four main ways entries can be added to the routing table—by the *ifconfig* command when an interface is configured, by the *route* command, by an ICMP redirect, or through an update from a dynamic protocol like RIP or OSPF. If dynamic protocols are used, the routing table is an example of a dynamic structure that can't be discovered by looking at configuration files.

Here is an example of a routing table from a FreeBSD system:

```
bsd1# netstat -rn
Routing tables


Internet:
Destination        Gateway              Flags    Refs      Use     Netif Expire
default            205.153.60.2         UGSc       0         0      xl0
127.0.0.1          127.0.0.1            UH         0         0      lo0
172.16.1/24        172.16.2.1           UGSc       0         7      xl1
172.16.2/24        link#2               UC         0         0      xl1
172.16.2.1         0:10:7b:66:f7:62     UHLW       2         0      xl1    913
172.16.2.255       ff:ff:ff:ff:ff:ff    UHLWb      0        18      xl1
172.16.3/24        172.16.2.1           UGSc       0         2      xl1
205.153.60         link#1               UC         0         0      xl0
205.153.60.1       0:0:a2:c6:e:42       UHLW       4         0      xl0    906
205.153.60.2       link#1               UHLW       1         0      xl0
205.153.60.5       0:90:27:9c:2d:c6     UHLW       0        34      xl0    987
205.153.60.255     ff:ff:ff:ff:ff:ff    UHLWb      1        18      xl0
205.153.61         205.153.60.1         UGSc       0         0      xl0
205.153.62         205.153.60.1         UGSc       0         0      xl0
205.153.63         205.153.60.1         UGSc       2         0      xl0
```

At first glance, output from other systems may be organized differently, but usually the same basic information is present. In this example, the *-n* option was used to suppress name resolution.

The first column gives the destination, while the second gives the interface or next hop to that destination. The third column gives the flags. These are often helpful in interpreting the first two columns. A U indicates the path is up or available, an H indicates the destination is a host rather than a network, and a G indicates a gateway or router. These are the most useful. Others shown in this table include b, indicating a broadcast address; S, indicating a static or manual addition; and W and c, indicating a route that was generated as a result of cloning. (These and other possibilities are described in detail in the Unix manpage for some versions of *netstat*.) The fourth column gives a reference count, i.e., the number of active uses for each of the routes. This is incremented each time a connection is built over the route (e.g., a Telnet connection is made using the route) and decremented when the connection is torn down. The fifth column gives the number of packets sent using this entry. The last entry is the interface that will be used.

If you are familiar with the basics of routing, you have seen these tables before. If not, an explanation of the first few lines of the table should help. The first entry indicates the default route. This was added statically at startup. The second entry is the loopback address for the machine. The third entry is for a remotely attached network. The destination network is a subnet from a Class B address space. The /24 is the subnet mask. Traffic to this network must go through *172.16.2.1*, a gateway that is defined with the next two entries. The fourth entry indicates that the network gateway, *172.16.2.1*, is on a network that has a direct attachment through the second interface *xl1*. The entry that follows gives the specifics, including the Ethernet address of the gateway's interface.

In general, it helps to have an idea of the interfaces and how they are configured before you get too deeply involved in routing tables. There are two quick ways to get this information—use the *-i* option with *netstat* or use the *ifconfig* command. Here is the output for the interfaces that *netstat* generates. This corresponds to the routing table just examined.

```
bsd1# netstat -i
Name  Mtu    Network       Address          Ipkts Ierrs   Opkts Oerrs  Coll
xl0   1500   <Link>        00.10.5a.e3.37.0c 2123     0     612     0     0
xl0   1500   205.153.60    205.153.60.247    2123     0     612     0     0
xl1   1500   <Link>        00.60.97.92.4a.7b  478     0      36     0     0
xl1   1500   172.16.2/24   172.16.2.13        478     0      36     0     0
lp0*  1500   <Link>                             0     0       0     0     0
tun0* 1500   <Link>                             0     0       0     0     0
sl0*  552    <Link>                             0     0       0     0     0
ppp0* 1500   <Link>                             0     0       0     0     0
lo0   16384  <Link>                             6     0       6     0     0
lo0   16384  127           localhost            6     0       6     0     0
```

For our purposes, we are interested in only the first four entries. (The other interfaces include the loop-back, *lo0*, and unused interfaces like *ppp0**, the PPP interface.) The first two entries give the Ethernet address and IP address for the *xl0* interface. The next two are for *xl1*. Notice that this also gives the number of input and output packets and errors as well. You can expect to see very large numbers for these. The very low numbers indicate that the system was recently restarted.

The format of the output may vary from system to system, but all will provide the same basic information. There is a lot more to *netstat* than this introduction shows. For example, *netstat* can be run periodically like *top*. We will return to *netstat* in future chapters.

lsof

lsof is a remarkable tool that is often overlooked. Written by Victor Abel, *lsof* lists open files on a Unix system. This might not seem a particularly remarkable service until you start thinking about the implications. An application that uses the filesystem, networked or otherwise, will have open files at some point. *lsof* offers a way to track that activity.

The program is available for a staggering variety of Unix systems, often in both source and binary formats. Although I will limit this discussion to networking related tasks, *lsof* is more properly an operating system tool than a networking tool. You may want to learn more about *lsof* than described here.

In its simplest form, *lsof* produces a list of all open files. You'll probably be quite surprised at the number of files that are open on a quiescent system. For example, on a FreeBSD system with no one else logged on, *lsof* listed 564 open files.

Here is an example of the first few lines of output from *lsof:*

```
bsd2# lsof
COMMAND    PID   USER   FD    TYPE     DEVICE    SIZE/OFF   NODE NAME
swapper      0   root   cwd   VDIR  116,131072        512      2 /
swapper      0   root   rtd   VDIR  116,131072        512      2 /
init         1   root   cwd   VDIR  116,131072        512      2 /
init         1   root   rtd   VDIR  116,131072        512      2 /
init         1   root   txt   VREG  116,131072     255940    157 /sbin/init
...
```

The most useful fields are the obvious ones, including the first three—the name of the command, the process ID, and its owner. The other fields and codes used in the fields are explained in the manpage for *lsof,* which runs about 30 pages.

It might seem that *lsof* returns too much information to be useful. Fortunately, it provides a number of options that will allow you to tailor the output to your needs. You can use *lsof* with the *-p* option to specify a specific process number or with the *-c* option to specify the name of a process. For example, the command *lsof -csendmail* will list all the files opened by *sendmail.* You only need to give enough of the name to uniquely identify the process. The *-N* option can be used to list files opened for the local computer on an NFS server. That is, when run on an NFS client, *lsof* shows files opened by the client. When run on a server, *lsof* will not show the files the server is providing to clients.

The *-i* option limits output to Internet and X.25 network files. If no address is given, all such files will be listed, effectively showing all open socket files on your network:

```
bsd2# lsof -i
COMMAND    PID    USER   FD   TYPE     DEVICE  SIZE/OFF NODE NAME
syslogd    105    root   4u   IPv4  0xc3dd8f00      0t0  UDP *:syslog
portmap    108  daemon   3u   IPv4  0xc3dd8e40      0t0  UDP *:sunrpc
portmap    108  daemon   4u   IPv4  0xc3e09d80      0t0  TCP *:sunrpc (LISTEN)
inetd      126    root   4u   IPv4  0xc3e0ad80      0t0  TCP *:ftp (LISTEN)
inetd      126    root   5u   IPv4  0xc3e0ab60      0t0  TCP *:telnet (LISTEN)
inetd      126    root   6u   IPv4  0xc3e0a940      0t0  TCP *:shell (LISTEN)
inetd      126    root   7u   IPv4  0xc3e0a720      0t0  TCP *:login (LISTEN)
inetd      126    root   8u   IPv4  0xc3e0a500      0t0  TCP *:finger (LISTEN)
```

```
inetd      126    root     9u   IPv4  0xc3dd8d80      0t0   UDP *:biff
inetd      126    root    10u   IPv4  0xc3dd8cc0      0t0   UDP *:ntalk
inetd      126    root    11u   IPv6  0xc3e0a2e0      0t0   TCP *:ftp
inetd      126    root    12u   IPv6  0xc3e0bd80      0t0   TCP *:telnet
inetd      126    root    13u   IPv6  0xc3e0bb60      0t0   TCP *:shell
inetd      126    root    14u   IPv6  0xc3e0b940      0t0   TCP *:login
inetd      126    root    15u   IPv6  0xc3e0b720      0t0   TCP *:finger
lpd        131    root     6u   IPv4  0xc3e0b500      0t0   TCP *:printer (LISTEN)
sendmail   137    root     4u   IPv4  0xc3e0b2e0      0t0   TCP *:smtp (LISTEN)
httpd      185    root    16u   IPv4  0xc3e0b0c0      0t0   TCP *:http (LISTEN)
httpd      198  nobody    16u   IPv4  0xc3e0b0c0      0t0   TCP *:http (LISTEN)
httpd      199  nobody    16u   IPv4  0xc3e0b0c0      0t0   TCP *:http (LISTEN)
httpd      200  nobody    16u   IPv4  0xc3e0b0c0      0t0   TCP *:http (LISTEN)
httpd      201  nobody    16u   IPv4  0xc3e0b0c0      0t0   TCP *:http (LISTEN)
httpd      202  nobody    16u   IPv4  0xc3e0b0c0      0t0   TCP *:http (LISTEN)
httpd    10408  nobody    16u   IPv4  0xc3e0b0c0      0t0   TCP *:http (LISTEN)
httpd    10409  nobody    16u   IPv4  0xc3e0b0c0      0t0   TCP *:http (LISTEN)
httpd    10410  nobody    16u   IPv4  0xc3e0b0c0      0t0   TCP *:http (LISTEN)
httpd    25233  nobody    16u   IPv4  0xc3e0b0c0      0t0   TCP *:http (LISTEN)
httpd    25236  nobody    16u   IPv4  0xc3e0b0c0      0t0   TCP *:http (LISTEN)
telnetd  58326    root     0u   IPv4  0xc3e0eb60      0t0   TCP bsd2.lander.edu:telne
t->sloan.lander.edu:1184 (ESTABLISHED)
telnetd  58326    root     1u   IPv4  0xc3e0eb60      0t0   TCP bsd2.lander.edu:telne
t->sloan.lander.edu:1184 (ESTABLISHED)
telnetd  58326    root     2u   IPv4  0xc3e0eb60      0t0   TCP bsd2.lander.edu:telne
t->sloan.lander.edu:1184 (ESTABLISHED)
perl     68936    root     4u   IPv4  0xc3dd8c00      0t0   UDP *:eicon-x25
ping     81206  nobody     3u   IPv4  0xc3e98f00      0t0   ICMP *:*
```

As you can see, this is not unlike the *-a* option with *netstat.* Apart from the obvious differences in the details reported, the big difference is that *lsof* will not report connections that do not have files open. For example, if a connection is being torn down, all files may already be closed. *netstat* will still report this connection while *lsof* won't. The preferred behavior will depend on what information you need.

If you specify an address, then only those files related to the address will be listed:

```
bsd2# lsof -i@sloan.lander.edu
COMMAND   PID USER    FD    TYPE     DEVICE SIZE/OFF NODE NAME
telnetd 73825 root     0u   IPv4 0xc3e0eb60      0t0  TCP bsd2.lander.edu:telnet->
sloan.lander.edu:1177 (ESTABLISHED)
telnetd 73825 root     1u   IPv4 0xc3e0eb60      0t0  TCP bsd2.lander.edu:telnet->
sloan.lander.edu:1177 (ESTABLISHED)
telnetd 73825 root     2u   IPv4 0xc3e0eb60      0t0  TCP bsd2.lander.edu:telnet->
sloan.lander.edu:1177 (ESTABLISHED)
```

One minor problem with this output is the identification of the *telnet* user as root—a consequence of root owning *telnetd,* the server's daemon. On some systems, you can use the PID with the *-p* option to track down the device entry and then use *lsof* on the device to discover the owner. Unfortunately, this won't work on many systems.

You can also use *lsof* to track an FTP transfer. You might want to do this to see if a transfer is making progress. You would use the *-p* option to see which files are open to the process. You can then use *-ad* to specify the device file descriptor along with *-r* to specify repeat mode. *lsof* will be run repeatedly, and you can see if the size of the file is changing.

Other uses of *lsof* are described in the manpage, the FAQ, and a quick-start guide supplied with the distribution. The latter is probably the best place to begin.

ifconfig

ifconfig is usually thought of as the command used to alter the configuration of the network interfaces. But, since you may need to know the current configuration of the interfaces before you make changes, *ifconfig* provides a mechanism to retrieve interface configurations. It will report the configuration of all the interfaces when called with the *-a* option or of a single interface when used with the interface's name.

Here are the results for the system we just looked at:

```
bsd1# ifconfig -a
xl0: flags=8843<UP,BROADCAST,RUNNING,SIMPLEX,MULTICAST> mtu 1500
        inet 205.153.60.247 netmask 0xffffff00 broadcast 205.153.60.255
        ether 00:10:5a:e3:37:0c
        media: 10baseT/UTP <half-duplex>
        supported media: autoselect 100baseTX <full-duplex> 100baseTX <half-dupl
ex> 100baseTX 10baseT/UTP <full-duplex> 10baseT/UTP <half-duplex> 10baseT/UTP
xl1: flags=8843<UP,BROADCAST,RUNNING,SIMPLEX,MULTICAST> mtu 1500
        inet 172.16.2.13 netmask 0xffffff00 broadcast 172.16.2.255
        ether 00:60:97:92:4a:7b
        media: 10baseT/UTP <half-duplex>
        supported media: autoselect 100baseTX <full-duplex> 100baseTX <half-dupl
ex> 100baseTX 10baseT/UTP <full-duplex> 10baseT/UTP 10baseT/UTP <half-duplex>
lp0: flags=8810<POINTOPOINT,SIMPLEX,MULTICAST> mtu 1500
tun0: flags=8010<POINTOPOINT,MULTICAST> mtu 1500
sl0: flags=c010<POINTOPOINT,LINK2,MULTICAST> mtu 552
ppp0: flags=8010<POINTOPOINT,MULTICAST> mtu 1500
lo0: flags=8049<UP,LOOPBACK,RUNNING,MULTICAST> mtu 16384
        inet 127.0.0.1 netmask 0xff000000
```

You can see that for the interfaces *xl0* and *xl1*, we are given a general status report. UP indicates that the interface is operational. If UP is missing, the interface is down and will not process packets. For Ethernet, the combination of BROADCAST, SIMPLEX, and MULTICAST is not surprising. The mtu is the largest frame size the interface will handle. Next, we have the IP number, address mask, and broadcast address. The Ethernet address comes next, although some systems (Solaris, for example) will suppress this if you aren't running the program as root. Finally, we see information about the physical interface connections.

You can ignore the entries for *lp0, tun0, sl0,* and *ppp0.* In fact, if you don't want to see these, you can use the combination *-au* to list just the interfaces that are up. Similarly, *-d* is used to list just the interfaces that are down.

While *netstat* allows you to get basic information on the interfaces, if your goal is configuration information, *ifconfig* is a better choice. First, as you can see, *ifconfig* supplies more of that sort of information. Second, on some systems, *netstat* may skip interfaces that haven't been configured. Finally, *ifconfig* also allows you to change parameters such as the IP addresses and masks. In particular, *ifconfig* is frequently used to shut down an interface. This is roughly equivalent to discon-necting the interface from the network. To shut down an interface, you use the *down* option. For example, *ifconfig xl1 down* will shut down the interface *xl1,* and *ifconfig xl1 up* will bring it back up. Of course, you must have root privileges to use *ifconfig* to change configurations.

Since *ifconfig* is used to configure interfaces, it is typically run automatically by one of the startup scripts when the system is booted. This is something to look for when you examine startup scripts. The use of *ifconfig* is discussed in detail in Craig Hunt's *TCP/IP Network Administration.*

arp

The ARP table on a system maps network addresses into MAC addresses. Of course, the ARP table applies only to directly connected devices, i.e., devices on the local network. Remote devices, i.e., devices that can be reached only by sending traffic through one or more routers, will not be added to the ARP table since you can't communicate with them directly. (However, the appropriate router interface will be added.)

Typically, addresses are added or removed automatically. If your system needs to communicate with another system on the local network whose MAC address is unknown, your system sends an ARP request, a broadcast packet with the destina-tion's IP address. If the system is accessible, it will respond with an ARP reply that includes its MAC address. Your system adds this to its ARP table and then uses this information to send packets directly to the destination. (A simple way to add an entry for a directly connected device to the ARP table is to *ping* the device you want added. *ping* is discussed in detail in Chapter 3.) Most systems are configured to drop entries from the ARP table if they aren't being used, although the length of the timeout varies from system to system.

At times, you may want to examine or even change entries in the ARP table. The *arp* command allows you to do this. When *arp* is invoked with the *-a* option, it reports the current contents of the ARP table. Here is an example from a Solaris system:

```
sol1# arp -a
Net to Media Table
Device  IP Address           Mask             Flags  Phys Addr
------  --------------------  ---------------- -----  ---------------
elxl0   205.153.60.1          255.255.255.255         00:00:a2:c6:0e:42
elxl0   205.153.60.53         255.255.255.255         00:e0:29:21:3c:0b
elxl0   205.153.60.55         255.255.255.255         00:90:27:43:72:70
elxl0   mail.lander.edu       255.255.255.255         00:90:27:9c:2d:c6
elxl0   sol1                  255.255.255.255 SP      00:60:97:58:71:b7
elxl0   pm3.lander.edu        255.255.255.255         00:c0:05:04:2d:78
elxl0   BASE-ADDRESS.MCAST.NET 240.0.0.0       SM      01:00:5e:00:00:00
```

The format or details may vary from system to system, but the same basic information should be provided.

For Solaris, the first column gives the interface for the connection. The next two are the IP address and its mask. (You can get just IP numbers by using the *-n* option.) There are four possible flags that may appear in the flags column. An S indicates a static entry, one that has been manually set rather than discovered. A P indicates an address that will be published. That is, this machine will provide this address should it receive an ARP request. In this case, the P flag is for the local machine, so it is natural that the machine would respond with this information. The flags U and M are used for unresolved and multicast addresses, respectively. The final column is the actual Ethernet address.

This information can be useful in several ways. It can be used to determine the Ethernet hardware in this computer, as well as the hardware in directly connected devices. The IEEE assigns to the manufacturers of Ethernet adapters unique identifiers to be used as the first three bytes of their Ethernet addresses. These addresses, known as *Organizationally Unique Identifiers* (OUI), can be found at the IEEE web page at *http://standards.ieee.org/regauth/oui/index.html*. In other words, the first three bytes of an Ethernet address identify the manufacturer. In this case, by entering on this web page 00 60 97, i.e., the first three bytes of the address 00 60 97 58 71 b7, we find that the host *sol1* has a 3COM Ethernet adapter. In the same manner we can discover that the host *205.153.60.1* is Bay Networks equipment.

OUI designations are not foolproof. The MAC address of a device may have been changed and may not have the manufacturer's OUI. And even if you can identify the manufacturer, in today's world of merger mania and takeovers, you may see an OUI of an acquired company that you don't recognize.

If some machines on your network are reachable but others aren't, or connectivity comes and goes, ARP problems may be the cause. (For an example of an ARP problem, see Chapter 12.) If you think you might have a problem with IP-to-Ethernet address resolution on your local network, *arp* is the logical tool to use to diagnose the problem. First, look to see if there is an entry for the destination and if it is correct. If it is missing, you can attempt to add it using the *-s* option. (You must be root.) If the entry is incorrect, you must first delete it with the *-d* option. Entries added with the *-s* option will not time out but will be lost on reboot. If you want to permanently add an entry, you can create a startup script to do this. In particular, in a script, *arp* can use the *-f* option to read entries from a file.

The usual reason for an incorrect entry in an *arp* table is a duplicated IP address somewhere on your network. Sometimes this is a typing mistake. Sometimes when setting up their computers, people will copy the configuration from other computers, including the supposedly unique IP number. A rogue DHCP server is another possibility. If you suspect one of your hosts is experiencing problems caused by a duplicate IP number on the network, you can shut down the interface on that computer or unplug it from the network. (This is less drastic than shutting down the computer, but that will also work.) Then you can *ping* the IP address in question from a second computer. If you get an answer, some other computer is using your IP address. Your *arp* table should give you the Ethernet address of the offending machine. Using its OUI will tell you the type of hardware. This usually won't completely locate the problem machine, but it is a start, particularly for unusual hardware.*

Scanning Tools

We've already discussed one reason why *ps* may not give a complete picture of your system. There is another much worse possibility. If you are having security problems, your copy of *ps* may be compromised. Crackers sometimes will replace *ps* with their own version that has been patched to hide their activities. In this event, you may have an additional process running on your system that provides a backdoor that won't show up under *ps*.

One way of detecting this is to use a port scanner to see which ports are active on your system. You could choose to do this from the compromised system, but you are probably better off doing this from a remote system known to be secure. This assumes, however, that the attacker hasn't installed a trapdoor on the compromised host that is masquerading as a legitimate service on a legitimate port.

---

* You can also use *arp* to deliberately publish a bad address. This will shut up a connection request that won't otherwise stop.

There are a large number of freely available port scanners. These include programs like *gtkportscan*, *nessus*, *portscan*, and *strobe*, to name just a few. They generally work by generating a connection request for each port number in the range being tested. If they receive a reply from the port, they add it to their list of open ports. Here is an example using *portscan*:

```
bsd1# portscan 205.153.63.239 1 10000 -vv
This is a portscanner - Rafael Barrero, Jr.
Email me at rbarrero@polymail.calpoly.edu
For further information. Enjoy!

Port: 7 -->      echo
Port: 9 -->      discard
Port: 13       -->      daytime
Port: 19       -->      chargen
Port: 21       -->      ftp
Port: 23       -->      telnet
Port: 25       -->      smtp
Port: 37       -->      time
Port: 79       -->      finger
Port: 111      -->      sunrpc
Port: 513      -->      login
Port: 514      -->      shell
```

The arguments are the destination address and beginning and ending port numbers. The result is a list of port numbers and service names for ports that answered.

Figure 2-1 shows another example of a port scanner running under Windows NT. This particular scanner is from Mentor Technologies, Inc., and can be freely downloaded from *http://www.mentortech.com/learn/tools/tools.shtml*. It is written in Java, so it can be run on both Windows and Unix machines but will require a Java runtime environment. It can also be run in command-line mode. Beware, this scanner is very slow when used with Windows.

Most administrators look on such utilities as tools for crackers, but they can have legitimate uses as shown here. Keep in mind that the use of these tools has political implications. You should be safe scanning your own system, but you are on very shaky ground if you scan other systems. These two tools make no real effort to hide what they are doing, so they are not difficult to detect. Stealth port scanners, however, send the packets out of order over extended periods of time and are, consequently, more difficult to detect. Some administrators consider port scans adequate justification for cutting connections or blocking all traffic from a site. Do not use these tools on a system without authorization. Depending on the circumstances, you may want to notify certain colleagues before you do a port scan even if you are authorized. In Chapter 12, we will return to port scanners and examine other uses, such as testing firewalls.

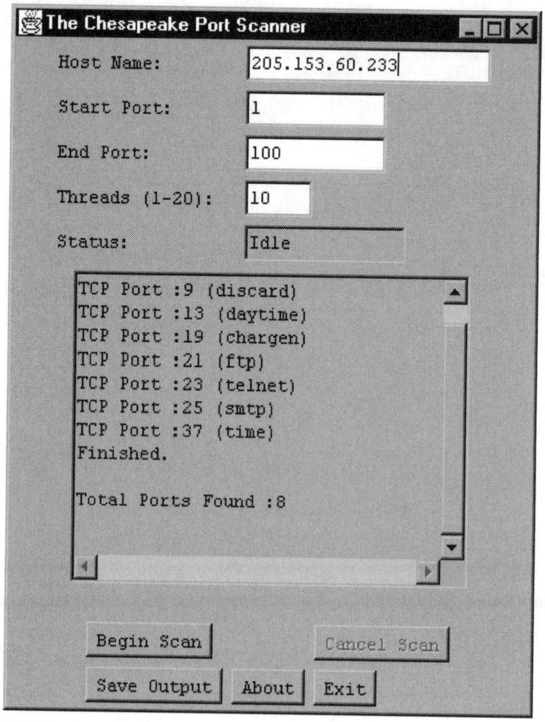

Figure 2-1. Chesapeake Port Scanner

One last word about these tools. Don't get caught up in using tools and overlook simpler tests. For example, you can check to see if *sendmail* is running by trying to connect to the SMTP port using *telnet*. In this example, the test not only tells me that *sendmail* is running, but it also tells me what version of *sendmail* is running:

```
lnx1# telnet 205.153.63.239 25
Trying 205.153.63.239...
Connected to 205.153.63.239.
Escape character is '^]'.
220 bsd4.lander.edu ESMTP Sendmail 8.9.3/8.9.3; Wed, 8 Mar 2000 09:38:02 -0500
(EST)
quit
221 bsd4.lander.edu closing connection
Connection closed by foreign host.
```

In the same spirit:

```
bsd1# ipfw list
ipfw: getsockopt(IP_FW_GET): Protocol not available
```

clearly shows *ipfw* is not running on this system. All I did was try to use it. This type of application-specific testing is discussed in greater detail in Chapter 10.

System Configuration Files

A major problem with configuration files under Unix is that there are so many of them in so many places. On a multiuser system that provides a variety of services, there may be scores of configuration files scattered among dozens of directories. Even worse, it seems that every implementation of Unix is different. Even different releases of the same flavor of Unix may vary. Add to this the complications that multiple applications contribute and you have a major undertaking. If you are running a number of different platforms, you have your work cut out for you.

For these reasons, it is unrealistic to attempt to give an exhaustive list of configuration files. It is possible, however, to discuss configuration files by categories. The categories can then serve as a guide or reminder when you construct your own lists so that you don't overlook an important group of files. Just keep in mind that what follows is only a starting point. You will have to discover your particular implementations of Unix one file at a time.

Basic Configuration Files

There are a number of fairly standard configuration files that seem to show up on most systems. These are usually, but not always, located in the */etc* directory. (For customization, you may see a number of files in the */usr/local* or */usr/opt* directories or their subdirectories.) When looking at files, this is clearly the first place to start. Your system will probably include many of the following: *defaultdomain, defaultroute, ethers, gateways, host.conf, hostname, hosts, hosts.allow, hosts.equiv, inetd.conf, localhosts, localnetworks, named.boot, netmasks, networks, nodename, nsswitch.conf, protocols, rc, rc.conf, rc.local, resolv.conf,* and *services.* You won't find all of these on a single system. Each version and release will have its own conventions. For example, Solaris puts the host's name in *nodename.*[*] With BSD, it is set in *rc.conf.* Customizations may change these as well. Thus, the locations and names of files will vary from system to system.

One starting point might be to scan all the files in */etc* and its subdirectories, trying to identify which ones are relevant. In the long run, you may want to know the role of all the files in */etc*, but you don't need to do this all at once.

There are a few files or groups of files that will be of particular interest. One of the most important is *inetd.conf.* While we can piece together what is probably being handled by *inetd* by using *ps* in combination with *netstat,* an examination of *inetd.conf* is usually much quicker and safer. On an unfamiliar system, this is

---

[*] The hostname may be used in other files as well so don't try to change the hostname by editing these files. Use the *hostname* command instead.

one of the first places you will want to look. Be sure to compare this to the output provided by *netstat*. Services that you can't match to running processes or *inetd* are a cause for concern.

You will also want to examine files like *host.conf, resolv.conf,* and *nsswitch.conf* to discover how name resolution is done. Be sure to examine files that establish trust relationships like *hosts.allow*. This is absolutely essential if you are having, or want to avoid, security problems. (There is more on some of these files in the discussion of *tcpwrappers* in Chapter 11.)

Finally, there is one group of these files, the *rc* files, that deserve particular attention. These are discussed separately in the later section on startup files and scripts.

Configuration Programs

Over the years, Unix has been heavily criticized because of its terse command-line interface. As a result, many GUI applications have been developed. System administration has not escaped this trend. These utilities can be used to display as well as change system configurations.

Once again, every flavor of Unix will be different. With Solaris, *admintool* was the torchbearer for years. In recent years, this has been superseded with *Solstice AdminSuite*. With FreeBSD, select the *configure* item from the menu presented when you run */stand/sysinstall*. With Linux you can use *linuxconf*. Both the menu and GUI versions of this program are common. The list goes on.

Kernel

It's natural to assume that examining the kernel's configuration might be an important first step. But while it may, in fact, be essential in resolving some key issues, in general, it is usually not the most productive place to look. You may want to postpone this until it seems absolutely necessary or you have lots of free time.

As you know, the first step in starting a system is loading and initializing the kernel. Network services rely on the kernel being configured correctly. Some services will be available only if first enabled in the kernel. While examining the kernel's configuration won't tell you which services are actually being used, it can give some insight into what is not available. For example, if the kernel is not configured to forward IP packets, then clearly the system is not being used as a router, even if it has multiple interfaces. On the other hand, it doesn't immediately follow that a system is configured as a firewall just because the kernel has been compiled to support filtering.

Changes to the kernel will usually be required only when building a new system, installing a new service or new hardware, or tuning system performance. Changing the kernel will not normally be needed to simply discover how a system is configured. However, changes may be required to use some of the tools described later in this book. For example, some versions of FreeBSD have not, by default, enabled the Berkeley packet filter pseudodriver. Thus, it is necessary to recompile the kernel to enable this before some packet capture software, such as *tcpdump*, can be run on these systems.

To recompile a kernel, you'll need to consult the documentation for your operating system for the specifics. Usually, recompiling a kernel first requires editing configuration files. This may be done manually or with the aid of a utility created for this task. For example, with Linux, the command *make config* runs an interactive program that sets appropriate parameters.* BSD uses a program called *config*. If you can locate the configuration files used, you can see how the kernel was configured. But, if the kernel has been rebuilt a number of times without following a consistent naming scheme, this can be surprisingly difficult.

As an example, on BSD-derived systems, the kernel configuration files are usually found in the directory */sys/arch/conf/kernel* where **arch** corresponds to the architecture of the system and **kernel** is the name of the kernel. With FreeBSD, the file might be */sys/i386/conf/GENERIC* if the kernel has not been recompiled. In Linux, the configuration file is *.config* in whatever directory the kernel was unpacked in, usually */usr/src/linux/*.

As you might expect, lines beginning with a # are comments. What you'll probably want to look for are lines specifying unusual options. For example, it is not difficult to guess that the following lines from a FreeBSD system indicate that the machine may be used as a firewall:

```
...
# Firewall options
options         IPFIREWALL
options         IPFIREWALL_VERBOSE_LIMIT=25
...
```

Some entries can be pretty cryptic, but hopefully there are some comments. The Unix manpages for a system may describe some options.

Unfortunately, there is very little consistency from one version of Unix to the next on how such files are named, where they are located, what information they may contain, or how they are used. For example, Solaris uses the file */etc/system* to

---

* You can also use *make xconfig* or *make menuconfig*. These are more interactive, allowing you to go back and change parameters once you have moved on. *make config* is unforgiving in this respect.

hold some directives, although there is little of interest in this file for our purposes. IRIX keeps its files in the */var/sysgen/system* directory. For Linux, take a look at */etc/conf.modules*. The list goes on.*

It is usually possible to examine or change selected system parameters for an existing kernel. For example, Solaris has the utilities *sysdef, prtconf,* and *ndd*. For our purposes, *ndd* is the most interesting and should provide the flavor of how such utilities work.

Specifically, *ndd* allows you to get or set driver configuration parameters. You will probably want to begin by listing configurable options. Specifying the driver (i.e., */dev/arp, /dev/icmp, /dev/ip, /dev/tcp,* and */dev/udp*) with the *?* option will return the parameters available for that driver. Here is an example:

```
sol1# ndd /dev/arp ?
?                            (read only)
arp_cache_report            (read only)
arp_debug                   (read and write)
arp_cleanup_interval        (read and write)
```

This shows three parameters that can be examined, although only two can be changed. We can examine an individual parameter by using its name as an argument. For example, we can retrieve the ARP table as shown here:

```
sol1# ndd /dev/arp arp_cache_report
ifname  proto addr      proto mask      hardware addr       flags
elxl0   205.153.060.053 255.255.255.255 00:e0:29:21:3c:0b
elxl0   205.153.060.055 255.255.255.255 00:90:27:43:72:70
elxl0   205.153.060.001 255.255.255.255 00:00:a2:c6:0e:42
elxl0   205.153.060.005 255.255.255.255 00:90:27:9c:2d:c6
elxl0   205.153.060.248 255.255.255.255 00:60:97:58:71:b7 PERM PUBLISH MYADDR
elxl0   205.153.060.150 255.255.255.255 00:c0:05:04:2d:78
elxl0   224.000.000.000 240.000.000.000 01:00:5e:00:00:00 PERM MAPPING
```

In this instance, it is fairly easy to guess the meaning of what's returned. (This output is for the same ARP table that we looked at with the *arp* command.) Sometimes, what's returned can be quite cryptic. This example returns the value of the IP forwarding parameter:

```
# ndd /dev/ip ip_forwarding
0
```

It is far from obvious how to interpret this result. In fact, 0 means never forward, 1 means always forward, and 2 means forward only when two or more interfaces are up. I've never been able to locate a definitive source for this sort of information, although a number of the options are described in an appendix to

---

* While general configuration parameters should be in a single file, a huge number of files are actually involved. If you have access to FreeBSD, you might look at */sys/conf/files* to get some idea of this. This is a list of the files FreeBSD uses.

W. Richard Stevens' *TCP/IP Illustrated*, vol. 1. If you want to change parameters, you can invoke the program interactively.

Other versions of Unix will have their own files and utilities. For example, BSD has the *sysctl* command. This example shows that IP forwarding is disabled:

```
bsd1# sysctl net.inet.ip.forwarding
net.inet.ip.forwarding: 0
```

The manpages provide additional guidance, but to know what to change, you may have to delve into the source code. With AIX, there is the *no* utility. As I have said before, the list goes on.

This brief description should give you a general idea of what's involved in gleaning information about the kernel, but you will want to go to the appropriate documentation for your system. It should be clear that it takes a fair degree of experience to extract this kind of information. Occasionally, there is a bit of information that can be obtained only this way, but, in general, this is not the most profitable place to start.

One last comment—if you are intent on examining the behavior of the kernel, you will almost certainly want to look at the messages it produces when booting. On most systems, these can be retrieved with the *dmesg* command. These can be helpful in determining what network hardware your system has and what drivers it uses. For hardware, however, I generally prefer opening the case and looking inside. Accessing the CMOS is another approach for discovering the hardware that doesn't require opening the box.

Startup Files and Scripts

Once the kernel is loaded, the swapper or scheduler is started and then the *init* process runs. This process will, in turn, run a number of startup scripts that will start the various services and do additional configuration chores.

After the standard configuration files, these are the next group of files you might want to examine. These will primarily be scripts, but may include configuration files read by the scripts. In general, it is a bad idea to bury configuration parameters within these scripts, but this is still done at times. You should also be prepared to read fairly cryptic shell code. It is hoped that most of these will be either in their pristine state, heavily commented, or both.

Look for three things when examining these files. First, some networking parameters may be buried in these files. You will not want to miss these. Next, there may be calls to network configuration utilities such as *route* or *ifconfig*. These are frequently customizations, so read these with a critical eye. Finally, networking applications such as *sendmail* may be started from these files. I strongly urge that you create a list of all applications that are run automatically at startup.

For systems derived from BSD, you should look for files in */etc* beginning with *rc*. Be sure to look at *rc.conf* and any *rc* files with extensions indicating a networking function of interest, e.g., *rc.firewall*. Realize that many of these will be templates for services that you may not be using. For example, if you see the file *rc.atm*, don't be too disappointed when you can't find your ATM connection.

Unix systems can typically be booted in one of several different states or run levels that determine which services are started. For example, run level 1 is single-user mode and is used for system maintenance. The services started by the different run levels vary somewhat among the different flavors of Unix. If your system is derived from System V, then the files will be in a half dozen or so directories in */etc*. These are named *rc1.d*, *rc2.d*, and so forth. The digit indicates the run level of the system when booted. Networking scripts are usually in *rc2.d*. In each directory, there will be scripts starting with an *S* or a *K* and a two-digit number. The rest of the name should give some indication of the function of the file. Files with names beginning with an *S* are started in numerical order when the system is rebooted. When the system shuts down, the files with *K* are run. (Some versions of Linux, such as Red Hat, follow this basic approach but group these directories together in the */etc/rc.d* directory. Others, such as Debian, follow the System V approach.)

There is one serious catch with all this. When versions of operating systems change, sometimes the locations of files change. For backward compatibility, links may be created to old locations. For example, on recent versions of Solaris, the network configuration file */etc/hosts* is actually a link to */etc/inet/hosts*. There are other important network configuration files that are really in */etc/inet*, not */etc*. Similarly, some of the startup scripts are really links to files in */etc/init.d*. If the link is somehow broken, you may find yourself editing the wrong version of a file and wondering why the system is ignoring your changes.

Other Files

There are several other categories of files that are worth mentioning briefly. If you have been following the steps just described, you will already have found most of these, but it may be worth mentioning them separately just in case you have overlooked something.

Application files

Once you have your list of applications that are started automatically, investigate how each application is configured. When it comes to configuration files, each application will follow its own conventions. The files may be grouped together, reside in a couple of directories, or have some distributed structure that spans a number of directories. For example, *sendmail* usually keeps configuration files together, usually in */etc* or in */etc/mail*. DNS may have a couple of files in */etc* to get things started, with the database files grouped together somewhere else. A web server like *apache* may have an extensive set of files distributed across a number of directories, particularly if you consider content. But beware, your particular implementation may vary from the norm—in that case, all bets are off. You will need to look for these on an application-by-application and a system-by-system basis.

Security files

It is likely you will have already discovered relevant security files at this point, but if you are having problems, this is something worth revisiting. There are several different categories to consider:

Trust relationships

Some files such as */etc/hosts.equiv* set up trust relationships with other computers. You will definitely want to review these. Keep in mind that users can establish their own trust relationships, so don't forget the *.rhost* file in home directories if you are having problems tied to specific users.

Traffic control

A number of files may be tied to general access or the control of traffic. These include configuration files for applications like *tcpwrappers* or firewall configuration files.

Application specific

Don't forget that individual applications may have security files as well. For example, the file */etc/ftpusers* may be used by *ftp* to restrict access. These are very easy to overlook.

Log files

One last category of files you might want to consider is log files. Strictly speaking, these are not configuration files. Apart from an occasional startup message, these may not tell you very much about your system's configuration. But occasionally, these will provide the missing puzzle piece for resolving a problem. Log files are described in much greater detail in Chapter 11.

Microsoft Windows

Networking with Windows can be quite complicated, since it may involve Microsoft's proprietary enhancements. Fortunately, Microsoft's approach to TCP/IP is pretty standard. As with Unix, you can approach the various versions of Windows by looking at configuration parameters or by using utilities to examine the current configuration. For the most part, you won't be examining files directly under Windows, at least for versions later than Windows for Workgroups. Rather, you'll use the utilities that Windows provides. (There are exceptions. For example, like Unix, Windows has *hosts, protocol,* and *services* files.)

If you are looking for basic information quickly, Microsoft provides one of two programs for this purpose, depending on which version of Windows you use. The utility *winipcfg* is included with Windows 95/98. A command-line program, *ipconfig,* is included with Windows NT and Windows 2000 and in Microsoft's TCP/IP stack for Windows for Workgroups. Both programs provide the same information. *winipcfg* produces a pop-up window giving the basic parameters such as the Ethernet address, the IP address, the default route, the name server's address, and so on (see Figure 2-2). You can invoke the program by entering the program name from *Run* on the start menu or in a DOS window. The most basic parameters will be displayed. Additional information can be obtained by using the */all* option or by clicking on the More Info >> button.

For *ipconfig,* start a DOS window. You can use the command switch */all* to get the additional details.

As in Unix, the utilities *arp, hostname,* and *netstat* are available. All require a DOS window to run. There are a few differences in syntax, but they work basically the same way and provide the same sorts of information. For example, *arp -a* will list all the entries in the ARP table:

```
C:\>arp -a

Interface: 205.153.63.30 on Interface 2
  Internet Address       Physical Address       Type
  205.153.63.1           00-00-a2-c6-28-44      dynamic
  205.153.63.239         00-60-97-06-22-22      dynamic
```

The command *netstat -r* gives the computer's routing table:

```
C:\>netstat -r

Route Table
=======================================================================
Interface List
0x1 ........................ MS TCP Loopback interface
0x2 ...00 10 5a a1 e9 08 ...... 3Com 3C90x Ethernet Adapter
0x3 ...00 00 00 00 00 00 ...... NdisWan Adapter
```

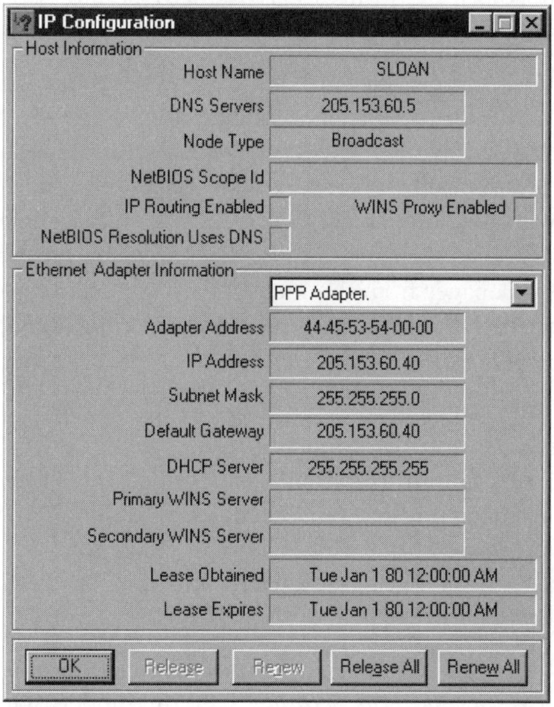

Figure 2-2. winipcfg

```
=============================================================================
=============================================================================
Active Routes:
Network Destination        Netmask          Gateway       Interface  Metric
        0.0.0.0          0.0.0.0     205.153.63.1   205.153.63.30       1
      127.0.0.0        255.0.0.0        127.0.0.1       127.0.0.1       1
   205.153.63.0    255.255.255.0   205.153.63.30   205.153.63.30       1
  205.153.63.30  255.255.255.255       127.0.0.1       127.0.0.1       1
 205.153.63.255  255.255.255.255   205.153.63.30   205.153.63.30       1
      224.0.0.0        224.0.0.0   205.153.63.30   205.153.63.30       1
255.255.255.255  255.255.255.255   205.153.63.30   205.153.63.30       1
=============================================================================

Active Connections

  Proto  Local Address          Foreign Address         State
  TCP    jsloan:1025            localhost:1028          ESTABLISHED
  TCP    jsloan:1028            localhost:1025          ESTABLISHED
  TCP    jsloan:1184            205.153.60.247:telnet   ESTABLISHED
  TCP    jsloan:1264            mail.lander.edu:pop3    TIME_WAIT
```

As you can see, the format is a little different, but it supplies the same basic information. (You can also use the command *route print* to list the routing table.) You can use *netstat -a* to get the active connections and services. There really isn't an

option that is analogous to *-i* in Unix's *netstat* (the option to display attached interfaces). For a listing of the basic syntax and available commands, try *netstat /?*.

While Windows does not provide *ps*, both Windows NT and Windows 2000 provide the Task Manager (*taskmgr.exe*), a utility that can be used to see or control
what is running. If you have the Windows Resource Kit, three additional utilities,
process viewer (*pviewer.exe*), process explode (*pview.exe*), and process monitor
(*pmon.exe*), are worth looking at. All four can be started by entering their names
at Start → Run. The Task Manager can also be started by pressing Ctrl-Alt-Delete
and selecting Task Manager from the menu or by right-clicking on a vacant area
on the task bar at the bottom of the screen and selecting Task Manger from the
menu.

You won't need NT's administrator privileges to use the DOS-based commands
just described. If you want to reconfigure the system or if you need additional
details, you will need to turn to the utilities provided by Windows. For NT, this
will require administrator privileges. (You'll also need administrative privileges to
make changes with *arp* or *route.*) This is available from Start → Settings → Control
Panel → Network or by following a similar path from My Computer. Select the
appropriate tab and fields as needed.

If you are interested in port scanners, a number are available. I have already mentioned that the *Chesapeake Port Scanner* will run under Windows. Scan the
Internet for others.

Finally, for the really brave of heart, you can go into the registry. But that's a subject for another book. (See Paul Robichaux's *Managing the Windows 2000 Registry* or Steven Thomas's *Windows NT 4.0 Registry.*)

3

Connectivity Testing

This chapter describes simple tests for individual network links and for end-to-end connectivity between networked devices. The tools described in this chapter are used to show that there is a functioning connection between two devices. These tools can also be used for more sophisticated testing, including the discovery of path characteristics and the general performance measurements. These additional uses are described in Chapter 4. Tools used for testing protocol issues related to connectivity are described in Chapter 9. You may want to turn next to these chapters if you need additional information in either of these areas.

This chapter begins with a quick review of cabling practices. If your cabling isn't adequate, that's the first thing you need to address. Next, there is a lengthy discussion of using *ping* to test connectivity along with issues that might arise when using *ping*, such as security problems. Next, I describe alternatives to *ping*. Finally, I discuss alternatives that run on Microsoft Windows platforms.

Cabling

For most managers, cabling is the most boring part of a network. Even administrators who are normally control freaks will often jump at the opportunity to delegate or cede responsibility for cabling to somebody else. It has none of the excitement of new equipment or new software. It is often hidden away in wiring closets, walls, and ceilings. When it is visible, it is usually in the way or an eyesore. The only time most managers think about cabling is when it is causing problems. Yet, unless you are one of a very small minority running a wireless network, it is the core of your network. Without adequate cabling, you don't have a network.

Although this is a book about software tools, not cabling, the topics are not unrelated. If you have a cabling problem, you may need to turn to the tools described later in this chapter to pinpoint the problem. Conversely, to properly use these tools, you can't ignore cabling, as it may be the real source of your problems.

If a cable is damaged, it won't be difficult to recognize the problem. But intermittent cabling problems can be a nightmare to solve. The problem may be difficult to recognize as a cabling problem. It may come and go, working correctly most of the time. The problem may arise in cables that have been in use for years. For example, I once watched a technician try to deal with a small classroom LAN that had been in use for more than five years and would fail only when the network was heavily loaded, i.e., if and only if there was a scheduled class in the room. The problem took weeks before what proved to be a cabling problem was resolved. In the meantime, several classes were canceled.

A full discussion of cabling practices, standards, and troubleshooting has been the topic of several books, so this coverage will be very selective. I am assuming that you are familiar with the basics. If not, several references in Appendix B provide a general but thorough introduction to cabling.

With cabling, as with most things, it is usually preferable to prevent problems than to have to subsequently deal with them. The best way to avoid cabling problems is to take a proactive approach. While some of the following suggestions may seem excessive, the costs are minimal when compared to what can be involved in solving a problem.

Installing New Cabling

If you are faced with a new installation, take the time to be sure it is done correctly from the start. While it is fairly straightforward to wire a few machines together in a home office, cabling should not generally be viewed as a do-it-yourself job. Large cabling projects should be left to trained professionals whenever possible.

Cabling is usually a large investment. Correcting cabling problems can be very costly in lost time both for diagnosing the problem and for correcting the problem. Also, cabling must conform to all applicable building and fire codes. For example, using nonplenum cabling in plenum spaces can, in the event of a fire, greatly endanger the safety of you and your fellow workers. (*Plenum cabling* is cabling designed to be used in *plenum spaces*, spaces used to recirculate air in a building. It uses materials that have low flame-spread and low smoke-producing properties.)

Cabling can also be very sensitive to its physical environment. Cable that runs too near fluorescent lights or large motors, e.g., elevator motors, can be problematic. Proximity to power lines can also cause problems. The network cable acts like an antenna, picking up other nearby electrical activity and introducing unwanted signals or noise onto the network. This can be highly intermittent and very difficult to identify. Concerns such as these should be enough to discourage you from doing the job yourself unless you are very familiar with the task.

Unfortunately, sometimes budget or organizational policies are such that you will have no choice but to do the job yourself or use internal personnel. If you must do the job yourself, take the time to learn the necessary skills before you begin. Get formal training if at all possible. Invest in the appropriate tools and test equipment to do the job correctly. And make sure you aren't violating any building or fire codes.

If the wiring is handled by others, you will need to evaluate whether those charged with the task really have the skill to complete the job. Most electricians and telephone technicians are not familiar with data cabling practices. Worse still, many don't realize this. So, if asked, they will reassure you they can do the job. If possible, use an installer who has been certified in data cabling. Once you have identified a likely candidate, follow up on her references. Ask for the names of some past customers and call those customers. If possible, ask to see some of her work.

When planning a project, you should install extra cable whenever feasible. It is much cheaper to pull extra cable as you go than to go back and install new cable or replace a faulty cable. You should also consider technologies that will support higher speeds than you are currently using. For example, if you are using 10-Mbps Ethernet to the desktop, you should install cable that will support 100 Mbps. In the past it has been a common recommendation to install fiber-optic cables to the desk as well, even if you aren't using fiber technologies at the desk at this time. Recent developments with copper cables have made this more of a judgment call. Certainly, you will want to pull spare fiber to any point your backbone may eventually include.

If at all feasible, cabling should be certified. This means that each cable is tested to ensure that it meets appropriate performance standards for the intended application. This can be particularly important for spare cabling. When it is time to use that cable, you don't want any nasty surprises.

Adequate documentation is essential. Maintenance will be much simpler if you follow cabling standards and use one of the more common structured cable schemes. More information can be found in the sources given in Appendix B.

Maintaining Existing Cabling

For existing cabling, you won't have as much latitude as with a new installation. You certainly won't want to go back and replace working cable just because it does not follow some set of standards. But there are several things you can do to make your life simpler when you eventually encounter problems.

The first step in cable management is knowing which cable is which and where each cable goes. Perhaps the most important tool for the management and troubleshooting of cabling is a good label maker. Even if you weren't around when the cable was originally installed, you should be able, over time, to piece together this information. You will also want to collect basic information about each cable such as cable types and lengths.

You will want to know which of your cables don't meet standards. If you have one of the more sophisticated cable testers, you can self-certify your cabling plant. You probably won't want to do either of these tasks all at once, but you may be able to do a little at a time. And you will definitely want to do it for any changes or additions you make.

Labeling Cables

This should be a self-explanatory topic. Unfortunately for some, this is not the case. I have very vivid memories of working with a wiring technician with years of experience. The individual had worked for major organizations and should have been quite familiar with labeling practices.

We were installing a student laboratory. The laboratory has a switch mounted in a box on the wall. Cabling went from the box into the wall and then through cable raceways down the length of the room. Along the raceway, it branched into raceways built into computer tables going to the individual computers. The problem should be clear. Once the cable disappears into the wall and raceways, it is impossible to match the end at the switch with the corresponding end that emerges at the computer.

While going over what needed to be done, I mentioned, needlessly I thought, that the cable should be clearly labeled. This was just one part of my usual lengthy litany. He thought for a moment and then said, "I guess I can do that." Then a puzzled expression came over his face and he added in dead earnest, "Which end do you want labeled?" I'd like to think he was just putting me on, but I don't think so.

You should use some method of attaching labels that is reasonably permanent. It can be very discouraging to find several labels lying on the floor beneath your equipment rack. Also, you should use a meaningful scheme for identifying your cables. *TIA/EIA-606 Administration Standard for Telecommunications Infrastructure of Commercial Buildings* provides one possibility. (See Appendix B for more information of TIA/EIA standards.) And, at the risk of stating the obvious, unless you can see the entire cable at the same time, it should be labeled at both ends.

Testing Cabling

Cable testing can be a simple, quick check for continuity or a complex set of measurements that carefully characterizes a cable's electrical properties. If you are in a hurry to get up and running, you may be limited to simple connectivity tests, but the more information you collect, the better prepared you will be to deal with future problems. If you must be up quickly, make definite plans to return and finish the job, and stick to those plans.

Link lights

Perhaps the simplest test is to rely on the network interface's *link lights*. Almost all networking equipment now has status lights that show, when lit, that you have functioning connections. If these do not light when you make a connection, you definitely have a problem somewhere. Keep in mind, however, a lit link light does not necessarily indicate the absence of a problem.

Many devices have additional indicators that give you more information. It is not uncommon to have a *transmit light* that blinks each time a packet is sent, a *receive light* that blinks each time a packet is received, and a *collision light* that blinks each time the device detects a collision. To get an idea of what is normal, look at the lights on other computers on the same network.

Typically, you would expect to see the receive light blinking intermittently as soon as you connect the device to an active network. Generally, anomalous behavior with the receive light indicates a problem somewhere else on your network. If it doesn't ever light, you may have a problem with your connection to the network. For example, you could be plugged into a hub that is not connected to the network. If the light is on all or most of the time, you probably have an overloaded network.

The transmit light should come on whenever you access the network but should remain off otherwise. You may be surprised, however, how often a computer will access the network. It will almost certainly blink several times when your computer is booted. If in doubt, try some basic networking tasks while watching for activity. If it does not light when you try to access the network, you have problems on that computer. If it stays lit, you not only have a problem but also are probably flooding the network with packets, thereby causing problems for others on the network as well. You may want to isolate this machine until the problem is resolved.

In the ideal network, from the user's perspective at least, the collision light should remain relatively inactive. However, excessive collision light flashing or even one that remains on most of the time may not indicate a problem. A collision is a very brief event. If the light only remained on for the length of the event, the flash would be too brief to be seen. Consequently, these lights are designed to remain on much longer than the actual event. A collision light that remains on doesn't necessarily mean that your network is saturated with collisions. On the other hand, this is something you'll want to investigate further.

For any of the cases in which you have an indication of a network overload, unless your network is completely saturated, you should be able to get some packets through. And you should see similar problems on every computer on that network segment. If your network is completely saturated, then you may have a malfunctioning device that is continuously transmitting. Usually, this can be easily located by turning devices off one at a time until the problem suddenly disappears.

If you have an indication of a network overload, you should look at the overall behavior and structure of your network. A good place to start is with *netstat* as discussed in Chapter 4. For a more thorough discussion of network performance monitoring, turn to Chapter 8.

One last word of warning—you may see anomalous behavior with any of these lights if your interface is misconfigured or has the wrong driver installed.

Cable testers

A wide variety of cable testers are available. Typically, you get what you pay for. Some check little more than continuity and the cable's pin-out (that the individual wires are connected to the appropriate pins). Others are extremely sophisticated and fully characterize the electrical properties of your cabling. These can easily cost thousands of dollars. Better testers typically consist of a pair of units—the actual tester and a termination device that creates a signal loop. These devices commonly check the following:

Wire-map (or pin-outs)

This checks to see if the corresponding pins on each end of a cable are correctly paired. Failure indicates an improperly terminated cable, such as crossed wires or faulty connections.

Near End Cross-Talk (NEXT)

This is a measure of how much a signal on one wire interferes with other signals on adjacent wires. High values can indicate improper termination or the wrong type of cable or connectors.

Attenuation

This measures how much of the original signal is lost over the length of the cable. As this is frequency dependent, this should be done at a number of different frequencies over the range used. It will determine the maximum data rates the cable can support. Problem causes include the wrong cable type, faulty connectors, and excessive lengths.

Impedance

This is the opposition to changes in current and arises from the resistance and the inductance of the cable. Impedance measurements may be useful for finding an impedance mismatch that may cause reflected signals at the point where cables are joined. It can also be useful in ascertaining whether or not you are using the right type of cable.

Attenuation to Cross-talk Ratio (ARC)

This is a comparison of signal strength to noise. Values that are too low indicate excessive cable length or poor connections.

Capacitance

This is the electrical field energy that can be stored in the cable. Anomalous values can indicate problems with the cable such as shorts or broken wires.

Length

By timing the return of a signal injected onto the cable, the length of a cable can be discovered. This can reveal how much cable is hidden in the walls, allowing you to verify that cable lengths are not exceeding the maximum allowed by the applicable standards.

The documentation with your cable tester will provide more details in understanding and using these tests.

The better cable testers may be preprogrammed with appropriate values for different types of cable, allowing you to quickly identify parameters that are out of specification. A good tester should also allow you to print or upload measurements into a database. This allows you to easily compare results over time to identify changes.

Other cable tests

In general, moving cables around is a poor way to test them. You may jiggle a nearby poor connection, changing the state of the problem. But if you can't afford a cable tester, you may have little choice.

If the cable in question is not installed in the wall, you can try to test it by swapping it with a cable known to be good. However, it is usually better to replace a working cable with a questionable cable and see if things continue to work rather than the other way around. This method is more robust to multiple failures. You will immediately know the status of the questionable cable. If you replace a questionable cable with a good cable and you still have problems, you clearly have a problem other than the cable. But you don't know if it is just a different problem or an additional problem. Of course, this approach ties up more systems.

Remember, electrical connectivity does not equate to network connectivity. I've seen technicians plug different subnets into the same hub and then wonder why the computers can't communicate.*

Testing Adapters

While most problems with adapters, such as Ethernet cards, are configuration errors, sometimes adapters do fail. Without getting into the actual electronics, there are generally three simple tests you can make with adapters. However, each has its drawbacks:

- If you have some doubts about whether the problem is in the adapter or network, you might try eliminating the bulk of the network from your tests. The easiest approach is to create a two-computer network using another working computer. If you use coaxial cable, simply run a cable known to be good between the computers and terminate each end appropriately. For twisted pair, use a crossover cable, i.e., a patch cable with send and receive crossed. If all is well, the computers should be able to communicate. If they don't, you should have a pretty clear idea of where to look next.

  The crossover cable approach is analogous to setting up a serial connection using a null modem. You may want to first try this method with two working computers just to verify you are using the right kind of cable. You should also be sure IP numbers and masks are set appropriately on each computer. Clearly, the drawbacks with this approach are shuffling computers around and finding the right cable. But if you have a portable computer available, the shuffling isn't too difficult.

- A second alternative is to use the configuration and test software provided by the adapter's manufacturer. If you bought the adapter as a separate purchase, you probably already have this software. If your adapter came with your computer, you may have to go to the manufacturer's web page and download the software. This approach can be helpful, particularly with configuration errors. For example, a combination adapter might be configured for coaxial cable while you are trying to use it with twisted pair. You may be able to change interrupts, DMA channels, memory locations, bus mastering configuration, and framing types with this software.

  Using diagnostic software has a couple of limitations. First, the software may not check for some problems and may seemingly absolve a faulty card. Second, the software may not be compatible with the operating system you

---

* There are also circumstances in which this will work, but mixing subnets this way is an extremely bad idea.

are using. This is particularly likely if you are using something like Linux or FreeBSD on an Intel platform.

- The third alternative is to swap the card for one that is known to work. This presumes that you have a spare card or are willing to remove one from another machine. It also presumes that you aren't having problems that may damage some other component in the computer or the new card. Even though I generally keep spare cards on hand, I usually leave this test until last whenever possible.

Software Testing with ping

Thus far, I have described ways to examine electrical and mechanical problems. The tools described in this section, *ping* and its variants, focus primarily on the software problems and the interaction of software with hardware. When these tools successfully communicate with remote systems, you have established basic connectivity. Your problem is almost certainly at a higher level in your system.

With these tools, you begin with the presumption that your hardware is working correctly. If the link light is out on the local host, these tools will tell you nothing you don't already know. But if you simply suspect a hardware problem somewhere on your network, these tools may help you locate the problem. Once you know the location of the problem, you will use the techniques previously described to resolve it. These tools can also provide insight when your hardware is marginal or when you have intermittent failures.

ping

While there are several useful programs for analyzing connectivity, unquestionably *ping* is the most commonly used program. As it is required by the IP RFC, it is almost always available as part of the networking software supplied with any system. In addition, numerous enhanced versions of *ping* are available at little or no cost. There are even web sites that will allow you to run *ping* from their sites.

Moreover, the basic idea has been adapted from IP networks to other protocols. For example, Cisco's implementation of *ping* has an optional keyword to check connectivity among routers using AppleTalk, DECnet, or IPX. *ping* is nearly universal.

ping was written by Mike Muuss.[*] Inspired by echo location, the name comes from sounds sonar makes. The name *ping* is frequently described as an acronym for Packet InterNet Groper. But, according to Muuss's web page, the acronym was applied to the program after the fact by someone else.

---

[*] For more on the background of *ping* as well as a review of the book *The Story About Ping*, an alleged allegory of the *ping* program, visit Muuss's web page at *http://ftp.arl.mil/~mike/ping.html*.

How ping Works

It is, in essence, a simple program based on a simple idea. (Muuss describes it as a 1000-line hack that was completed in about one evening.) One network device sends a request for a reply to another device and records the time the request was sent. The device receiving the request sends a packet back. When the reply is received, the round-trip time for packet propagation can be calculated. The receipt of a reply indicates a working connection. This elapsed time provides an indication of the length of the path. Consistency among repeated queries gives an indication of the quality of the connection. Thus, *ping* answers two basic questions. Do I have a connection? How good is that connection? In this chapter, we will focus on the first question, returning to the second question in the next chapter.

Clearly, for the program to work, the networking protocol must support this query/response mechanism. The *ping* program is based on Internet Control Message Protocol (ICMP), part of the TCP/IP protocol. ICMP was designed to pass information about network performance between network devices and exchange error messages. It supports a wide variety of message types, including this query/response mechanism.

The normal operation of *ping* relies on two specific ICMP messages, ECHO_REQUEST and ECHO_REPLY, but it may respond to ICMP messages other than ECHO_REPLY when appropriate. In theory, all TCP/IP-based network equipment should respond to an ECHO_REQUEST by returning the packet to the source, but this is not always the case.

Simple examples

The default behavior of *ping* will vary among implementations. Typically, implementations have a wide range of command-line options so that the behavior discussed here is generally available. For example, implementations may default to sending a single packet, a small number of packets, or a continuous stream of packets. They may respond with a set of round-trip transmission times or with a simple message. The version of *ping* that comes with the Solaris operating system sends, by default, a single ICMP packet. It responds that the destination is alive or that no answer was received. In this example, an ECHO_REPLY was received:

```
sol1# ping 205.153.63.30
205.153.63.30 is alive
sol1#
```

In this example, no response was received before the program timed out:

```
sol1# ping www.microsoft.com
no answer from microsoft.com
sol1#
```

Note that *ping* can be used with an IP number or with a hostname, as shown by these examples.

Other implementations will, by default, repeatedly send ECHO_REQUESTs until interrupted. FreeBSD is an example:

```
bsd1# ping www.bay.com
PING www.bay.com (204.80.244.66): 56 data bytes
64 bytes from 204.80.244.66: icmp_seq=0 ttl=112 time=180.974 ms
64 bytes from 204.80.244.66: icmp_seq=1 ttl=112 time=189.810 ms
64 bytes from 204.80.244.66: icmp_seq=2 ttl=112 time=167.653 ms
^C
--- www.bay.com ping statistics ---
3 packets transmitted, 3 packets received, 0% packet loss
round-trip min/avg/max/stddev = 167.653/179.479/189.810/9.107 ms
bsd1#
```

The execution of the program was interrupted with a Ctrl-C, at which point the summary statistics were printed. Without an interrupt, the program will continue indefinitely. With the appropriate command-line option, *-s*, similar output can be obtained with Solaris.

Interpreting results

Before I go into the syntax of *ping* and the ways it might be used, it is worth getting a clear understanding of what results might be returned by *ping*. The simplest results are seen with Solaris, a message simply stating, in effect, that the reply packet was received or was not received. With FreeBSD, we receive a great deal more information. It repeatedly sends packets and reports results for each packet, as well as providing a summary of results. In particular, for each packet we are given the size and source of each packet, an ICMP sequence number, a *Time-To-Live* (TTL) count, and the round-trip times. (The TTL field is explained later.) Of these, the sequence number and round-trip times are the most revealing when evaluating basic connectivity.

When each ECHO_REQUEST packet is sent, the time the packet is sent is recorded in the packet. This is copied into the corresponding ECHO_REPLY packet by the remote host. When an ECHO_REPLY packet is received, the elapsed time is calculated by comparing the current time to the time recorded in the packet, i.e., the time the packet was sent. This difference, the elapsed time, is reported, along with the sequence number and the TTL, which comes from the packet's header. If no ECHO_REPLY packet is received that matches a particular sequence number, that packet is presumed lost. The size and the variability of elapsed times will depend on the number and speed of intermediate links as well as the congestion on those links.

An obvious question is "What values are reasonable?" Typically, this is highly dependent on the networks you cross and the amount of activity on those networks. For example, these times are taken from a PPP link with a 28.8-Kbps modem:

```
64 bytes from 205.153.60.42: icmp_seq=0 ttl=30 time=225.620 ms
64 bytes from 205.153.60.42: icmp_seq=1 ttl=30 time=213.652 ms
64 bytes from 205.153.60.42: icmp_seq=2 ttl=30 time=215.306 ms
64 bytes from 205.153.60.42: icmp_seq=3 ttl=30 time=194.782 ms
64 bytes from 205.153.60.42: icmp_seq=4 ttl=30 time=199.562 ms
...
```

The following times were for the same link only moments later:

```
64 bytes from 205.153.60.42: icmp_seq=0 ttl=30 time=1037.367 ms
64 bytes from 205.153.60.42: icmp_seq=1 ttl=30 time=2119.615 ms
64 bytes from 205.153.60.42: icmp_seq=2 ttl=30 time=2269.448 ms
64 bytes from 205.153.60.42: icmp_seq=3 ttl=30 time=2209.715 ms
64 bytes from 205.153.60.42: icmp_seq=4 ttl=30 time=2493.881 ms
...
```

There is nothing wrong here. The difference is that a file download was in progress on the link during the second set of measurements.

In general, you can expect very good times if you are staying on a LAN. Typically, values should be well under 100 ms and may be less than 10 ms. Once you move onto the Internet, values may increase dramatically. A coast-to-coast, round-trip time will take at least 60 ms when following a mythical straight-line path with no congestion. For remote sites, times of 200 ms may be quite good, and times up to 500 ms may be acceptable. Much larger times may be a cause for concern. Keep in mind these are very rough numbers.

You can also use *ping* to calculate a rough estimate of the *throughput* of a connection. (Throughput and related concepts are discussed in greater detail in Chapter 4.) Send two packets with different sizes across the path of interest. This is done with the *-s* option, which is described later in this chapter. The difference in times will give an idea of how much longer it takes to send the additional data in the larger packet. For example, say it takes 30 ms to ping with 100 bytes and 60 ms with 1100 bytes. Thus, it takes an additional 30 ms round trip or 15 ms in one direction to send the additional 1000 bytes or 8000 bits. The throughput is roughly 8000 bits per 15 ms or 540,000 bps. The difference between two measurements is used to eliminate overhead. This is extremely crude. It makes no adjustment for other traffic and gives a composite picture for all the links on a path. Don't try to make too much out of these numbers.

It may seem that the TTL field could be used to estimate the number of hops on a path. Unfortunately, this is problematic. When a packet is sent, the TTL field is initialized and is subsequently decremented by each router along the path. If it reaches zero, the packet is discarded. This imposes a finite lifetime on all packets, ensuring that, in the event of a routing loop, the packet won't remain on the network indefinitely. Unfortunately, the TTL field may or may not be reset at the remote machine and, if reset, there is little consistency in what it is set to. Thus, you need to know very system-specific information to use the TTL field to estimate the number of hops on a path.

A steady stream of replies with reasonably consistent times is generally an indication of a healthy connection. If packets are being lost or discarded, you will see jumps in the sequence numbers, the missing numbers corresponding to the lost packets. Occasional packet loss probably isn't an indication of any real problem. This is particularly true if you are crossing a large number of routers or any congested networks. It is particularly common for the first packet in a sequence to be lost or have a much higher elapsed time. This behavior is a consequence of the need to do ARP resolution at each link along the path for the first packet. Since the ARP data is cached, subsequent packets do not have this overhead. If, however, you see a large portion of the packets being lost, you may have a problem somewhere along the path.

The program will also report duplicate and damaged packets. Damaged packets are a cause for real concern. You will need to shift into troubleshooting mode to locate the source of the problem. Unless you are trying to *ping* a broadcast address, you should not see duplicate packets. If your computers are configured to respond to ECHO_REQUESTs sent to broadcast addresses, you will see lots of duplicate packets. With normal use, however, duplicate responses could indicate a routing loop. Unfortunately, *ping* will only alert you to the problem; its underlying mechanism cannot explain the cause of such problems.

In some cases you may receive other ICMP error messages. Typically from routers, these can be very informative and helpful. For example, in the following, an attempt is made to reach a device on a nonexistent network:

```
bsd1# ping 172.16.4.1
PING 172.16.4.1 (172.16.4.1): 56 data bytes
36 bytes from 172.16.2.1: Destination Host Unreachable
Vr HL TOS  Len   ID Flg  off TTL Pro  cks      Src      Dst
 4  5  00 5400 5031   0 0000  fe  01 0e49 172.16.2.13  172.16.4.1

36 bytes from 172.16.2.1: Destination Host Unreachable
Vr HL TOS  Len   ID Flg  off TTL Pro  cks      Src      Dst
 4  5  00 5400 5034   0 0000  fe  01 0e46 172.16.2.13  172.16.4.1

^C
--- 172.16.4.1 ping statistics ---
2 packets transmitted, 0 packets received, 100% packet loss
```

Since the router has no path to the network, it returns the ICMP DESTINATION_ HOST_UNREACHABLE message. In general, you will receive a `Destination Host Unreachable` *warning* or a `Destination Network Unreachable` *warning* if the problem is detected on the machine where *ping* is being run. If the problem is detected on a device trying to forward a packet, you will receive only a `Destination Host Unreachable` warning.

In the next example, an attempt is being made to cross a router that has been configured to deny traffic from the source:

```
bsd1# ping 172.16.3.10
PING 172.16.3.10 (172.16.3.10): 56 data bytes
36 bytes from 172.16.2.1: Communication prohibited by filter
Vr HL TOS  Len   ID Flg  off TTL Pro  cks      Src       Dst
 4  5  00 5400 5618   0 0000  ff  01 0859 172.16.2.13  172.16.3.10

36 bytes from 172.16.2.1: Communication prohibited by filter
Vr HL TOS  Len   ID Flg  off TTL Pro  cks      Src       Dst
 4  5  00 5400 561b   0 0000  ff  01 0856 172.16.2.13  172.16.3.10

^C
--- 172.16.3.10 ping statistics ---
2 packets transmitted, 0 packets received, 100% packet loss
```

The warning `Communication prohibited by filter` indicates the packets are being discarded. Be aware that you may be blocked by filters without seeing this message. Consider the following example:

```
bsd1# ping 172.16.3.10
PING 172.16.3.10 (172.16.3.10): 56 data bytes
^C
--- 172.16.3.10 ping statistics ---
6 packets transmitted, 0 packets received, 100% packet loss
```

The same filter was used on the router, but it was applied to traffic leaving the network rather than inbound traffic. Hence, no messages were sent. Unfortunately, *ping* will often be unable to tell you why a packet is unanswered.

While these are the most common ICMP messages you will see, *ping* may display a wide variety of messages. A listing of ICMP messages can be found in RFC 792. A good discussion of the more common messages can be found in Eric A. Hall's *Internet Core Protocols: The Definitive Guide*. Most ICMP messages are fairly self-explanatory if you are familiar with TCP/IP.

Options

A number of options are generally available with *ping*. These vary considerably from implementation to implementation. Some of the more germane options are described here.

Several options control the number of or the rate at which packets are sent. The *-c* option will allow you to specify the number of packets you want to send. For example, *ping -c10* would send 10 packets and stop. This can be very useful if you are running *ping* from a script.

The commands *-f* and *-l* are used to flood packets onto a network. The *-f* option says that packets should be sent as fast as the receiving host can handle them. This can be used to stress-test a link or to get some indication of the comparative performance of interfaces. In this example, the program is run for about 10 seconds on each of two different destinations:

```
bsd1# ping -f 172.16.2.12
PING 172.16.2.12 (172.16.2.12): 56 data bytes
..^C
--- 172.16.2.12 ping statistics ---
27585 packets transmitted, 27583 packets received, 0% packet loss
round-trip min/avg/max/stddev = 0.303/0.310/0.835/0.027 ms
bsd1# ping -f 172.16.2.20
PING 172.16.2.20 (172.16.2.20): 56 data bytes
.^C
--- 172.16.2.20 ping statistics ---
5228 packets transmitted, 5227 packets received, 0% packet loss
round-trip min/avg/max/stddev = 1.535/1.736/6.463/0.363 ms
```

In the first case, the destination was a 200-MHz Pentium with a PCI adapter. In the second, the destination was a 50-MHz 486 with an ISA adapter. It is not surprising that the first computer was more than five times faster. But remember, it may not be clear whether the limiting factor is the source or the receiver unless you do multiple tests. Clearly, use of this option could cripple a host. Consequently, the option requires root privileges to run and may not be included in some implementations.

The *-l* option takes a count and sends out that many packets as fast as possible. It then falls back to normal mode. This could be used to see how the router handles a flood of packets. Use of this command is also restricted to root.

The *-i* option allows the user to specify the amount of time in seconds to wait between sending consecutive packets. This could be a useful way to space out packets for extended runs or for use with scripts. In general, the effect of an occasional *ping* packet is negligible when compared to the traffic already on all but the slowest of links. Repeated packets or packet flooding can, however, add considerably to traffic and congestion. For that reason, you should be very circumspect in using any of these options (and perhaps *ping* in general).

The amount and form of the data can be controlled to a limited extent. The *-n* option restricts output to numeric form. This is useful if you are having DNS problems. Implementations also typically include options for more detailed output, typically *-v* for verbose output, and for fewer details, typically *-q* and *-Q* for quiet output.

The amount and nature of the data in the frame can be controlled using the *-s* and *-p* options. The packet size option, *-s*, allows you to specify how much data to send. If set too small, less than 8, there won't be space in the packet for a time-stamp. Setting the packet size can help in diagnosing a problem caused by path *Maximum Transmission Unit* (MTU) settings (the largest frame size that can be sent on the path) or fragmentation problems. (Fragmentation is dividing data among multiple frames when a single packet is too large to cross a link. It is handled by the IP portion of the protocol stack.) The general approach is to increase packet sizes up to the maximum allowed to see if at some point you have problems. When this option isn't used, *ping* defaults to 64 bytes, which may be too small a packet to reveal some problems. Also remember that *ping* does not count the IP or ICMP header in the specified length so your packets will be 28 bytes larger than you specify.

You could conceivably see MTU problems with protocols, such as PPP, that use escaped characters as well.* With escaped characters, a single character may be replaced by two characters. The expansion of escaped characters increases the size of the data frame and can cause problems with MTU restrictions or fragmentation.

The *-p* option allows you to specify a pattern for the data included within the packet after the timestamp. You might use this if you think you have data-dependent problems. The FreeBSD manpage for *ping* notes that this sort of problem might show up if you lack sufficient "transitions" in your data, i.e., your data is all or almost all ones or all or almost all zeros. Some serial links are particularly vulnerable to this sort of problem.

There are a number of other options not discussed here. These provide control over what interfaces are used, the use of multicast packets, and so forth. The flags presented here are from FreeBSD and are fairly standard. Be aware, however, that different implementations may use different flags for these options. Be sure to consult your documentation if things don't work as expected.

Using ping

To isolate problems using *ping*, you will want to run it repeatedly, changing your destination address so that you work your way through each intermediate device to your destination. You should begin with your *loopback* interface. Use either `localhost` or `127.0.0.1`. Next, *ping* your interface by IP number. (Run *ifconfig -a* if in doubt.) If either of these fails, you know that you have a problem with the host.

Next, try a host on a local network that you know is operational. Use its IP address rather than its hostname. If this fails, there are several possibilities. If other

---

* Generally there are better ways to deal with problems with PPP. For more information, see Chapter 15 in *Using and Managing PPP*, by Andrew Sun.

hosts are able to communicate on the local network, then you likely have problems with your connection to the network. This could be your interface, the cable to your machine, or your connection to a hub or switch. Of course, you can't rule out configuration errors such as media type on the adapter or a bad IP address or mask.

Next, try to reach the same host by name rather than number. If this fails, you almost certainly have problems with name resolution. Even if you have this problem, you can continue using *ping* to check your network, but you will need to use IP addresses.

Try reaching the near and far interfaces of your router. This will turn up any basic routing problems you may have on your host or connectivity problems getting to your router.

If all goes well here, you are ready to ping remote computers. (You will need to know the IP address of the intermediate devices to do this test. If in doubt, read the section on *traceroute* in the next chapter.) Realize, of course, that if you start having failures at this point, the problem will likely lie beyond your router. For example, your ICMP ECHO_REQUEST packets may reach the remote machine, but it may not have a route to your machine to use for the ICMP ECHO_REPLY packets.

When faced with failure at this point, your response will depend on who is responsible for the machines beyond your router. If this is still part of your network, you will want to shift your tests to machines on the other side of the router and try to work in both directions.

If these machines are outside your responsibility or control, you will need to enlist the help of the appropriate person. Before you contact this person, however, you should collect as much information as you can. There are three things you may want to do. First, go back to using IP numbers if you have been using names. As said before, if things start working, you have a name resolution problem.

Second, if you were trying to ping a device several hops beyond your router, go back to closer machines and try to zero in on exactly where you first encountered the problem.

Finally, be sure to probe from more than one machine. While you may have a great deal of confidence in your local machine at this point, your discussion with the remote administrator may go much more smoothly if you can definitely say that you are seeing this problem from multiple machines instead of just one. In general, this stepwise approach is the usual approach for this type of problem.

Sometimes, you may be more interested in investigating connectivity over time. For example, you might have a connection that seems to come and go. By running *ping* in the background or from a script, you may be able to collect useful information. For example, with some routing protocols, updates have a way of becoming synchronized, resulting in periodic loading on the network. If you see increased delays, for example every 30 seconds, you might be having that sort of problem. Or, if you lose packets every time someone uses the elevator, you might look at the path your cable takes.

If you are looking at performance over a long period of time, you will almost certainly want to use the *-i* option to space out your packets in a more network-friendly manner. This is a reasonable approach to take if you are experiencing occasional outages and need to document the time and duration of the outages. You should also be aware that over extended periods of time, you may see changes in the paths the packets follow.

Problems with ping

Up to this point, I have been describing how *ping* is normally used. I now describe some of the complications faced when using *ping*.

First, the program does not exist in isolation, but depends on the proper functioning of other elements of the network. In particular, *ping* usually depends upon ARP and DNS. As previously noted, if you are using a hostname rather than an IP address as your destination, the name of the host will have to be resolved before *ping* can send any packets. You can bypass DNS by using IP addresses.

It is also necessary to discover the host's link-level address for each host along the path to the destination. Although this is rarely a problem, should ARP resolution fail, then *ping* will fail. You could avoid this problem, in part, by using static ARP entries to ensure that the ARP table is correct. A more common problem is that the time reported by *ping* for the first packet sent will often be distorted since it reflects both transit times and ARP resolution times. On some networks, the first packet will often be lost. You can avoid this problem by sending more than one packet and ignoring the results for the first packet.

The correct operation of your network will depend on considerations that do not affect *ping*. In such situations, *ping* will work correctly, but you will still have link problems. For example, if there are problems with the configuration of the path MTU, smaller *ping* packets may zip through the network while larger application packets may be blocked. S. Lee Henry described a problem in which she could *ping* remote systems but could not download web pages.[*] While her particular

---

[*] "Systems Administration: You Can't Get There from Here," *Server/Workstation Expert*, May 1999. This article can be found in PDF format at *http://sw.expert.com/C4/SE.C4.MAY.99.pdf*.

problem was highly unusual, it does point out that a connection can appear to be working, but still have problems.

The opposite can be true as well. Often *ping* will fail when the connection works for other uses. For various reasons, usually related to security, some system administrators may block ICMP packets in general or ECHO_REQUEST packets in particular. Moreover, this practice seems to be increasing. I've even seen a site block *ping* traffic at its DNS server.

Security and ICMP

Unfortunately, *ping* in particular, and ICMP packets in general, have been implicated in several recent denial-of-service attacks. But while these attacks have used *ping*, they are not inherently problems with *ping*. Nonetheless, network administrators have responded as though *ping* was the problem (or at least the easiest way to deal with the problem), and this will continue to affect how and even if *ping* can be used in some contexts.

Smurf Attacks

In a *Smurf Attack*, ICMP ECHO_REQUEST packets are sent to the broadcast address of a network. Depending on how hosts are configured on the network, some may attempt to reply to the ECHO_REQUEST. The resulting flood of responses may degrade the performance of the network, particularly at the destination host.

With this attack, there are usually three parties involved—the attacker who generates the original request; an intermediary, sometimes called a reflector or multiplier, that delivers the packet onto the network; and the victim. The attacker uses a forged source address so that the ECHO_REPLY packets are returned, not to the attacker, but to a "spoofed" address, i.e., the victim. The intermediary may be either a router or a compromised host on the destination network.

Because there are many machines responding to a single request, little of the attacker's bandwidth is used, while much of the victim's bandwidth may be used. Attackers have developed tools that allow them to send ECHO_REQUESTs to multiple intermediaries at about the same time. Thus, the victim will be overwhelmed by ECHO_REPLY packets from multiple sources. Notice also that congestion is not limited to just the victim but may extend through its ISP all the way back to the intermediaries' networks.

The result of these attacks is that many sites are now blocking ICMP ECHO_ REQUEST traffic into their network. Some have gone as far as to block all ICMP traffic. While understandable, this is not an appropriate response. First, it blocks legitimate uses of these packets, such as checking basic connectivity. Second, it may not be effective. In the event of a compromised host, the ECHO_REQUEST may originate within the network. At best, blocking pings is only a temporary solution.

A more appropriate response requires taking several steps. First, you should configure your routers so they will not forward broadcast traffic onto your network from other networks. How you do this will depend on the type of router you have, but solutions are available from most vendors.

Second, you may want to configure your hosts so they do not respond to ECHO_REQUESTs sent to broadcast addresses. It is easy to get an idea of which hosts on your network respond to these broadcasts. First, examine your ARP table, then ping your broadcast address, and then look at your ARP table again for new entries.*

Finally, as a good network citizen, you should install filters on your access router to prevent packets that have a source address not on your network from leaving your network. This limits not only Smurf Attacks but also other attacks based on spoofed addresses from originating on your network. These filters should also be applied to internal routers as well as access routers. (This assumes you are providing forwarding for other networks!)

If you follow these steps, you should not have to disable ICMP traffic. For more information on Smurf Attacks, including information on making these changes, visit *http://www.cert.org/advisories/CA-1998-01.html.* You might also look at RFC 2827.

Ping of Death

The specifications for TCP/IP have a maximum packet size of 65536 octets or bytes. Unfortunately, some operating systems behave in unpredictable ways if they receive a larger packet. Systems may hang, crash, or reboot. With a *Ping of Death* (or *Ping o' Death*) *Attack*, the packet size option for *ping* is used to send a slightly oversized packet to the victim's computer. For example, on some older machines, the command *ping -s 65510 172.16.2.1* (use *-l* rather than *-s* on old Windows systems) will send a packet, once headers are added, that causes this problem to the host *172.16.2.1.* (Admittedly, I have some misgivings about giving an explicit command, but this has been widely published and some of you may want to test your systems.)

This is basically an operating system problem. Large packets must be fragmented when sent. The destination will put the pieces in a buffer until all the pieces have

---

* At one time, you could test your site by going to *http://www.netscan.org*, but this site seems to have disappeared.

arrived and the packet can be reassembled. Some systems simply don't do adequate bounds checking, allowing memory to be trashed.

Again, this is not really a problem with *ping*. Any oversized packet, whether it is an ICMP packet, TCP packet, or UDP packet, will cause the same problem in susceptible operating systems. (Even IPX has been mentioned.) All *ping* does is supply a trivial way to exploit the problem. The correct way to deal with this problem is to apply the appropriate patch to your operating system. Blocking ICMP packets at your router will not protect you from other oversized packets. Fortunately, most systems have corrected this problem, so you are likely to see it only if you are running older systems.*

Other problems

Of course, there may be other perceived problems with *ping*. Since it can be used to garner information about a network, it can be seen as a threat to networks that rely on security through obscurity. It may also be seen as generating unwanted or unneeded traffic. For these and previously cited reasons, ICMP traffic is frequently blocked at routers.

Blocking is not the only difficulty that routers may create. Routers may assign extremely low priorities to ICMP traffic rather than simply block such traffic. This is particularly true for routers implementing quality of service protocols. The result can be much higher variability in traffic patterns. *Network Address Translation* (NAT) can present other difficulties. Cisco's implementation has the router responding to ICMP packets for the first address in the translation pool regardless of whether it is being used. This might not be what you would have expected.

In general, blocking ICMP packets, even just ECHO_REQUEST packets, is not desirable. You lose a valuable source of information about your network and inconvenience users who may have a legitimate need for these messages. This is often done as a stopgap measure in the absence of a more comprehensive approach to security.

Interestingly, even if ICMP packets are being blocked, you can still use *ping* to see if a host on the local subnet is up. Simply clear the ARP table (typically *arp -ad*), ping the device, and then examine the ARP table. If the device has been added to the ARP table, it is up and responding.

One final note about *ping*. It should be obvious, but *ping* checks only connectivity, not the functionality of the end device. During some network changes, I once used *ping* to check to see if a networked printer had been reconnected yet. When I was finally able to ping the device, I sent a job to the printer. However,

---

* For more information on this attack, see *http://www.cert.org/advisories/CA-1996-26.html.*

my system kept reporting that the job hadn't printed. I eventually got up and walked down the hall to the printer to see what was wrong. It had been reconnected to the network, but someone had left it offline. Be warned, it is very easy to read too much into a successful ping.

Alternatives to ping

Variants to *ping* fall into two general categories, those that add to *ping*'s functionality and those that are alternatives to *ping*. An example of the first is *fping,* and an example of the second is *echoping.*

fping

Written by Roland Schemers of Stanford University, *fping* extends *ping* to support multiple hosts in parallel. Typical output is shown in this example:

```
bsd1# fping 172.16.2.10 172.16.2.11 172.16.2.12 172.16.2.13 172.16.2.14
172.16.2.13 is alive
172.16.2.10 is alive
172.16.2.12 is alive
172.16.2.14 is unreachable
172.16.2.11 is unreachable
```

Notice that five hosts are being probed at the same time and that the results are reported in the order replies are received.

This works the same way *ping* works, through sending and receiving ICMP messages. It is primarily designed to be used with files. Several command-line options are available, including the *-f* option for reading a list of devices to probe from a file and the *-u* option used to print only those systems that are unreachable. For example:

```
bsd1# fping -u 172.16.2.10 172.16.2.11 172.16.2.12 172.16.2.13 172.16.2.14
172.16.2.14
172.16.2.11
```

The utility of this form in a script should be self-evident.

echoping

Several tools similar to *ping* don't use ICMP ECHO_REQUEST and ECHO_REPLY packets. These may provide an alternative to *ping* in some contexts.

One such program is *echoping.* It is very similar to *ping.* It works by sending packets to one of several services that may be offered over TCP and UDP—ECHO, DISCARD, CHARGEN, and HTTP. Particularly useful when ICMP messages are being blocked, *echoping* may work where *ping* fails.

If none of these services is available, *echoping* cannot be used. Unfortunately, ECHO and CHARGEN have been used in the *Fraggle* denial of service attacks. By sending the output from CHARGEN (a character-generation protocol) to ECHO, the network can be flooded. Consequently, many operating systems are now shipped with these services disabled. Thus, the program may not be as useful as *ping*. With Unix, these services are controlled by *inetd* and could be enabled if desired and if you have access to the destination machine. But these services have limited value, and you are probably better off disabling them.

In this example, I have previously enabled ECHO on *lnx1*:

```
bsd1# echoping -v lnx1

This is echoping, version 2.2.0.

Trying to connect to internet address 205.153.61.177  to transmit 256 bytes...
Connected...
Sent (256 bytes)...
256 bytes read from server.
Checked
Elapsed time: 0.004488 seconds
```

This provides basically the same information as *ping*. The *-v* option simply provides a few more details. The program defaults to TCP and ECHO. Command-line options allow UDP packet or the other services to be selected.

When *ping* was first introduced in this chapter, we saw that *www.microsoft.com* could not be reached by *ping*. Nor can it be reached using *echoping* in its default mode. But, as a web server, port 80 should be available. This is in fact the case:

```
bsd1# echoping -v -h /ms.htm www.microsoft.com:80

This is echoping, version 2.2.0.

Trying to connect to internet address 207.46.130.14 (port 80) to transmit 100
bytes...
Connected...
Sent (100 bytes)...
2830 bytes read from server.
Elapsed time: 0.269319 seconds
```

Clearly, Microsoft is blocking ICMP packets. In this example, we could just as easily have turned to our web browser. Sometimes, however, this is not the case.

An obvious question is "Why would you need such a tool?" If you have been denied access to a network, should you be using such probes? On the other hand, if you are responsible for the security of a network, you may want to test your configuration. What can users outside your network discover about your network? If this is the case, you'll need these tools to test your network.

arping

Another interesting and useful variant of *ping* is *arping. arping* uses ARP requests and replies instead of ICMP packets. Here is an example:

```
bsd2# arping -v -c3 00:10:7b:66:f7:62
This box:   Interface: ep0  IP: 172.16.2.236   MAC address: 00:60:97:06:22:22
ARPING 00:10:7b:66:f7:62
60 bytes from 172.16.2.1 (00:10:7b:66:f7:62): icmp_seq=0
60 bytes from 172.16.2.1 (00:10:7b:66:f7:62): icmp_seq=1
60 bytes from 172.16.2.1 (00:10:7b:66:f7:62): icmp_seq=2

--- 00:10:7b:66:f7:62 statistics ---
3 packets transmitted, 3 packets received,   0% unanswered
2 packets transmitted, 2 packets received,   0% unanswered
```

In this case, I've used the MAC address, but the IP address could also be used. The *-v* option is for verbose, while *-c3* limits the run to three probes. Verbose doesn't really add a lot to the default output, just the first line identifying the source. If you just want the packets sent, you can use the *-q,* or quiet, option.

This tool has several uses. First, it is a way to find which IP addresses are being used. It can also be used to work backward, i.e., to discover IP addresses given MAC addresses. For example, if you have captured non-IP traffic (e.g., IPX, etc.) and you want to know the IP address for the traffic's source, you can use *arping* with the MAC address. If you just want to check connectivity, *arping* is also a useful tool. Since ARP packets won't be blocked, this should work even when ICMP packets are blocked. You could also use this tool to probe for ARP entries in a router. Of course, due to the nature of ARP, there is not a lot that this tool can tell you about devices not on the local network.

Other programs

There are other programs that can be used to check connectivity. Two are described later in this book. *nmap* is described in Chapter 6, and *hping* is described in Chapter 9. Both are versatile tools that can be used for many purposes.

A number of *ping* variants and extended versions of *ping* are also available, both freely and commercially. Some extend *ping*'s functionality to the point that the original functionality seems little more than an afterthought. Although only a few examples are described here, don't be fooled into believing that these are all there are. A casual web search should turn up many, many more.

Finally, don't forget the obvious. If you are interested in checking only basic connectivity, you can always try programs like *telnet* or your web browser. While this is generally not a recommended approach, each problem is different, and you should use whatever works. (For a discussion of the problems with this approach, see the sidebar "Using Applications to Test Connectivity.")

Using Applications to Test Connectivity

One all-too-common way of testing a new installation is to see if networking applications are working. The cable is installed and connected, the TCP/IP stack is configured, and then a web browser is started to see if the connection is working. If you can hit a couple of web sites, then everything is alright and no further testing is needed.

This is understandably an extremely common way to test a connection. It can be particularly gratifying to see a web page loading on a computer you have just connected to your network. But it is also an extremely poor way to test a connection.

One problem is that the software stack you use to test the connection is designed to hide problems from users. If a packet is lost, the stack will transparently have the lost packet resent without any indication to the user. You could have a connection that is losing 90% of its packets. The problem would be immediately obvious when using *ping*. But with most applications, this would show up only as a slow response. Other problems include locally cached information or the presence of proxy servers on the network.

Unfortunately, web browsers seem to be the program of choice for testing a connection. This, of course, is the worst possible choice. The web's slow response is an accepted fact of life. What technician is going to blame a slow connection on his shoddy wiring when the alternative is to blame the slow connection on the Web? What technician would even consider the possibility that a slow web response is caused by a cable being too close to a fluorescent light?

The only thing testing with an application will really tell you is whether a connection is totally down. If you want to know more than that, you will have to do real testing.

Microsoft Windows

The various versions of Windows include implementations of *ping*. With the Microsoft implementation, there are a number of superficial differences in syntax and somewhat less functionality. Basically, however, it works pretty much as you might expect. The default is to send four packets, as shown in the two following examples. In the first, we successfully ping the host *www.cabletron.com*:

```
C:\>ping www.cabletron.com

Pinging www.cabletron.com [204.164.189.90] with 32 bytes of data:

Reply from 204.164.189.90: bytes=32 time=100ms TTL=239
Reply from 204.164.189.90: bytes=32 time=100ms TTL=239
```

```
Reply from 204.164.189.90: bytes=32 time=110ms TTL=239
Reply from 204.164.189.90: bytes=32 time=90ms TTL=239

C:\>
```

In the next example, we are unable to reach *www.microsoft.com* for reasons previously explained:

```
C:\>ping www.microsoft.com

Pinging microsoft.com [207.46.130.149] with 32 bytes of data:

Request timed out.
Request timed out.
Request timed out.
Request timed out.
```

Note that this is run in a DOS window. If you use *ping* without an argument, you will get a description of the basic syntax and a listing of the various options:

```
C:\>ping

Usage: ping [-t] [-a] [-n count] [-l size] [-f] [-i TTL] [-v TOS]
            [-r count] [-s count] [[-j host-list] | [-k host-list]]
            [-w timeout] destination-list

Options:
    -t              Ping the specifed host until interrupted.
    -a              Resolve addresses to hostnames.
    -n count        Number of echo requests to send.
    -l size         Send buffer size.
    -f              Set Don't Fragment flag in packet.
    -i TTL          Time To Live.
    -v TOS          Type Of Service.
    -r count        Record route for count hops.
    -s count        Timestamp for count hops.
    -j host-list    Loose source route along host-list.
    -k host-list    Strict source route along host-list.
    -w timeout      Timeout in milliseconds to wait for each reply.
```

Notice that the flooding options, fortunately, are absent and that the *-t* option is used to get an output similar to that used in most of our examples. The implementation does not provide a summary at the end, however.

In addition to Microsoft's implementation of *ping*, numerous other versions—as well as more generic tools or toolkits that include a *ping*-like utility—are available. Most are free or modestly priced. Examples include *tjping*, *trayping*, and *winping*, but many more are available, including some interesting variations. For example, *trayping* monitors a connection in the background. It displays a small heart in the system tray as long as the connection is up. As availability changes frequently, if you need another version of *ping*, search the Web.

4

Path Characteristics

In the last chapter, we attempted to answer a fundamental question, "Do we have a working network connection?" We used tools such as *ping* to verify basic connectivity. But simple connectivity is not enough for many purposes. For example, an ISP can provide connectivity but not meet your needs or expectations. If your ISP is not providing the level of service you think it should, you will need something to base your complaints on. Or, if the performance of your local network isn't adequate, you will want to determine where the bottlenecks are located before you start implementing expensive upgrades. In this chapter, we will try to answer the question, "Is our connection performing reasonably?"

We will begin by looking at ways to determine which links or individual connections compose a path. This discussion focuses on the tool *traceroute*. Next, we will turn to several tools that allow us to identify those links along a path that might cause problems. Once we have identified individual links of interest, we will examine some simple ways to further characterize the performance of those links, including estimating the bandwidth of a connection and measuring the available throughput.

Path Discovery with traceroute

This section describes *traceroute*, a tool used to discover the links along a path. While this is the first step in investigating a path's behavior and performance, it is useful for other tasks as well. In the previous discussion of *ping*, it was suggested that you work your way, hop by hop, toward a device you can't reach to discover the point of failure. This assumes that you know the path.

Path discovery is also an essential step in diagnosing routing problems. While you may fully understand the structure of your network and know what path you want your packets to take through your network, knowing the path your packets actually take is essential information and may come as a surprise.

Once packets leave your network, you have almost no control over the path they actually take to their destination. You may know very little about the structure of adjacent networks. Path discovery can provide a way to discover who their ISP is, how your ISP is connected to the world, and other information such as peering arrangements. *traceroute* is the tool of choice for collecting this kind of information.

The *traceroute* program was written by Van Jacobson and others. It is based on a clever use of the *Time-To-Live* (TTL) field in the IP packet's header. The TTL field, described briefly in the last chapter, is used to limit the life of a packet. When a router fails or is misconfigured, a routing loop or circular path may result. The TTL field prevents packets from remaining on a network indefinitely should such a routing loop occur. A packet's TTL field is decremented each time the packet crosses a router on its way through a network. When its value reaches 0, the packet is discarded rather than forwarded. When discarded, an ICMP TIME_ EXCEEDED message is sent back to the packet's source to inform the source that the packet was discarded. By manipulating the TTL field of the original packet, the program *traceroute* uses information from these ICMP messages to discover paths through a network.

traceroute sends a series of UDP packets with the destination address of the device you want a path to.* By default, *traceroute* sends sets of three packets to discover each hop. *traceroute* sets the TTL field in the first three packets to a value of 1 so that they are discarded by the first router on the path. When the ICMP TIME_EXCEEDED messages are returned by that router, *traceroute* records the source IP address of these ICMP messages. This is the IP address of the first hop on the route to the destination.

Next, three packets are sent with their TTL field set to 2. These will be discarded by the second router on the path. The ICMP messages returned by this router reveal the IP address of the second router on the path. The program proceeds in this manner until a set of packets finally has a TTL value large enough so that the packets reach their destination.

Typically, when the probe packets finally have an adequate TTL and reach their destination, they will be discarded and an ICMP PORT_UNREACHABLE message will be returned. This happens because *traceroute* sends all its probe packets with what should be invalid port numbers, i.e., port numbers that aren't usually used. To do this, *traceroute* starts with a very large port number, typically 33434, and

---

* *tracert*, a Windows variant of *traceroute*, uses ICMP rather than UDP. *tracert* is discussed later in this chapter.

increments this value with each subsequent packet. Thus, each of the three packets in a set will have three different unlikely port numbers. The receipt of ICMP PORT_UNREACHABLE messages is the signal that the end of the path has been reached. Here is a simple example of using *traceroute*:

```
bsd1# traceroute 205.160.97.122
traceroute to 205.160.97.122 (205.160.97.122), 30 hops max, 40 byte packets
 1   205.153.61.1 (205.153.61.1)  1.162 ms  1.068 ms  1.025 ms
 2   cisco (205.153.60.2)  4.249 ms  4.275 ms  4.256 ms
 3   165.166.36.17 (165.166.36.17)  4.433 ms  4.521 ms  4.450 ms
 4   e0.r01.ia-gnwd.Infoave.Net (165.166.36.33)  5.178 ms  5.173 ms  5.140 ms
 5   165.166.125.165 (165.166.125.165)  13.171 ms  13.277 ms  13.352 ms
 6   165.166.125.106 (165.166.125.106)  18.395 ms  18.238 ms  18.210 ms
 7   atm12-0-10-mp.r01.ia-clma.infoave.net (165.166.126.3)  18.816 ms  18.934 ms
18.893 ms
 8   Serial5-1-1.GW1.RDU1.ALTER.NET (157.130.35.69)  26.658 ms  26.484 ms  26.855
ms
 9   Fddi12-0-0.GW2.RDU1.ALTER.NET (137.39.40.231)  26.692 ms  26.697 ms  26.490
ms
10   smatnet-gw2.customer.ALTER.NET (157.130.36.94)  27.736 ms  28.101 ms  27.738
ms
11   rcmt1-S10-1-1.sprintsvc.net (205.244.203.50)  33.539 ms  33.219 ms  32.446 m
s
12   rcmt3-FE0-0.sprintsvc.net (205.244.112.22)  32.641 ms  32.724 ms  32.898 ms
13   gwd1-S3-7.sprintsvc.net (205.244.203.13)  46.026 ms  50.724 ms  45.960 ms
14   gateway.ais-gwd.com (205.160.96.102)  47.828 ms  50.912 ms  47.823 ms
15   pm3-02.ais-gwd.com (205.160.97.41)  63.786 ms  48.432 ms  48.113 ms
16   user58.ais-gwd.com (205.160.97.122)  200.910 ms  184.587 ms  202.771 ms
```

The results should be fairly self-explanatory. This particular path was 16 hops long. Reverse name lookup is attempted for the IP address of each device, and, if successful, these names are reported in addition to IP addresses. Times are reported for each of the three probes sent. They are interpreted in the same way as times with *ping*. (However, if you just want times for one hop, *ping* is generally a better choice.)

Although no packets were lost in this example, should a packet be lost, an asterisk is printed in the place of the missing time. In some cases, all three times may be replaced with asterisks. This can happen for several reasons. First, the router at this hop may not return ICMP TIME_EXCEEDED messages. Second, some older routers may incorrectly forward packets even though the TTL is 0. A third possibility is that ICMP messages may be given low priority and may not be returned in a timely manner. Finally, beyond some point of the path, ICMP packets may be blocked.

Other routing problems may exist as well. In some instances *traceroute* will append additional messages to the end of lines in the form of an exclamation point and a letter. !H, !N, and !P indicate, respectively, that the host, network, or protocol is unreachable. !F indicates that fragmentation is needed. !S indicates a source route failure.

Options

Two options control how much information is printed. Name resolution can be disabled with the *-n* option. This can be useful if name resolution fails for some reason or if you just don't want to wait on it. The *-v* option is the verbose flag. With this flag set, the source and packet sizes of the probes will be reported for each packet. If other ICMP messages are received, they will also be reported, so this can be an important option when troubleshooting.

Several options may be used to alter the behavior of *traceroute*, but most are rarely needed. An example is the *-m* option. The TTL field is an 8-bit number allowing a maximum of 255 hops. Most implementations of *traceroute* default to trying only 30 hops before halting. The *-m* option can be used to change the maximum number of hops tested to any value up to 255.

As noted earlier, *traceroute* usually receives a PORT_UNREACHABLE message when it reaches its final destination because it uses a series of unusually large port numbers as the destination ports. Should the number actually match a port that has a running service, the PORT_UNREACHABLE message will not be returned. This is rarely a problem since three packets are sent with different port numbers, but, if it is, the *-p* option lets you specify a different starting port so these ports can be avoided.

Normally, *traceroute* sends three probe packets for each TTL value with a timeout of three seconds for replies. The default number of packets per set can be changed with the *-q* option. The default timeout can be changed with the *-w* option.

Additional options support how packets are routed. See the manpage for details on these if needed.

Complications with traceroute

The information *traceroute* supplies has its limitations. In some situations, the results returned by *traceroute* have a very short shelf life. This is particularly true for long paths crossing several networks and ISPs.

You should also recall that a router, by definition, is a computer with multiple network interfaces, each with a different IP address. This raises an obvious question: which IP address should be returned for a router? For *traceroute*, the answer is dictated by the mechanism it uses to discover the route. It can report only the address of the interface receiving the packet. This means a quite different path will be reported if *traceroute* is run in the reverse direction.

Here is the output when the previous example is run again from what was originally the destination to what was originally the source, i.e., with the source and destination exchanged:

```
C:\>tracert 205.153.61.178

Tracing route to 205.153.61.178 over a maximum of 30 hops

    1    132 ms    129 ms    129 ms  pm3-02.ais-gwd.com [205.160.97.41]
    2    137 ms    130 ms    129 ms  sprint-cisco-01.ais-gwd.com [205.160.97.1]
    3    136 ms    129 ms    139 ms  205.160.96.101
    4    145 ms    150 ms    140 ms  rcmt3-S4-5.sprintsvc.net [205.244.203.53]
    5    155 ms    149 ms    149 ms  sl-gw2-rly-5-0-0.sprintlink.net [144.232.184.85]
    6    165 ms    149 ms    149 ms  sl-bb11-rly-2-1.sprintlink.net [144.232.0.77]
    7    465 ms    449 ms    399 ms  sl-gw11-dc-8-0-0.sprintlink.net [144.232.7.198]
    8    155 ms    159 ms    159 ms  sl-infonet-2-0-0-T3.sprintlink.net [144.228.220.6]
    9    164 ms    159 ms    159 ms  atm4-0-10-mp.r01.ia-gnvl.infoave.net [165.166.126.
4]
   10    164 ms    169 ms    169 ms  atm4-0-30.r1.scgnvl.infoave.net [165.166.125.105]
   11    175 ms    179 ms    179 ms  165.166.125.166
   12    184 ms    189 ms    195 ms  e0.r02.ia-gnwd.Infoave.Net [165.166.36.34]
   13    190 ms    179 ms    180 ms  165.166.36.18
   14    185 ms    179 ms    179 ms  205.153.60.1
   15    174 ms    179 ms    179 ms  205.153.61.178

Trace complete.
```

There are several obvious differences. First, the format is slightly different because this example was run using Microsoft's implementation of *traceroute*, *tracert*. This, however, should present no difficulty.

A closer examination shows that there are more fundamental differences. The second trace is not simply the first trace in reverse order. The IP addresses are not the same, and the number of hops is different.

There are two things going on here. First, as previously mentioned, *traceroute* reports the IP number of the interface where the packet arrives. The reverse path will use different interfaces on each router, so different IP addresses will be reported. While this can be a bit confusing at first glance, it can be useful. By running *traceroute* at each end of a connection, a much more complete picture of the connection can be created.

Figure 4-1 shows the first six hops on the path starting from the source for the first trace as reconstructed from the pair of traces. We know the packet originates at *205.153.61.178*. The first trace shows us the first hop is *205.153.61.1*. It leaves this router on interface *205.153.60.1* for *205.153.60.2*. The second of these addresses is just the next hop in the first trace. The first address comes from the second trace. It is the last hop before the destination. It is also reasonable in that we have two addresses that are part of the same class C network. With IP networks, the ends of a link are part of the link and must have IP numbers consistent with a single network.

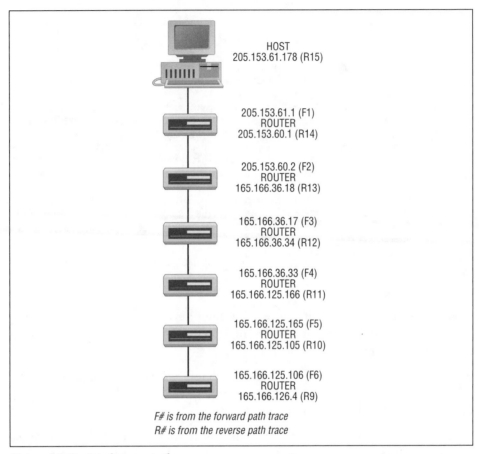

Figure 4-1. First six hops on path

From the first trace, we know packets go from the *205.153.60.2* to *165.166.36.17.* From the reverse trace, we are able to deduce that the other end of the *165.166. 36.17* link is *165.166.36.18.* Or, equivalently, the outbound interface for the *205. 153.60.2* router has the address *165.166.36.18.*

In the same manner, the next router's inbound interface is *165.166.36.17,* and its outbound interface is *165.166.36.34.* This can be a little confusing since it appears that these last three addresses should be on the same network. On closer examination of this link and adjacent links, it appears that this class B address is using a subnet mask of */20.* With this assumption, the addresses are consistent.

We can proceed in much the same manner to discover the next few links. However, when we get to the seventh entry in the first trace (or to the eighth entry working backward in the second trace), the process breaks down. The reason is simple—we have asymmetric paths across the Internet. This also accounts for the difference in the number of hops between the two traces.

In much the same way we mapped the near end of the path, the remote end can be reconstructed as well. The paths become asymmetric at the seventh router when working in this direction. Figure 4-2 shows the first four hops. We could probably fill in the remaining addresses for each direction by running *traceroute* to the specific machine where the route breaks down, but this probably isn't worth the effort.

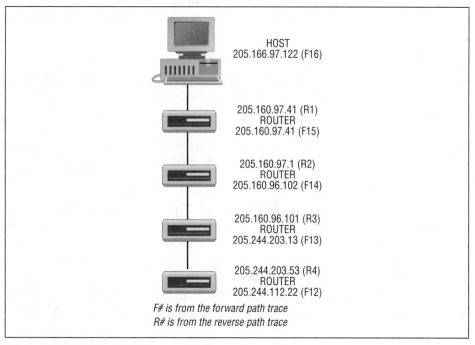

HOST
205.166.97.122 (F16)

205.160.97.41 (R1)
ROUTER
205.160.97.41 (F15)

205.160.97.1 (R2)
ROUTER
205.160.96.102 (F14)

205.160.96.101 (R3)
ROUTER
205.244.203.13 (F13)

205.244.203.53 (R4)
ROUTER
205.244.112.22 (F12)

F# is from the forward path trace
R# is from the reverse path trace

Figure 4-2. First four hops on reverse path

One possible surprise in Figure 4-2 is that we have the same IP number, *205.160.97.41*, on each interface at the first hop. The explanation is that dial-in access is being used. The IP number *205.166.97.122* is assigned to the host when the connection is made. *205.160.97.41* must be the access router. This numbering scheme is normal for an access router.

Although we haven't constructed a complete picture of the path(s) between these two computers, we have laid out the basic connection to our network through our

ISP. This is worth working out well in advance of any problems. When you suspect problems, you can easily ping these intermediate routers to pinpoint the exact location of a problem. This will tell you whether it is your problem or your ISP's problem. This can also be nice information to have when you call your ISP.

To construct the bidirectional path using the technique just described, you need access to a second, remote computer on the Internet from which you can run *traceroute*. Fortunately, this is not a problem. There are a number of sites on the Internet, which, as a service to the network community, will run *traceroute* for you. Often called *looking glasses*, such sites can provide a number of other services as well. For example, you may be able to test how accessible your local DNS setup is by observing how well *traceroute* works. A list of such sites can be found at *http://www.traceroute.org*. Alternately, the search string "web traceroute" or "traceroute looking glass" will usually turn up a number of such sites with most search engines.

In theory, there is an alternative way to find this type of information with some implementations of *traceroute*. Some versions of *traceroute* support *loose source routing*, the ability to specify one or more intermediate hops that the packets must go through. This allows a packet to be diverted through a specific router on its way to its destination. (*Strict source routing* may also be available. This allows the user to specify an exact path through a network. While loose source routing can take any path that includes the specified hops, strict source routing must exactly follow the given path.)

To construct a detailed list of all devices on a path, the approach is to use *traceroute* to find a path from the source host to itself, specifying a route through a remote device. Packets leave the host with the remote device as their initial destination. When the packets arrive at the remote device, that device replaces the destination address with the source's address, and the packets are redirected back to the source. Thus, you get a picture of the path both coming and going. (Of course, source routing is not limited to just this combination of addresses.)

At least, that is how it should work in theory. In practice, many devices no longer support source routing. Unfortunately, source routing has been used in IP spoofing attacks. Packets sent with a spoofed source address can be diverted so they pass through the spoofed device's network. This approach will sometimes slip packets past firewalls since the packet seems to be coming from the right place.

This is shown in Figure 4-3. Without source routing, the packet would come into the firewall on the wrong interface and be discarded. With source routing, the packet arrives on the correct interface and passes through the firewall. Because of problems like this, source routing is frequently disabled.

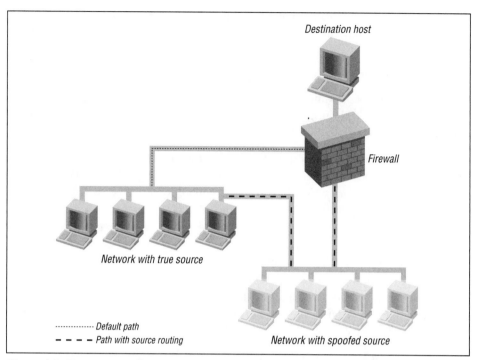

Figure 4-3. IP source spoofing

One final word of warning regarding *traceroute*—buggy or nonstandard implementations exist. Nonstandard isn't necessarily bad; it just means you need to watch for differences. For example, see the discussion of *tracert* later in this chapter. Buggy implementations, however, can really mislead you.

Path Performance

Once you have a picture of the path your traffic is taking, the next step in testing is to get some basic performance numbers. Evaluating path performance will mean doing three types of measurements. Bandwidth measurements will give you an idea of the hardware capabilities of your network, such as the maximum capacity of your network. Throughput measurements will help you discover what capacity your network provides in practice, i.e., how much of the maximum is actually available. Traffic measurements will give you an idea of how the capacity is being used.

My goal in this section is not a definitive analysis of performance. Rather, I describe ways to collect some general numbers that can be used to see if you have a reasonable level of performance or if you need to delve deeper. If you want to go beyond the quick-and-dirty approaches described here, you might consider some of the more advanced tools described in Chapter 9. The tools mentioned here should help you focus your efforts.

Performance Measurements

Several terms are used, sometimes inconsistently, to describe the capacity or performance of a link. Without getting too formal, let's review some of these terms to avoid potential confusion.

Two factors determine how long it takes to send a packet or frame across a single link. The amount of time it takes to put the signal onto the cable is known as the *transmission time* or *transmission delay*. This will depend on the *transmission rate* (or interface speed) and the size of the frame. The amount of time it takes for the signal to travel across the cable is known as the *propagation time* or *propagation delay*. Propagation time is determined by the type of media used and the distance involved. It often comes as a surprise that a signal transmitted at 100 Mbps will have the same propagation delay as a signal transmitted at 10 Mbps. The first signal is being transmitted 10 times as fast, but, once it is on a cable, it doesn't propagate any faster. That is, the difference between 10 Mbps and 100 Mbps is not the speed the bits travel, but the length of the bits.

Once we move to multihop paths, a third consideration enters the picture—the delay introduced from processing packets at intermediate devices such as routers and switches. This is usually called the *queuing delay* since, for the most part, it arises from the time packets spend in queues within the device. The total delay in delivering a packet is the sum of these three delays. Transmission and propagation delays are usually quite predictable and stable. Queuing delays, however, can introduce considerable variability.

The term *bandwidth* is typically used to describe the capacity of a link. For our purposes, this is the transmission rate for the link.* If we can transmit onto a link at 10 Mbps, then we say we have a bandwidth of 10 Mbps.

Throughput is a measure of the amount of data that can be sent over a link in a given amount of time. Throughput estimates, typically obtained through measurements based on the bulk transfer of data, are usually expressed in bits per second or packets per second. Throughput is frequently used as an estimate of the bandwidth of a network, but bandwidth and throughput are really two different things. Throughput measurement may be affected by considerable overhead that is not included in bandwidth measurements. Consequently, throughput is a more realistic estimator of the actual performance you will see.

---

* My apologies to any purist offended by my somewhat relaxed, pragmatic definition of bandwidth.

Throughput is generally an end-to-end measurement. When dealing with multihop paths, however, the bandwidths may vary from link to link. The *bottleneck bandwidth* is the bandwidth of the slowest link on a path, i.e., the link with the lowest bandwidth. (While introduced here, bottleneck analysis is discussed in greater detail in Chapter 12.)

Additional metrics will sometimes be needed. The best choice is usually task dependent. If you are sending real-time audio packets over a long link, you may want to minimize both delay and variability in the delay. If you are using FTP to do bulk transfers, you may be more concerned with the throughput. If you are evaluating the quality of your link to the Internet, you may want to look at bottleneck bandwidth for the path. The development of reliable metrics is an active area of research.

Bandwidth Measurements

We will begin by looking at ways to estimate bandwidth. Bandwidth really measures the capabilities of our hardware. If bandwidth is not adequate, you will need to reexamine your equipment.

ping revisited

The preceding discussion should make clear that the times returned by *ping*, although frequently described as propagation delays, really are the sum of the transmission, propagation, and queuing delays. In the last chapter, we used *ping* to calculate a rough estimate of the bandwidth of a connection and noted that this treatment is limited since it gives a composite number.

We can refine this process and use it to estimate the bandwidth for a link along a path. The basic idea is to first calculate the path behavior up to the device on the closest end of the link and then calculate the path behavior to the device at the far end of the link. The difference is then used to estimate the bandwidth for the link in question. Figure 4-4 shows the basic arrangement.

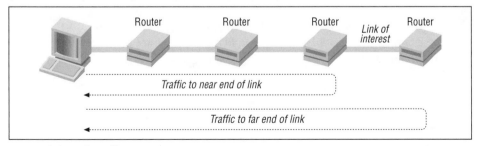

Figure 4-4. Link traffic measurements

This process requires using *ping* four times. First, ping the near end of a link with two different packet sizes. The difference in the times will eliminate the propagation and queuing delays along the path (assuming they haven't changed too much) leaving the time required to transmit the additional data in the larger packet. Next, use the same two packet sizes to ping the far end of the link. The difference in the times will again eliminate the overhead. Finally, the difference in these two differences will be the amount of time to send the additional data over the last link in the path. This is the round-trip time. Divide this number by two and you have the time required to send the additional data in one direction over the link. The bandwidth is simply the amount of additional data sent divided by this last calculated time.*

Table 4-1 shows the raw data for the second and third hops along the path shown in Figure 4-1. Packets sizes are 100 and 1100 bytes.

Table 4-1. Raw data

IP address	Time for 100 bytes	Time for 1100 bytes
205.153.61.1	1.380 ms	5.805 ms
205.153.60.2	4.985 ms	12.823 ms
165.166.36.17	8.621 ms	26.713 ms

Table 4-2 shows the calculated results. The time difference was divided by two (RRT correction), then divided into 8000 bits (the size of the data in bits), and then multiplied by 1000 (milliseconds-to-seconds correction.). The results, in bps, were then converted to Mbps. If several sets of packets are sent, the minimums of the times can be used to improve the estimate.

Table 4-2. Calculated bandwidth

Near link	Far link	Time difference	Estimated bandwidth
205.153.61.1	205.153.60.2	3.413 ms	4.69 Mbps
205.153.60.2	165.166.36.17	10.254 ms	1.56 Mbps

Clearly, doing this manually is confusing, tedious, and prone to errors. Fortunately, several tools based on this approach greatly simplify the process. These tools also improve accuracy by using multiple packets.

---

* The formula for bandwidth is $BW = 16 \times (P_l - P_s)/(t_{2l} - t_{2s} - t_{1l} + t_{1s})$. The larger and smaller packet sizes are P_l and P_s bytes, t_{1l} and t_{1s} are the *ping* times for the larger and smaller packets to the nearer interface in seconds, and t_{2l} and t_{2s} are the *ping* times for the larger and smaller packets to the distant interface in seconds. The result is in bits per second.

pathchar

One tool that automates this process is *pathchar*. This tool, written by Van Jacobson several years ago, seems to be in a state of limbo. It has, for several years, been available as an alpha release, but nothing seems to have been released since. Several sets of notes or draft notes are available on the Web, but there appears to be no manpage for the program. Nonetheless, the program remains available and has been ported to several platforms. Fortunately, a couple of alternative implementations of the program have recently become available. These include *bing, pchar, clink,* and *tmetric.*

One strength of *pathchar* and its variants is that they can discover the bandwidth of each link along a path using software at only one end of the path. The method used is basically that described earlier for *ping,* but *pathchar* uses a large number of packets of various sizes. Here is an example of running *pathchar*:

```
bsd1# pathchar 165.166.0.2
pathchar to 165.166.0.2 (165.166.0.2)
 mtu limited to 1500 bytes at local host
 doing 32 probes at each of 45 sizes (64 to 1500 by 32)
 0 205.153.60.247 (205.153.60.247)
 |    4.3 Mb/s,    1.55 ms (5.88 ms)
 1 cisco (205.153.60.2)
 |    1.5 Mb/s,    -144 us (13.5 ms)
 2 165.166.36.17 (165.166.36.17)
 |     10 Mb/s,    242 us (15.2 ms)
 3 e0.r01.ia-gnwd.Infoave.Net (165.166.36.33)
 |    1.2 Mb/s,    3.86 ms (32.7 ms)
 4 165.166.125.165 (165.166.125.165)
 |    ?? b/s,    2.56 ms (37.7 ms)
 5 165.166.125.106 (165.166.125.106)
 |     45 Mb/s,    1.85 ms (41.6 ms),  +q 3.20 ms (18.1 KB) *4
 6 atm1-0-5.r01.ncchrl.infoave.net (165.166.126.1)
 |     17 Mb/s,    0.94 ms (44.3 ms),  +q 5.83 ms (12.1 KB) *2
 7 h10-1-0.r01.ia-chrl.infoave.net (165.166.125.33)
 |    ?? b/s,     89 us (44.3 ms),  1% dropped
 8 dns1.InfoAve.Net (165.166.0.2)
 8 hops, rtt 21.9 ms (44.3 ms), bottleneck 1.2 Mb/s, pipe 10372 bytes
```

As *pathchar* runs, it first displays a message describing how the probing will be done. From the third line of output, we see that *pathchar* is using 45 different packet sizes ranging from 64 to 1500 bytes. (1500 is the local host's MTU.) It uses 32 different sets of these packets for each hop. Thus, this eight-hop run generated 11,520 test packets plus an equal number of replies.

The bandwidth and delay for each link is given. *pathchar* may also include information on the queuing delay (links 5 and 6 in this example). As you can see, *pathchar* is not always successful in estimating the bandwidth (see the links numbered 4 and

7) or the delay (see link numbered 1). With this information, we could go back to Figure 4-1 and fill in link speeds for most links.

As *pathchar* runs, it shows a countdown as it sends out each packet. It will display a line that looks something like this:

```
1:  31   288   0      3
```

The `1:` refers to the hop count and will be incremented for each successive hop on the path. The next number counts down, giving the number of sets of probes remaining to be run for this link. The third number is the size of the current packet being sent. Both the second and third numbers should be changing rapidly. The last two numbers give the number of packets that have been dropped so far on this link and the average round-trip time for this link.

When the probes for a hop are complete, this line is replaced with a line giving the bandwidth, incremental propagation delay, and round-trip time. *pathchar* uses the minimum of the observed delays to improve its estimate of bandwidth.

Several options are available with *pathchar*. Of greatest interest are those that control the number and size of the probe packet used. The option *-q* allows the user to specify the number of sets of packets to send. The options *-m* and *-M* control the minimum and maximum packet sizes, respectively. The option *-Q* controls the step size from the smallest to largest packet sizes. As a general rule of thumb, more packets are required for greater accuracy, particularly on busy links. The option *-n* turns off DNS resolution, and the option *-v* provides for more output.

pathchar is not without problems. One problem for *pathchar* is hidden or unknown transmission points. The first link reports a bandwidth of 4.3 Mbps. From *traceroute*, we only know of the host and the router at the end of the link. This is actually a path across a switched LAN with three segments and two additional transmission points at the switches. The packet is transmitted onto a 10-Mbps network, then onto a 100-Mbps backbone, and then back onto a 10 Mbps network before reaching the first router. Consequently, there are three sets of transmission delays rather than just one, and a smaller than expected bandwidth is reported.

You will see this problem with store-and-forward switches, but it is not appreciable with cut-through switches. (See the sidebar "Types of Switches" if you are unfamiliar with the difference between cut-through and store-and-forward switches.) In a test in which another switch, configured for cut-through, was added to this network, almost no change was seen in the estimated bandwidth with *pathchar*. When the switch was reconfigured as a store-and-forward switch, the reported bandwidth on the first link dropped to 3.0 Mbps.

Types of Switches

Devices may minimize queuing delays by forwarding frames as soon as possible. In some cases, a device may begin retransmitting a frame before it has finished receiving that frame. With Ethernet frames, for example, the destination address is the first field in the header. Once this has been read, the out interface is known and transmission can begin even though much of the original frame is still being received. Devices that use this scheme are called *cut-through* devices.

The alternative is to wait until the entire frame has arrived before retransmitting it. Switches that use this approach are known as *store-and-forward* devices.

Cut-through devices have faster throughput than store-and-forward switches because they begin retransmitting sooner. Unfortunately, cut-through devices may forward damaged frames, frames that a store-and-forward switch would have discarded. The problem is that the damage may not be discovered by the cut-through device until after retransmission has already begun. Store-and-forward devices introduce longer delays but are less likely to transmit damaged frames since they can examine the entire frame before retransmitting it. Store-and-forward technology is also required if interfaces operate at different speeds. Often devices can be configured to operate in either mode.

This creates a problem if you are evaluating an ISP. For example, it might appear that the fourth link is too slow if the contract specifies T1 service. This might be the case, but it could just be a case of a hidden transmission point. Without more information, this isn't clear.

Finally, you should be extremely circumspect about running *pathchar*. It can generate a huge amount of traffic. The preceding run took about 40 minutes to complete. It was run from a host on a university campus while the campus was closed for Christmas break and largely deserted. If you are crossing a slow link and have a high path MTU, the amount of traffic can effectively swamp the link. Asymmetric routes, routes in which the path to a device is different from the path back, changing routes, links using tunneling, or links with additional padding added can all cause problems.

bing

One alternative to *pathchar* is *bing*, a program written by Pierre Beyssac. Where *pathchar* gives the bandwidth for every link along a path, *bing* is designed to measure point-to-point bandwidth. Typically, you would run *traceroute* first if you don't already know the links along a path. Then you would run *bing* specifying the near and far ends of the link of interest on the command line. This example measures the bandwidth of the third hop in Figure 4-1:

```
bsd1# bing -e10 -c1 205.153.60.2 165.166.36.17
BING    205.153.60.2 (205.153.60.2) and 165.166.36.17 (165.166.36.17)
        44 and 108 data bytes
1024 bits in 0.835ms: 1226347bps, 0.000815ms per bit
1024 bits in 0.671ms: 1526080bps, 0.000655ms per bit
1024 bits in 0.664ms: 1542169bps, 0.000648ms per bit
1024 bits in 0.658ms: 1556231bps, 0.000643ms per bit
1024 bits in 0.627ms: 1633174bps, 0.000612ms per bit
1024 bits in 0.682ms: 1501466bps, 0.000666ms per bit
1024 bits in 0.685ms: 1494891bps, 0.000669ms per bit
1024 bits in 0.605ms: 1692562bps, 0.000591ms per bit
1024 bits in 0.618ms: 1656958bps, 0.000604ms per bit

--- 205.153.60.2 statistics ---
bytes   out    in   dup  loss   rtt (ms): min        avg        max
   44   10    10          0%               3.385      3.421      3.551
  108   10    10          0%               3.638      3.684      3.762

--- 165.166.36.17 statistics ---
bytes   out    in   dup  loss   rtt (ms): min        avg        max
   44   10    10          0%               3.926      3.986      4.050
  108   10    10          0%               4.797      4.918      4.986

--- estimated link characteristics ---
estimated throughput 1656958bps
minimum delay per packet 0.116ms (192 bits)

average statistics (experimental) :
packet loss: small 0%, big 0%, total 0%
average throughput 1528358bps
average delay per packet 0.140ms (232 bits)
weighted average throughput 1528358bps

resetting after 10 samples.
```

The output begins with the addresses and packet sizes followed by lines for each pair of probes. Next, *bing* returns round-trip times and packet loss data. Finally, it returns several estimates of throughput.[*]

In this particular example, we have specified the options *-e10* and *-c1*, which limit the probe to one cycle using 10 pairs of packets. Alternatively, you can omit these options and watch the output. When the process seems to have stabilized, enter a Ctrl-C to terminate the program. The summary results will then be printed. Interpretation of these results should be self-explanatory.

---

[*] The observant reader will notice that *bing* reported throughput, not bandwidth. Unfortunately, there is a lot of ambiguity and inconsistency surrounding these terms.

bing allows for a number of fairly standard options. These options allow controlling the number of packet sizes, suppressing name resolution, controlling routing, and obtaining verbose output. See the manpage if you have need of these options.

Because *bing* uses the same mechanism as *pathchar*, it will suffer the same problems with hidden transmission points. Thus, you should be circumspect when using it if you don't fully understand the topology of the network. While *bing* does not generate nearly as much traffic as *pathchar*, it can still place strains on a network.

Packet pair software

One alternative approach that is useful for measuring bottleneck bandwidth is the *packet pair* or *packet stretch* approach. With this approach, two packets that are the same size are transmitted back-to-back. As they cross the network, whenever they come to a slower link, the second packet will have to wait while the first is being transmitted. This increases the time between the transmission of the packets at this point on the network. If the packets go onto another faster link, the separation is preserved. If the packets subsequently go onto a slower link, then the separation will increase. When the packets arrive at their destination, the bandwidth of the slowest link can be calculated from the amount of separation and the size of the packets.

It would appear that getting this method to work requires software at both ends of the link. In fact, some implementations of packet pair software work this way. However, using software at both ends is not absolutely necessary since the acknowledgment packets provided with some protocols should preserve the separation.

One assumption of this algorithm is that packets will stay together as they move through the network. If other packets are queued between the two packets, the separation will increase. To avoid this problem, a number of packet pairs are sent through the network with the assumption that at least one pair will stay together. This will be the pair with the minimum separation.

Several implementations of this algorithm exist. *bprobe* and *cprobe* are two examples. At the time this was written, these were available only for the IRIX operating system on SGI computers. Since the source code is available, this may have changed by the time you read this.

Compared to the *pathchar* approach, the packet pair approach will find only the bottleneck bandwidth rather than the bandwidth of an arbitrary link. However, it does not suffer from the hidden hop problem. Nor does it create the levels of traffic characteristic of *pathchar*. This is a technology to watch.

Throughput Measurements

Estimating bandwidth can provide a quick overview of hardware performance. But if your bandwidth is not adequate, you are limited in what you can actually do—install faster hardware or contract for faster service. In practice, it is often not the raw bandwidth of the network but the bandwidth that is actually available that is of interest. That is, you may be more interested in the throughput that you can actually achieve.

Poor throughput can result not only from inadequate hardware but also from architectural issues such as network design. For example, a broadcast domain that is too large will create problems despite otherwise adequate hardware. The solution is to redesign your network, breaking apart or segmenting such domains *once you have a clear understanding of traffic patterns.*

Equipment configuration errors may also cause poor performance. For example, some Ethernet devices may support full duplex communication if correctly configured but will fall back to half duplex otherwise. The first step toward a solution is recognizing the misconfiguration. Throughput tests are the next logical step in examining your network.

Throughput is typically measured by timing the transfer of a large block of data. This may be called the *bulk transfer capacity* of the link. There are a number of programs in this class besides those described here. The approach typically requires software at each end of the link. Because the software usually works at the application level, it tests not only the network but also your hardware and software at the endpoints.

Since performance depends on several parts, when you identify that a problem exists, you won't immediately know where the problem is. Initially, you might try switching to a different set of machines with different implementations to localize the problem. Before you get too caught up in your testing, you'll want to look at the makeup of the actual traffic as described later in this chapter. In extreme cases, you may need some of the more advanced tools described later in this book.

One simple quick-and-dirty test is to use an application like FTP. Transfer a file with FTP and see what numbers it reports. You'll need to convert these to a bit rate, but that is straightforward. For example, here is the final line for a file transfer:

```
1294522 bytes received in 1.44 secs (8.8e+02 Kbytes/sec)
```

Convert 1,294,522 bytes to bits by multiplying by 8 and then dividing by the time, 1.44 seconds. This gives about 7,191,789 bps.

One problem with this approach is that the disk accesses required may skew your results. There are a few tricks you can use to reduce this, but if you need the added accuracy, you are better off using a tool that is designed to deal with such a problem. *ttcp*, for example, overcomes the disk access problem by repeatedly sending the same data from memory so that there is no disk overhead.

ttcp

One of the oldest bulk capacity measurement tools is *ttcp*. This was written by Mike Muuss and Terry Slattery. To run the program, you first need to start the server on the remote machine using, typically, the *-r* and *-s* options. Then the client is started with the options *-t* and *-s* and the hostname or address of the server. Data is sent from the client to the server, performance is measured, the results are reported at each end, and then both client and server terminate. For example, the server might look something like this:

```
bsd2# ttcp -r -s
ttcp-r: buflen=8192, nbuf=2048, align=16384/0, port=5001  tcp
ttcp-r: socket
ttcp-r: accept from 205.153.60.247
ttcp-r: 16777216 bytes in 18.35 real seconds = 892.71 KB/sec +++
ttcp-r: 11483 I/O calls, msec/call = 1.64, calls/sec = 625.67
ttcp-r: 0.0user 0.9sys 0:18real 5% 15i+291d 176maxrss 0+2pf 11478+28csw
```

The client side would look like this:

```
bsd1# ttcp -t -s 205.153.63.239
ttcp-t: buflen=8192, nbuf=2048, align=16384/0, port=5001  tcp  -> 205.153.63.239
ttcp-t: socket
ttcp-t: connect
ttcp-t: 16777216 bytes in 18.34 real seconds = 893.26 KB/sec +++
ttcp-t: 2048 I/O calls, msec/call = 9.17, calls/sec = 111.66
ttcp-t: 0.0user 0.5sys 0:18real 2% 16i+305d 176maxrss 0+2pf 3397+7csw
```

The program reports the amount of information transferred, indicates that the connection is being made, and then gives the results, including raw data, throughput, I/O call information, and execution times. The number of greatest interest is the transfer rate, 892.71 KB/sec (or 893.26 KB/sec). This is about 7.3 Mbps, which is reasonable for a 10-Mbps Ethernet connection. (But it is not very different from our quick-and-dirty estimate with FTP.)

These numbers reflect the rate at which data is transferred, not the raw capacity of the line. Relating these numbers to bandwidth is problematic since more bits are actually being transferred than these numbers would indicate. The program reports sending 16,777,216 bytes in 18.35 seconds, but this is just the data. On Ethernet with an MTU of 1500, each buffer will be broken into 6 frames. The first will carry an IP and TCP header for 40 more bytes. Each of the other 5 will have an IP header for 20 more bytes each. And each will be packaged as an Ethernet frame costing an additional 18 bytes each. And don't forget the Ethernet preamble. All this additional overhead should be included in a calculation of raw capacity.

Poor throughput numbers typically indicate congestion but that may not always be the case. Throughput will also depend on configuration issues such as the TCP window size for your connection. If your window size is not adequate, it will drastically affect performance. Unfortunately, this problem is not uncommon for older systems on today's high-speed links.

The *-u* option allows you to check UDP throughput. A number of options give you some control over the amount and the makeup of the information transferred. If you omit the *-s* option, the program uses standard input and output. This option allows you to control the data being sent.*

The nice thing about *ttcp* is that a number of implementations are readily available. For example, it is included as an undocumented command in the Enterprise version of Cisco IOS 11.2 and later. At one time, a Java version of *ttcp* was freely available from Chesapeake Computer Consultants, Inc., (now part of Mentor Technologies, Inc.). This program would run on anything with a Java interpreter including Windows machines. The Java version supported both a Windows and a command-line interface. Unfortunately, this version does not seem to be available anymore, but you might want to try tracking down a copy.

netperf

Another program to consider is *netperf,* which had its origin in the Information Networks Division of Hewlett-Packard. While not formally supported, the program does appear to have informal support. It is freely available, runs on a number of Unix platforms, and has reasonable documentation. It has also been ported to Windows. While not as ubiquitous as *ttcp*, it supports a much wider range of tests.

Unlike with *ttcp*, the client and server are two separate programs. The server is *netserver* and can be started independently or via *inetd*. The client is known as *netperf.* In the following example, the server and client are started on the same machine:

```
bsd1# netserver
Starting netserver at port 12865
bsd1# netperf
TCP STREAM TEST to localhost : histogram
Recv    Send    Send
```

---

* In fact, *ttcp* can be used to transfer files or directories between machines. At the destination, use `ttcp` `-r | tar xvpf` – and, at the source, use `tar cf - ` *directory*`| ttcp -t` *dest_machine*.

```
Socket Socket  Message  Elapsed
Size   Size    Size     Time      Throughput
bytes  bytes   bytes    secs.     10^6bits/sec

16384  16384   16384    10.00     326.10
```

This tests the loop-back interface, which reports a throughput of 326 Mbps.

In the next example, *netserver* is started on one host:

```
bsd1# netserver
Starting netserver at port 12865
```

Then *netperf* is run with the *-H* option to specify the address of the server:

```
bsd2# netperf -H 205.153.60.247
TCP STREAM TEST to 205.153.60.247 : histogram
Recv    Send    Send
Socket Socket  Message  Elapsed
Size   Size    Size     Time      Throughput
bytes  bytes   bytes    secs.     10^6bits/sec

16384  16384   16384    10.01     6.86
```

This is roughly the same throughput we saw with *ttcp*. *netperf* performs a number of additional tests. In the next test, the transaction rate of a connection is measured:

```
bsd2# netperf -H 205.153.60.247 -tTCP_RR
TCP REQUEST/RESPONSE TEST to 205.153.60.247 : histogram
Local /Remote
Socket Size  Request  Resp.   Elapsed  Trans.
Send   Recv  Size     Size    Time     Rate
bytes  Bytes bytes    bytes   secs.    per sec

16384  16384 1        1       10.00    655.84
16384  16384
```

The program contains several scripts for testing. It is also possible to do various stream tests with *netperf*. See the document that accompanies the program if you have these needs.

iperf

If *ttcp* and *netperf* don't meet your needs, you might consider *iperf*. *iperf* comes from the National Laboratory for Applied Network Research (NLANR) and is a very versatile tool. While beyond the scope of this chapter, *iperf* can also be used to test UDP bandwidth, loss, and jitter. A Java frontend is included to make *iperf* easier to use. This utility has also been ported to Windows.

Here is an example of running the server side of *iperf* on a FreeBSD system:

```
bsd2# iperf -s -p3000
------------------------------------------------------------
Server listening on TCP port 3000
```

```
TCP window size: 16.0 KByte (default)
------------------------------------------------------------
[  4] local 172.16.2.236 port 3000 connected with 205.153.63.30 port 1133
[ ID] Interval        Transfer       Bandwidth
[  4]  0.0-10.0 sec   5.6 MBytes    4.5 Mbits/sec
^C
```

Here is the client side under Windows:

```
C:\>iperf -c205.153.60.236
 -p3000
------------------------------------------------------------
Client connecting to 205.153.60.236, TCP port 3000
TCP window size:  8.0 KByte (default)
------------------------------------------------------------
[ 28] local 205.153.63.30 port 1133 connected with 205.153.60.236 port 3000
[ ID] Interval        Transfer       Bandwidth
[ 28]  0.0-10.0 sec   5.6 MBytes    4.5 Mbits/sec
```

Notice the use of Ctrl-C to terminate the server side. In TCP mode, *iperf* is compatible with *ttcp* so it can be used as the client or server.

iperf is a particularly convenient tool for investigating whether your TCP window is adequate. The *-w* option sets the socket buffer size. For TCP, this is the window size. Using the *-w* option, you can step through various window sizes and see how they impact throughput. *iperf* has a number of other strengths that make it worth considering.

Other related tools

You may also want to consider several similar or related tools. *treno* uses a *traceroute*-like approach to calculate bulk capacity, path MTU, and minimum RTP. Here is an example:

```
bsd2# treno 205.153.63.30
 MTU=8166  MTU=4352  MTU=2002  MTU=1492 .........
Replies were from sloan.lander.edu [205.153.63.30]
    Average rate: 3868.14 kbp/s (3380 pkts in + 42 lost = 1.2%) in 10.07 s
Equilibrium rate:     0 kbp/s (0 pkts in + 0 lost =   0%) in    0 s
Path properties: min RTT was  13.58 ms, path MTU was 1440 bytes
XXX Calibration checks are still under construction, use -v
```

treno is part of a larger Internet traffic measurement project at NLANR. *treno* servers are scattered across the Internet.

In general, *netperf, iperf,* and *treno* offer a wider range of features, but *ttcp* is generally easier to find.

Evaluating Internet Service Providers

When you sign a contract with an ISP to provide a level of service, say T1 access, what does this mean? The answer is not obvious.

ISPs sell services based, in some sense, on the total combined expected usage of all users. That is, they sell more capacity than they actually have, expecting levels of usage by different customers to balance out. If everyone tries to use their connection at once, there won't be enough capacity. But the idea is that this will rarely happen. To put it bluntly, ISPs oversell their capacity.

This isn't necessarily bad. Telephone companies have always done this. And, apart from Mother's Day and brief periods following disasters, you can almost always count on the phone system working. When you buy T1 Internet access, the assumption is that you will not be using that line to its full capacity all the time. If everyone used their connection to full capacity all the time, the price of those connections would be greatly increased. If you really need some guaranteed level of service, talk to your ISP. They may be able to provide guarantees if you are willing to pay for them.

But for the rest of us, the question is "What can we reasonably expect?" At a minimum, a couple of things seem reasonable. First, the ISP should have a connection to the Internet that well exceeds the largest connections that they are selling. For example, if they are selling multiple T1 lines, they should have a connection that is larger than a T1 line, e.g., a T3 line. Otherwise, if more that one customer is using the link, then no one can operate at full capacity. Since two customers using the link at the same time is very likely, having only a T1 line would violate the basic assumption that the contracted capacity is available.

Second, the ISP should be able to provide a path through their network to their ISP that operates in excess of the contracted speed. If you buy T1 access that must cross a 56-Kbps line to reach the rest of the Internet, you don't really have T1 access.

Finally, ISPs should have multiple peering arrangements (connections to the global Internet) so that if one connection goes down, there is an alternative path available.

Of course, your ISP may feel differently. And, if the price is really good, your arrangement may make sense. Clearly, not all service arrangements are the same. You'll want to come to a clear understanding with your ISP if you can. Unfortunately, with many ISPs, the information you will need is a closely guarded secret. As always, caveat emptor.

Traffic Measurements with netstat

In the ideal network, throughput numbers, once you account for overhead, will be fairly close to your bandwidth numbers. But few of us have our networks all to ourselves. When throughput numbers are lower than expected, which is usually the case, you'll want to account for the difference. As mentioned before, this could be hardware or software related. But usually it is just the result of the other traffic on your network. If you are uncertain of the cause, the next step is to look at the traffic on your network.

There are three basic approaches you can take. First, the quickest way to get a summary of the activity on a link is to use a tool such as *netstat*. This approach is described here. Or you can use packet capture to look at traffic. This approach is described in Chapter 5. Finally, you could use SNMP-based tools like *ntop*. SNMP tools are described in Chapter 7. Performance analysis tools using SNMP are described in Chapter 8.

The program *netstat* was introduced in Chapter 2. Given that *netstat*'s role is to report network data structures, it should come as no surprise that it might be useful in this context. To get a quick picture of the traffic on a network, use the *-i* option. For example:

```
bsd2# netstat -i
Name  Mtu   Network    Address            Ipkts Ierrs   Opkts Oerrs  Coll
lp0*  1500  <Link>                            0     0       0     0     0
ep0   1500  <Link>     00.60.97.06.22.22 13971293     0 1223799     1     0
ep0   1500  205.153.63 bsd2               13971293     0 1223799     1     0
tun0* 1500  <Link>                            0     0       0     0     0
sl0*  552   <Link>                            0     0       0     0     0
ppp0* 1500  <Link>                            0     0       0     0     0
lo0   16384 <Link>                          234     0     234     0     0
lo0   16384 127        localhost            234     0     234     0     0
```

The output shows the number of packets processed for each interface since the last reboot. In this example, interface *ep0* has received 13,971,293 packets (`Ipkts`) with no errors (`Ierrs`), has sent 1,223,799 packets (`Opkts`) with 1 error (`Oerrs`), and has experienced no collisions (`Coll`). A few errors are generally not a cause for alarm, but the percentage of either error should be quite low, certainly much lower than 0.1% of the total packets. Collisions can be higher but should be less than 10% of the traffic. The collision count includes only those involving the interface. A high number of collisions is an indication that your network is too heavily loaded, and you should consider segmentation. This particular computer is on a switch, which explains the absence of collision. Collisions are seen only on shared media.

If you want output for a single interface, you can specify this with the *-I* option.
For example:

```
bsd2# netstat -Iep0
Name  Mtu   Network       Address            Ipkts Ierrs    Opkts Oerrs  Coll
ep0   1500  <Link>        00.60.97.06.22.22 13971838    0 1223818     1     0
ep0   1500  205.153.63    bsd2              13971838    0 1223818     1     0
```

(This was run a couple of minutes later so the numbers are slightly larger.)

Implementations vary, so your output may look different but should contain the
same basic information. For example, here is output under Linux:

```
lnx1# netstat -i
Kernel Interface table
Iface   MTU Met    RX-OK RX-ERR RX-DRP RX-OVR    TX-OK TX-ERR TX-DRP TX-OVR Flg
eth0   1500   0  7366003      0      0      0    93092      0      0      0 BMRU
eth1   1500   0   289211      0      0      0    18581      0      0      0 BRU
lo     3924   0      123      0      0      0      123      0      0      0 LRU
```

As you can see, Linux breaks down lost packets into three categories—errors,
drops, and overruns.

Unfortunately, the numbers *netstat* returns are cumulative from the last reboot of
the system. What is really of interest is how these numbers have changed recently,
since a problem could develop and it would take a considerable amount of time
before the actual numbers would grow enough to reveal the problem.[*]

One thing you may want to try is stressing the system in question to see if this
increases the number of errors you see. You can use either *ping* with the *-l* option
or the *spray* command. (*spray* is discussed in greater detail in Chapter 9.)

First, run *netstat* to get a current set of values:

```
bsd2# netstat -Iep0
Name  Mtu   Network       Address            Ipkts Ierrs    Opkts Oerrs  Coll
ep0   1500  <Link>        00.60.97.06.22.22 13978296    0 1228137     1     0
ep0   1500  205.153.63    bsd2              13978296    0 1228137     1     0
```

Next, send a large number of packets to the destination. In this example, 1000
UDP packets were sent:

```
bsd1# spray -c1000 205.153.63.239
sending 1000 packets of lnth 86 to 205.153.63.239 ...
        in 0.09 seconds elapsed time
        464 packets (46.40%) dropped
Sent:   11267 packets/sec, 946.3K bytes/sec
Rcvd:   6039 packets/sec, 507.2K bytes/sec
```

---

[*] *System Performance Tuning* by Mike Loukides contains a script that can be run at regular intervals so
that differences are more apparent.

Notice that this exceeded the capacity of the network as 464 packets were dropped. This may indicate a congested network. More likely, the host is trying to communicate with a slower machine. When *spray* is run in the reverse direction, no packets are dropped. This indicates the latter explanation. Remember, *spray* is sending packets as fast as it can, so don't make too much out of dropped packets.

Finally, rerun *nestat* to see if any problems exist:

```
bsd2# netstat -Iep0
Name  Mtu   Network      Address              Ipkts Ierrs   Opkts Oerrs  Coll
ep0   1500  <Link>       00.60.97.06.22.22 13978964     0 1228156     1     0
ep0   1500  205.153.63   bsd2              13978964     0 1228156     1     0
```

No problems are apparent in this example.

If problems are indicated, you can get a much more detailed report with the *-s* option. You'll probably want to pipe the output to *more* so it doesn't disappear off the top of the screen. The amount of output data can be intimidating but can give a wealth of information. The information is broken down by protocol and by error types such as bad checksums or incomplete headers.

On some systems, such as FreeBSD, a summary of the nonzero values can be obtained by using the *-s* option twice, as shown in this example:

```
bsd2# netstat -s -s
ip:
        255 total packets received
        255 packets for this host
        114 packets sent from this host
icmp:
        ICMP address mask responses are disabled
igmp:
tcp:
        107 packets sent
            81 data packets (8272 bytes)
            26 ack-only packets (25 delayed)
        140 packets received
            77 acks (for 8271 bytes)
            86 packets (153 bytes) received in-sequence
        1 connection accept
        1 connection established (including accepts)
        77 segments updated rtt (of 78 attempts)
        2 correct ACK header predictions
        62 correct data packet header predictions
udp:
        115 datagrams received
        108 broadcast/multicast datagrams dropped due to no socket
        7 delivered
        7 datagrams output
```

A summary for a single protocol can be obtained with the *-p* option to specify the protocol. The next example shows the nonzero statistics for TCP:

```
bsd2# netstat -p tcp -s -s
tcp:
        147 packets sent
                121 data packets (10513 bytes)
                26 ack-only packets (25 delayed)
        205 packets received
                116 acks (for 10512 bytes)
                122 packets (191 bytes) received in-sequence
        1 connection accept
        1 connection established (including accepts)
        116 segments updated rtt (of 117 attempts)
        2 correct ACK header predictions
        88 correct data packet header predictions
```

This can take a bit of experience to interpret. Begin by looking for statistics showing a large number of errors. Next, identify the type of errors. Typically, input errors are caused by faulty hardware. Output errors are a problem on or at the local host. Data corruption, such as faulty checksums, frequently occurs at routers. And, as noted before, congestion is indicated by collisions. Of course, these are generalizations, so don't read too much into them.

Microsoft Windows

Most of the tools we have been discussing are available in one form or another for Windows platforms. Microsoft's implementation of *traceroute*, known as *tracert*, has both superficial and fundamental differences from the original implementation. Like *ping*, *tracert* requires a DOS window to run. We have already seen an example of its output. *tracert* has fewer options, and there are some superficial differences in their flags. But most of *traceroute*'s options are rarely used anyway, so this isn't much of a problem.

A more fundamental difference between Microsoft's *tracert* and its Unix relative is that *tracert* uses ICMP packets rather than UDP packets. This isn't necessarily bad, just different. In fact, if you have access to both *traceroute* and *tracert*, you may be able to use this to your advantage in some unusual circumstances. Its behavior may be surprising in some cases. One obvious implication is that routers that block ICMP messages will block *tracert*, while *traceroute*'s UDP packets will be passed.

As noted earlier in this chapter, Mentor's Java implementation of *ttcp* runs under Windows if you can find it. Both *netperf* and *iperf* have also been ported to Windows. Another freely available program worth considering is *Qcheck* from Ganymede Software, Inc. This program requires that Ganymede's *Performance Endpoints* software be installed on systems at each end of the link. This software is also provided at no cost and is available for a wide variety of systems ranging from Windows to MVS. In addition to supporting IP, the software supports SPX and IPX protocols. The software provides *ping*-like connectivity checks, as well as response time and throughput measurements.

As noted in Chapter 2, Microsoft also provides its own version of *netstat*. The options of interest here are *-e* and *-s*. The *-e* option gives a brief summary of activity on any Ethernet interface:

```
C:\>netstat -e
Interface Statistics

                              Received               Sent

Bytes                          9840233            2475741
Unicast packets                  15327              16414
Non-unicast packets               9268                174
Discards                             0                  0
Errors                               0                  0
Unknown protocols                  969
```

The *-s* option gives the per-protocol statistics:

```
C:\>netstat -s

IP Statistics

    Packets Received                    = 22070
    Received Header Errors              = 0
    Received Address Errors             = 6
    Datagrams Forwarded                 = 0
    Unknown Protocols Received          = 0
    Received Packets Discarded          = 0
    Received Packets Delivered          = 22064
    Output Requests                     = 16473
    Routing Discards                    = 0
    Discarded Output Packets            = 0
    Output Packet No Route              = 0
    Reassembly Required                 = 0
    Reassembly Successful               = 0
    Reassembly Failures                 = 0
    Datagrams Successfully Fragmented   = 0
    Datagrams Failing Fragmentation     = 0
    Fragments Created                   = 0

ICMP Statistics

                              Received    Sent
    Messages                  20          8
    Errors                    0           0
    Destination Unreachable   18          8
    Time Exceeded             0           0
    Parameter Problems        0           0
    Source Quenchs            0           0
    Redirects                 0           0
```

```
    Echos                        0          0
    Echo Replies                 0          0
    Timestamps                   0          0
    Timestamp Replies            0          0
    Address Masks                0          0
    Address Mask Replies         0          0

TCP Statistics

    Active Opens                       = 489
    Passive Opens                      = 2
    Failed Connection Attempts         = 69
    Reset Connections                  = 66
    Current Connections                = 4
    Segments Received                  = 12548
    Segments Sent                      = 13614
    Segments Retransmitted             = 134

UDP Statistics

    Datagrams Received     = 8654
    No Ports               = 860
    Receive Errors         = 0
    Datagrams Sent         = 2717
```

Interpretation is basically the same as with the Unix version.

5

Packet Capture

Packet capture and analysis is the most powerful technique that will be discussed in this book—it is the ultimate troubleshooting tool. If you really want to know what is happening on your network, you will need to capture traffic. No other tool provides more information.

On the other hand, no other tool requires the same degree of sophistication to use. If misused, it can compromise your system's security and invade the privacy of your users. Of the software described in this book, packet capture software is the most difficult to use to its full potential and requires a thorough understanding of the underlying protocols to be used effectively. As noted in Chapter 1, you must ensure that what you do conforms to your organization's policies and any applicable laws. You should also be aware of the ethical implications of your actions.

This chapter begins with a discussion of the type of tools available and various issues involved in traffic capture. Next I describe *tcpdump*, a ubiquitous and powerful packet capture tool. This is followed by a brief description of other closely related tools. Next is a discussion of *ethereal*, a powerful protocol analyzer that is rapidly gaining popularity. Next I describe some of the problems created by traffic capture. The chapter concludes with a discussion of packet capture tools available for use with Microsoft Windows platforms.

Traffic Capture Tools

Packet capture is the real-time collection of data as it travels over networks. Tools for the capture and analysis of traffic go by a number of names including *packet sniffers, packet analyzers, protocol analyzers,* and even *traffic monitors.* Although there is some inconsistency in how these terms are used, the primary difference is in how much analysis or interpretation is provided after a packet is captured.

Packet sniffers generally do the least amount of analysis, while protocol analyzers provide the greatest level of interpretation. Packet analyzers typically lie somewhere in between. All have the capture of raw data as a core function. Traffic monitors typically are more concerned with collecting statistical information, but many support the capture of raw data. Any of these may be augmented with additional functions such as graphing utilities and traffic generators. This chapter describes *tcpdump*, a packet sniffer, several analysis tools, and *ethereal*, a protocol analyzer.

While packet capture might seem like a low-level tool, it can also be used to examine what is happening at higher levels, including the application level, because of the way data is encapsulated. Since application data is encapsulated in a generally transparent way by the lower levels of the protocol stack, the data is basically intact when examined at a lower level.* By examining network traffic, we can examine the data generated at the higher levels. (In general, however, it is usually much easier to debug an application using a tool designed for that application. Tools specific to several application-level protocols are described in Chapter 10.)

Packet capture programs also require the most technical expertise of any program we will examine. A thorough understanding of the underlying protocol is often required to interpret the results. For this reason alone, packet capture is a tool that you want to become familiar with well before you need it. When you are having problems, it will also be helpful to have comparison systems so you can observe normal behavior. The time to learn how your system works is before you have problems. This technique cannot be stressed enough—do a baseline run for your network periodically and analyze it closely so you know what traffic you expect to see on your network before you have problems.

Access to Traffic

You can capture traffic only on a link that you have access to. If you can't get traffic to an interface, you can't capture it with that interface. While this might seem obvious, it may be surprisingly difficult to get access to some links on your network. On some networks, this won't be a problem. For example, 10Base2 and 10Base5 networks have shared media, at least between bridges and switches. Computers connected to a hub are effectively on a shared medium, and the traffic is exposed. But on other systems, watch out!

Clearly, if you are trying to capture traffic from a host on one network, it will never see the local traffic on a different network. But the problem doesn't stop

---

* There are two obvious exceptions. The data may be encrypted, or the data may be fragmented among multiple packets.

there. Some networking devices, such as bridges and switches, are designed to contain traffic so that it is seen only by parts of the local network. On a switched network, only a limited amount of traffic will normally be seen at any interface.* Traffic will be limited to traffic to or from the host or to multicast and broadcast traffic. If this includes the traffic you are interested in, so much the better. But if you are looking at general network traffic, you will use other approaches.

Not being able to capture data on an interface has both positive and negative ramifications. The primary benefit is that it is possible to control access to traffic with an appropriate network design. By segmenting your network, you can limit access to data, improving security and enhancing privacy.

Lack of access to data can become a serious problem, however, when you must capture that traffic. There are several basic approaches to overcome this problem. First, you can try to physically go to the traffic by using a portable computer to collect the data. This has the obvious disadvantage of requiring that you travel to the site. This may not be desirable or possible. For example, if you are addressing a security problem, it may not be feasible to monitor at the source of the suspected attack without revealing what you are doing. If you need to collect data at multiple points simultaneously, being at different places at the same time is clearly not possible by yourself.

Another approach is to have multiple probe computers located throughout your network. For example, if you have computers on your network that you can reach using *telnet*, *ssh*, X Window software, or *vnc*, you can install the appropriate software on each. Some software has been designed with remote probing in mind. For example, Microsoft's *netmon* supports the use of a Windows platform as a probe for collecting traffic. Data from the agents on these machines can be collected by a central management station. Some RMON probes will also do this. (*vnc* and *ssh* are described in Chapter 11. *netmon* is briefly described later in this chapter, and RMON is described in Chapter 8.)

When dealing with switches, there are two common approaches you can take. (Several other techniques that I can't recommend are described later in this chapter.) One approach is to augment the switch with a spare hub. Attach the hub to the switch and move from the switch to the hub only the connections that need to be examined. You could try replacing the switch with a hub, but this can be disruptive and, since a hub inherently has a lower capacity, you may have more traffic than the hub can handle. Augmenting the switch with a hub is a better solution.

---

* This assumes the switches have been running long enough to have a reasonably complete address table. Most switches forward traffic onto all ports if the destination address is unknown. So when they are first turned on, switches look remarkably like hubs.

Buying a small portable hub to use in establishing a probe point into your network is certainly worth the expense. Because you will be connecting a hub to a switch, you will be using both crossover and patch cables. Be sure you work out the details of the cabling well before you have to try this approach on a problematic network. Alternately, there are several commercially available devices designed specifically for patching into networks. These devices include monitoring switches, fiber splitters, and devices designed to patch into 100-Mbps links or links with special protocols. If your hardware dictates such a need, these devices are worth looking into.

Here is a riddle for you—when is a hub not a hub? In recent years, the distinction between hubs and switches has become blurred. For example, a 10/100 autoswitching hub may be implemented, internally, as a 10-Mbps hub and a 100-Mbps hub connected by a dual-port switch. With such a device, you may not be able to see all the traffic. In the next few years, true hubs may disappear from the market. You may want to keep this in mind when looking for a hub for traffic monitoring.

A second possibility with some switches is to duplicate the traffic from one port onto another port. If your switch supports this, it can be reconfigured dynamically to copy traffic to a monitoring port. Other ports continue functioning normally so the monitoring appears transparent to the rest of the switch's operation. This technique is known by a variety of names. With Bay Network products, this is known as *conversation steering*. Cisco refers to this as *monitoring* or using a *spanning* port. Other names include *port aliasing* and *port mirroring*.

Unfortunately, many switches either don't support this behavior or place limitations on what can be done. For instance, some switches will allow traffic to be redirected only to a high-speed port. Implementation details determining exactly what can be examined vary greatly. Another problem is that some types of errors will be filtered by the switch, concealing possible problems. For example, if there are any framing errors, these will typically be discarded rather than forwarded. Normally, discarding these packets is exactly what you want the switch to do, just not in this context. You'll have to consult the documentation with your switch to see what is possible.

Capturing Data

Packet capture may be done by software running on a networked host or by hardware/software combinations designed specifically for that purpose. Devices designed specifically for capturing traffic often have high-performance interfaces that can capture large amounts of data without loss. These devices will also capture frames with framing errors—frames that are often silently discarded with more conventional interfaces. More conventional interfaces may not be able to keep up with high traffic levels so packets will be lost. Programs like *tcpdump* give summary statistics, reporting the number of packets lost. On moderately loaded networks, however, losing packets should not be a problem. If dropping packets becomes a problem, you will need to consider faster hardware or, better yet, segmenting your network.

Packet capture software works by placing the network interface in *promiscuous mode.*[*] In normal operations, the network interface captures and passes on to the protocol stack only those packets with the interface's unicast address, packets sent to a multicast address that matches a configured address for the interface, or broadcast packets. In promiscuous mode, all packets are captured regardless of their destination address.

While the vast majority of interfaces can be placed in promiscuous mode, a few are manufactured not to allow this. If in doubt, consult the documentation for your interface. Additionally, on Unix systems, the operating system software must be configured to allow promiscuous mode. Typically, placing an interface in promiscuous mode requires root privileges.

tcpdump

The *tcpdump* program was developed at the Lawrence Berkeley Laboratory at the University of California, Berkeley, by Van Jacobson, Craig Leres, and Steven McCanne. It was originally developed to analyze TCP/IP performance problems. A number of features have been added over time although some options may not be available with every implementation. The program has been ported to a wide variety of systems and comes preinstalled on many systems.

For a variety of reasons, *tcpdump* is an ideal tool to begin with. It is freely available, runs on many Unix platforms, and has even been ported to Microsoft Windows. Features of its syntax and its file format have been used or supported by a large number of subsequent programs. In particular, its capture software, *libpcap*, is frequently used by other capture programs. Even when proprietary programs with additional features exist, the universality of *tcpdump* makes it a compelling choice. If you work with a wide variety of platforms, being able to use the same program on all or most of the platforms can easily outweigh small advantages proprietary programs might have. This is particularly true if you use the programs on

---

[*] On a few systems you may need to manually place the interface in promiscuous mode with the *ifconfig* command before running the packet capture software.

an irregular basis or don't otherwise have time to fully master them. It is better to know a single program well than several programs superficially. In such situations, special features of other programs will likely go unused.

Since *tcpdump* is text based, it is easy to run remotely using a Telnet connection. Its biggest disadvantage is a lack of analysis, but you can easily capture traffic, move it to your local machine, and analyze it with a tool like *ethereal*. Typically, I use *tcpdump* in text-only environments or on remote computers. I use *ethereal* in a Microsoft Windows or X Window environment and to analyze *tcpdump* files.

Using tcpdump

The simplest way to run *tcpdump* is interactively by simply typing the program's name. The output will appear on your screen. You can terminate the program by typing Ctrl-C. But unless you have an idle network, you are likely to be overwhelmed by the amount of traffic you capture. What you are interested in will likely scroll off your screen before you have a chance to read it.

Fortunately, there are better ways to run *tcpdump*. The first question is how you plan to use *tcpdump*. Issues include whether you also plan to use the host on which *tcpdump* is running to generate traffic in addition to capturing traffic, how much traffic you expect to capture, and how you will determine that the traffic you need has been captured.

There are several very simple, standard ways around the problem of being overwhelmed by data. The Unix commands *tee* and *script* are commonly used to allow a user to both view and record output from a Unix session. (Both *tee* and *script* are described in Chapter 11.) For example, *script* could be started, *tcpdump* run, and *script* stopped to leave a file that could be examined later.

The *tee* command is slightly more complicated since *tcpdump* must be placed in line mode to display output with *tee*. This is done with the *-l* option. The syntax for capturing a file with *tee* is:

```
bsd1# tcpdump -l | tee outfile
```

Of course, additional arguments would probably be used.

Using multiple Telnet connections to a host or multiple windows in an X Window session allows you to record in one window while taking actions to generate traffic in another window. This approach can be very helpful in some circumstances.

An alternative is to use *telnet* to connect to the probe computer. The session could be logged with many of the versions of *telnet* that are available. Be aware, however, that the Telnet connection will generate considerable traffic that may become part of your log file unless you are using filtering. (Filtering, which is discussed

later in this chapter, allows you to specify the type of traffic you want to examine.)
The additional traffic may also overload the connection, resulting in lost packets.

Another alternative is to run *tcpdump* as a detached process by including an *&* at
the end of the command line. Here is an example:

```
bsd1# tcpdump -w outfile &
[1] 70260
bsd1# tcpdump: listening on xl0
```

The command starts *tcpdump*, prints a process number, and returns the user
prompt along with a message that *tcpdump* has started. You can now enter commands to generate the traffic you are interested in. (You really have a prompt at
this point; the message from *tcpdump* just obscures it.) Once you have generated
the traffic of interest, you can terminate *tcpdump* by issuing a *kill* command using
the process number reported when *tcpdump* was started. (You can use the *ps*
command if you have forgotten the process number.)

```
bsd1# kill 70260
153 packets received by filter
0 packets dropped by kernel
[1]    Done                    tcpdump -w outfile
```

You can now analyze the capture file. (Running *tcpdump* as a detached process
can also be useful when you are trying to capture traffic that might not show up
for a while, e.g., RADIUS or DNS exchanges. You might want to use the *nohup*
command to run it in the background.)

Yet another approach is to use the *-w* option to write the captured data directly to
a file. This option has the advantage of collecting raw data in binary format. The
data can then be replayed with *tcpdump* using the *-r* option. The binary format
decreases the amount of storage needed, and different filters can be applied to the
file without having to recapture the traffic. Using previously captured traffic is an
excellent way of fine-tuning filters to be sure they work as you expect. Of course,
you can selectively analyze data captured as text files in Unix by using the many
tools Unix provides, but you can't use *tcpdump* filtering on text files. And you can
always generate a text file from a *tcpdump* file for subsequent analysis with Unix
tools by simply redirecting the output. To capture data you might type:

```
bsd1# tcpdump -w rawfile
```

The data could be converted to a text file with:

```
bsd1# tcpdump -r rawfile   > textfile
```

This approach has several limitations. Because the data is being written directly to
a file, you must know when to terminate recording without actually seeing the
traffic. Also, if you limit what is captured with the original run, the data you
exclude is lost. For these reasons, you will probably want to be very liberal in

what you capture, offsetting some of the storage gains of the binary format. Clearly, each approach has its combination of advantages and disadvantages. If you use *tcpdump* very much, you will probably need each from time to time.

tcpdump Options

A number of command-line options are available with *tcpdump*. Roughly speaking, options can be separated into four broad categories—commands that control the program operations (excluding filtering), commands that control how data is displayed, commands that control what data is displayed, and filtering commands. We will consider each category in turn.

Controlling program behavior

This class of command-line options affects program behavior, including the way data is collected. We have already seen two examples of control commands, *-r* and *-w*. The *-w* option allows us to redirect output to a file for later analysis, which can be extremely helpful if you are not sure exactly how you want to analyze your data. You can subsequently play back capture data using the *-r* option. You can repeatedly apply different display options or filters to the data until you have found exactly the information you want. These options are extremely helpful in learning to use *tcpdump* and are essential for documentation and sharing.

If you know how many packets you want to capture or if you just have an upper limit on the number of packets, the *-c* option allows you to specify that number. The program will terminate automatically when that number is reached, eliminating the need to use a *kill* command or Ctrl-C. In the next example, *tcpdump* will terminate after 100 packets are collected:

```
bsd1# tcpdump -c100
```

While limiting packet capture can be useful in some circumstances, it is generally difficult to predict accurately how many packets need to be collected.

If you are running *tcpdump* on a host with more than one network interface, you can specify which interface you want to use with the *-i* option. Use the command *ifconfig -a* to discover what interfaces are available and what networks they correspond to if you aren't sure. For example, suppose you are using a computer with two class C interfaces, *xl0* with an IP address of *205.153.63.238* and *xl1* with an IP address of *205.153.61.178*. Then, to capture traffic on the *205.153.61.0* network, you would use the command:

```
bsd1# tcpdump -i xl1
```

Without an explicitly identified interface, *tcpdump* defaults to the lowest numbered interface.

The *-p* option says that the interface should not be put into promiscuous mode. This option would, in theory, limit capture to the normal traffic on the interface— traffic to or from the host, multicast traffic, and broadcast traffic. In practice, the interface might be in promiscuous mode for some other reason. In this event, *-p* will not turn promiscuous mode off.

Finally, *-s* controls the amount of data captured. Normally, *tcpdump* defaults to some maximum byte count and will only capture up to that number of bytes from individual packets. The actual number of bytes depends on the pseudodevice driver used by the operating system. The default is selected to capture appropriate headers, but not to collect packet data unnecessarily. By limiting the number of bytes collected, privacy can be improved. Limiting the number of bytes collected also decreases processing and buffering requirements.

If you need to collect more data, the *-s* option can be used to specify the number of bytes to collect. If you are dropping packets and can get by with fewer bytes, *-s* can be used to decrease the number of bytes collected. The following command will collect the entire packet if its length is less than or equal to 200 bytes:

```
bsd1# tcpdump -s200
```

Longer packets will be truncated to 200 bytes.

If you are capturing files using the *-w* option, you should be aware that the number of bytes collected will be what is specified by the *-s* option at the time of capture. The *-s* option does not apply to files read back with the *-r* option. Whatever you captured is what you have. If it was too few bytes, then you will have to recapture the data.

Controlling how information is displayed

The *-a, -n, -N,* and *-f* options determine how address information is displayed. The *-a* option attempts to force network addresses into names, the *-n* option prevents the conversion of addresses into names, the *-N* option prevents domain name qualification, and the *-f* option prevents remote name resolution. In the following, the remote site *www.cisco.com* (*192.31.7.130*) is pinged from *sloan.lander.edu* (*205.153.63.30*) without an option, with *-a,* with *-n,* with *-N,* and with *-f,* respectively. (The options *-c1 host 192.31.7.130* restricts capture to one packet to or from the host *192.31.7.130.*)

```
bsd1# tcpdump -c1 host 192.31.7.130
tcpdump: listening on xl0
14:16:35.897342 sloan.lander.edu > cio-sys.cisco.com: icmp: echo request
bsd1# tcpdump -c1 -a host 192.31.7.130
tcpdump: listening on xl0
14:16:14.567917 sloan.lander.edu > cio-sys.cisco.com: icmp: echo request
bsd1# tcpdump -c1 -n host 192.31.7.130
tcpdump: listening on xl0
```

```
14:17:09.737597 205.153.63.30 > 192.31.7.130: icmp: echo request
bsd1# tcpdump -c1 -N host 192.31.7.130
tcpdump: listening on xl0
14:17:28.891045 sloan > cio-sys: icmp: echo request
bsd1# tcpdump -c1 -f host 192.31.7.130
tcpdump: listening on xl0
14:17:49.274907 sloan.lander.edu > 192.31.7.130: icmp: echo request
```

Clearly, the *-a* option is the default.

Not using name resolution can eliminate the overhead and produce terser output. If the network is broken, you may not be able to reach your name server and will find yourself with long delays, while name resolution times out. Finally, if you are running *tcpdump* interactively, name resolution will create more traffic that will have to be filtered out.

The *-t* and *-tt* options control the printing of timestamps. The *-t* option suppresses the display of the timestamp while *-tt* produces unformatted timestamps. The following shows the output for the same packet using *tcpdump* without an option, with the *-t* option, and with the *-tt* option, respectively:

```
12:36:54.772066 sloan.lander.edu.1174 > 205.153.63.238.telnet: . ack 3259091394
win 8647 (DF)

sloan.lander.edu.1174 > 205.153.63.238.telnet: . ack 3259091394 win 8647 (DF)

934303014.772066 sloan.lander.edu.1174 > 205.153.63.238.telnet: . ack 3259091394
win 8647 (DF)
```

The *-t* option produces a more terse output while the *-tt* output can simplify subsequent processing, particularly if you are writing scripts to process the data.

Controlling what's displayed

The verbose modes provided by *-v* and *-vv* options can be used to print some additional information. For example, the *-v* option will print TTL fields. For less information, use the *-q*, or quiet, option. Here is the output for the same packet presented with the *-q* option, without options, with the *-v* option, and with the *-vv* option, respectively:

```
12:36:54.772066 sloan.lander.edu.1174 > 205.153.63.238.telnet: tcp 0 (DF)

12:36:54.772066 sloan.lander.edu.1174 > 205.153.63.238.telnet: . ack 3259091394
win 8647 (DF)

12:36:54.772066 sloan.lander.edu.1174 > 205.153.63.238.telnet: . ack 3259091394
win 8647 (DF) (ttl 128, id 45836)

12:36:54.772066 sloan.lander.edu.1174 > 205.153.63.238.telnet: . ack 3259091394
win 8647 (DF) (ttl 128, id 45836)
```

This additional information might be useful in a few limited contexts, while the quiet mode provides shorter output lines. In this instance, there was no difference between the results with *-v* and *-vv*, but this isn't always the case.

The *-e* option is used to display link-level header information. For the packet from the previous example, with the *-e* option, the output is:

```
12:36:54.772066 0:10:5a:a1:e9:8 0:10:5a:e3:37:c ip 60:
sloan.lander.edu.1174 > 205.153.63.238.telnet: . ack 3259091394 win 8647 (DF)
```

0:10:5a:a1:e9:8 is the Ethernet address of the 3Com card in *sloan.lander.edu,* while *0:10:5a:e3:37:c* is the Ethernet address of the 3Com card in *205.153.63.238.* (We can discover the types of adapters used by looking up the OUI portion of these addresses, as described in Chapter 2.)

For the masochist who wants to decode packets manually, the *-x* option provides a hexadecimal dump of packets, excluding link-level headers. A packet displayed with the *-x* and *-vv* options looks like this:

```
13:57:12.719718 bsd1.lander.edu.1657 > 205.153.60.5.domain: 11587+ A? www.
microsoft.com. (35) (ttl 64, id 41353)
                        4500 003f a189 0000 4011 c43a cd99 3db2
                        cd99 3c05 0679 0035 002b 06d9 2d43 0100
                        0001 0000 0000 0000 0377 7777 096d 6963
                        726f 736f 6674 0363 6f6d 0000 0100 01
```

Please note that the amount of information displayed will depend on how many bytes are collected, as determined by the *-s* option. Such hex listings are typical of what might be seen with many capture programs.

Describing how to do such an analysis in detail is beyond the scope of this book, as it requires a detailed understanding of the structure of packets for a variety of protocols. Interpreting this data is a matter of taking packets apart byte by byte or even bit by bit, realizing that the interpretation of the results at one step may determine how the next steps will be done. For header formats, you can look to the appropriate RFC or in any number of books. Table 5-1 summarizes the analysis for this particular packet, but every packet is different. This particular packet was a DNS lookup for *www.microsoft.com.* (For more information on decoding packets, see Eric A. Hall's *Internet Core Protocols: The Definitive Guide.*)

Table 5-1. Packet analysis summary

Raw data in hex	Interpretation
IP header	
First 4 bits of 45	IP version—4
Last 4 bits of 45	Length of header multiplier—5 (times 4 or 20 bytes)

Table 5-1. Packet analysis summary (continued)

Raw data in hex	Interpretation
00	Type of service
00 3f	Packet length in hex—63 bytes
a1 89	ID
First 3 bits of 00	000—flags, none set
Last 13 bits of 00 00	Fragmentation offset
40	TTL—64 hops
11	Protocol number in hex—UDP
c4 3a	Header checksum
cd 99 3d b2	Source IP—205.153.61.178
cd 99 3c 05	Destination IP—205.153.60.5
UDP header	
06 79	Source port
00 35	Destination port—DNS
00 2b	UDP packet length—43 bytes
06 d9	Header checksum
DNS message	
2d 43	ID
01 00	Flags—query with recursion desired
00 01	Number of queries
00 00	Number of answers
00 00	Number of authority RRs
00 00	Number of additional RRs
Query	
03	Length—3
77 77 77	String—"www"
09	Length—9
6d 69 63 72 6f 73 6f 66 74	String—"microsoft"
03	Length—3
63 6f 6d	String—"com"
00	Length—0
00 01	Query type—IP address
00 01	Query class—Internet

This analysis was included here primarily to give a better idea of how packet analysis works. Several programs that analyze packet data from a *tcpdump* trace file are described later in this chapter. Unix utilities like *strings*, *od*, and *hexdump* can also make the process easier. For example, in the following example, this makes it easier to pick out *www.microsoft.com* in the data:

```
bsd1# hexdump -C tracefile
00000000  d4 c3 b2 a1 02 00 04 00  00 00 00 00 00 00 00 00  |................|
00000010  c8 00 00 00 01 00 00 00  78 19 06 38 66 fb 0a 00  |........x..8f...|
00000020  4d 00 00 00 4d 00 00 00  00 00 a2 c6 0e 43 00 60  |M...M........C.`|
00000030  97 92 4a 7b 08 00 45 00  00 3f a1 89 00 00 40 11  |..J{..E..?....@.|
00000040  c4 3a cd 99 3d b2 cd 99  3c 05 06 79 00 35 00 2b  |.:..=...<..y.5.+|
00000050  06 d9 2d 43 01 00 00 01  00 00 00 00 00 00 03 77  |..-C...........w|
00000060  77 77 09 6d 69 63 72 6f  73 6f 66 74 03 63 6f 6d  |ww.microsoft.com|
00000070  00 00 01 00 01                                    |.....|
00000075
```

The *-vv* option could also be used to get as much information as possible.

Hopefully, you will have little need for the *-x* option. But occasionally you may encounter a packet that is unknown to *tcpdump,* and you have no choice. For example, some of the switches on my local network use a proprietary implementation of a spanning tree protocol to implement virtual local area networks (VLANs). Most packet analyzers, including *tcpdump*, won't recognize these. Fortunately, once you have decoded one unusual packet, you can usually easily identify similar packets.

Filtering

To effectively use *tcpdump*, it is necessary to master the use of filters. Filters permit you to specify what traffic you want to capture, allowing you to focus on just what is of interest. This can be absolutely essential if you need to extract a small amount of traffic from a massive trace file. Moreover, tools like *ethereal* use the *tcpdump* filter syntax for capturing traffic, so you'll want to learn the syntax if you plan to use these tools.

If you are absolutely certain that you are not interested in some kinds of traffic, you can exclude traffic as you capture. If you are unclear of what traffic you want, you can collect the raw data to a file and apply the filters as you read back the file. In practice, you will often alternate between these two approaches.

Filters at their simplest are keywords added to the end of the command line. However, extremely complex commands can be constructed using logical and relational operators. In the latter case, it is usually better to save the filter to a file and use the *-F* option. For example, if *testfilter* is a text file containing the filter host 205.153.63.30, then typing tcpdump -Ftestfilter is equivalent to typing the command *tcpdump host 205.153.63.30.* Generally, you will want to use this feature with complex filters only. However, you can't combine filters on the command line with a filters file in the same command.

Address filtering. It should come as no surprise that filters can select traffic based on addresses. For example, consider the command:

```
bsd1# tcpdump host 205.153.63.30
```

This command captures all traffic to and from the host with the IP address 205. 153.63.30. The host may be specified by IP number or name. Since an IP address has been specified, you might incorrectly guess that the captured traffic will be limited to IP traffic. In fact, other traffic, such as ARP traffic, will also be collected by this filter. Restricting capture to a particular protocol requires a more complex filter. Nonintuitive behavior like this necessitates a thorough testing of all filters.

Addresses can be specified and restricted in several ways. Here is an example that uses the Ethernet address of a computer to select traffic:

```
bsd1# tcpdump ether host 0:10:5a:e3:37:c
```

Capture can be further restricted to traffic flows for a single direction, either to a host or from a host, using *src* to specify the source of the traffic or *dst* to specify the destination. The next example shows a filter that collects traffic sent to the host at *205.153.63.30* but not from it:

```
bsd1# tcpdump dst 205.153.63.30
```

Note that the keyword *host* was omitted in this example. Such omissions are OK in several instances, but it is always safer to include these keywords.

Multicast or broadcast traffic can be selected by using the keyword *multicast* or *broadcast,* respectively. Since multicast and broadcast traffic are specified differently at the link level and the network level, there are two forms for each of these filters. The filter *ether multicast* captures traffic with an Ethernet multicast address, while *ip multicast* captures traffic with an IP multicast address. Similar qualifiers are used with broadcast traffic. Be aware that multicast filters may capture broadcast traffic. As always, test your filters.

Traffic capture can be restricted to networks as well as hosts. For example, the following command restricts capture to packets coming from or going to the 205.153. 60.0 network:

```
bsd1# tcpdump net 205.153.60
```

The following command does the same thing:

```
bsd1# tcpdump net 205.153.60.0 mask 255.255.255.0
```

Although you might guess otherwise, the following command does not work properly due to the final `.0`:

```
bsd1# tcpdump net 205.153.60.0
```

Be sure to test your filters!

Protocol and port filtering. It is possible to restrict capture to specific protocols such as IP, Appletalk, or TCP. You can also restrict capture to services built on top of these protocols, such as DNS or RIP. This type of capture can be done in three ways—by using a few specific keywords known by *tcpdump*, by protocol using the *proto* keyword, or by service using the *port* keyword.

Several of these protocol names are recognized by *tcpdump* and can be identified by keyword. The following command restricts the traffic captured to IP traffic:

```
bsd1# tcpdump ip
```

Of course, IP traffic will include TCP traffic, UDP traffic, and so on.

To capture just TCP traffic, you would use:

```
bsd1# tcpdump tcp
```

Recognized keywords include *ip*, *igmp*, *tcp*, *udp*, and *icmp*.

There are many transport-level services that do not have recognized keywords. In this case, you can use the keywords *proto* or *ip proto* followed by either the name of the protocol found in the */etc/protocols* file or the corresponding protocol number. For example, either of the following will look for OSPF packets:

```
bsd1# tcpdump ip proto ospf
bsd1# tcpdump ip proto 89
```

Of course, the first works only if there is an entry in */etc/protocols* for OSPF.

Built-in keywords may cause problems. In these examples, the keyword *tcp* must either be escaped or the number must be used. For example, the following is fine:

```
bsd#1 tcpdump ip proto 6
```

On the other hand, you can't use *tcp* with *proto*.

```
bsd#1 tcpdump ip proto tcp
```

will generate an error.

For higher-level services, services built on top of the underlying protocols, you must use the keyword *port*. Either of the following will collect DNS traffic:

```
bsd#1 tcpdump port domain
bds#1 tcpdump port 53
```

In the former case, the keyword *domain* is resolved by looking in */etc/services*. When there may be ambiguity between transport-layer protocols, you may further restrict ports to a particular protocol. Consider the command:

```
bsd#1 tcpdump udp port domain
```

This will capture DNS name lookups using UDP but not DNS zone transfers using TCP. The two previous commands would capture both.

Packet characteristics. Filters can also be designed based on packet characteristics such as packet length or the contents of a particular field. These filters must include a relational operator. To use length, the keyword *less* or *greater* is used. Here is an example:

```
bsd1# tcpdump greater 200
```

This command collects packets longer than 200 bytes.

Looking inside packets is a little more complicated in that you must understand the structure of the packet's header. But despite the complexity, or perhaps because of it, this technique gives you the greatest control over what is captured. (If you are charged with creating a firewall using a product that requires specifying offsets into headers, practicing with *tcpdump* could prove invaluable.)

The general syntax is ***proto [expr : size]***. The field *proto* indicates which header to look into—*ip* for the IP header, *tcp* for the TCP header, and so forth. The *expr* field gives an offset into the header indexed from 0. That is, the first byte in a header is number 0, the second byte is number 1, and so forth. Alternately, you can think of *expr* as the number of bytes in the header to skip over. The *size* field is optional. It specifies the number of bytes to use and can be 1, 2, or 4.

```
bsd1# tcpdump "ip[9] = 6"
```

looks into the IP header at the tenth byte, the protocol field, for a value of 6. Notice that this must be quoted. Either an apostrophe or double quotes should work, but a backquote will not work.

```
bsd1# tcpdump tcp
```

is an equivalent command since 6 is the protocol number for TCP.

This technique is frequently used with a mask to select specific bits. Values should be in hex. Comparisons are specified using the syntax *&* followed by a bit mask. The next example extracts the first byte from the Ethernet header (i.e., the first byte of the destination address), extracts the low-order bit, and makes sure the bit is not 0:[*]

```
bsd1# tcpdump 'ether[0] & 1 != 0'
```

This will match multicast and broadcast packets.

With both of these examples, there are better ways of matching the packets. For a more realistic example, consider the command:

```
bsd1# tcpdump "tcp[13] & 0x03 != 0"
```

---

[*] The astute reader will notice that this test could be more concisely written as *=1* rather than *!=0*. While it doesn't matter for this example, using the second form simplifies testing in some cases and is a common idiom. In the next command, the syntax is simpler since you are testing to see if multiple bits are set.

This filter skips the first 13 bytes in the TCP header, extracting the flag byte. The mask *0x03* selects the first and second bits, which are the FIN and SYN bits. A packet is captured if either bit is set. This will capture setup or teardown packets for a TCP connection.

It is tempting to try to mix in relational operators with these logical operators. Unfortunately, expressions like *tcp src port > 23* don't work. The best way of thinking about it is that the expression *tcp src port* returns a value of true or false, not a numerical value, so it can't be compared to a number. If you want to look for all TCP traffic with a source port with a value greater than 23, you must extract the port field from the header using syntax such as *"tcp[0:2] & 0xffff > 0x0017"*.

Compound filters. All the examples thus far have consisted of simple commands with a single test. Compound filters can be constructed in *tcpdump* using logical operator and, or, and not. These are often abbreviated &&, ||, and ! respectively. Negation has the highest precedence. Precedence is left to right in the absence of parentheses. While parentheses can be used to change precedence, remember that they must be escaped or quoted.

Earlier it was noted that the following will not limit capture to just IP traffic:

```
bsd1# tcpdump host 205.153.63.30
```

If you really only want IP traffic in this case, use the command:

```
bsd1# tcpdump host 205.153.63.30 and ip
```

On the other hand, if you want all traffic to the host except IP traffic, you could use:

```
bsd1# tcpdump host 205.153.63.30 and not ip
```

If you need to capture all traffic to and from the host and all non-IP traffic, replace the and with an or.

With complex expressions, you have to be careful of the precedence. Consider the two commands:

```
bsd1# tcpdump host lnx1 and udp or arp
bsd1# tcpdump "host lnx1 and (udp or arp)"
```

The first will capture all UDP traffic to or from *lnx1* and all ARP traffic. What you probably want is the second, which captures all UDP or ARP traffic to or from *lxn1*. But beware, this will also capture ARP broadcast traffic. To beat a dead horse, be sure to test your filters.

I mentioned earlier that running *tcpdump* on a remote station using *telnet* was one way to collect data across your network, except that the Telnet traffic itself would be captured. It should be clear now that the appropriate filter can be used to avoid this problem. To eliminate a specific TCP connection, you need four pieces of information—the source and destination IP addresses and the source and destination port numbers. In practice, the two IP addresses and the well-known port number is often enough.

For example, suppose you are interested in capturing traffic on the host *lnx1*, you are logged onto the host *bsd1*, and you are using *telnet* to connect from *bsd1* to *lnx1*. To capture all the traffic at *lnx1*, excluding the Telnet traffic between *bsd1* and *lnx1*, the following command will probably work adequately in most cases:

```
lnx1# tcpdump -n "not (tcp port telnet and host lnx1 and host bsd1)"
```

We can't just exclude Telnet traffic since that would exclude all Telnet traffic between *lnx1* and any host. We can't just exclude traffic to or from one of the hosts because that would exclude non-Telnet traffic as well. What we want to exclude is just traffic that is Telnet traffic, has *lnx1* as a host, and has *bsd1* as a host. So we take the negation of these three requirements to get everything else.

While this filter is usually adequate, this filter excludes all Telnet sessions between the two hosts, not just yours. If you really want to capture other Telnet traffic between *lnx1* and *bsd1*, you would need to include a fourth term in the negation giving the ephemeral port assigned by *telnet*. You'll need to run *tcpdump* twice, first to discover the ephemeral port number for your current session since it will be different with every session, and then again with the full filter to capture the traffic you are interested in.

One other observation—while we are not reporting the traffic, the traffic is still there. If you are investigating a bandwidth problem, you have just added to the traffic. You can, however, minimize this traffic during the capture if you write out your trace to a file on *lnx1* using the *-w* option. This is true, however, only if you are using a local filesystem. Finally, note the use of the *-n* option. This is required to prevent name resolution. Otherwise, *tcpdump* would be creating additional network traffic in trying to resolve IP numbers into names as noted earlier.

Once you have mastered the basic syntax of *tcpdump*, you should run *tcpdump* on your own system without any filters. It is worthwhile to do this occasionally just to see what sorts of traffic you have on your network. There are likely to be a number of surprises. In particular, there may be router protocols, switch topology information exchange, or traffic from numerous PC-based protocols that you aren't expecting. It is very helpful to know that this is normal traffic so when you have problems you won't blame the problems on this strange traffic.

This has not been an exhaustive treatment of *tcpdump,* but I hope that it adequately covers the basics. The manpage for *tcpdump* contains a wealth of additional information, including several detailed examples with explanations. One issue I have avoided has been how to interpret *tcpdump* data. Unfortunately, this depends upon the protocol and is really beyond the scope of a book such as this. Ultimately, you must learn the details of the protocols. For TCP/IP, Richard W. Stevens' *TCP/IP Illustrated,* vol. 1, *The Protocols* has extensive examples using *tcpdump.* But the best way to learn is to use *tcpdump* to examine the behavior of working systems.

Analysis Tools

As previously noted, one reason for using *tcpdump* is the wide variety of support tools that are available for use with *tcpdump* or files created with *tcpdump.* There are tools for sanitizing the data, tools for reformatting the data, and tools for presenting and analyzing the data.

sanitize

If you are particularly sensitive to privacy or security concerns, you may want to consider *sanitize*, a collection of five Bourne shell scripts that reduce or condense *tcpdump* trace files and eliminate confidential information. The scripts renumber host entries and select classes of packets, eliminating all others. This has two primary uses. First, it reduces the size of the files you must deal with, hopefully focusing your attention on a subset of the original traffic that still contains the traffic of interest. Second, it gives you data that can be distributed or made public (for debugging or network analysis) without compromising individual privacy or revealing too much specific information about your network. Clearly, these scripts won't be useful for everyone. But if internal policies constrain what you can reveal, these scripts are worth looking into.

The five scripts included in *sanitize* are *sanitize-tcp, sanitize-syn-fin, sanitize-udp, sanitize-encap,* and *sanitize-other.* Each script filters out inappropriate traffic and reduces the remaining traffic. For example, all non-TCP packets are removed by *sanitize-tcp* and the remaining TCP traffic is reduced to six fields—an unformatted timestamp, a renumbered source address, a renumbered destination address, the source port, a destination address, and the number of data bytes in the packet.

```
934303014.772066 205.153.63.30.1174 > 205.153.63.238.23: . ack 3259091394 win 8647
(DF)
                    4500 0028 b30c 4000 8006 2d84 cd99 3f1e
                    cd99 3fee 0496 0017 00ff f9b3 c241 c9c2
                    5010 21c7 e869 0000 0000 0000 0000
```

would be reduced to **934303014.772066 1 2 1174 23 0**. Notice that the IP numbers have been replaced with 1 and 2, respectively. This will be done in a consistent manner with multiple packets so you will still be able to compare addresses within a single trace. The actual data reported varies from script to script. Here is an example of the syntax:

```
bsd1# sanitize-tcp tracefile
```

This runs *sanitize-tcp* over the *tcpdump* trace file *tracefile*. There are no arguments.

tcpdpriv

The program *tcpdpriv* is another program for removing sensitive information from *tcpdump* files. There are several major differences between *tcpdpriv* and *sanitize*. First, as a shell script, *sanitize* should run on almost any Unix system. As a compiled program, this is not true of *tcpdpriv*. On the other hand, *tcpdpriv* supports the direct capture of data as well as the analysis of existing files. The captured packets are written as a *tcpdump* file, which can be subsequently processed.

Also, *tcpdpriv* allows you some degree of control over how much of the original data is removed or scrambled. For example, it is possible to have an IP address scrambled but retain its class designation. If the *-C4* option is chosen, an IP address such as *205.153.63.238* might be replaced with *193.0.0.2*. Notice that address classes are preserved—a class C address is replaced with a class C address.

There are a variety of command-line options that control how data is rewritten, several of which are mandatory. Many of the command-line options will look familiar to *tcpdump* users. The program does not allow output to be written to a terminal, so it must be written directly to a file or redirected. While a useful program, the number of required command-line options can be annoying. There is some concern that if the options are not selected properly, it may be possible to reconstruct the original data from the scrambled data. In practice, this should be a minor concern.

As an example of using *tcpdpriv*, the following command will scramble the file *tracefile*:

```
bsd1# tcpdpriv -P99 -C4 -M20 -r tracefile -w outfile
```

The *-P99* option preserves (doesn't scramble) the port numbers, *-C4* preserves the class identity of the IP addresses, and *-M20* preserves multicast addresses. If you want the data output to your terminal, you can pipe the output to *tcpdump*:

```
bsd1# tcpdpriv -P99 -C4 -M20 -r tracefile -w- | tcpdump -r-
```

The last options look a little strange, but they will work.

tcpflow

Another useful tool is *tcpflow*, written by Jeremy Elson. This program allows you to capture individual TCP flows or sessions. If the traffic you are looking at includes, say, three different Telnet sessions, *tcpflow* will separate the traffic into three different files so you can examine each individually. The program can reconstruct data streams regardless of out-of-order packets or retransmissions but does not understand fragmentation.

tcpflow stores each flow in a separate file with names based on the source and destination addresses and ports. For example, SSH traffic (port 22) between *172. 16.2.210* and *205.153.63.30* might have the filename *172.016.002.210.00022-205.153.063.030.01071,* where 1071 is the ephemeral port created for the session.

Since *tcpflow* uses *libpcap*, the same packet capture library *tcpdump* uses, capture filters are constructed in exactly the same way and with the same syntax. It can be used in a number of ways. For example, you could see what cookies are being sent during an HTTP session. Or you might use it to see if SSH is really encrypting your data. Of course, you could also use it to capture passwords or read email, so be sure to set permissions correctly.

tcp-reduce

The program *tcp-reduce* invokes a collection of shell scripts to reduce the packet capture information in a *tcpdump* trace file to one-line summaries for each connection. That is, an entire Telnet session would be summarized by a single line. This could be extremely useful in getting an overall picture of how the traffic over a link breaks down or for looking quickly at very large files.

The syntax is quite simple.

```
bsd1# tcp-reduce tracefile > outfile
```

will reduce *tracefile*, putting the output in *outfile*. The program *tcp-summary*, which comes with *tcp-reduce*, will further summarize the results. For example, on my system I traced a system briefly with *tcpdump*. This process collected 741 packets. When processed with *tcp-reduce*, this revealed 58 TCP connections. Here is an example when results were passed to *tcp-summary*:

```
bsd1# tcp-reduce out-file | tcp-summary
```

This example produced the following five-line summary:

proto	# conn	KBytes	% SF	% loc	% ngh
www	56	35	25	0	0
telnet	1	1	100	0	0
pop-3	1	0	100	0	0

In this instance, this clearly shows that the HTTP traffic dominated the local network traffic.

tcpshow

The program *tcpshow* decodes a *tcpdump* trace file. It represents an alternative to using *tcpdump* to decode data. The primary advantage of *tcpshow* is much nicer formatting for output. For example, here is the *tcpdump* output for a packet:

```
12:36:54.772066 sloan.lander.edu.1174 > 205.153.63.238.telnet: . ack
3259091394 win 8647 (DF) b
```

Here is corresponding output from *tcpshow* for the same packet:

```
-----------------------------------------------------------------------
Packet 1
TIME:   12:36:54.772066
LINK:   00:10:5A:A1:E9:08 -> 00:10:5A:E3:37:0C type=IP
  IP:   sloan -> 205.153.63.238 hlen=20 TOS=00 dgramlen=40 id=B30C
        MF/DF=0/1 frag=0 TTL=128 proto=TCP cksum=2D84
 TCP:   port 1174 -> telnet seq=0016775603 ack=3259091394
        hlen=20 (data=0) UAPRSF=010000 wnd=8647 cksum=E869 urg=0
DATA:   <No data>
-----------------------------------------------------------------------
```

The syntax is:

```
bsd1# tcpshow < trace-file
```

There are numerous options.

tcpslice

The program *tcpslice* is a simple but useful program for extracting pieces or merging *tcpdump* files. This is a useful utility for managing larger *tcpdump* files. You specify a starting time and optionally an ending time for a file, and it extracts the corresponding records from the source file. If multiple files are specified, it extracts packets from the first file and then continues extracting only those packets from the next file that have a later timestamp. This prevents duplicate packets if you have overlapping trace files.

While there are a few options, the basic syntax is quite simple. For example, consider the command:

```
bsd1# tcpslice 934224220.0000 in-file > out-file
```

This will extract all packets with timestamps after 934224220.0000. Note the use of an unformatted timestamp. This is the same format displayed with the *-tt* option with *tcpdump*. Note also the use of redirection. Because it works with binary files, *tcpslice* will not allow you to send output to your terminal. See the manpage for additional options.

tcptrace

This program is an extremely powerful *tcpdump* file analysis tool. The program *tcptrace* is strictly an analysis tool, not a capture program, but it works with a variety of capture file formats. The tool's primary focus is the analysis of TCP connections. As such, it is more of a network management tool than a packet analysis tool. The program provides several levels of output or analysis ranging from very brief to very detailed.

While for most purposes *tcptrace* is used as a command-line tool, *tcptrace* is capable of producing several types of output files for plotting with the X Window program *xplot*. These include *time sequence graphs, throughput graphs,* and graphs of *round-trip times*. Time sequence graphs (*-S* option) are plots of sequence numbers over time that give a picture of the activity on the network. Throughput graphs (*-T* option), as the name implies, plot throughput in bytes per second against time. While throughput gives a picture of the volume of traffic on the network, round-trip times give a better picture of the delays seen by individual connections. Round-trip time plots (*-R* option) display individual round-trip times over time. For other graphs and graphing options, consult the documentation.

For normal text-based operations, there are an overwhelming number of options and possibilities. One of the most useful is the *-l* option. This produces a long listing of summary statistics on a connection-by-connection basis. What follows is an example of the information provided for a single brief Telnet connection:

```
TCP connection 2:
        host c:        sloan.lander.edu:1230
        host d:        205.153.63.238:23
        complete conn: yes
        first packet:  Wed Aug 11 11:23:25.151274 1999
        last packet:   Wed Aug 11 11:23:53.638124 1999
        elapsed time:  0:00:28.486850
        total packets: 160
        filename:      telnet.trace
   c->d:                              d->c:
      total packets:        96           total packets:        64
      ack pkts sent:        95           ack pkts sent:        64
      pure acks sent:       39           pure acks sent:       10
      unique bytes sent:   119           unique bytes sent:  1197
      actual data pkts:     55           actual data pkts:     52
      actual data bytes:   119           actual data bytes:  1197
      rexmt data pkts:       0           rexmt data pkts:       0
      rexmt data bytes:      0           rexmt data bytes:      0
      outoforder pkts:       0           outoforder pkts:       0
      pushed data pkts:     55           pushed data pkts:     52
      SYN/FIN pkts sent:   1/1           SYN/FIN pkts sent:   1/1
      mss requested:      1460 bytes     mss requested:      1460 bytes
      max segm size:        15 bytes     max segm size:       959 bytes
      min segm size:         1 bytes     min segm size:         1 bytes
```

avg segm size:	2	bytes	avg segm size:	23	bytes
max win adv:	8760	bytes	max win adv:	17520	bytes
min win adv:	7563	bytes	min win adv:	17505	bytes
zero win adv:	0	times	zero win adv:	0	times
avg win adv:	7953	bytes	avg win adv:	17519	bytes
initial window:	15	bytes	initial window:	3	bytes
initial window:	1	pkts	initial window:	1	pkts
ttl stream length:	119	bytes	ttl stream length:	1197	bytes
missed data:	0	bytes	missed data:	0	bytes
truncated data:	1	bytes	truncated data:	1013	bytes
truncated packets:	1	pkts	truncated packets:	7	pkts
data xmit time:	28.479	secs	data xmit time:	27.446	secs
idletime max:	6508.6	ms	idletime max:	6709.0	ms
throughput:	4	Bps	throughput:	42	Bps

This was produced by using *tcpdump* to capture all traffic into the file *telnet.trace* and then executing *tcptrace* to process the data. Here is the syntax required to produce this output:

```
bsd1# tcptrace -l telnet.trace
```

Similar output is produced for each TCP connection recorded in the trace file. Obviously, a protocol (like HTTP) that uses many different sessions may overwhelm you with output.

There is a lot more to this program than covered in this brief discussion. If your primary goal is analysis of network performance and related problems rather than individual packet analysis, this is a very useful tool.

trafshow

The program *trafshow* is a packet capture program of a different sort. It provides a continuous display of traffic over the network, giving repeated snapshots of traffic. It displays the source address, destination address, protocol, and number of bytes. This program would be most useful in looking for suspicious traffic or just getting a general idea of network traffic.

While *trafshow* can be run on a text-based terminal, it effectively takes over the display. It is best used in a separate window of a windowing system. There are a number of options, including support for packet filtering using the same filter format as *tcpdump*.

xplot

The *xplot* program is an X Windows plotting program. While it is a general purpose plotting program, it was written as part of a thesis project for TCP analysis by David Clark. As a result, some support for plotting TCP data (oriented toward network analysis) is included with the package. It is also used by *tcptrace*. While a powerful and useful program, it is not for the faint of heart. Due to the lack of documentation, the program is easiest to use with *tcptrace* rather than as a stand-alone program.

Other Packet Capture Programs

We have discussed *tcpdump* in detail because it is the most widely available packet capture program for Unix. Many implementations of Unix have proprietary packet capture programs that are comparable to *tcpdump*. For example, Sun Microsystems' Solaris provides *snoop*. (This is a replacement for *etherfind,* which was supplied with earlier versions of the Sun operating system.)

Here is an example of using *snoop* to capture five packets:

```
sol1> snoop -c5
Using device /dev/elxl (promiscuous mode)
172.16.2.210 -> sol1           TELNET C port=28863
        sol1 -> 172.16.2.210 TELNET R port=28863 /dev/elxl (promiscuo
172.16.2.210 -> sol1           TELNET C port=28863
172.16.2.210 -> sloan.lander.edu TCP D=1071 S=22      Ack=143990 Seq=3737542069
Len=60 Win=17520
sloan.lander.edu -> 172.16.2.210 TCP D=22 S=1071      Ack=3737542129 Seq=143990
Len=0 Win=7908
snoop: 5 packets captured
```

As you can see, it is used pretty much the same way as *tcpdump*. (Actually, the output has a slightly more readable format.) *snoop*, like *tcpdump*, supports a wide range of options and filters. You should have no trouble learning *snoop* if you have ever used *tcpdump*.

Other systems will provide their own equivalents (for example, AIX provides *iptrace*). While the syntax is different, these tools are used in much the same way.

Packet Analyzers

Even with the tools just described, the real limitation with *tcpdump* is interpreting the data. For many uses, *tcpdump* may be all you need. But if you want to examine the data within packets, a packet sniffer is not enough. You need a packet analyzer. A large number of packet analyzers are available at tremendous prices. But before you start spending money, you should consider *ethereal*.

ethereal

ethereal is available both as an X Windows program for Unix systems and as a Microsoft Windows program. It can be used as a capture tool and as an analysis tool. It uses the same capture engine and file format as *tcpdump,* so you can use the same filter syntax when capturing traffic, and you can use *ethereal* to analyze *tcpdump* files. Actually, *ethereal* supports two types of filters, capture filters based on *tcpdump* and display filters used to control what you are looking at. Display filters use a different syntax and are described later in this section.

Using ethereal

Usually *ethereal* will be managed entirely from a windowing environment. While it can be run with command-line options, I've never encountered a use for these. (There is also a text-based version, *tethereal*.) When you run *ethereal*, you are presented with a window with three initially empty panes. The initial screen is similar to Figure 5-1 except the panes are empty. (These figures are for the Windows implementation of *ethereal*, but these windows are almost identical to the Unix version.) If you have a file you want to analyze, you can select File → Open. You can either load a *tcpdump* file created with the *-w* option or a file previously saved from *ethereal*.

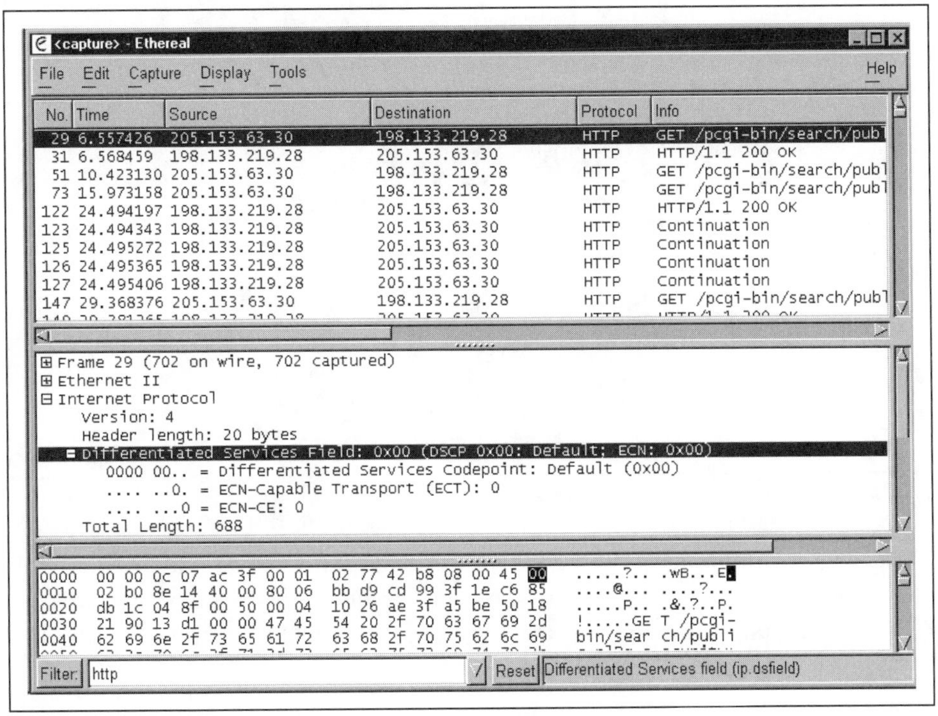

Figure 5-1. ethereal

To capture data, select Capture → Start. You will be presented with a Capture Preferences screen like the one shown in Figure 5-2. If you have multiple interfaces, you can select which one you want to use with the first field. The Count: field is used to limit the number of packets you will collect. You can enter a capture filter, using *tcpdump* syntax, in the Filter: field. If you want your data automatically saved to a file, enter that in the File: field. The fifth field allows you to limit the number of bytes you collect from the packet. This can be useful if you are interested only in header information and want to keep your files small. The first of the four buttons allows you to switch between promiscuous and nonpromiscuous mode. With the latter, you'll collect only traffic sent to or from your machine rather than everything your machine sees. Select the second button if you want to see traffic as it is captured. The third button selects automatic scrolling. Finally, the last button controls name resolution. Name resolution really slows *ethereal* down. Don't enable name resolution if you are going to display packets in real time! Once you have everything set, click on OK to begin capturing data.

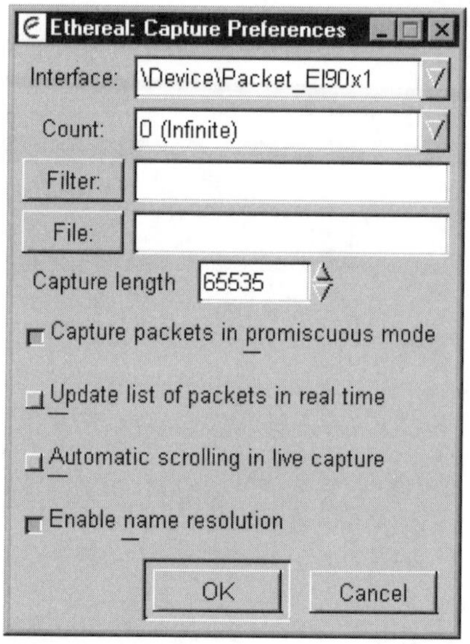

Figure 5-2. ethereal Capture Preferences

While you are capturing traffic, *ethereal* will display a Capture window that will give you counts for the packets captured in real time. This window is shown in Figure 5-3. If you didn't say how many frames you wanted to capture on the last screen, you can use the Stop button to end capture.

Once you have finished capturing data, you'll want to go back to the main screen shown in Figure 5-1. The top pane displays a list of the captured packets. The lower panes display information for the packet selected in the top pane. The packet to be dissected is selected in the top pane by clicking on it. The second pane then displays a protocol tree for the packet, while the bottom pane displays

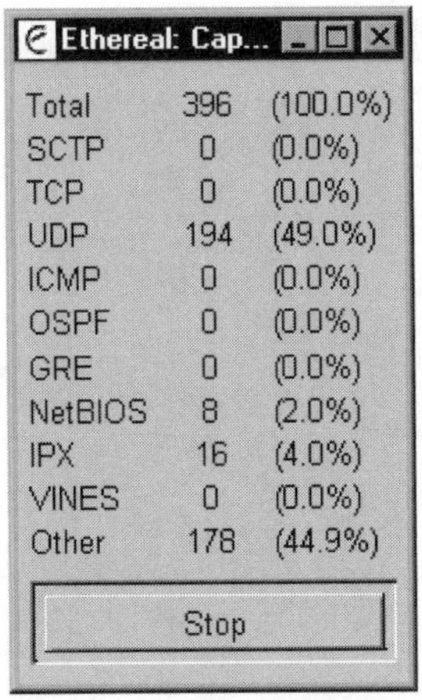

Figure 5-3. ethereal Capture

the raw data in hex and ASCII. The layout of *ethereal* is shown in Figure 5-1. You'll probably want to scroll through the top pane until you find the traffic of interest. Once you have selected a packet, you can resize the windows as needed. Alternately, you can select Display → Show Packet in New Window to open a separate window, allowing you to open several packets at once.

The protocol tree basically displays the structure of the packet by analyzing the data and determining the header type and decoding accordingly. Fields can be expanded or collapsed by clicking on the plus or minus next to the field, respectively. In the figure, the Internet Protocol header has been expanded and the Type-Of-Service (TOS) field in turn has been expanded to show the various values of the TOS flags. Notice that the raw data for the field selected in the second pane is shown in bold in the bottom pane. This works well for most protocols, but if you are using some unusual protocol, like other programs, *ethereal* will not know what to do with it.

ethereal has several other useful features. For example, you can select a TCP packet from the main pane and then select Tools → Follow TCP Stream. This tool collects information from all the packets in the TCP session and displays the information. Unfortunately, while convenient at times, this feature makes it just a little too easy to capture passwords or otherwise invade users' privacy.

The Tools → Summary gives you the details for data you are looking at. An example is shown in Figure 5-4.

There are a number of additional features that I haven't gone into here. But what I described here is more than enough for most simple tasks.

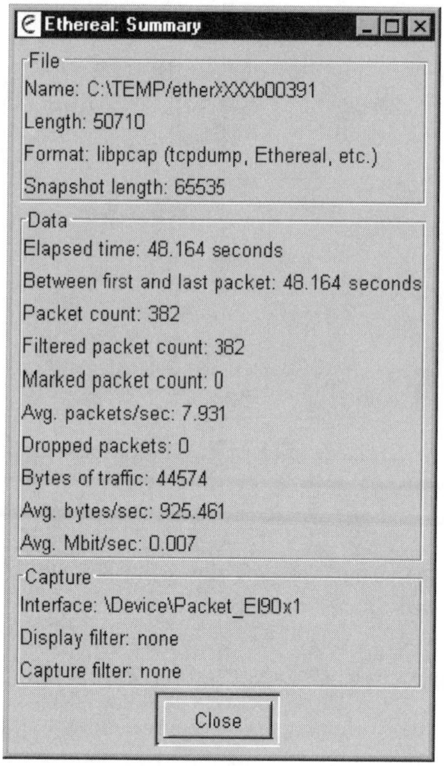

Figure 5-4. ethereal Summary

Display filters

Display filters allow you to selectively display data that has been captured. At the bottom of the window shown in Figure 5-1, there is a box for creating display filters. As previously noted, display filters have their own syntax. The *ethereal* documentation describes this syntax in great detail. In this case, I have entered *http* to limit the displayed traffic to web traffic. I could just as easily enter any number of other different protocols—*ip*, *udp*, *icmp*, *arp*, *dns*, etc.

The real power of *ethereal*'s display filters comes when you realize that you don't really need to understand the syntax of display filters to start using them. You can select a field from the center pane and then select Display → Match Selected, and *ethereal* will construct and apply the filter for you. Of course, not every field is useful, but it doesn't take much practice to see what works and what doesn't work.

The primary limitation of this approach comes in constructing compound filters. If you want to capture all the traffic to or from a computer, you won't be able to match a single field. But you should be able to discover the syntax for each of the pieces. Once you know that `ip.src==205.153.63.30` matches all IP traffic with *205.153.63.30* as its source and that `ip.dst==205.153.63.30` matches all IP traffic to *205.153.63.30*, it isn't difficult to come up with the filter you need, `ip.src==205.153.63.30` or `ip.dst==205.153.63.30`. Display filters are really very intuitive, so you should have little trouble learning how to use them.

Perhaps more than any other tool described in this book, *ethereal* is constantly being changed and improved. While this book was being written, new versions were appearing at the rate of about once a month. So you should not be surprised if *ethereal* looks a little different from what is described here. Fortunately, *ethereal* is a well-developed program that is very intuitive to use. You should have little trouble going on from here.

Dark Side of Packet Capture

What you can do, others can do. Pretty much anything you can discover through packet capture can be discovered by anyone else using packet capture in a similar manner. Moreover, some technologies that were once thought to be immune to packet capture, such as switches, are not as safe as once believed.

Switch Security

Switches are often cited as a way to protect traffic from sniffing. And they really do provide some degree of protection from casual sniffing. Unfortunately, there are several ways to defeat the protection that switches provide.

First, many switches will operate as hubs, forwarding traffic out on every port, whenever their address tables are full. When first initialized, this is the default behavior until the address table is built. Unfortunately, tools like *macof*, part of the *dsniff* suite of tools, will flood switches with MAC addresses overflowing a switch's address table. If your switch is susceptible, all you need to do to circumvent security is run the program.

Second, if two machines have the same MAC address, some switches will forward traffic to both machines. So if you want copies of traffic sent to a particular machine on your switch, you can change the MAC address on your interface to match the target devices' MAC address. This is easily done on many Unix computers with the *ifconfig* command.

A third approach, sometimes called *ARP poisoning*, is to send a forged ARP packet to the source device. This can be done with a tool like *arpredirect*, also part of *dsniff*. The idea is to substitute the packet capture device's MAC address for the destination's MAC address. Traffic will be sent to a packet capture device, which can then forward the traffic to its destination. Of course, the forged ARP packets can be sent to any number of devices on the switch.

The result, with any of these three techniques, is that traffic will be copied to a device that can capture it. Not all switches are susceptible to all of these attacks. Some switches provide various types of port security including static ARP assignments. You can also use tools like *arpwatch* to watch for suspicious activities on your network. (*arpwatch* is described in Chapter 6.) If sniffing is a concern, you may want to investigate what options you have with your switches.

While these techniques could be used to routinely capture traffic as part of normal management, the techniques previously suggested are preferable. Flooding the address table can significantly degrade network performance. Duplicating a MAC address will allow you to watch traffic only to a single host. ARP poisoning is a lot of work when monitoring more than one host and can introduce traffic delays. Consequently, these aren't really techniques that you'll want to use if you have a choice.

Protecting Yourself

Because of the potential for abuse, you should be very circumspect about who has access to packet capture tools. If you are operating in a Unix-only environment, you may have some success in restricting access to capture programs. packet capture programs should always be configured as privileged commands. If you want to allow access to a group of users, the recommended approach is to create an administrative group, restrict execution of packet capture programs to that group, and give group membership only to a small number of trusted individuals. This amounts to setting the SUID bit for the program, but limiting execution to the owner and any group members.

With some versions of Unix, you might even consider recompiling the kernel so the packet capture software can't be run on machines where it isn't needed. For example, with FreeBSD, it is very straightforward to disable the Berkeley packet filter in the kernel. (With older versions of FreeBSD, you needed to explicitly enable it.) Another possibility is to use interfaces that don't support promiscuous mode. Unfortunately, these can be hard to find.

There is also software that can be used to check to see if your interface is in promiscuous mode. You can do this manually with the *ifconfig* command. Look for PROMISC in the flags for the interface. For example, here is the output for one interface in promiscuous mode:

```
bsd2# ifconfig ep0
ep0: flags=8943<UP,BROADCAST,RUNNING,PROMISC,SIMPLEX,MULTICAST> mtu 1500
        inet 172.16.2.236 netmask 0xffffff00 broadcast 172.16.2.255
        inet6 fe80::260:97ff:fe06:2222%ep0 prefixlen 64 scopeid 0x2
        ether 00:60:97:06:22:22
        media: 10baseT/UTP
        supported media: 10baseT/UTP
```

Of course, you'll want to check every interface.

Alternately, you could use a program like *cpm, check promiscuous mode* from CERT/CC. *lsof,* described in Chapter 11, can be used to look for large open files that might be packet sniffer output. But if you have Microsoft Windows computers on your network or allow user-controlled computers on your network, this approach isn't enough.

While it may appear that packet capture is a purely passive activity that is undetectable, this is often not the case. There are several techniques and tools that can be used to indicate packet capture or to test remote interfaces to see if they are in promiscuous mode. One of the simplest techniques is to turn your packet capture software on, ping an unused IP address, and watch for DNS queries trying to resolve that IP address. An unused address should be ignored. If someone is trying to resolve the address, it is likely they have captured a packet.

Another possibility is the tool *antisniff* from L0pht Heavy Industries. This is a commercial tool, but a version is available for noncommercial uses. There are subtle changes in the behavior of an interface when placed in promiscuous mode. This tool is designed to look for those changes. It can probe the systems on a network, examine their responses, and usually determine which devices have an interface in promiscuous mode.

Another approach is to restructure your network for greater security. To the extent you can limit access to traffic, you can reduce the packet capture. Use of virtual LANs can help, but no approach is really foolproof. Ultimately, strong encryption is your best bet. This won't stop sniffing, but it will protect your data. Finally, it is always helpful to have clearly defined policies. Make sure your users know that unauthorized packet capture is not acceptable.

Microsoft Windows

In general, it is inadvisable to leave packet capture programs installed on Windows systems unless you are quite comfortable with the physical security you provide for those machines. Certainly, packet capture programs should never be installed on publicly accessible computers using consumer versions of Windows.

The programs *WinDump95* and *WinDump* are ports of *tcpdump* to Windows 95/98 and Windows NT, respectively. Each requires the installation of the appropriate drivers. They are run in DOS windows and have the same basic syntax as *tcpdump*. As *tcpdump* has already been described, there is little to add here.

ethereal is also available for Windows and, on the whole, works quite well. The one area in which the port doesn't seem to work is in sending output directly to a printer. However, printing to files works nicely so you can save any output you want and then print it.

One of the more notable capture programs available for Windows platforms is *netmon* (Network Monitor), a basic version of which is included with Windows NT Server. The *netmon* program was originally included with Windows NT 3.5 as a means of collecting data to send to Microsoft's technical support. As such, it was not widely advertised. Figure 5-5 shows the packet display window.

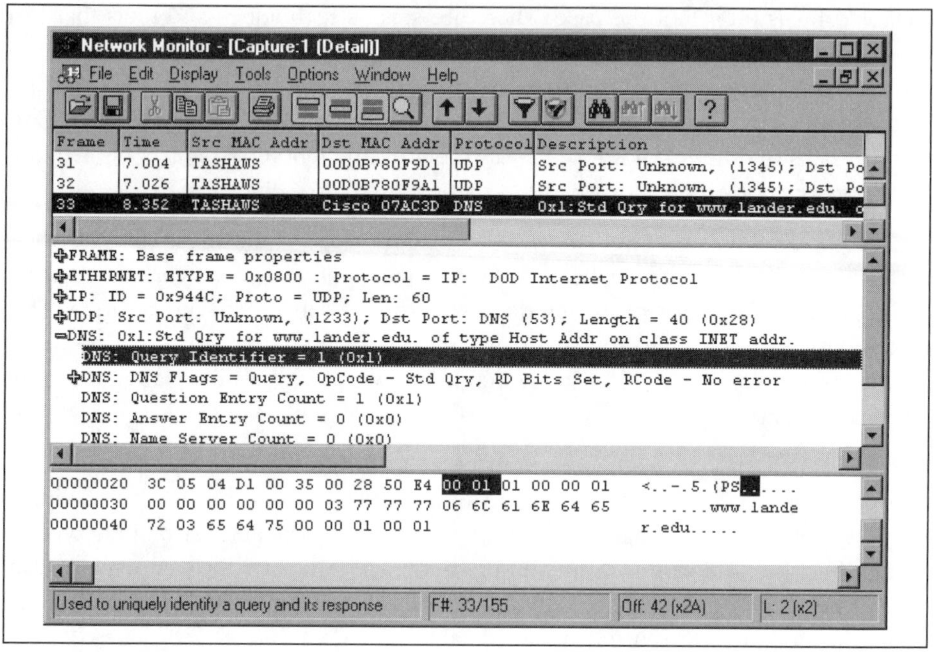

Figure 5-5. netmon for Windows

The basic version supplied with Windows NT Server is quite limited in scope. It restricts capture to traffic to or from the server and severely limits the services it provides. The full version is included as part of the Systems Management Server (SMS), part of the BackOffice suite, and is an extremely powerful program. Of concern with any capture and analysis program is what protocols can be effectively decoded. As might be expected, *netmon* is extremely capable when dealing with Microsoft protocols but offers only basic decoding of Novell protocols. (For Novell protocols, consider Novell's *LANalyzer.*)

One particularly nice feature of *netmon* is the ability to set up collection agents on any Windows NT workstation and have them collect data remotely. The collected data resides with the agent until needed, thus minimizing traffic over the network.

The program is, by default, not installed. The program can be added as a service under network configuration in the setup window. It is included under Administrative Tools (Common). The program, once started, is very intuitive and has a strong help system.

6

Device Discovery and Mapping

The earlier chapters in this book focused on collecting information on the smaller parts of a network, such as the configuration of an individual computer or the path between a pair of computers. Starting with this chapter, we will broaden our approach and look at tools more suited to collecting information on IP networks as a whole. The next three closely related chapters deal with managing and troubleshooting devices distributed throughout a network. This chapter focuses on device discovery and mapping. Additional techniques and tools for this purpose are presented in Chapter 7, once *Simple Network Management Protocol* (SNMP) has been introduced. Chapter 8 focuses on the collection of information on traffic patterns and device utilization throughout the network.

This chapter begins with a brief discussion of the relationship between network management and troubleshooting. This is followed by a discussion of ways to map out the IP addresses that are being used on your network and ways to find which IP addresses correspond to which hosts. This is followed by a description of ways to discover more information on these hosts based on the network services they support and other forensic information. The chapter briefly discusses scripting tools, then describes the network mapping and monitoring tool, *tkined*. The chapter concludes with a brief description of related tools for use with Microsoft Windows platforms.

Troubleshooting Versus Management

Some of the tools in the next few chapters may seem only marginally related to troubleshooting. This is not a totally unfair judgment. Of course, troubleshooting is an unpredictable business, and any tools that can provide information may be useful in some circumstances. Often you will want to use tools that were designed with another purpose in mind.

But these tools were not included just on the off chance they might be useful. Many of the tools described here, while typically used for management, are just as useful for troubleshooting. In a very real sense, troubleshooting and management are just different sides of the same coin. Ideally, management deals with problems before they happen, while troubleshooting deals with problems after the fact. With this in mind, it is worth reviewing management software with an eye on how it can be used as troubleshooting software.

Characteristics of Management Software

Everyone seems to have a different idea of exactly what management software should do. Ideally, network management software will provide the following:

Discovery and mapping

Discovery includes both the automatic detection of all devices on a network and the collection of basic information about each device, such as the type of each device, its MAC address and IP address, the type of software being used, and, possibly, the services it provides. Mapping is the creation of a graphical representation of the network showing individual interconnections as well as overall topology.

Event monitoring

Once a picture of the network has been created, each device may be monitored to ensure continuous operation. This can be done passively, by waiting for the device to send an update or alert, or by actively polling the device.

Remote configuration

You should be able to connect to each device and then examine and change its configuration. It should also be possible to collectively track configuration information, such as which IP addresses are in use.

Metering and performance management

Information on resource utilization should be collected. Ideally, this information should be available in a usable form for purposes such as trend analysis and capacity planning.

Software management

Being able to install and configure software remotely is rapidly becoming a necessity in larger organizations. Being able to track licensing can be essential to avoid legal problems. Version management is also important.

Security and accounting

Depending on the sensitivity of data, the organization's business model, and access and billing policies, it may be necessary to control or track who is using what on the network.

It doesn't take much imagination to see how most of these functions relate to troubleshooting. This chapter focuses on discovery and mapping. Chapter 7 will discuss event monitoring and the remote configuration of hardware and software. Metering and performance management are discussed in Chapter 8. Security is discussed throughout the next three chapters as appropriate.

Discovery and Mapping Tools

A wide range of tools is available. At the low end are *point tools*—tools designed to deal with specific tasks or closely related tasks. Several of the tools we will examine, such as *arpwatch* and *nmap*, fall in this category. Such tools tend to be well focused and do their job well. Typically, they are very easy to learn to use and are usually free or quite inexpensive.

Also found at the low end are toolkits and scripting languages for creating your own applications. Unlike most prebuilt tools, these can be extremely difficult to both learn and use, but they often give you the greatest degree of control. The quality of the final tool will ultimately depend on how much effort and skill you put into its creation. The initial outlay may be modest, but the development time can be extremely costly. Nonetheless, some people swear by this approach. The idea is that time is spent once to develop a tool that saves time each time it is used. We will look very briefly at the scripting language *Tcl* and its extensions. The primary goal here will be to describe the issues and provide information on how to get started.

At the middle of the range are integrated packages. This type of software addresses more than one aspect of network management. They typically include network discovery, mapping, and monitoring programs but may include other functionality as well. Typically they are straightforward to use but don't perform well with very large, diverse networks.

Finally, at the high end are frameworks. Roughly, these are packages that can be easily extended. Since you can extend functionality by adding modules, frameworks are better suited for larger, diverse networks. But be warned, dividing lines among these last categories are not finely drawn.

Unfortunately, at the time of this writing, there aren't many freely available packages at these higher levels. The leading contenders are really works in progress. *tkined* is described in this chapter and the next because it seemed, at the time this was written, to be further along and fairly stable. But there are at least two other projects making rapid progress in this area that are worth considering. The work of Open Network Management Systems (*http://www.opennms.org*) is truly outstanding and making terrific progress. The other is the *GxSNMP SNMP Manager* (*http://www.gxsnmp.org*), a part of the GNOME project. Both are open source (*http://opensource.org*) projects, and both appear to have a committed base of supporters and are likely to be successful. At the time this was written, both had begun to release viable tools, particularly the Open Network Management Systems folks. (Linux users may want to also consider *Cheops*.)

Selecting a Product

It may seem strange that a book devoted to noncommercial software would recommend buying software, but network management is one area in which you should at least consider the possibility. Commercial products are not without problems, but noncommercial mapping and management tools are relatively scarce. Depending on the size of the network you are dealing with, you may have little choice but to consider commercial products at this time.

The key factors are the size of your network, the size of your budget, and the cost of a nonfunctioning network. With point tools, you will be forced to put the pieces together. Certainly, this is something you can do with a small network. If you are responsible for a single LAN or small number of LANs and if you can tolerate being down for a few hours at a time, then you can probably survive with the noncommercial tools described here. But if you are responsible for a larger network or one that is rapidly changing, then you should consider commercial tools. While these may be quite expensive, they may be essential for a large network. And if you are really dealing with a large number of machines, the cost per machine may not be that high.

Even if you feel compelled to buy commercial management software, you should read the rest of this chapter. Several of the point tools described here can be used in conjunction with commercial tools. Some of these tools, because they are designed for a single function, will perform better than commercial tools that attempt to do everything. In a few instances, noncommercial tools address issues not addressed by commercial tools.

Device Discovery

The first step in managing a network is discovering which devices are on the network. There are some fairly obvious reasons why this is important. You will need to track address usage to manage services such as DNS. You may need this information to verify licensing information. From a security perspective, you will want to know if there are any devices on your network that shouldn't be there. And one particularly compelling reason for a complete picture of your network is IP address management.

IP Address Management

Management of IP addresses is often cited as the most common problem faced in the management of an IP network. There are two goals in IP management— keeping track of the addresses in use so you know what is available and keeping track of the devices associated with each assigned IP address.

Several developments over the last few years have helped to lessen the problems of IP management. First, DHCP servers, systems that automatically allocate and track IP addresses, help when dynamic allocation is appropriate. But there are a number of reasons why a system may require a static IP address. Any resource or server—time server, name server, and so on—should be given a static address. Network devices like switches and routers require static addresses. Some sites require reverse DNS lookup before allowing access. The easiest way to provide this is with a static IP address and with an appropriate DNS entry.* Even when such issues don't apply, the cost and complexity of DHCP services may prevent their use. And even if you use DHCP, there is nothing to prevent a user from incorrectly assigning a static IP address in the middle of the block of addresses you have reserved for DNS assignment.

Another development that has helped is automatic testing of newly assigned addresses. While earlier implementations of TCP/IP stacks sometimes neglected to test whether an IP address was being used, most systems, when booted, now first check to see if an IP address is in use before using it. The test, known as *gratuitous ARP*, sends out an ARP request for the IP address about to be used. If anyone replies, the address must already be in use. Of course, this test works only when the other machine is turned on. You may set up a machine with everything appearing to work correctly, only to get a call later in the day. Once such a problem has been detected, you will need to track it down.

While these and similar developments have gone a long way toward lessening the problems of IP management and duplicate IP addresses, IP management remains a headache on many networks. Ideally, you will keep careful records as IP addresses are assigned, but mistakes are unavoidable. Thus, an automated approach is often desirable.

The simplest way to collect MAC/IP address pairs is to ping the address and then examine your ARP table. The ping is necessary since most ARP tables are flushed frequently. At one time, it was possible to ping a broadcast address and get a number of replies at once. Most hosts are now configured to ignore ICMP requests sent to broadcast addresses. (See the discussion of Smurf Attacks in Chapter 3.)

---

* Strictly speaking, static addresses are not mandatory in every case. Support for dynamic DNS, or DDNS, has been available for several years. With DDNS, DNS entries can be mapped to dynamically assigned IP addresses. Unfortunately, many sites still do not use it.

You will need to repeat ping scans very frequently if you want to get a picture over time. It is a simple matter to create a script that automates the process of pinging a range of IP addresses, particularly if you use a tool like *fping*. You'll need the output from the *arp* command if you want the MAC addresses. And you certainly will want to do some cleanup with *sort* or *sed*.

Fortunately, there is a class of tools that simplifies this process—IP scanner or *ping* scanner. These are usually very simple tools that send ICMP ECHO_REQUEST packets in a systematic manner to each IP address in a range of IP addresses and then record any replies. (These tools are not limited to using just ECHO_REQUEST packets.)

nmap

The program *nmap* is a multifunction tool that supports IP scanning. It also provides port scanning and stack fingerprinting. (Stack fingerprinting is described later in this chapter.) *nmap* is an extremely feature-rich program with lots of versatility. For many of its uses, root privileges are required, although some functions work without root privileges.

nmap certainly could have been described in Chapter 2, when port scanners were introduced. But if all you want is a port scan for a single machine, using *nmap* is overkill.* Nonetheless, if you only want as few programs as possible and you need some of the other functionality that *nmap* provides, then you can probably get by with just *nmap*.

To use *nmap* as a port scanner, the only information you need is the IP address or hostname of the target:

```
bsd1# nmap sol1

Starting nmap V. 2.12 by Fyodor (fyodor@dhp.com, www.insecure.org/nmap/)
Interesting ports on sol1.lander.edu (172.16.2.233):
Port    State    Protocol  Service
21      open     tcp       ftp
23      open     tcp       telnet
25      open     tcp       smtp
37      open     tcp       time
111     open     tcp       sunrpc
515     open     tcp       printer
540     open     tcp       uucp
6000    open     tcp       X11

Nmap run completed -- 1 IP address (1 host up) scanned in 1 second
```

---

* There are also reasons, as will become evident, why you might not want *nmap* too freely available on your network.

The results should be self-explanatory. You can specify several IP addresses or you can span a segment by specifying an address with a mask if you want to scan multiple devices or addresses. The next example will scan all the addresses on the same subnet as the *lnx1* using a class C network mask:

```
bsd1# nmap lnx1/24
```

While *nmap* skips addresses that don't respond, this can still produce a lot of output.

Fortunately, *nmap* will recognize a variety of address range options. Consider:

```
bsd1# nmap 172.16.2.230-235,240
```

This will scan seven IP addresses—those from *172.16.2.230* through *172.16.2.235* inclusive and *172.16.2.240*. You can use *172.16.2.** to scan everything on the subnet. Be warned, however, that the shell you use may require you to use an escape sequence for the * to work correctly. For example, with C-shell, you could use *172.16.2.**. You should also note that the network masks do not have to align with a class boundary. For example, /29 would scan eight hosts by working through the possibilities generated by changing the three low-order bits of the address.

If you want to just do an IP scan to discover which addresses are currently in use, you can use the *-sP* option. This will do a *ping*-like probe for each address on the subnet:

```
bsd1# nmap -sP lnx1/24

Starting nmap V. 2.12 by Fyodor (fyodor@dhp.com, www.insecure.org/nmap/)
Host    (172.16.2.0) seems to be a subnet broadcast address (returned 3 extra
pings).  Skipping host.
Host cisco.lander.edu (172.16.2.1) appears to be up.
Host    (172.16.2.12) appears to be up.
Host    (172.16.2.230) appears to be up.
Host bsd2.lander.edu. (172.16.2.232) appears to be up.
Host sol1.lander.edu (172.16.2.233) appears to be up.
Host lnx1.lander.edu (172.16.2.234) appears to be up.
Host    (172.16.2.255) seems to be a subnet broadcast address (returned 3 extra
pings).  Skipping host.
Nmap run completed -- 256 IP addresses (6 hosts up) scanned in 1 second
```

You should be warned that this particular scan uses both an ordinary ICMP packet and a TCP ACK packet to port 80 (HTTP). This second packet will get past routers that block ICMP packets. If an RST packet is received, the host is up and the address is in use. Unfortunately, some intrusion detection software that will ignore the ICMP packet will flag the TCP ACK as an attack. If you want to use only ICMP packets, use the *-PI* option. For example, the previous scan could have been done using only ICMP packets with the command:

```
bsd1# nmap -sP -PI lnx1/24
```

In this case, since the devices are on the same subnet and there is no intervening firewall, the same machines are found.

Unfortunately, *nmap* stretches the limits of what might be considered appropriate at times. In particular, *nmap* provides a number of options for stealth scanning. There are two general reasons for using stealth scanning. One is to probe a machine without being detected. This can be extremely difficult if the machine is actively watching for such activity.

The other reason is to slip packets past firewalls. Because firewall configuration can be quite complex and because it can be very difficult to predict traffic patterns, many firewalls are configured in ways that allow or block broad, generic classes of traffic. This minimizes the number of rules that need to be applied and improves the throughput of the firewall. But blocking broad classes of traffic also means that it may be possible to sneak packets past such firewalls by having them look like legitimate traffic. For example, external TCP connections may be blocked by discarding the external SYN packets used to set up a connection. If a SYN/ACK packet is sent from the outside, most firewalls will assume the packet is a response for a connection that was initiated by an internal machine. Consequently, the firewall will pass the packet. With these firewalls, it is possible to construct such a packet and slip it through the firewall to see how an internal host responds.

nmap has several types of scans that are designed to do stealth probes. These include *-sF*, *-sX*, and *-sN*. (You can also use the *-f* option to break stealth probes into lots of tiny fragments.) But while these stealth packets may slip past firewalls, they should all be detected by any good intrusion detection software running on the target. You may want to try these on your network just to see how well your intrusion detection system works or to investigate how your firewall responds. But if you are using these to do clandestine scans, you should be prepared to be caught and to face the consequences.

Another questionable feature of *nmap* is the ability to do decoy scans. This option allows you to specify additional forged IP source addresses. In addition to the probe packets that are sent with the correct source address, other similar packets are sent with forged source addresses. The idea is to make it more difficult to pinpoint the real source of the attack since only a few of the packets will have the correct source address. Not only does this create unnecessary network traffic, but it can create problems for hosts whose addresses are spoofed. If the probed site automatically blocks traffic from probing sites, it will cut off the spoofed sites as well as the site where the probe originated. Clearly, this is not what you really want to do. This calls into question any policy that simply blocks sites without further investigation. Such systems are also extremely vulnerable to denial-of-service attacks. Personally, I can see no legitimate use for this feature and would be happy to see it dropped from *nmap*.

But while there are some questionable options, they are easily outnumbered by useful options. If you want your output in greater detail, you might try the *-v* or the *-d* option. If information is streaming past you on the screen too fast for you to read, you can log the output to a file in human-readable or machine-parseable form. Use, respectively, the *-o* or *-m* options along with a filename. The *-h* option will give a brief summary of *nmap*'s many options. You may want to print this to use while you learn *nmap*.

If you are using *nmap* to do port scans, you can use the *-p* option to specify a range of ports. Alternatively, the *-F*, or fast scan option, can be used to limit scans to ports in your services file. You'll certainly want to consider using one or the other of these. Scanning every possible port on a network can take a lot of time and generate a lot of traffic. A number of other options are described in *nmap*'s documentation.

Despite the few negative things I have mentioned, *nmap* really is an excellent tool. You will definitely want to add it to your collection.

arpwatch

Active scans, such as those we have just seen with *nmap*, have both advantages and disadvantages. They allow scans of remote networks and give a good snapshot of the current state of the network. The major disadvantage is that these scans will identify only machines that are operational when you do the scan. If a device is on for only short periods at unpredictable times, it can be virtually impossible to catch by scanning. Tools that run constantly, like *arpwatch*, provide a better picture of activity over time.

For recording IP addresses and their corresponding MAC addresses, *arpwatch* is my personal favorite. It is a very simple tool that does this very well. Basically, *arpwatch* places an interface in promiscuous mode and watches for ARP packets. It then records IP/MAC address pairs. The primary limitation to *arpwatch* comes from being restricted to local traffic. It is not a tool that can be used across networks. If you need to watch several networks, you will need to start *arpwatch* on each of those networks.

The information can be recorded in one of four ways. Data may be written directly to the system console, to the system's *syslog* file, or to a user-specified text file, or it can be sent as an email to root. (*syslog* is described in Chapter 11.) Output to the console or the *syslog* file is basically the same. An entry will look something like:

```
Mar 30 15:16:29 bsd1 arpwatch: new station 172.16.2.234 0:60:97:92:4a:6
```

Of course, with the *syslog* file, these messages will be interspersed with many other messages, but you can easily use *grep* to extract them. For example, to write all the messages from *arpwatch* that were recorded in */var/log/messages* into the file */temp/arp.data*, you can use the command:

```
bsd1# grep arpwatch /var/log/messages > /tmp/arp.list
```

If your *syslog* file goes by a different name or you want output in a different output file, you will need to adjust names accordingly. This approach will include other messages from *arpwatch* as well, but you can easily delete those that are not of interest.

Email looks like:

```
From: arpwatch (Arpwatch)
To: root
Subject: new station (lnx1.lander.edu)

          hostname: lnx1.lander.edu
        ip address: 172.16.2.234
  ethernet address: 0:60:97:92:4a:6
   ethernet vendor: 3Com
         timestamp: Thursday, March 30, 2000 15:16:29 -0500
```

Email output has the advantage of doing name resolution for the IP address, and it gives the vendor for the MAC address. The vendor name is resolved using information in the file *ethercodes.dat*. This file, as supplied with *arpwatch*, is not particularly complete or up-to-date, but you can always go to the IEEE site as described in Chapter 2 if you need this data for a particular interface. If you do this, don't forget to update the *ethercodes.dat* file on your system.

arpwatch can also record raw data to a file. This is typically the file *arp.dat*, but you can specify a different file with the *-f* option. The default location for *arp.dat* seems to vary with systems. The manpage for *arpwatch* specifies */usr/operator/arpwatch* as the default home directory, but this may not be true for some ports. If you use an alternative file, be sure to give its full pathname. Whether you use *arp.dat* or another file, the file must exist before you start *arpwatch*. The format is pretty sparse:

```
0:60:97:92:4a:6 172.16.2.234    954447389      lnx1
```

Expect a lot of entries the first few days after you start *arpwatch* as it learns your network. This can be a little annoying at first, but once most machines are recorded, you shouldn't see much traffic—only new or changed addresses. These should be very predictable. Of particular concern are frequently changing addresses. The most likely explanation for a single address change is that a computer has been replaced by another. Although less likely, a new adapter would also explain the change.

Frequent or unexplained changes deserve greater scrutiny. It could simply mean someone is using two computers. Perhaps a user is unplugging his desktop machine in order to plug in his portable. But it can also mean that someone is trying to hide something they are doing. On many systems, both the MAC and IP addresses can be easily changed. A cracker will often change these addresses to cover her tracks. Or a cracker could be using ARP poisoning to redirect traffic.

Here is an example of an email report for an address change:

```
From: arpwatch (Arpwatch)
To: root
Subject: changed ethernet address

             hostname: <unknown>
           ip address: 205.153.63.55
     ethernet address: 0:e0:29:21:88:83
      ethernet vendor: <unknown>
 old ethernet address: 0:e0:29:21:89:d9
  old ethernet vendor: <unknown>
            timestamp: Monday, April 3, 2000 4:57:16 -0400
   previous timestamp: Monday, April 3, 2000 4:52:33 -0400
                delta: 4 minutes
```

Notice that the subject line will alert you to the nature of the change. This change was followed shortly by another change as shown here:

```
From: arpwatch (Arpwatch)
To: root
Subject: flip flop

             hostname: <unknown>
           ip address: 205.153.63.55
     ethernet address: 0:e0:29:21:89:d9
      ethernet vendor: <unknown>
 old ethernet address: 0:e0:29:21:88:83
  old ethernet vendor: <unknown>
            timestamp: Monday, April 3, 2000 9:40:47 -0400
   previous timestamp: Monday, April 3, 2000 9:24:07 -0400
                delta: 16 minutes
```

This is basically the same sort of information, but *arpwatch* labels the first as a changed address and subsequent changes as flip-flops.

If you are running DHCP and find *arpwatch*'s output particularly annoying, you may want to avoid *arpwatch*. But if you are having problems with DHCP, *arpwatch* might, in limited circumstances, be useful.

Device Identification

At times it can be helpful to identify the operating system used on a remote machine. For example, you may need to identify systems vulnerable to some recently disclosed security hole. Or if you are faced with a duplicate IP address, identifying the type of machine is usually the best first step in locating it. Using *arp* to discover the type of hardware may be all that you will need to do. If you have identified the interface as a Cisco interface and you have only a half dozen Cisco devices on your network, you should be able to easily find the one with the duplicate address. If, on the other hand, you can identify it only as one of several hundred PCs, you'll want more information. Knowing the operating system on the computer may narrow your search.

The obvious, simple strategies are usually the best place to start, since these are less likely to offend anyone. Ideally, you will have collected additional information as you set systems up, so all you'll need to do is consult your database, DHCP records, or DNS files or, perhaps, give the user a call. But if your records are incomplete, you'll need to probe the device.

Begin by using *telnet* to connect to the device to check for useful banners. Often login banners are changed or suppressed, so don't restrict yourself to just the Telnet port. Here is an example of trying the SMTP port (25):

```
bsd1# telnet 172.16.2.233 25
Trying 172.16.2.233...
Connected to 172.16.2.233.
Escape character is '^]'.
220 sol1. ESMTP Sendmail 8.9.1b+Sun/8.9.1; Fri, 2 Jun 2000 09:02:45 -0400 (EDT)
quit
221 sol1. closing connection
Connection closed by foreign host.
```

This simple test tells us the host is *sol1*, and it is using a Sun port of *sendmail.* The most likely ports to try are FTP (21), Telnet (23), SNMP (25), HTTP (80), POP2 (109), POP3 (110), and NTTP (119), but, depending on the systems, others may be informative as well.

Often, you don't even have to get the syntax correct to get useful information. Here is an example of an ill-formed GET request (the REQUEST_URI is omitted) sent using *telnet*:

```
bsd1# telnet 172.16.2.230 80
Trying 172.16.2.230...
Connected to 172.16.2.230.
Escape character is '^]'.
GET HTTP/1.0
HTTP/1.1 400 Bad Request
Server: Microsoft-IIS/4.0
...
```

Additional output has been omitted, but the system has been identified in the last line shown. (See Chapter 10 for other examples.)

Port scanning is one of the tools described in Chapter 2 that can also be used here. To do the tests described in Chapter 2, you need change only the host address. The interpretation of the results is the same. The only thing you need worry about is the possibility that some of the services you are testing may be blocked by a firewall. Of course, the presence or absence of a service may provide insight into the role of the device. An obvious example is an open HTTP port. If it is open, you are looking at a web server (or, possibly, a machine misconfigured as a web server) and can probably get more information by using your web browser on the site.

When these obvious tests fail, as they often will, you'll need a more sophisticated approach such as stack fingerprinting.

Stack Fingerprinting

The standards that describe TCP/IP stack implementations are incomplete in the sense that they sometimes do not address how the stack should respond in some degenerate or pathological situations. For example, there may be no predefined way for dealing with a packet with contradictory flags or with a meaningless sequence of inconsistent packets. Since these situations should not normally arise, implementers are free to respond in whatever manner they see fit. Different implementations respond in different ways.

There are also optional features that stack implementers may or may not choose to implement. The presence or absence of such support is another useful clue to the identity of a system. Even when behavior is well defined, some TCP/IP stacks do not fully conform to standards. Usually, the differences are minor inconsistencies that have no real impact on performance or interoperability. For example, if an isolated FIN packet is sent to an open port, the system should ignore the packet. Microsoft Windows, among others, will send a RESET instead of ignoring the packet. This doesn't create any problems for either of the devices involved, but it can be used to distinguish systems.

Collectively, these different behaviors can be exploited to identify which operating system (OS) is being used on a remote system. A carefully chosen set of packets is sent and the responses are examined. It is necessary only to compare the responses seen against a set of known behaviors to deduce the remote system. This technique is known as *stack fingerprinting* or *OS fingerprinting*.

A fingerprinting program will be successful only if it has a set of anomalies or, to mix metaphors, a *signature* that distinguishes the device of interest from other devices. Since devices change and new devices are introduced, it is not uncommon for a stack fingerprinting program not to know the signature for some devices. Ideally, the program will have a separate signature file or database so that it can be easily updated. From the user's perspective, it may also be helpful to have more than one program since each may be able to identify devices unknown to the other. Consequently, both *queso* and the stack fingerprinting option for *nmap* are described here.

It should also be noted that *passive fingerprinting* is possible. With passive fingerprinting, the idea is to examine the initialization packets that come into your machine. Of course, this will only identify systems that try to contact you, but this can be a help in some circumstances, particularly with respect to security. In some ways, this approach is more reliable. When a remote machine sends the first packet, it must fill in all the fields in the headers. When you probe a remote machine, many of the fields in the headers in the reply packet will have been copied directly from your probe packets. If you are interested in this approach, you might want to look at *siphon* or *pOf.*

 When using stack fingerprinting, whether active or passive, you must realize that you are fingerprinting the machine you are actually communicating with. Normally, that is exactly what you want. But if there is a proxy server between your machine and the target, you will fingerprint the proxy server, not the intended target.

---

queso

A number of programs do stack fingerprinting. One simple program that works well is *queso.* Its sole function is stack fingerprinting. The syntax is straightforward:

```
bsd1# queso 172.16.2.230
172.16.2.230:80 * Windoze 95/98/NT
```

By default, *queso* probes the HTTP port (80). If that port is not in use, *queso* will tell you to try another port:

```
bsd1# queso 172.16.2.1
172.16.2.1:80   *- Not Listen, try another port
```

You can do this with the *-p* option. In this example, the Telnet port is being checked:

```
bsd1# queso -p23 172.16.2.1
172.16.2.1:23   * Cisco 11.2(10a), HP/3000 DTC, BayStack Switch
```

This is not a definitive answer, but it has certainly narrowed down the field.

You can call *queso* with multiple addresses by simply putting all the addresses on the command line. You can also use subnet masks, as shown in the following:

```
bsd1# queso -p23 172.16.2.232/29
172.16.2.233:23 * Solaris 2.x
172.16.2.234:23 * Linux 2.1.xx
172.16.2.235:23 *- Not Listen, try another port
172.16.2.236:23 * Dead Host, Firewalled Port or Unassigned IP
172.16.2.237:23 * Dead Host, Firewalled Port or Unassigned IP
172.16.2.238:23 * Dead Host, Firewalled Port or Unassigned IP
```

Notice from this example that mask selection doesn't have to fall on a class boundary.

queso maintains a separate configuration file. If it doesn't recognize a system, it will prompt you to update this file:

```
bsd1# queso -p23 205.153.60.1
205.153.60.1:23 *- Unknown OS, pleez update /usr/local/etc/queso.conf
```

You can update this file with the *-w* option. *queso* can identify a hundred or so different systems. It is not a particularly fast program but gives acceptable results. It can take several seconds to scan each machine on the same subnet. If you invoke *queso* without any argument, it will provide a brief summary of its options.

nmap Revisited

You can also do stack fingerprinting with *nmap* by using the *-O* option:

```
bsd1# nmap -O 172.16.2.230

Starting nmap V. 2.12 by Fyodor (fyodor@dhp.com, www.insecure.org/nmap/)
WARNING: OS didn't match until the 2 try
Interesting ports on  (172.16.2.230):
Port    State       Protocol  Service
21      open        tcp         ftp
80      open        tcp         http
135     open        tcp         loc-srv
139     open        tcp         netbios-ssn
443     open        tcp         https
1032    open        tcp         iad3
6666    open        tcp         irc-serv
7007    open        tcp         afs3-bos

TCP Sequence Prediction: Class=trivial time dependency
                         Difficulty=0 (Trivial joke)
Remote operating system guess: Windows NT4 / Win95 / Win98

Nmap run completed -- 1 IP address (1 host up) scanned in 5 seconds
```

You can suppress most of the port information by specifying a particular port. For example:

```
bsd1# nmap -p80 -O 172.16.2.230

Starting nmap V. 2.12 by Fyodor (fyodor@dhp.com, www.insecure.org/nmap/)
Interesting ports on  (172.16.2.230):
Port    State       Protocol  Service
80      open        tcp         http

TCP Sequence Prediction: Class=trivial time dependency
                         Difficulty=0 (Trivial joke)
Remote operating system guess: Windows NT4 / Win95 / Win98

Nmap run completed -- 1 IP address (1 host up) scanned in 1 second
```

You will probably want to do this if you are scanning a range of machines to save time. However, if you don't restrict *nmap* to a single port, you are more likely to get a useful answer.

Results can be vague at times. This is what *nmap* returned on one device:

```
...
Remote OS guesses: Cisco Catalyst 1900 switch or Netopia 655-U/POTS ISDN Router,
 Datavoice TxPORT PRISM 3000 T1 CSU/DSU 6.22/2.06, MultiTech CommPlete Controlle
 r, IBM MVS TCP/IP stack V. 3.2, APC MasterSwitch Network Power Controller, AXIS
 or Meridian Data Network CD-ROM server, Meridian Data Network CD-ROM Server (V4.
 20 Nov 26 1997), WorldGroup BBS (MajorBBS) w/TCP/IP
```

The correct answer is none of the above. A system that may not be recognized by *nmap* may be recognized by *queso* or vice versa.

Scripts

Since most networks have evolved over time, they are frequently odd collections of equipment for which no single tool may be ideal. And even when the same tool can be used, differences in equipment may necessitate minor differences in how the tool is used. Since many of the tasks may need to be done on a regular basis, it should come as no surprise that scripting languages are a popular way to automate these tasks. Getting started can be labor intensive, but if your current approach is already labor intensive, it can be justified.

You will want to use a scripting language with extensions that support the collection of network data. To give an idea of this approach, *Tcl* and its extensions are briefly described here. Even if you don't really want to write your own tools, you may want to consider one of the tools based on *Tcl* that are freely available, most notably *tkined*.

Tcl was selected because it is provides a natural introduction to *tkined*. Of course, there are other scripting languages that you may want to consider. Perl is an obvious choice. Several packages and extensions are available for system and network administration. For example, you may want to look at *spidermap*. This is a set of Perl scripts that do network scans. For SNMP-based management, you'll probably want to get Simon Leinen's SNMP extensions *SNMP_Session.pm* and *BER.pm*. (Other tools you might also look at include *mon* and *nocol*.)

Tcl/Tk and scotty

Tool Command Language, or *Tcl* (pronounced "tickle"), is a scripting language that is well suited for network administration. *Tcl* was developed in the late 1980s by John Ousterhout, then a faculty member at UC Berkeley. *Tcl* was designed to be a generic, embeddable, and extensible interpreted language. Users frequently cite studies showing *Tcl* requires one-tenth the development time required by C/ C++. Its major weakness is that it is not well suited for computationally intensive tasks, but that shouldn't pose much of a problem for network management. You can also write applets or *tclets* (pronounced "tik-lets") in *Tcl.*

Tcl can be invoked interactively using the shell *tclsh* (pronounced "ticklish") or with scripts. You may need to include a version number as part of the name. Here is an example:

```
bsd2# tclsh8.2
%
```

This really is a shell. You can change directories, print the working directory, copy files, remove files, and so forth, using the usual Unix commands. You can use the *exit* command to leave the program.

One thing that makes *Tcl* interesting is the number and variety of extensions that are available. *Tk* is a set of extensions that provides the ability to create GUIs in an X Window environment. These extensions make it easy to develop graphical interfaces for tools. *Tk* can be invoked interactively using the windowing shell *wish*. Both *Tcl* and *Tk* are implemented as C library packages that can be included in programs if you prefer.

scotty, primarily the work of Jürgen Schönwälder, adds network management extensions to *Tcl/Tk*. The *tnm* portion of *scotty* adds network administration support. The *tkined* portion of *scotty*, described in the next section, is a graphical network administration program. What *tnm* adds is a number of network management commands. These include support for a number of protocols including ICMP, UDP, DNS, HTTP, Sun's RPC, NTP, and, most significantly, SNMP. In addition, there are several sets of commands that simplify writing network applications. The *netdb* command gives access to local network databases such as */etc/hosts*, the *syslog* command supports sending messages to the system logging facilities, and the *job* command simplifies scheduling tasks. A few examples should give an idea of how these commands could be used.

You can invoke the *scotty* interpreter directly as shown here. In this example, the *netdb* command is used to list the */etc/host* table on a computer:

```
bsd4# scotty
% netdb hosts
{localhost.lander.edu 1.0.0.127} {bsd4.lander.edu 239.63.153.205} {bsd4.lander.e
du. 239.63.153.205} {bsd1.lander.edu 231.60.153.205} {sol1.lander.edu 233.60.153
.205} {lnx1.lander.edu 234.60.153.205}
% exit
```

The results are returned with each entry reduced to the canonical name and IP address in brackets. Here is the host table for the same system:

```
bsd4# cat /etc/hosts
127.0.0.1               localhost.lander.edu localhost
205.153.63.239          bsd4.lander.edu bsd4
205.153.63.239          bsd4.lander.edu.
205.153.60.231          bsd1.lander.edu bsd1
205.153.60.233          sol1.lander.edu sol1
205.153.60.234          lnx1.lander.edu lnx1
```

Note that there is not a separate entry for the alias bsd4.

Here are a few examples of other commands. In the first example, the name of the protocol with a value of 1 is looked up in */etc/protocols* using the *netdb* command:

```
% netdb protocols name 1
icmp
```

In the second example, a reverse DNS lookup is done for the host at *205.153.63.30:*

```
% dns name 205.153.63.30
sloan.lander.edu
```

Finally, an ICMP ECHO_REQUEST is sent to *www.cisco.com:*

```
% icmp echo www.cisco.com
{www.cisco.com 321}
```

The response took 321 ms. Other commands, such as *snmp*, require multiple steps to first establish a session and then access information. (Examples are given in Chapter 7.) If you are interested in using these tools in this manner, you will first want to learn *Tcl*. You can then consult the manpages for these extensions. A number of books and articles describe *Tcl*, some of them listed in Appendix B. The source is freely available for all these tools.

Mapping or Diagramming

At this point, you should have a good idea of how to find out what is on your network. The next step is to put together a picture of how everything interconnects. This is usually referred to as *mapping* but may go by other names such as *network drawing* or *diagramming*. This can be absolutely essential if you are dealing with topology-related problems.

A wide spectrum of approaches may be taken. At one extreme, you could simply use the collected data and some standard drawing utility to create your map. Clearly, some graphics software is better suited than others for this purpose. For example, special icons for different types of equipment are particularly nice. But almost any software should be usable to a degree. I have even put together passable diagrams using the drawing features in Microsoft Excel.

Manual diagramming is usually practical only for a single segment or a very small network. But there might be times when this will be desirable for larger networks—for example, you may be preparing graphics for a formal presentation. This, however, should be an obvious exception, not a routine activity.

In the middle of the spectrum are programs that will both discover and draw the network. When using tools with automatic discovery, you will almost certainly want to clean up the graphics. It is extremely hard to lay out a graph in an aesthetically pleasing manner when doing it manually. You can forget about a computer doing a good job automatically.

Another closely related possibility is to use scripting tools to update the files used by a graphing utility. The graphic utility can then display the new or updated map with little or no additional interaction. While this is a wonderful learning opportunity, it really isn't a practical solution for most people with real time constraints.

At the other extreme, mapping tools are usually part of more comprehensive management packages. Automatic discovery is the norm for these. Once the map is created, additional management functions—including basic monitoring to ensure that devices and connections still work and to collect performance data—are performed.

Ideally, these programs will provide a full graphic display that is automatically generated, includes every device on the network, provides details of the nature and state of the devices, updates the map in real time, and requires a minimum of user input. Some tools are well along the path to this goal.

There are problems with automatic discovery. First, you'll want to be careful when you specify the networks to be analyzed and keep an eye on things whenever you change this. It is not that uncommon to make an error and find that you are mapping devices well beyond your network. And, as explained later in this chapter, not everyone will be happy about this.

Also, many mapping programs do a poor job of recognizing topology. For example, in a virtual LAN, a single switch may be logically part of two different networks. Apart from proprietary tools, don't expect many map programs to recognize and handle these devices correctly. Each logical device may be drawn as a separate device. If you are relying solely on ICMP ECHO_REQUEST packets, unmanaged hubs and switches will not be recognized at all, while managed hubs and switches will be drawn as just another device on the network without any indication of the role they play in the network topology.

Even with automatic discovery, network mapping and management tools may presuppose that you know the basic structure of your network. At a minimum, you must know the address range for your network. It seems very unlikely that a legitimate administrator would not have this information. If for some bizarre reason you don't have this information, you might begin by looking at the routing tables and NAT tables in your router, DNS files, DHCP configurations, or Internic registration information. You might also use *traceroute* to identify intermediate segments and routers.

tkined

An excellent example of a noncommercial, open source mapping program is *tkined*. This is a network editor that can be used as a standalone tool or as a framework for an extensible network management system. At its simplest, it can be used to construct a network diagram. Figure 6-1 is an example of a simple network map that has been constructed using *tkined* tools. (Actually, as will be explained, this map was "discovered" rather than drawn, but don't worry about this distinction for now.)

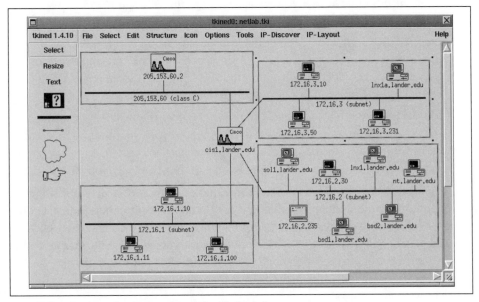

Figure 6-1. A network map constructed with tkined

Drawing maps with tkined

Manually drawing a map like this is fairly straightforward, although somewhat tedious for all but the smallest networks. You begin by starting *tkined* under an X Window session. (This discussion assumes you are familiar with using an X Window application.) You should see the menu bar across the top window just under the titlebar, a toolbar to the left, and a large, initially blank work area called the canvas.

To create a map, follow these steps:

1. Add the devices to the canvas. Begin by clicking* on the *machine icon* on the toolbar on the left. This is the icon with the question mark in the middle. With this tool selected, each time you click over the canvas, a copy of this icon will be inserted on the canvas at the cursor.

   You can change the appearance of each of these icons to reflect the type of device it represents. First, click on Select on the toolbar (not Select on the menu). Next, select the icon or icons you want to change. You select single icons by clicking on them. Multiple icons can be selected by Shift-clicking on each in turn. As you select devices, small boxes are displayed at the corners of the icon. Once you have selected the icons of interest, go to the *icon* pull-down menu and select the icon you want from the appropriate submenu. Notice that the icon on the toolbar changes. (You could make this change before inserting devices if you wish and insert the selected icon that way.)

2. Label each device. Right-click on each device in turn. From the pop-up menu, select Edit All Attributes..., enter the appropriate name and IP address for each device, and then select Set Values. Once you have done this, right-click on the icon again and select Label with Attribute..., select either name or address depending on your preference, and then click on Accept.

3. Add the networks. This is done with the tool below the machine icon (the thick bar). Select this tool by clicking on it. Click where you want the bar to begin on the canvas. Move the mouse to where you want the network icon to end and click a second time. You can label networks in the same way you label nodes.

4. Connect devices to the networks. You can join devices to a network using the next tool on the toolbar, the thin line with little boxes at either end. Select this tool, click on the device you want to join to the network, and then click on the appropriate network icon. As you move the mouse, a line from the icon to the mouse pointer will be shown. When you click on the network, the line should be attached to both the device and the network. If it disappears, your aim was off. Try again.

   At this point, you will probably want to rearrange your drawing to tidy things up. You can move icons by dragging them with the middle mouse button. (If your mouse doesn't have three buttons, try holding down both the left and right buttons simultaneously.)

5. Group devices and networks. This allows you to collapse a subnet into a single icon. You can open whichever subnets you need to work with at the moment and leave the rest closed. For large networks, this is essential. Otherwise, the map becomes too cluttered to use effectively.

---

* Unless otherwise noted, *clicking* means clicking with the left mouse button.

To combine devices, use the Select tool to select the devices and the network. Then select Structure → Group. You can use this same menu to select Ungroup, Expand, and Collapse for your groups. You can edit the group label as desired in the previously discussed manner.

Autodiscovery with tkined

For a small network, manually drawing a diagram doesn't take very long. But for large networks, this can be a very tedious process. Fortunately, *tkined* provides tools for the automatic discovery of nodes and the automatic layout of maps.

You begin with Tools → IP-Discover. What this does is add the IP Discover menu to the menu bar. The first two items on this menu are Discover IP Network and Discover Route. These tools will attempt to discover either the devices on a network or the routers along a path to a remote machine. When one of these is selected, a pop-up box queries you for the network number or remote device of interest. Unfortunately, *tkined* seems to support only class-based discovery, so you must specify a class B or a class C address (although you can specify a portion of a class B network by giving a class C style subnet address, e.g., 172.16.1.0). It also tends to be somewhat unpredictable or quirky when trying to discover multiple networks. If you are using subnets on a class B address, what seems to work best is to run separate discovery sessions and then cut and paste the results together. This is a little bit of a nuisance, but it is not too bad. This was what was actually done to create Figure 6-1.

Figure 6-2 shows the output generated in discovering a route across the network and one of the subnets for the network shown in Figure 6-1. This window is automatically created by *tkined* and shows its progress during the discovery process. Note that it is sending out a flood of ICMP ECHO_REQUEST packets in addition to the *traceroute*-style discovery packets, the ICMP network mask queries, and the SNMP queries shown here.

If you do end up piecing together a network map, other previously discussed tools, such as *traceroute*, can be very helpful. You might also want to look at your routing tables with *netstat*.

There are a couple of problems in using *tkined*. Foremost is the problem of getting everything installed correctly. You will need to install *Tcl*, then *Tk*, and then *scotty*. *scotty* can be very particular about which version of *Tcl* and *Tk* are installed. You will also need to make sure everything is in the default location or that the environmental variables are correctly set. Fortunately, packages are available for some systems, such as Linux, that take care of most of these details automatically. Also, *tkined* will not warn you if you exit without saving any changes you have made.

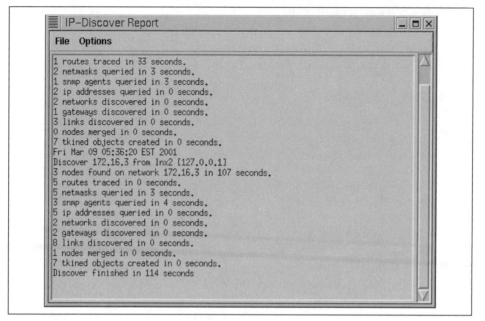

Figure 6-2. Route and network discovery with tkined

Politics and Security

You should have a legitimate reason and the authority to use the tools described here. Some of these tools directly probe other computers on the network. Even legitimate uses of these tools can create surprises for users and may, in some instances, result in considerable ill will and mistrust. For example, doing security probes to discover weaknesses in your network may be a perfectly reasonable thing to do, provided that is your responsibility. But you don't want these scans to come as a surprise to your users. I, for one, strongly resent unexpected probing of my computer regardless of the reason. Often, a well-meaning individual has scanned a network only to find himself with a lot of explaining to do. The list of people who have made this mistake includes several big names in the security community.

With the rise of personal firewalls and monitoring tools, more and more users are monitoring what is happening on their local networks and at their computers. Not all of these users really understand the results returned by these tools, so you should be prepared to deal with misunderstandings. Reactions can be extreme, even from people who should know enough to put things in context.

The first time I used *CiscoWorks* for Windows, the program scanned the network with, among others, CMIP packets. This, of course, is a perfectly natural thing to do. Unfortunately, another machine on the network had been configured in a manner that, when it saw the packet, it began blocking all subsequent packets from the management station. It then began logging all subsequent traffic from the management station as attacks. This included the System Messaged Blocks (SMB) that are a normal part of the network background noise created by computers running Microsoft Windows. A couple of days later I received a very concerned email regarding a 10-page log of attacks originating from the management station. To make matters worse, the clock on the "attacked" computer was off a couple of hours. The times recorded for the alleged attacks didn't fall in the block of time I had run *CiscoWorks*. It did include, however, blocks of times I knew the management station was offline. Before it was all sorted out, my overactive imagination had turned it into a malicious attack with a goal of casting blame on the management station when it was nothing more than a misunderstanding.*

It is best to deal with such potential problems in advance by clearly stating what you will be doing and why. If you can't justify it, then perhaps you should reconsider exactly why you are doing it. A number of sites automatically block networks or hosts they receive scans from. And within some organizations, unauthorized scanning may be grounds for dismissal. You should consider developing a formal policy clearly stating when and by whom scanning may and may not be done.

This leads to an important point: you really should have a thorough understanding of how scanning tools work before you use them. For example, some SNMP tools have you enter a list of the various SNMP passwords (community strings) you use on your network. In the automatic discovery mode, it will probe for SNMP devices by trying each of these passwords in turn on each machine on the network. This is intended to save the network manager from having to enter this information for each individual device. However, it is a simple matter for scanned machines to capture these passwords. Tools like *dsniff* are designed specifically for that purpose. I strongly recommend watching the behavior of whatever scanning tools you use with a tool like *tcpdump* or *ethereal* to see what it is actually doing.

Unfortunately, some of the developers of these tools can't seem to decide whether they are writing for responsible users or crackers. As previously noted, some tools include questionable features, such as support stealth scans or forged IP addresses. In general, I have described only those features for which I can see a legitimate use. However, sometimes there is no clear dividing line. For example, forged IP addresses can be useful in testing firewalls. When I have described such features, I assume that you will be able to distinguish between appropriate and inappropriate uses.

---

* This problem could have been lessened if both had been running NTP. NTP is discussed in Chapter 11.

Microsoft Windows

Traditionally, commercial tools for network management have typically been developed for Unix platforms rather than Windows. Those available under Windows tended not to scale well. In the last few years this has been changing rapidly, and many of the standard commercial tools are now available for Windows platforms.

A number of packages support IP scanning under Windows. These include freeware, shareware, and commercial packages. Generally, these products are less sophisticated than similar Unix tools. For example, stealth scanning is usually lacking under Windows. (Personally, I'm not sure this is something to complain about.)

Nonetheless, there are a number of very impressive noncommercial tools for Windows. In fact, considering the quality and functionality of some of these free packages, it is surprising that the commercial packages are so successful. But free software, particularly in network management, seems to have a way of becoming commercial software over time—once it has matured and developed a following.

Cyberkit

One particularly impressive tool is Luc Neijens' *cyberkit*. The package works well, has a good help system, and implements a wide range of functions in one package. In addition to IP scanning, the program includes, among others, *ping, traceroute, finger, whois, nslookup*, and NTP synchronization.

With *cyberkit*, you can scan a range of addresses within an address space or you can read a set of addresses from a file. Figure 6-3 shows an example of such a scan.

Here you can see how to specify a range of IP addresses. The button to the right of the Address Range field will assist you in specifying an address range or entering a filename. If you want to use a file, you need enter only the path and name of a text file containing a set of addresses, one address per line. Notice that you can use the same tab to resolve addresses or do port scans of each address. There are a number of other tools you might consider. *getif*, which makes heavy use of SNMP, is described in Chapter 7. You might also want to look at *Sam Spade*. (*Sam Spade* is particularly helpful when dealing with spamming and other email related problems.)

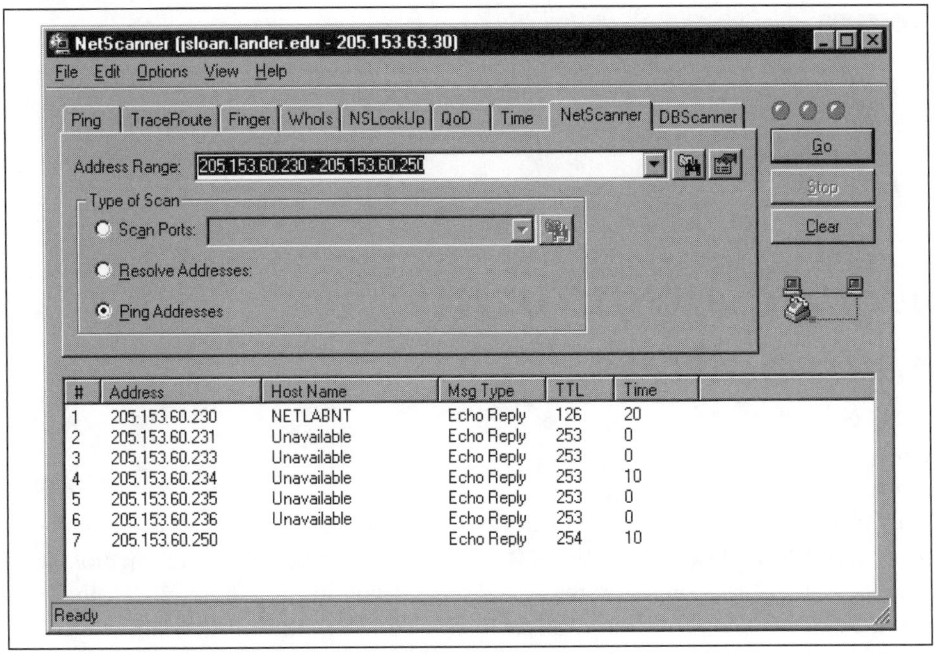

Figure 6-3. IP scan with cyberkit

Other Tools for Windows

The good news is that *Tcl, Tk, scotty,* and *tkined* are all available for Windows platforms. *Tcl* and *Tk* seem to be pretty stable ports. *tkined* is usually described as an early alpha port but seems to work fairly well. You'll want a three-button mouse. The interface is almost identical to the Unix version, and I have moved files between Windows and Unix platforms without problems. For example, you could create maps on one and move them to another for monitoring. Moreover, the *tnm* extensions have been used as the basis for additional tools available for Windows.

If you use Microsoft Exchange Server, a topology diagramming tool called *emap* can be downloaded from Microsoft. It will read an Exchange directory and automatically generate a *Visio* diagram for your site topology. Of course, you'll need *Visio* to view the results.

Finally, if you are using NetBIOS, you might want to look at the *nbtstat* utility. This command displays protocol statistics and current TCP connections using Net-BIOS over TCP/IP (NBT). You can use this command to poll remote NetBIOS name tables among other things. The basic syntax is returned if you call the program with no options.

7

Device Monitoring with SNMP

This chapter is about monitoring devices with *Simple Network Management Protocol (SNMP)*. It describes how SNMP can be used to retrieve information from remote systems, to monitor systems, and to alert you to problems. While other network management protocols exist, SNMP is currently the most commonly used. While SNMP has other uses, our primary focus will be on monitoring systems to ensure that they are functioning properly and to collect information when they aren't. The material in this chapter is expanded upon in Chapter 8.

This chapter begins with a brief review of SNMP. This description is somewhat informal but should serve to convey enough of the basic ideas to get you started if you are unfamiliar with SNMP. If you are already familiar with the basic concepts and vocabulary, you can safely skip over this section. Next I describe NET SNMP—a wonderful tool for learning about SNMP that can be used for many simple tasks. Network monitoring using *tkined* is next, followed by a few pointers to tools for Microsoft Windows.

Overview of SNMP

SNMP is a management protocol allowing a management program to communicate, configure, or control remote devices that have embedded SNMP agents. The basic idea behind SNMP is to have a program or *agent* running on the remote system that you can communicate with over the network. This *agent* then can monitor systems and collect information. Software on a management station sends messages to the remote agent requesting information or directing it to perform some specific task. While communication is usually initiated by the management station, under certain conditions the agent may send an unsolicited message or *trap* back to the management station.

SNMP provides a framework for network management. While SNMP is not the only management protocol or, arguably, even the best management protocol, SNMP is almost universal. It has a small footprint, can be implemented fairly quickly, is extensible, is well documented, and is an open standard. It resides at the application level of the TCP/IP protocol suite. On the other hand, SNMP, particularly Version 1, is not a secure protocol; it is poorly suited for real-time applications, and it can return an overwhelming amount of information.

SNMP is an evolving protocol with a confusing collection of abbreviations designating the various versions. Only the major versions are mentioned here. Understanding the major distinctions among versions can be important, because there are a few things you can't do with earlier versions and because of differences in security provided by the different versions. However, the original version, SNMPv1, is still widely used and will be the primary focus of this chapter. Generally, the later versions are backward compatible, so differences in versions shouldn't cause too many operational problems.

The second version has several competing variants. SNMPv2 Classic has been superseded by community-based SNMPv2 or SNMPv2c. Two more secure supersets of SNMPv2c are SNMPv2u and SNMPv2*. SNMPv2c is the most common of the second versions and is what is usually meant when you see a reference to SNMPv2. SNMPv2 has not been widely adopted, but its use is growing. SNMP-NG or SNMPv3 attempts to resolve the differences between SNMPv2u and SNMPv2*. It is too soon to predict how successful SNMPv3 will be, but it also appears to be growing in popularity.

Although there are usually legitimate reasons for the choice of terms, the nomenclature used to describe SNMP can be confusing. For example, parameters that are monitored are frequently referred to as *objects,* although *variables* might have been a better choice and is sometimes used. Basically, objects can be thought of as data structures.

Sometimes, the specialized nomenclature doesn't seem to be worth the effort. For example, SNMP uses *community strings* to control access. In order to gain access to a device, you must give the community string. If this sounds a lot like a password to you, you are not alone. The primary difference is the way community strings are used. The same community strings are often shared by a group or community of devices, something frowned upon with passwords. Their purpose is more to logically group devices than to provide security.

An SNMP *manager*, software on a central management platform, communicates with an SNMP *agent*, software located in the managed device, through SNMP *messages*. With SNMPv1 there are five types of messages. GET_REQUEST, GET_NEXT_REQUEST, and SET_REQUEST are sent by the manager to the agent to request an action. In the first two cases, the agent is asked to supply information, such as the value of an object. The SET_REQUEST message asks the agent to change the value of an object.

The remaining messages, GET_RESPONSE and TRAP, originate at the agent. The agent replies to the first three messages with the GET_RESPONSE message. In each case, the exchange is initiated by the manager. With the TRAP message, the action is initiated by the agent. Like a hardware interrupt on a computer, the TRAP message is the agent's way of getting the attention of the manager. Traps play an essential role in network management in that they alert you to problems needing attention. Knowing that a device is down is, of course, the first step to correcting the problem. And it always helps to be able to tell a disgruntled user that you are aware of the problem and are working on it. Traps are as close as SNMP gets to real-time processing. Unfortunately, for many network problems (such as a crashed system) traps may not be sent. Even when traps are sent, they could be discarded by a busy router. UDP is the transport protocol, so there is no error detection for lost packets. Figure 7-1 summarizes the direction messages take when traveling between the manager and agent.

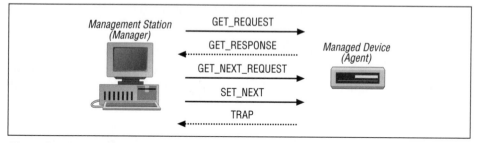

Figure 7-1. SNMP messages

For a management station to send a packet, it must know the IP address of the agent, the appropriate community string or password used by the agent, and the name of the identifier for the variable or object referenced. Unfortunately, SNMPv1 is very relaxed about community strings. These are sent in clear text and can easily be captured by a packet sniffer. One of the motivating factors for SNMPv2 was to provide greater security. Be warned, however, SNMPv2c uses plain text community strings.

Most systems, by default, use `public` for the read-only community string and `private` for the read/write community string. When you set up SNMP access on a device, you will be given the opportunity to change these. If you don't want your system to be reconfigurable by anyone on the Internet, you should change these. When communicating with devices, use read-only community strings whenever possible and read/write community strings only when necessary. Use filters to block all SNMP traffic into or out of your network. Most agents will also allow you to restrict which devices you can send and receive SNMP messages to and from. Do this! For simplicity and clarity, the examples in this chapter have been edited to use `public` and `private`. These are not the community strings I actually use.

Another advantage to SNMPv2 is that two additional messages have been added. GET_BULK_REQUEST will request multiple pieces of data with a single query, whereas GET_REQUEST generates a separate request for each piece of data. This can considerably improve performance. The other new message, INFORM_REQUEST, allows one manager to send unsolicited information to another.

Collectively, the objects are variables defined in the *Management Information Base* (MIB). Unfortunately, MIB is an overused term that means slightly different things in different contexts. There are some formal rules for dealing with MIBs—MIB formats are defined by *Structure of Management Information* (SMI), the syntax rules for MIB entries are described in *Abstract Syntax Notation One* (ASN.1), and how the syntax is encoded is given by *Basic Encoding Rules* (BER). Unless you are planning to delve into the implementation of SNMP or decode hex dumps, you can postpone learning SMI, ASN.1, and BER. And because of the complexity of these rules, I advise against looking at hex dumps. Fortunately, programs like *ethereal* do a good job of decoding these packets, so I won't discuss these rules in this book.

The actual objects that are manipulated are identified by a unique, authoritative *object identifier* (OID). Each OID is actually a sequence of integers separated by decimal points, sometimes called *dotted notation*. For example, the OID for a system's description is *1.3.6.1.2.1.1.1*. This OID arises from the standardized organization of all such objects, part of which is shown in Figure 7-2. The actual objects are the leaves of the tree. To eliminate any possibility of ambiguity among objects, they are named by giving their complete path from the root of the tree to the leaf.

As you can see from the figure, nodes are given both names and numbers. Thus, the OID can also be given by specifying the names of each node or *object descriptor*. For example, *iso.org.dod.internet.mgmt.mib-2.system.sysDescr* is the object descriptor that corresponds to the object identifier *1.3.6.1.2.1.1.1*. The more

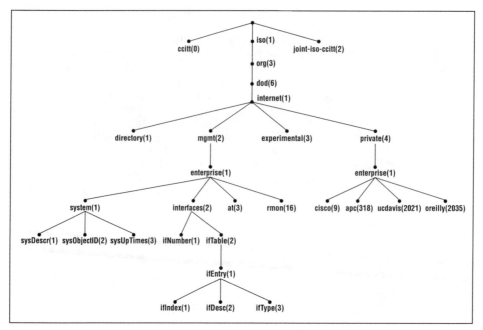

Figure 7-2. Partial OID structure

concise numerical names are used within the agents and within messages. The nonnumeric names are used at the management station for the convenience of users. Objects are coded directly into the agents and manipulated by object descriptors. While management stations can mechanically handle object descriptors, they must be explicitly given the mappings between object descriptors and object identifiers if you want to call objects by name. This is one role of the MIB files that ship with devices and load onto the management station. These files also tell the management station which identifiers are valid.

As you might guess from Figure 7-2, this is not a randomly created tree. Through the standardization process, a number of identifiers have been specified. In particular, the *mib-2* subtree has a number of subtrees or *groups* of interest. The *system* group, *1.3.6.1.2.1.1*, has nodes used to describe the system such as *sysDescr(1)*, *sysObjectID(2)*, *sysUpTime(3)*, and so on. These should be pretty self-explanatory. Although not shown in the figure, the *ip(4)* group has a number of objects such as *ipForwarding(1)*, which indicates whether IP packets will be forwarded, and *ipDefaultTTL(2)*, which gives the default TTL when it isn't specified by the transport layer. The *ip* group also has three tables including the *ipRouteTable(20)*. While this information can be gleaned from RFC 1213, which defines the MIB, several books that present this material in a more accessible form are listed in Appendix B. Fortunately, there are tools that can be used to investigate MIBs directly.

In addition to standard entries, companies may register private or *enterprise* MIBs. These have extensions specific to their equipment. Typically, these MIBs must be added to those on the management station if they are not already there. They are usually shipped with the device or can be downloaded over the Internet. Each company registers for a node under the *enterprises* node (*1.3.6.1.4.1*). These extensions are under their respective registered nodes.

If you are new to SNMP, this probably seems pretty abstract. Appendix B also lists and discusses a number of sources that describe the theory and architecture of SNMP in greater detail. But you should know enough at this point to get started. The best way to come to terms with SNMP and the structure of managed objects is by experimentation, and that requires tools. I will try to clarify some of these concepts as we examine SNMP management tools.

SNMP-Based Management Tools

There are several extremely powerful and useful noncommercial SNMP tools. Tools from the NET SNMP project, *scotty*, and *tkined* are described here.

NET SNMP (UCD SNMP)

The University of California at Davis implementation of SNMP (*UCD SNMP*) has its origin in a similar project at Carnegie Mellon University under Steve Waldbusser (*CMU SNMP*). In the mid-nineties, the CMU project languished. During this period, the UCD project was born. The UCD project has greatly expanded the original CMU work and is flourishing, thanks to the work of Wes Hardaker. The CMU project reemerged for a while with a somewhat different focus and has seen a lot of support in the Linux community. Both are excellent. While only UCD SNMP will be described here, the basics of each are so similar that you should have no problem using CMU SNMP once you are familiar with UCD SNMP. Very recently, UCD SNMP has been renamed NET SNMP to reflect some organizational changes.

NET SNMP is actually a set of tools, a SNMP library, and an extensible agent. The source code is available and runs on a number of systems. Binaries are also available for some systems, including Microsoft Windows. NET SNMP supports SNMPv1, SNMPv2c, and SNMPv3.

Admittedly, the NET SNMP toolset is not ideal for the routine management of a large network. But it is ideal for learning about SNMP, is not an unreasonable toolset for occasional tasks on smaller networks, and can be particularly useful in debugging SNMP problems, in part because it separates SNMP functions into individual utilities. The agent software is a logical choice for systems using Linux or FreeBSD and is extensible. Most, but not all, of the utilities will be described.

snmpget

In the last section, it was stated that there are three messages that can be sent by a management station: GET_REQUEST, GET_NEXT_REQUEST, and SET_REQUEST. NET SNMP provides utilities to send each of these messages—*snmpget*, *snmpgetnext*, and *snmpset*, respectively. In order to retrieve the value of an object, it is necessary to specify the name or IP address of the remote host, a community string for the host, and the OID of the object. For example:

```
bsd4# snmpget 172.16.1.5 public .1.3.6.1.2.1.1.1.0
system.sysDescr.0 = "APC Embedded PowerNet SNMP Agent (SW v2.2, HW vB2, Mod: AP9
605, Mfg 08/10/96, SN: WA9632270847, Agent Loader v1.0)"
```

There are a couple of points to make about the OID. First, notice the 0 at the end. This is an offset into the data. It is a common error to omit this. If you are looking at a table, you would use the actual offset into the table instead of a 0. For example, the description of the third interface in the interface table would have the OID ifDescr.3.

Second, the leading dot is important. NET SNMP will attempt to attach a prefix to any OIDs not beginning with a dot. By default, the prefix is 1.3.6.1.2.1, but you can change this by setting the environment variable *PREFIX*. In this example, we have specified the OID explicitly. Without the leading dot, *snmpget* would have added the prefix to what we had, giving an OID that was too long. On the other hand, you could just use 1.1.0 without the leading dot and you would get the same results. Initially, using the prefix can be confusing, but it can save a lot of typing once you are used to it.

Of course, you can also use names rather than numbers, provided the appropriate MIB is available. This is shown in the next two examples:

```
bsd4# snmpget 172.16.1.5 public iso.org.dod.internet.mgmt.mib-2.system.sysDescr.0
system.sysDescr.0 = "APC Embedded PowerNet SNMP Agent (SW v2.2, HW vB2, Mod: AP9
605, Mfg 08/10/96, SN: WA9632270847, Agent Loader v1.0)"
bsd4# snmpget 172.16.1.5 public system.sysDescr.0
system.sysDescr.0 = "APC Embedded PowerNet SNMP Agent (SW v2.2, HW vB2, Mod: AP9
605, Mfg 08/10/96, SN: WA9632270847, Agent Loader v1.0)"
```

In the first case, the full path was given, and in the second the prefix was used. (Don't forget the trailing 0.) Numbers and names can be mixed:

```
bsd4# snmpget 172.16.1.5 public .1.3.6.internet.2.1.system.1.0
system.sysDescr.0 = "APC Embedded PowerNet SNMP Agent (SW v2.2, HW vB2, Mod: AP9
605, Mfg 08/10/96, SN: WA9632270847, Agent Loader v1.0)"
```

(Frankly, I can't see much reason for doing this.)

Also, if the MIB is known, you can do a random-access lookup for unique node names:

```
bsd4# snmpget 172.16.1.5 public upsBasicIdentModel.0
enterprises.apc.products.hardware.ups.upsIdent.upsBasicIdent.upsBasicIdentModel.
0 = "APC Smart-UPS 700 "
```

In this example, only the final identifier in the OID, **upsBasicIdentMode.0**, is given, and the MIB is searched to construct the full OID. This can be particularly helpful if you want to query several objects with a single *snmpget*. You can also use multiple OIDs in the same *snmpget* command to retrieve the values of several objects.

Configuration and options

Before we look further at the NET SNMP commands, let's discuss configuration and options. For the most part, these tools share the same configuration files and options. (A few exceptions will be noted when appropriate.) The general configuration file is *snmp.conf* and is typically in the */usr/local/share/snmp*, */usr/local/lib/ snmp*, or *$HOME/.snmp* directory. This search path can be overridden by setting the *SNMPCONFPATH* environment variable. Further documentation can be found in the *snmp.conf* Unix manpage. This manpage also describes environment variables.

One particular concern in configuring the software is the proper installation of MIBs. As noted earlier, use of the name form of OIDs works only if the appropriate MIB[*] is loaded. Devices may have more than one MIB associated with them. In the examples just presented, we have been interacting with an SNMP-controlled uninterruptible power supply (UPS) manufactured by APC Corp. With this device, we can use the standard default MIB-II defined in RFC 1213. This standard MIB defines objects used by most devices. If you have correctly installed the software, this MIB should be readily available. There are two additional MIBs that may be installed for this particular device. The first is the IETF MIB, which defines a generic UPS. This is the UPS-MIB defined by RFC 1628. The third MIB, PowerNet-MIB, contains APC Corp.'s custom extensions. These last two MIBs came on a diskette with the SNMP adapter for this particular UPS.

To install these MIBs, the files are first copied to the appropriate directory, */usr/ local/share/snmp* in this case. (You may also want to rename them so that all your MIB files have consistent names.) Next, the environment variable *MIBS* is set so the MIBs will be loaded. This can be a colon-delimited list of individual MIB names, but setting *MIBS* to **ALL** is usually simpler. On a Windows computer, use the command:

```
C:\usr\bin>set MIBS=ALL
```

---

[*] When *a* MIB is loaded, it becomes part of *the* MIB. Don't say I didn't warn you.

On a Unix system using the Bash shell, you would use:

```
export MIBS=ALL
```

For the C-shell, use:

```
setenv MIBS ALL
```

Of course, this may vary depending on the shell you use.

Alternately, you can use the environment variable *MIBFILES* to specify filenames. There is also a command-line option with most of these utilities, *-m*, to load specific MIBs. If the MIBs are not installed correctly, you will not be able to use names from the MIB, but you can still access objects by their numerical OIDs.

The NET SNMP commands use the same basic syntax and command-line options. For example, the earlier discussion on OID usage applies to each command. This is described in the *variables* manpage. The manpages for the individual commands are a little sparse. This is because the descriptions of the options have been collected together on the *snmpcmd* manpage. Options applicable to a specific command can be displayed by using the *-h* option.

Let's return to *snmpget* and look at some of the available options. The *-O* options control how output is formatted. The default is to print the text form of the OID:

```
bsd4# snmpget 172.16.1.5 public .1.3.6.1.4.1.318.1.1.1.1.1.1.0
enterprises.apc.products.hardware.ups.upsIdent.upsBasicIdent.upsBasicIdentModel.
0 = "APC Smart-UPS 700 "
```

-On forces the OID to be printed numerically:

```
bsd4# snmpget -On 172.16.1.5 public .1.3.6.1.4.1.318.1.1.1.1.1.1.0
.1.3.6.1.4.1.318.1.1.1.1.1.1.0 = "APC Smart-UPS 700 "
```

Sometimes the value of an object will be a cryptic numerical code. By default, a description will be printed. For example:

```
bsd4# snmpget 172.16.1.5 public ip.ipForwarding.0
ip.ipForwarding.0 = not-forwarding(2)
```

Here, the actual value of the object is 2. This description can be suppressed with the *-Oe* option:

```
bsd4# snmpget -Oe 172.16.1.5 public ip.ipForwarding.0
ip.ipForwarding.0 = 2
```

This could be useful in eliminating any confusion about the actual stored value, particularly if you are going to use the value subsequently with a SET command.

Use the *-Os*, *-OS*, and *-Of* commands to control the amount of information included in the OID. The *-Os* option displays the final identifier only:

```
bsd4# snmpget -Os 172.16.1.5 public enterprises.318.1.1.1.1.1.1.0
upsBasicIdentModel.0 = "APC Smart-UPS 700 "
```

The *-OS* option is quite similar to *-Os* except that the name of the MIB is placed before the identifier:

```
sd4# snmpget -OS 172.16.1.5 public enterprises.318.1.1.1.1.1.1.0
PowerNet-MIB::upsBasicIdentModel.0 = "APC Smart-UPS 700 "
```

-Of forces the display of the full OID:

```
bsd4# snmpget -Of 172.16.1.5 public enterprises.318.1.1.1.1.1.1.0
.iso.org.dod.internet.private.enterprises.apc.products.hardware.ups.upsIdent.
upsBasicIdent.upsBasicIdentModel.0 = "APC Smart-UPS 700 "
```

This leaves no question about what you are looking at.

There are a number of additional options. The *-V* option will return the program's version. The version of SNMP used can be set with the *-v* option, either 1, 2c, or 3. The *-d* option can be used to dump all SNMP packets. You can set the number of retries and timeouts with the *-r* and *-t* options. These few options just scratch the surface. The syntax for many of these options has changed recently, so be sure to consult the *snmpcmd* manpage for more options and details for the version you use.

snmpgetnext, snmpwalk, and snmptable

Sometimes you will want to retrieve several related values that are stored together within the agent. Several commands facilitate this sort of retrieval. The *snmpgetnext* command is very similar to the *snmpget* command. But while *snmpget* returns the value of the specified OID, *snmpgetnext* returns the value of the next object in the MIB tree:

```
bsd4# snmpget -Os 172.16.1.5 public sysDescr.0
sysDescr.0 = APC Embedded PowerNet SNMP Agent (SW v2.2, HW vB2, Mod: AP9605, Mfg
  08/10/96, SN: WA9632270847, Agent Loader v1.0)
bsd4# snmpgetnext -Os 172.16.1.5 public sysDescr.0
sysObjectID.0 = OID: smartUPS700
bsd4# snmpgetnext -Os 172.16.1.5 public sysObjectID.0
sysUpTime.0 = Timeticks: (77951667) 9 days, 0:31:56.67
bsd4# snmpgetnext -Os 172.16.1.5 public sysUpTime.0
sysContact.0 = Sloan
```

As you can see from this example, *snmpgetnext* can be used to walk through a sequence of values. Incidentally, this is one of the few cases in which it is OK to omit the trailing 0. This command can be particularly helpful if you don't know the next identifier.

If you want all or most of the values of adjacent objects, the *snmpwalk* command can be used to retrieve a subtree. For example:

```
bsd4# snmpwalk 172.16.1.5 public system
system.sysDescr.0 = APC Embedded PowerNet SNMP Agent (SW v2.2, HW vB2, Mod:
AP9605, Mfg 08/10/96, SN: WA9632270847, Agent Loader v1.0)
system.sysObjectID.0 = OID: enterprises.apc.products.system.smartUPS.smartUPS700
system.sysUpTime.0 = Timeticks: (78093618) 9 days, 0:55:36.18
```

```
system.sysContact.0 = Sloan
system.sysName.0 = Equipment Rack APC
system.sysLocation.0 = Network Laboratory
system.sysServices.0 = 72
```

Be prepared to be overwhelmed if you don't select a small subtree. You probably wouldn't want to walk the *mib-2* or *enterprises* subtree:

```
bsd4# snmpwalk 172.16.2.1 public enterprises | wc
    3320    10962   121987
```

In this example, the *enterprises* subtree is 3320 lines long. Nonetheless, even with large subtrees this can be helpful to get a quick idea of what is out there. For example, you might pipe output from a subtree you aren't familiar with to *head* or *more* so you can skim it.

Some objects are stored as tables. It can be painful to work with these tables one item at a time, and once you have them, they can be almost unreadable. *snmptable* is designed to address this need. Here is an example of a small route table from a Cisco 3620 router:

```
bsd4# snmptable -Cb -Cw 80 172.16.2.1 public ipRouteTable
SNMP table: ip.ipRouteTable
```

Dest	IfIndex	Metric1	Metric2	Metric3	Metric4	NextHop	Type
0.0.0.0	0	0	-1	-1	-1	205.153.60.2	indirect
172.16.1.0	2	0	-1	-1	-1	172.16.1.1	direct
172.16.2.0	3	0	-1	-1	-1	172.16.2.1	direct
172.16.3.0	4	0	-1	-1	-1	172.16.3.1	direct
205.153.60.0	1	0	-1	-1	-1	205.153.60.250	direct
205.153.61.0	0	0	-1	-1	-1	205.153.60.1	indirect
205.153.62.0	0	0	-1	-1	-1	205.153.60.1	indirect
205.153.63.0	0	0	-1	-1	-1	205.153.60.1	indirect

```
SNMP table ip.ipRouteTable, part 2
```

Proto	Age	Mask	Metric5	Info
local	33	0.0.0.0	-1	.ccitt.nullOID
local	0	255.255.255.0	-1	.ccitt.nullOID
local	0	255.255.255.0	-1	.ccitt.nullOID
local	0	255.255.255.0	-1	.ccitt.nullOID
local	0	255.255.255.0	-1	.ccitt.nullOID
local	33	255.255.255.0	-1	.ccitt.nullOID
local	33	255.255.255.0	-1	.ccitt.nullOID
local	33	255.255.255.0	-1	.ccitt.nullOID

Even with *snmptable*, it can be a little tricky to get readable output. In this case, I have used two options to help. *-Cb* specifies a brief header. *-Cw 80* defines a maximum column width of 80 characters, resulting in a multipart table. You can also specify the column delimiter with the *-Cf* option, and you can suppress headers altogether with the *-CH* option. (There are also a *snmpbulkget* and a *snmpbulkwalk* if you are using SNMPv2.)

snmpset

The *snmpset* command is used to change the value of objects by sending SET_ REQUEST messages. The syntax of this command is a little different from previous commands since you must also specify a value and a type for the value. You will also need to use a community string that provides read/write access:

```
bsd4# snmpset 172.16.1.5 private sysContact.0 s "el Zorro"
system.sysContact.0 = el Zorro
```

In this example, the system contact was set using a quote-delimited string. Legitimate types include integers (*i*), strings (*s*), hex strings (*x*), decimal strings (*d*), null objects (*n*), object ID (*o*), time ticks (*t*), and IP addresses (*a*), among others.

People often think of SNMP as being appropriate only for collecting information, not as a general configuration tool, since SNMP only allows objects to be retrieved or set. However, many objects are configuration parameters that control the operation of the system. Moreover, agents can react to changes made to objects by running scripts, and so on. With the appropriate agent, virtually any action can be taken.[*] For example, you could change entries in an IP routing table, enable or disable a second interface on a device, or enable or disable IP forwarding. With an SNMP-controlled UPS, you could shut off power to a device. What you can do, and will want to do, will depend on both the device and the context. You will need to study the documentation for the device and the applicable MIBs to know what is possible on a case-by-case basis.

snmptranslate

In all the preceding examples, I have specified an OID. An obvious question is how did I know the OID? Available OIDs are determined by the design of the agent and are described by its MIB. There are several different approaches you can take to discover the contents of a MIB. The most direct approach is to read the MIB. This is not a difficult task if you don't insist on understanding every detail. You'll be primarily interested in the object definitions.

Here is an example of the definition of the system contact (*sysContact*) taken from MIB-II (RFC 1213):

```
sysContact OBJECT-TYPE
            SYNTAX  DisplayString (SIZE (0..255))
            ACCESS  read-write
            STATUS  mandatory
            DESCRIPTION
```

---

[*] In an extremely interesting interview of John Romkey by Carl Malamud on this topic, Romkey describes an SNMP-controlled toaster. The interview was originally on the Internet radio program *Geek of the Week* (May 29, 1993). At one time, it was available on audio tape from O'Reilly & Associates (ISBN 1-56592-997-7). Visit *http://town.hall.org/radio/Geek* and follow the link to Romkey.

```
                    "The textual identification of the contact person
                    for this managed node, together with information
                    on how to contact this person."
        ::= { system 4 }
```

The object name is in the first line. The next line says the object's type is a string and specifies its maximum size. The third line tells us that this can be read or written. In addition to *read-write*, an object may be designated *read-only* or *not-accessible*. While some objects may not be implemented in every agent, this object is required, as shown in the next line. Next comes the description. The last line tells where the object fits into the MIB tree. This is the fourth node in the *system* group.

With an enterprise MIB, there is usually some additional documentation that explains what is available. With standard MIBs like this one, numerous descriptions in books on SNMP describe each value in detail. These can be very helpful since they are usually accompanied by tables or diagrams that can be scanned quickly. See Appendix B for specific suggestions.

NET SNMP provides two tools that can be helpful. We have already discussed *snmpwalk*. Another useful tool is *snmptranslate*. This command is designed to present a MIB in a human-readable form. *snmptranslate* can be used in a number of different ways. First, it can be used to translate between the text and numeric form of an object. For example:

```
bsd4# snmptranslate system.sysContact.0
.1.3.6.1.2.1.1.4.0
```

We can get the numeric form with the *-On* option as shown in the next two examples:

```
bsd4# snmptranslate -On .1.3.6.1.2.1.1.4.0
system.sysContact.0

bsd4# snmptranslate -Ofn system.sysContact.0
.iso.org.dod.internet.mgmt.mib-2.system.sysContact.0
```

snmptranslate can be a little particular about prefixes. In the previous example, *sysContact.0* would not have been sufficient. You can get around this with the *-IR* option. (This is usually the default for most NET SNMP commands.)

```
bsd4# snmptranslate -IR sysContact.0
.1.3.6.1.2.1.1.4.0
```

You can also use regular expression matching. For example:

```
bsd4# snmptranslate -On -Ib 'sys.*ime'
system.sysUpTime
```

Notice the use of single quotes. (This option can return a few surprises at times as well.)

You get extended information by using the *-Td* option:

```
bsd4# snmptranslate -Td system.sysContact
.1.3.6.1.2.1.1.4
sysContact OBJECT-TYPE
  -- FROM        SNMPv2-MIB, RFC1213-MIB
  -- TEXTUAL CONVENTION DisplayString
  SYNTAX        OCTET STRING (0..255)
  DISPLAY-HINT  "255a"
  MAX-ACCESS    read-write
  STATUS        current
  DESCRIPTION   "The textual identification of the contact person for this
        managed node, together with information on how to contact
        this person.  If no contact information is known, the value
        is the zero-length string."
::= { iso(1) org(3) dod(6) internet(1) mgmt(2) mib-2(1) system(1) 4 }
```

This is basically what we saw in the MIB but in a little more detail. (By the way, the lines starting with -- are just comments embedded in the MIB.)

We can use *snmptranslate* to generate a tree representation for subtrees by using the *-Tp* option. For example:

```
bsd4# snmptranslate -Tp system
+--system(1)
   |
   +-- -R-- String    sysDescr(1)
   |         Textual Convention: DisplayString
   |         Size: 0..255
   +-- -R-- ObjID     sysObjectID(2)
   +-- -R-- TimeTicks sysUpTime(3)
   +-- -RW- String    sysContact(4)
   |         Textual Convention: DisplayString
   |         Size: 0..255
   +-- -RW- String    sysName(5)
   |         Textual Convention: DisplayString
   |         Size: 0..255
   +-- -RW- String    sysLocation(6)
   |         Textual Convention: DisplayString
   |         Size: 0..255
   +-- -R-- Integer   sysServices(7)
   +-- -R-- TimeTicks sysORLastChange(8)
   |         Textual Convention: TimeStamp
   |
   +--sysORTable(9)
      |
      +--sysOREntry(1)
         |
         +-- ---- Integer    sysORIndex(1)
         +-- -R-- ObjID      sysORID(2)
         +-- -R-- String     sysORDescr(3)
         |         Textual Convention: DisplayString
         |         Size: 0..255
         +-- -R-- TimeTicks sysORUpTime(4)
                   Textual Convention: TimeStamp
```

Don't forget the final argument or you'll get the entire MIB. There are also options to print all objects in labeled form (*-Tl*), numeric form (*-To*), or symbolic form (*-Tt*), but frankly, I've never found much use for these. These options simply give too much data. One last word of warning: if you have trouble using *snmptranslate*, the first thing to check is whether your MIBs are correctly loaded.

snmpnetstat

snmpnetstat is an SNMP analog to *netstat*. Using SNMP, it will provide *netstat*-like information from remote systems. Many of the major options are the same as with *netstat*. A few examples will show how this tool is used.

The *-an* option will show the sockets in open mode:

```
bsd4# snmpnetstat 172.16.2.234 public -an
Active Internet (tcp) Connections (including servers)
Proto Local Address              Foreign Address            (state)
tcp    *.ftp                     *.*                        LISTEN
tcp    *.telnet                  *.*                        LISTEN
tcp    *.smtp                    *.*                        LISTEN
tcp    *.http                    *.*                        LISTEN
tcp    *.sunrpc                  *.*                        LISTEN
tcp    *.printer                 *.*                        LISTEN
tcp    *.659                     *.*                        LISTEN
tcp    *.680                     *.*                        LISTEN
tcp    *.685                     *.*                        LISTEN
tcp    *.690                     *.*                        LISTEN
tcp    *.1024                    *.*                        LISTEN
tcp    172.16.2.234.telnet       sloan.1135                 ESTABLISHED
Active Internet (udp) Connections
Proto Local Address
udp    *.sunrpc
udp    *.snmp
udp    *.who
udp    *.657
udp    *.668
udp    *.678
udp    *.683
udp    *.688
udp    *.1024
udp    *.nfsd
```

Notice that with *snmpnetstat*, the options are listed at the end of the command.

The *-r* option gives the route table. Here is a route table from a Cisco 3620 router:

```
bsd4# snmpnetstat 172.16.2.1 public -rn
Routing tables
Destination            Gateway            Flags    Interface
default                205.153.60.2       UG       if0
172.16.1/24            172.16.1.1         U        Ethernet0/1
172.16.2/24            172.16.2.1         U        Ethernet0/2
172.16.3/24            172.16.3.1         U        Ethernet0/3
```

```
205.153.60            205.153.60.250   U      Ethernet0/0
205.153.61            205.153.60.1     UG     if0
205.153.62            205.153.60.1     UG     if0
205.153.63            205.153.60.1     UG     if0
```

In each of these examples, the *-n* option is used to suppress name resolution.

Here are the packet counts for the interfaces from the same router:

```
bsd4# snmpnetstat 172.16.2.1 public -i
Name         Mtu Network       Address        Ipkts Ierrs  Opkts Oerrs Queue
Ethernet0/1  1500 172.16.1/24  172.16.1.1     219805     0 103373     0     0
Ethernet0/0  1500 205.153.60   205.153.60.250 406485     0 194035     0     0
Ethernet0/2  1500 172.16.2/24  172.16.2.1     177489     1 231011     0     0
Ethernet0/3  1500 172.16.3/24  172.16.3.1      18175     0  97954     0     0
Null0        1500                                  0     0      0     0     0
```

As with *netstat*, the *-i* option is used.

As a final example, the *-s* option is used with the *-P* option to get general statistics with output restricted to a single protocol, in this case IP:

```
bsd4# snmpnetstat 172.16.2.1 public -s -P ip
ip:
        533220 total datagrams received
        0 datagrams with header errors
        0 datagrams with an invalid destination address
        231583 datagrams forwarded
        0 datagrams with unknown protocol
        0 datagrams discarded
        301288 datagrams delivered
        9924 output datagram requests
        67 output datagrams discarded
        4 datagrams with no route
        0 fragments received
        0 datagrams reassembled
        0 reassembly failures
        0 datagrams fragmented
        0 fragmentation failures
        0 fragments created
```

This should all seem very familiar to *netstat* users.

snmpstatus

The *snmpstatus* command is a quick way to get a few pieces of basic information from an agent:

```
bsd4# snmpstatus 172.16.2.1 public
[172.16.2.1]=>[Cisco Internetwork Operating System Software
IOS (tm) 3600 Software (C3620-IO3-M), Version 12.0(7)T,  RELEASE SOFTWARE (fc2)
Copyright (c) 1986-1999 by Cisco Systems, Inc.
Compiled Wed 08-Dec-99 10:08 by phanguye] Up: 11 days, 1:31:43.66
Interfaces: 5, Recv/Trans packets: 1113346/629074 | IP: 533415/9933
```

It gets the IP address, text description, time since the system was booted, total received and transmitted packets, and total received and transmitted IP packets.

Agents and traps

In addition to management software, NET SNMP also includes the agent *snmpd*. As with any agent, *snmpd* responds to SNMP messages, providing basic management for the host on which it is run. *snmpd* uses the *snmpd.conf* configuration file (not to be confused with *snmp.conf*, the configuration file for the utilities). *snmpd* functionality will depend, in part, on what is enabled by its configuration file. The distribution comes with the MIB *UCD-SNMP-MIB.txt* and the file *EXAMPLE.conf*, an example configuration file that is fairly well documented. The manpage for *snmpd. conf* provides additional information.

At a minimum, you'll want to edit the security entries. The *com2sec* entry is used to set the community names for a host or network. The *group* entry defines an access class. For example, consider these three lines from a configuration file:

```
com2sec    local    172.16.2.236    private
...
group    MyRWGroup v1    local
...
access  MyRWGroup ""    any    noauth   prefix   all   all   none
```

The first line sets the community string to `private` for the single host *172.16.2. 236*. The last two establish that this host is using SNMPv1 and has both read and write privileges.

Even without further editing of the configuration file, the agent provides a number of useful pieces of information. These include things like information on processes (*prTable*), memory usage (*memory*), processor load (*laTable*), and disk usage (*dskTable*). For example, here is the disk information from a Linux system:

```
bsd4# snmpwalk 172.16.2.234 public dskTable
enterprises.ucdavis.dskTable.dskEntry.dskIndex.1 = 1
enterprises.ucdavis.dskTable.dskEntry.dskPath.1 = /
enterprises.ucdavis.dskTable.dskEntry.dskDevice.1 = /dev/sda1
enterprises.ucdavis.dskTable.dskEntry.dskMinimum.1 = 10000
enterprises.ucdavis.dskTable.dskEntry.dskMinPercent.1 = -1
enterprises.ucdavis.dskTable.dskEntry.dskTotal.1 = 202182
enterprises.ucdavis.dskTable.dskEntry.dskAvail.1 = 133245
enterprises.ucdavis.dskTable.dskEntry.dskUsed.1 = 58497
enterprises.ucdavis.dskTable.dskEntry.dskPercent.1 = 31
enterprises.ucdavis.dskTable.dskEntry.dskErrorFlag.1 = 0
enterprises.ucdavis.dskTable.dskEntry.dskErrorMsg.1 =
```

Most of the entries are just what you would guess. The *dskPath* entry says we are looking at the root partition. The *dskDevice* gives the path to the partition being examined, */dev/sda1*. The next two items are parameters for triggering error messages. The *dskTotal* entry is the size of the partition in kilobytes. This partition is

202MB. The next two entries, *dskAvail* and *dskUsed*, give the amount of available and used space; 31% of the disk is in use. Here is the output from *df* for the same system:

```
lnx1# df -k /
Filesystem          1k-blocks      Used Available Use% Mounted on
/dev/sda1              202182     58497    133245  31% /
```

The last two entries are objects used to signal errors. By editing the configuration file, you can get information on other partitions. Brief descriptions for each object are included within the MIB, *UCD-SNMP-MIB.txt*. Directions for changing the configuration file are given in the example file.

It is also possible to extend the agent. This will allow you to run external programs or scripts. The output, in its simplest form, is limited to a single line and an exit code that can be retrieved as an MIB object. For example, the following line could be added to the configuration file:

```
exec datetest /bin/date -j -u
```

Here, *exec* is a keyword, *datetest* is a label, */bin/date* is the command, and the rest of the line is treated as a set of arguments and parameters to the command. The *-j* option prevents a query to set the date, and *-u* specifies Coordinated Universal time. The command is run by the agent each time you try to access the object. For example, *snmpwalk* could be used to retrieve the following information:

```
bsd4# snmpwalk 172.16.2.236 private extTable
enterprises.ucdavis.extTable.extEntry.extIndex.1 = 1
enterprises.ucdavis.extTable.extEntry.extNames.1 = datetest
enterprises.ucdavis.extTable.extEntry.extCommand.1 = /bin/date -j -u
enterprises.ucdavis.extTable.extEntry.extResult.1 = 0
enterprises.ucdavis.extTable.extEntry.extOutput.1 = Mon Jun 26 14:10:50 GMT 2000
enterprises.ucdavis.extTable.extEntry.extErrFix.1 = 0
enterprises.ucdavis.extTable.extEntry.extErrFixCmd.1 =
```

You should be able to recognize the label, command with options, exit code, and output in this table. The command will be run each time you retrieve a value from this table.

Running *snmpd* on a system is straightforward. As root, type **snmpd**, and it will immediately fork and return the prompt. There are several options you can use. If you don't want it to fork, you can use the *-f* option. This is useful with options that return additional runtime information. I've found that it is also useful when testing the configuration file. I'll start *snmpd* in one window and test the configuration in another. When I'm ready to change configurations, I jump back to the original window and kill and restart the process. Of course, you can always use *ps* to look up the process and then send the process a *-HUP* signal. Or you could use *snmpset* to set the OID *versionUpdateConfig* to 1 to force a reload of the configuration file:

```
bsd4# snmpset 172.16.2.236 private versionUpdateConfig.0 i 1
enterprises.ucdavis.version.versionUpdateConfig.0 = 1
```

Take your pick, but you must reload the file before changes will take effect.

It is possible to use *snmpd* options in a couple of ways to trace packet exchanges. You can use the options *-f*, *-L*, and *-d*, respectively, to prevent forking, to redirect messages to standard output, and to dump packets. Here is an example:

```
bsd4# snmpd -f -L -d
UCD-SNMP version 4.1.2

Received 49 bytes from 205.153.63.30:1055
0000: 30 82 00 2D  02 01 00 04  06 70 75 62  6C 69 63 A0    0..-.....public.
0016: 82 00 1E 02  02 0B 78 02  01 00 02 01  00 30 82 00    ......x......0..
0032: 10 30 82 00  0C 06 08 2B  06 01 02 01  01 06 00 05    .0.....+........
0048: 00                                                    .

Received SNMP packet(s) from 205.153.63.30
  GET message
    -- system.sysLocation.0
    >> system.sysLocation.0 = 303 Laura Lander Hall

Sending 70 bytes to 205.153.63.30:1055
0000: 30 82 00 42  02 01 00 04  06 70 75 62  6C 69 63 A2    0..B.....public.
0016: 82 00 33 02  02 0B 78 02  01 00 02 01  00 30 82 00    ..3...x......0..
0032: 25 30 82 00  21 06 08 2B  06 01 02 01  01 06 00 04    %0..!..+........
0048: 15 33 30 33  20 4C 61 75  72 61 20 4C  61 6E 64 65    .303 Laura Lande
0064: 72 20 48 61  6C 6C                                    r Hall
```

This is probably more information than you want. As previously noted, you probably don't want to delve into the hex. You can replace the *-d* option with the *-V* option to get a verbose display but without the dump:

```
bsd4# snmpd -f -L -V
UCD-SNMP version 4.1.2
Received SNMP packet(s) from 205.153.63.30
  GET message
    -- system.sysLocation.0
    >> system.sysLocation.0 = 303 Laura Lander Hall
```

This should give you an adequate idea of what is going on for most troubleshooting needs. See the manpage for other options.

NET SNMP also includes two applications for dealing with traps. *snmptrapd* starts a daemon to receive and respond to traps. It uses the configuration file *snmptrapd.conf*. The *snmptrap* is an application used to generate traps. While these can be useful in troubleshooting, their use is arcane to say the least. You will need to edit the appropriate MIB files before using these. There are simpler ways to test traps.

scotty

scotty was introduced in Chapter 6. Now that we've talked a little about SNMP, here are a few more examples of using *scotty*. These are based on examples given in one of the *README* files that comes with *scotty*. Since you will have to install *scotty* to get *tkined*, it is helpful to know a few *scotty* commands to test your setup. These *scotty* commands also provide a quick-and-dirty way of getting a few pieces of information.

To use SNMP with *scotty*, you must first establish an SNMP session:

```
lnx1# scotty
% set s [snmp session -address 172.16.1.5 -community private]
snmp0
```

Once you have a session, you can retrieve a single object, multiple objects, the successor of an object, or subtrees. Here are some examples:

```
% $s get sysDescr.0
{1.3.6.1.2.1.1.1.0 {OCTET STRING} {APC Embedded PowerNet SNMP Agent (SW v2.2, HW
  vB2, Mod: AP9605, Mfg 08/10/96, SN: WA9632270847, Agent Loader v1.0)}}
% $s get "sysDescr.0 sysContact.0"
{1.3.6.1.2.1.1.1.0 {OCTET STRING} {APC Embedded PowerNet SNMP Agent (SW v2.2, HW
  vB2, Mod: AP9605, Mfg 08/10/96, SN: WA9632270847, Agent Loader v1.0)}} {1.3.6.1
  .2.1.1.4.0 {OCTET STRING} {Sloan <jsloan@lander.edu>}}
% $s getnext sysUpTime.0
{1.3.6.1.2.1.1.4.0 {OCTET STRING} {Sloan <jsloan@lander.edu>}}
% $s getnext [mib successor system]
{1.3.6.1.2.1.1.1.0 {OCTET STRING} {APC Embedded PowerNet SNMP Agent (SW v2.2, HW
  vB2, Mod: AP9605, Mfg 08/10/96, SN: WA9632270847, Agent Loader v1.0)}} {1.3.6.1
  .2.1.1.2.0 {OBJECT IDENTIFIER} PowerNet-MIB!smartUPS700} {1.3.6.1.2.1.1.3.0 Time
  Ticks {4d 22:27:07.42}} {1.3.6.1.2.1.1.4.0 {OCTET STRING} {Joe Sloan}} {1.3.6.1.
  2.1.1.5.0 {OCTET STRING} {APC UPS}} {1.3.6.1.2.1.1.6.0 {OCTET STRING} {214 Laura
  Lander Hall, Equipment Rack}} {1.3.6.1.2.1.1.7.0 INTEGER 72} {1.3.6.1.2.1.2.1.0
  INTEGER 1} {1.3.6.1.2.1.2.1.0 INTEGER 1}
```

Once you know the syntax, it is straightforward to change the value of objects as can be seen here:

```
% $s set [list [list sysContact.0 "OCTET STRING" "Joe Sloan"] ]
{1.3.6.1.2.1.1.4.0 {OCTET STRING} {Joe Sloan}}
% $s get sysContact.0
{1.3.6.1.2.1.1.4.0 {OCTET STRING} {Joe Sloan}}
```

Notice that after the object is set, I have retrieved it to verify the operation. I strongly recommend doing this each time you change something.

If you aren't familiar with *Tcl*, then defining a trap handler will seem arcane. Here is an example:

```
% % proc traphandler {ip list} {
       set msg "SNMP trap from $ip:"
       foreach vb $list {
           append msg " [mib name [lindex $vb 0]]=\"[lindex $vb 2]\""
       }
       puts stderr $msg
   }
% set t [snmp session -port 162]
snmp1
% $t bind "" trap {traphandler %A "%V"}
```

Once the trap handler is defined, we can test it by interrupting the power to the UPS by unplugging the UPS.* This test generated the following trap messages:

```
% SNMP trap from 172.16.1.5: sysUpTime.0="2d 21:15:50.44" snmpTrapOID.0="PowerNe
t-MIB!upsOnBattery" smartUPS700="57:41:52:4E:49:4E:47:3A:20:54:68:65:20:55:50:53
:20:6F:6E:20:73:65:72:69:61:6C:20:70:6F:72:74:20:31:20:69:73:20:6F:6E:20:62:61:7
4:74:65:72:79:20:62:61:63:6B:75:70:20:70:6F:77:65:72:2E" snmpTrapEnterprise.0="a
pc"
SNMP trap from 172.16.1.5: sysUpTime.0="2d 21:15:50.55" snmpTrapOID.0="1.3.6.1.2
.1.33.2.0.1" upsEstimatedMinutesRemaining="31" upsSecondsOnBattery="0" upsConfig
LowBattTime="2" snmpTrapEnterprise.0="upsTraps"
SNMP trap from 172.16.1.5: sysUpTime.0="2d 21:15:50.66" snmpTrapOID.0="1.3.6.1.2
.1.33.2.0.3" upsAlarmId="12" upsAlarmDescr="UPS-MIB!upsAlarmInputBad" snmpTrapEn
terprise.0="upsTraps"
SNMP trap from 172.16.1.5: sysUpTime.0="2d 21:15:55.27" snmpTrapOID.0="1.3.6.1.2
.1.33.2.0.4" upsAlarmId="11" upsAlarmDescr="UPS-MIB!upsAlarmOnBattery" snmpTrapE
nterprise.0="upsTraps"
SNMP trap from 172.16.1.5: sysUpTime.0="2d 21:15:55.38" snmpTrapOID.0="1.3.6.1.2
.1.33.2.0.4" upsAlarmId="12" upsAlarmDescr="UPS-MIB!upsAlarmInputBad" snmpTrapEn
terprise.0="upsTraps"
SNMP trap from 172.16.1.5: sysUpTime.0="2d 21:15:55.50" snmpTrapOID.0="PowerNet-
MIB!powerRestored" smartUPS700="49:4E:46:4F:52:4D:41:54:49:4F:4E:3A:20:4E:6F:72:
6D:61:6C:20:70:6F:77:65:72:20:68:61:73:20:62:65:65:6E:20:72:65:73:74:6F:72:65:64
:20:74:6F:20:74:68:65:20:55:50:53:20:6F:6E:20:73:65:72:69:61:6C:20:70:6F:72:74:2
0:31:2E" snmpTrapEnterprise.0="apc"
```

From this example, you can see a sequence of traps as the power is lost and restored. Most messages should be self-explanatory, and all are explained in the UPS documentation.

Generating traps is much simpler. In this example, a session is started and a trap is sent to that session:

```
% set u [snmp session -port 162 -address 172.16.2.234]
snmp2
% $u trap coldStart ""
```

---

* This is OK with this particular UPS. In fact, it's suggested in the documentation. However, you don't want to do this with just any UPS. While UPSs are designed to deal with power interruptions, some are not necessarily designed to deal with the ground being removed, as happens when you unplug a UPS.

You can terminate a session without exiting *scotty* with the *destroy* command:

```
% $u destroy
```

If you are thinking about writing *Tcl* scripts, this should give you an idea of the power of the *tnm* extensions supplied by *scotty*.

If you aren't familiar with the syntax of *Tcl*, these examples will seem fairly opaque but should give you an idea of what is possible. You could try these on your system as presented here, but if you are really interested is doing this sort of thing, you'll probably want to learn some *Tcl* first. Several sources of information are given in Appendix B.

tkined

tkined was introduced in the last chapter. Here we will look at how it can be used to retrieve information and do basic monitoring. *tkined* is a versatile tool, and only some of the more basic features will be described here. This should be enough to get you started and help you decide if *tkined* is the right tool for your needs. A small test network is shown in Figure 7-3. (We will be looking at this network, along with minor variations, in the following examples.)

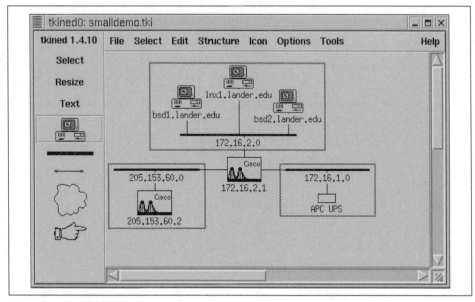

Figure 7-3. Demo network

ICMP monitoring

ICMP monitoring periodically sends an ECHO_REQUEST packet to a remote device to see if the connection is viable. (We've seen examples of this before.)

SNMP monitoring is superior when available since it can be used to retrieve additional information. But if the device doesn't support SNMP, or if you don't have SNMP access, ICMP monitoring may be your only option. Your ISP, for example, probably won't give you SNMP access to their routers even though you depend on them.

To use ICMP monitoring with *tkined*, use Tools → IP-Monitor. This will add an IP-Monitor menu to the menu bar. Next, select a device on your map by clicking on the Select tool and then the device's icon. Now, use IP-Monitor → Check Reachability. (See Figure 7-4.) Since the idea of monitoring is to alert you to problems, if your device is reachable, you shouldn't see any changes. If the device is nearby and it won't create any problems, you can test your setup by disconnecting the device from the network. The device's icon should turn red and start flashing. A message will also be displayed on the map under the icon.

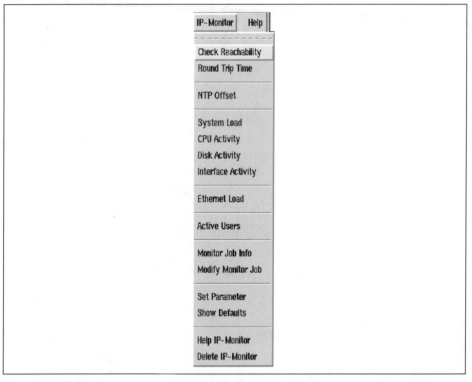

Figure 7-4. IP-Monitor menu

If the device is in a collapsed group, the icon for the group will flash. Thus, you don't have to have an icon displayed for every device you are monitoring. You could start a monitor on each device of interest, put related devices into a group, and collapse the group. By creating a number of groups, all collapsed, you can monitor a large number of machines from a small, uncluttered map and still be able to drill down on a problem.

When you reconnect the device, the icon should turn black and then stop flashing. It may take a minute to see these changes. By default, the system polls devices every 60 seconds. You can check which devices are being monitored by selecting IP-Monitor → Monitor Job Info. A pop-up box will display a list of the monitors that are running.

If you want to change parameters, select IP-Monitor → Modify Monitor Job. This will bring up a box displaying a list of running jobs. Select the job of interest by clicking on it, then click on the Modify button. The box listing jobs will be replaced by a box giving job parameters, as shown in Figure 7-5.

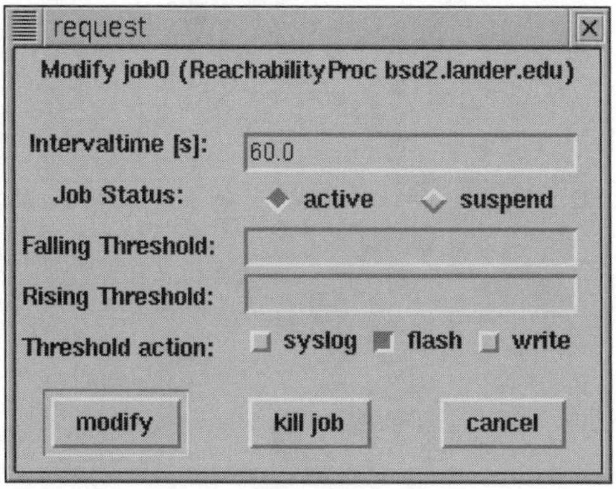

Figure 7-5. Monitor job parameters

You can reset the polling rate by changing the Intervaltime field. The next two radio buttons allow you to suspend or restart a suspended job. The two Threshold fields allow you to establish limits on response times. If your system normally responds within, say, 100ms, you could set Rising Threshold to 200ms. If the quality of the connection degrades so that response time rises above 200ms, the system will alert you. The Threshold Action buttons allow you to say how you want to be notified when thresholds are crossed. Finally, you can commit to the changes, terminate the job, or cancel any changes.

If you are really interested in tracking how response time is changing, you can select IP-Monitor → Round Trip Time. A small box will appear on the map, partially obscuring the icon. (You can drag it to a more convenient location.) This is called a *stripchart* and will plot round-trip times against time. You can change parameters using IP-Monitor → Modify Monitor Job. You can change labels and scale by right-clicking on the chart.

Figure 7-6 shows two stripcharts. The chart in the upper right really isn't very revealing since the device is on the local network and everything is working OK. The latest round-trip time is displayed below the stripchart and is updated dynamically. A device does not have to be integrated into the map. The site *www.infoave. net*, an ISP at the bottom of the figure, has been added to the site and is being monitored. This icon is partially obscured by a slider used to adjust the scale. Other ICMP monitoring options, shown in Figure 7-4, are available.

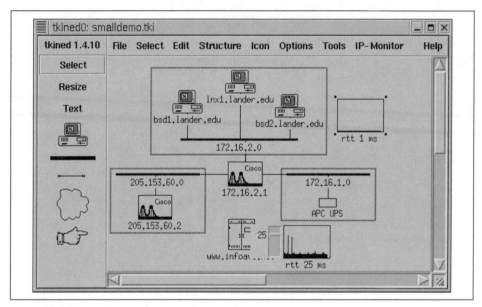

Figure 7-6. Map with stripcharts

SNMP traps

Before you begin using *tkined* for SNMP-based monitoring, you want to make sure the appropriate MIBs are installed. These will usually be located in a common *mibs* directory under the *tnm* library directory, e.g., */usr/lib/tnm2.1.10/mibs* or */usr/ local/lib/tnm2.1.10/mibs*. You will want to copy any enterprise MIB you plan to use to that directory. Next, you should verify that the files are compatible. Try loading them into *scotty* with the *mib load* command, e.g., *mib load toaster.mib*. If the file loads without comment, you are probably OK. Finally, you will want to edit the *init.tcl* file to automatically load the MIBs. Ideally, you will have a site-specific version of the file for changes, but you can edit the standard default file. You will want to add a line that looks something like `lappend tnm(mibs) toaster.mib`. You are now ready to start *tkined* and do SNMP-based monitoring.

The first step is to go to Tools → SNMP-Monitor. This will add the SNMP-Monitor menu to the menu bar. This menu is shown in Figure 7-7. To receive traps, select

SNMP-Monitor → Trap Sink. A pop-up box will give you the option of listening to or ignoring traps. Select the Listen button and click on Accept to start receiving traps. At this point, the station is now configured to receive traps.

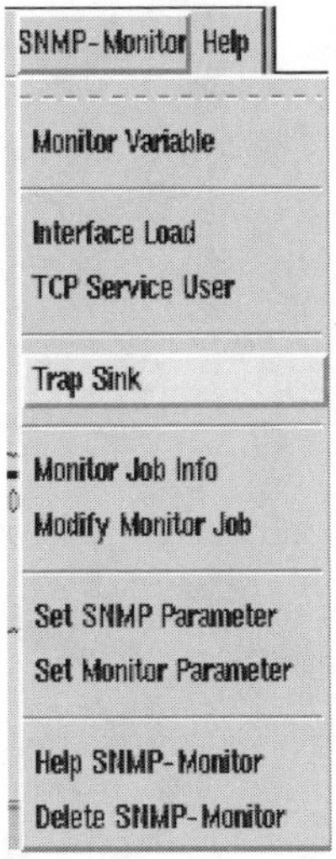

Figure 7-7. SNMP-Monitor menu

To test that this is really working, we need to generate some traps for the system to receive. If you are a *scotty* user, you might use the code presented in the last section. For this example, a UPS that was being monitored was unplugged. Regardless of how the trap is generated, *tkined* responds in the same way. The device icon blinks, a message is written on the map, and a new window, shown in Figure 7-8, is displayed with the trap messages generated by the UPS. Note that the duration of this problem was under 5 seconds. It is likely this event would have been missed with polling.

Examining MIBs

Tools → SNMP Tree provides one way of examining MIBs. Or, if you prefer, you can use Tools → SNMP-Browser. The SNMP Tree command displays a graphical representation of a subtree of the MIB. This is shown in Figure 7-9.

Menu items allow you to focus in on a particular subtree. For example, the MIB-2 menu shows the various subtrees under the MIB-2 node. The Enterprises menu shows various enterprise MIBs that have been loaded. You simply select the MIB of interest from the menu, and it will be displayed in the window. You can click on an item on the tree and a pop-up window will give you the option of displaying a description of the item, retrieving its value, changing its value, or displaying just the

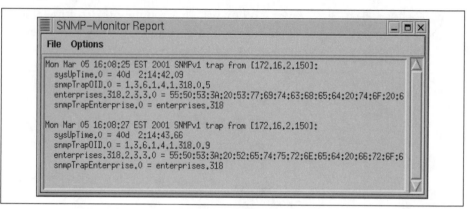

Figure 7-8. SNMP monitor report

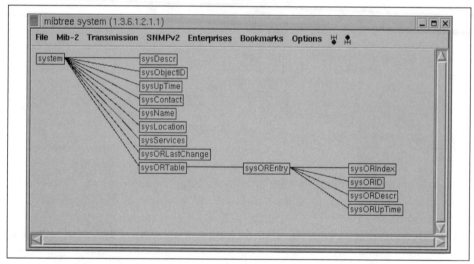

Figure 7-9. SNMP tree

subtree of the node in question. Of course, you will need to select a system before you can retrieve system-specific information.

The SNMP-Browser option provides much the same functionality but displays information in a different format. If you select SNMP-Browser → MIB Browser, you will be given a text box listing the nodes below the *internet* node (*.1.3.6.1*) of the MIB tree. If you click on any of these nodes, the text box will be replaced with one of the nodes under the selected node. In this manner, you can move down the MIB tree. After the first box, you will also be given the option to move up the tree or, if appropriate, to the previous or next node in the subtree. If you reach a leaf, you will be given a description of the object, as shown in Figure 7-10. If the object can be changed, you will be given that choice as well.

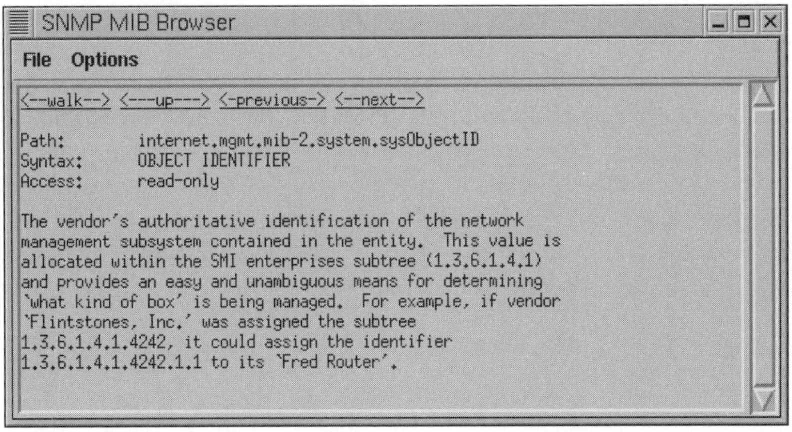

Figure 7-10. MIB Browser

You are also given the option to walk a subtree. This option will attempt to retrieve all the object values for leaves under the current node. This can be quite lengthy depending on where you are in the tree. Figure 7-11 shows the last few entries under *ip*. Most of the values have scrolled off the window.

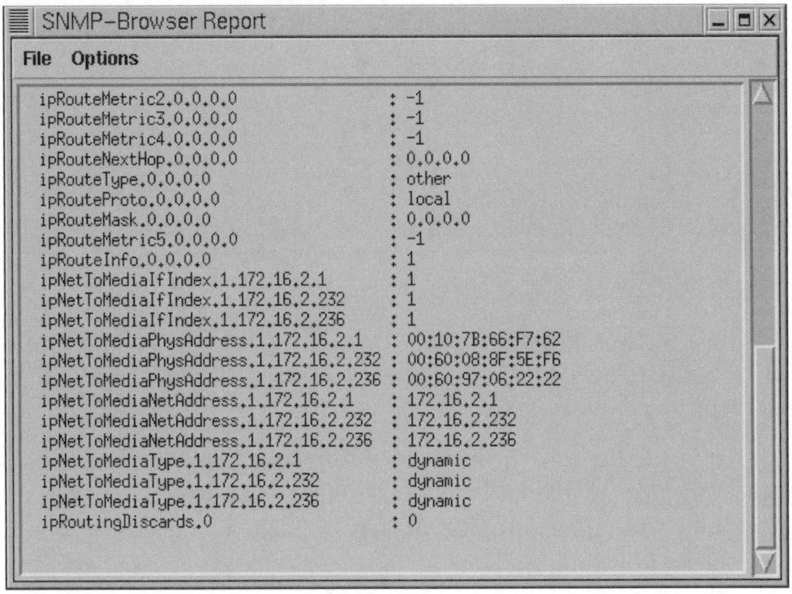

Figure 7-11. Walk for IP

SNMP Tree provides a nice visual display, but it can be a little easier to move around with the MIB Browser. Take your choice.

Monitoring SNMP objects

In much the same way you monitor devices, you can monitor SNMP objects. First, you will need to identify the object you want to monitor. This can be done using the techniques just described. With MIB Browser you can select monitoring at a leaf. Alternately, you can select SNMP-Monitor → Monitor Variable. This is a little easier if you already know the name of the object you want to monitor. A pop-up box will request the name of the object to monitor. Type in the name of the object and click on Start. (Don't forget to select a system first.) A stripchart will be created on your map displaying the values for the monitored object.

Other commands

Tools → SNMP Trouble installs the SNMP-Trouble menu. The name is somewhat misleading. Generally, the SNMP-Trouble menu provides quick ways to collect common, useful information. First, it can be used to locate SNMP-aware devices on your network. By selecting multiple devices on the map and then choosing SNMP-Trouble → SNMP Devices, *tkined* will poll each of the devices. The output for the test network is shown in Figure 7-12.

```
┌─────────────────────────────────────────────────────────────────┐
│ ▓  SNMP−Trouble Report                                 _ □ ✕    │
├─────────────────────────────────────────────────────────────────┤
│  File   Options                                                  │
├─────────────────────────────────────────────────────────────────┤
│ SNMP devices:                                              △    │
│ APC UPS                      [<172.16.2.150>]                    │
│ cis1.lander.edu              [<172.16.2.1>]                      │
│ bsd4.lander.edu              [<172.16.2.236>]                    │
│ lnx1.lander.edu              [172.16.2.234] noResponse           │
│ bsd1.lander.edu              [172.16.2.231] noResponse           │
│ 205.153.60.2                 [205.153.60.2] noResponse           │
│                                                            ▽    │
└─────────────────────────────────────────────────────────────────┘
```

Figure 7-12. SNMP devices

Please note that noResponse does not necessarily mean that the device is down or that it doesn't support SNMP. For example, it may simply mean that you are not using the correct community string.

The SNMP-Trouble menu also provides menu options that will return some of the more commonly needed pieces of information such as system information, ARP tables, IP routing tables, interface information, or TCP connections. A few of these reports are shown in Figure 7-13.

Caveats

tkined is a fine program, but it does have a couple of problems. As noted in the last chapter, it will let you exit without saving changes. Another problem is that it doesn't recover well from one particular type of user error. When you are through

```
╔══════════════════════════════════════════════════════════════════╗
║ ▤▤ SNMP-Trouble Report                                    _ □ ☒   ║
╠══════════════════════════════════════════════════════════════════╣
║  File  Options                                                     ║
╟──────────────────────────────────────────────────────────────────╢
║ IP addresses of APC UPS [172.16.2.150]:                        ▲  ║
║ ifIndex ipAdEntAddr      ipAdEntNetMask ipAdEntBcastAddr          ║
║    1   172.16.2.150    255.255.255.0       1                      ║
║                                                                   ║
║ Routing Table of APC UPS [172.16.2.150]:                         ║
║ ipRouteDest      ipRouteNextHop   ipRouteMask    IfIndex  Type    Proto  ║
║ 0.0.0.0          0.0.0.0          0.0.0.0             1   other   local  ║
║                                                                   ║
║ ARP Table of APC UPS [172.16.2.150]:                             ║
║ ifIndex PhysAddress       NetAddress      Type       Vendor      ║
║    1   00:10:7B:66:F7:62 172.16.2.1     dynamic                  ║
║    1   00:60:08:8F:5E:F6 172.16.2.232   dynamic                  ║
║                                                                   ║
║ TCP Connections of APC UPS [172.16.2.150]:                       ║
║ State         LocalAddress      LocalPort  RemoteAddress    RemotePort ║
║ listen             0.0.0.0          www        0.0.0.0           0 ║
║                                                                   ║
║ [172.16.2.150:161] [Mon Mar 05 16:32:10 EST 2001]:               ║
║    tcpRtoAlgorithm.0 : rsre                                       ║
║    tcpRtoMin.0       : 0                                          ║
║    tcpRtoMax.0       : 0                                          ║
║    tcpMaxConn.0      : 14                                         ║
║    tcpActiveOpens.0  : 0                                          ║
║    tcpPassiveOpens.0 : 0                                      ▼   ║
╚══════════════════════════════════════════════════════════════════╝
```

Figure 7-13. SNMP-Trouble reports

with a window or display, you should shrink the window rather than closing it. If you close the window, *tkined* will not automatically reopen it for you. When you later use a command that needs the closed window, it will appear that *tkined* has simply ignored your command. Usually, you can simply unload and then reload the menu that contains the selection used to initially create the window. Typically, the last item on a menu (for example, see Figure 7-4 and Figure 7-7) will remove or delete the menu and unload the subsystem. Then go to the Tools menu and reload the menu. The appropriate subsystem will be reloaded, correcting the problem. This can be very frustrating when you first encounter it, but it is easy to work around or avoid once you know to look for it.

One other problem with *tkined* is that it uses a single community string when talking with devices. This can be changed with Set SNMP Parameters, which is available on several menus. But if you are using different community strings within your network or prefer using read-only strings most of the time but occasionally need to change something, changing the community string can be a nuisance. Overall, these few problems seem to be minor inconveniences for an otherwise remarkably useful program. The program has a number of additional features— such as sending reports to the *syslog* system—that were not discussed here. You should, however, have a pretty good idea of how to get started using *tkined* from this discussion.

Non-SNMP Approaches

Of course, SNMP is not the only way to retrieve information or monitor systems. For example, a number of devices now have small HTTP servers built in that allow remote configuration and management. These can be particularly helpful in retrieving information. With Unix, it is possible to remotely log on to a system using *telnet* or *ssh* over a network connection and reconfigure the host. There is probably very little I can say about using these approaches that you don't already know or that isn't obvious. There is one thing that you undoubtedly know, but that is all too easy to forget—*don't make any changes that will kill your connection.*[*]

Some remote-access programs provide a greater degree of control than others. In a Microsoft Windows environment, where traditionally there is only one user on a system, a remote control program may take complete control of the remote system. On a multiuser system such as a Unix-based system, the same software may simply create another session on the remote host. Although these programs are not specifically designed with network management in mind, they work well as management tools.

While these approaches will allow you to actively retrieve information or reconfigure devices, the remote systems are basically passive entities. There are, however, other monitoring tools that you could consider. *Big Brother* (*bb*) is one highly regarded package. It is a web-based, multiplatform monitor. It is available commercially and, for some uses, noncommercially.

Microsoft Windows

SNMP is implemented as a Win32 service. It is available for the more recent versions of Windows but must be installed from the distribution CD-ROM. Installation and setup is very straightforward but varies from version to version.

Windows SNMP Setup

With NT, SNMP is installed from the Network applet under the Control Panel. Select Add under the Services tab, then select SNMP Services from the Select Network Service pop-up box. You will then be prompted for your distribution CD-ROM. Once it is installed, a pop-up box called Microsoft SNMP Properties will appear. You use the three tabs on this box to configure SNMP. The Agent tab is used to set the contact and location. The Traps tab is used to set the Community

---

[*] One precaution that some administrators use is connecting the console port of crucial devices to another device that should remain reachable—a port on a terminal server, a modem, or even a serial port on a nearby server. If you take this "milking-machine" approach, be sure this portal is secure.

name and address of the management station that will receive the traps. Use the Add button in the appropriate part of the box. The Security tab is used to set the community strings, privileges, and addresses for the management stations. Be sure to select the radio button Accept SNMP Packets for These Hosts if you want to limit access. If you experience problems running SNMP, try reinstalling the latest service pack from Microsoft.

Installation with Windows 98 is similar, but at the Select Network Service prompt, you must click Have Disk. The SNMP agent can be found in the *Tools\Reskit* *Netadmin\SNMP* directory on the installation disk. SNMP is not included with the original distribution of Windows 95 but can be installed from the Resource Kit or downloaded from Microsoft. On later releases, it can be found on the distribution disk in *Admin\Ntools\SNMP*.

With Windows 2000, instead of using the Network applet, you will use the Add/ Remove Programs applets. Select Add/Remove Windows Components. From the Windows Components Wizard, select Management and Monitoring Tools. Click on Next to install SNMP. To configure SNMP, start the Administrative Tools applet, and select Services and then SNMP Services. You'll be given more choices, but you can limit yourself to the same three tabs as with Windows NT.

For further details on installation and configuration of SNMP on Windows platforms, look first to the Windows help system. You might also look at James D. Murray's *Windows NT SNMP*.

SNMP Tools

NET SNMP is available both in source and binary form for Windows. With the binary version I downloaded, it was necessary to move all the subdirectories up to *C:\usr* to get things to work. Although the program still needs a little polish, it works well enough. As noted in Chapter 6, *tkined* is also available under Windows.

One very nice freeware program for Windows, written by Philippe Simonet, is *getif*. This provides both SNMP services as well as other basic network services. It is intuitively organized as a window with a tab for each service.

To begin using *getif*, you must begin with the Parameters tab. You identify and set the community strings for the remote host here. Having done this, clicking on Start will retrieve the basic information contained in the *system* group. This is shown in Figure 7-14. Even if you know this information, it is a good idea to get it again just to make sure everything is working correctly.

Once this has been done, many of the other services simply require selecting the appropriate tab and clicking on Start. For example, you can retrieve the device's interface, address, routing, and ARP tables this way.

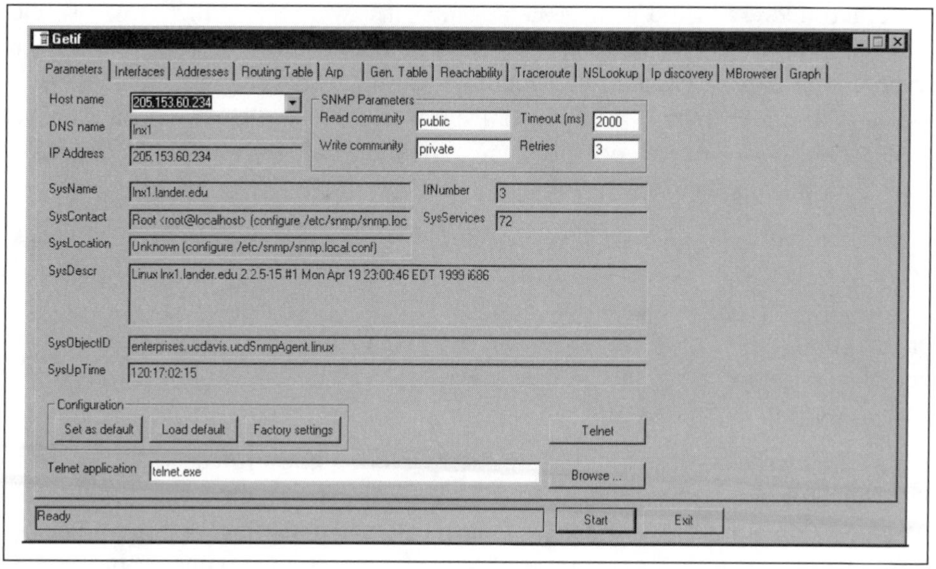

Figure 7-14. getif Parameters tab

The Reachability tab will allow you to send an ICMP ECHO_REQUEST and will also test if several common TCP ports, such as HTTP, TELNET, SMTP, and so on, are open. The Traceroute tab does both a standard ICMP traceroute and an SNMP traceroute. An SNMP traceroute constructs the route from the route tables along the path. Of course, all the intervening routers must be SNMP accessible using the community strings set under the Parameters tab. The NSLookup tab does a name service lookup. The IP Discovery tab does simple IP scanning.

The MBrowser tab provides a graphical interface to NET SNMP. This is shown in Figure 7-15. In the large pane in the upper left, the MIB tree is displayed. You can expand and collapse subtrees as needed. You can select a subtree by clicking on its root node. If you click on Walk, all readable objects in the subtree will be queried and displayed in the lower pane. You can also use this display to set objects.

The Graph tab will be discussed in Chapter 8.

Other Options

Apart from SNMP, there are a number of remote administration options including several third-party commercial tools. If remote access is the only consideration, *vnc* is an excellent choice. In particular, the viewer requires no installation. It is under 200KB so it can be run from a floppy disk. It provides a very nice way to access an X Window session on a Unix system from a PC even if you don't want to use it for management. Installation of the server binary is very straightforward. However, *vnc* will not provide multiuser access to Windows and can be sluggish

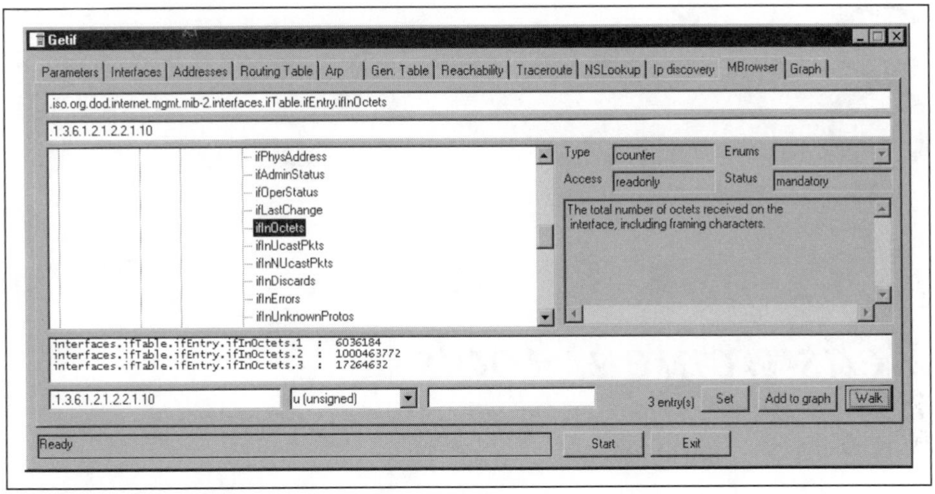

Figure 7-15. getif MBrowser tab

over low-bandwidth connections such as dial-up lines. Under these circumstances, you might consider *Microsoft Terminal Server,* Microsoft Corporation's thin client architecture, which supports remote access. (See Chapter 11 for more information on *vnc.*)

For other administrative tasks, there are a number of utilities that are sold as part of Microsoft's Resource Kits. While not free, these are generally modestly priced, and many of the tools can be downloaded from the Web at no cost. Some tools, while not specifically designed for remote troubleshooting, can be used for that purpose if you are willing to allow appropriate file sharing. These include the *System Policy Editor, Registry Editor, System Monitor,* and *Net Watcher,* among others. These are all briefly described by the Windows help system and more thoroughly in Microsoft published documentation.

8

Performance Measurement Tools

Everything on your network may be working, but using it can still be a frustrating experience. Often, a poorly performing system is worse than a broken system. As a user on a broken system, you know when to give up and find something else to do. And as an administrator, it is usually much easier to identify a component that isn't working at all than one that is still working but performing poorly. In this chapter, we will look at tools and techniques used to evaluate network performance.

This chapter begins with a brief overview of the types of tools available. Then we look at *ntop*, an excellent tool for watching traffic on your local network. Next, I describe *mrtg*, *rrd*, and *cricket*—tools for collecting traffic data from remote devices over time. RMON, monitoring extensions to SNMP, is next. We conclude with tools for use on Microsoft Windows systems.

Don't overlook the obvious! Although we will look at tools for measuring traffic, user dissatisfaction is probably the best single indicator of the health of your network. If users are satisfied, you needn't worry about theoretical problems. And if users are screaming at your door, then it doesn't matter what the numbers prove.

What, When, and Where

Network performance will depend on many things—on the applications you are using and how they are configured, on the hosts running these applications, on the networking devices, on the structure and design of the network as a whole, and on how these pieces interact with one another. Even though the focus of this chapter is restricted to network performance, you shouldn't ignore the other pieces of the puzzle. Problems may arise from the interaction of these pieces, or a problem with one of the pieces may look like a problem with another piece. A misconfigured or poorly designed application can significantly increase the amount of traffic on a network. For example, Version 1.1 of the HTTP protocol provides for persistent connections that can significantly reduce traffic. Not using this particular feature is unlikely to be a make or break issue. My point is, if you look only at the traffic on a network without considering software configurations, you may seem to have a hardware capacity problem when a simple change in software might lessen the problem and, at a minimum, buy you a little more time.

This chapter will focus on tools used to collect information on network performance. The first step in analyzing performance is measuring traffic. In addition to problem identification and resolution, this should be done as part of capacity planning and capacity management (tuning). Several books listed in Appendix B provide general discussions of application and host performance analysis.

Of the issues related to measuring network traffic, the most important ones are what to measure, how often, and where. Although there are no simple answers to any of these questions, what to measure is probably the hardest of the three. It is extremely easy to end up with so much data that you don't have time to analyze it. Or you may collect data that doesn't match your needs or that is in an unusable format. If you keep at it, eventually you will learn from experience what is most useful. Take the time to think about how you will use the data before you begin. Be as goal directed as possible. Just realize that, even with the most careful planning, when faced with a new, unusual problem, you'll probably think of something you wish you had been measuring.

If you are looking at the performance of your system over time, then data at just one point in time will be of little value. You will need to collect data periodically. How often you collect will depend on the granularity or frequency of the events you want to watch. For many tasks, the ideal approach is one that periodically condenses and eventually discards older data.

Unless your network is really unusual, the level of usage will vary with the time of day, the day of the week, and the time of the year. Most performance related problems will be most severe at the busiest times. In telephony, the hour when traffic is heaviest is known as the *busy hour*, and planning centers around traffic at this time. In a data network, for example, the busy hour may be first thing in the morning when everyone is logging on and checking their email, or it could be at noon when everyone is web surfing over their lunch hour.

Knowing usage patterns can simplify data collection since you'll need to do little collecting when the network is underutilized. Changes in usage patterns can indicate fundamental changes in your network that you'll want to be able to identify and explain. Finally, knowing when your network is least busy should give you an idea of the most convenient times to do maintenance.

I have divided traffic-measurement tools into three rough categories based on where they are used within a network. Tools that allow you to capture traffic coming into or going out of a particular machine are called *host-monitoring* tools. Tools that place an interface in promiscuous mode and allow you to capture all the traffic at an interface are called *point-monitoring* tools. Finally, tools that build a global picture of network traffic by querying other hosts (which are in turn running either host-monitoring or point-monitoring tools) are called *network-monitoring* tools. Both host monitoring and point monitoring should have a minimal impact on network traffic. With the exception of DNS traffic, they shouldn't be generating additional traffic. This is not true for network-monitoring tools.

Because of their roles within a network, devices such as switches and routers don't easily fit into this classification scheme. If a single switch interconnects all devices in a subnet, then it will see all the local traffic. If, however, multiple switches are used and you aren't mirroring traffic, each switch will see only part of the traffic. Routers will see only traffic moving between networks. While this is ideal for measuring traffic between local and remote devices, it is not helpful in understanding strictly local traffic. The problem should be obvious. If you monitor the wrong device, you may easily miss bottlenecks or other problems. Before collecting data, you need to understand the structure of your network so you can understand what traffic is actually being seen. This is one reason the information in Chapter 6, is important.

Finally, you certainly won't want to deal with raw data on a routine basis. You will want tools that present the data in a useful manner. For time-series data, graphs and summary statistics are usually the best choice.

Host-Monitoring Tools

We have already discussed host-monitoring tools in several different parts of this book, particularly Chapter 2 and Chapter 4. An obvious example of a host-monitoring tool is *netstat*. You will recall that the *-i* option will give a cumulative picture of the traffic into and out of a computer.

Although easy to overlook, any tool that logs traffic is a host-monitoring tool of sorts. These are generally not too useful after the fact, but you may be able to piece together some information from them. A better approach is to configure the software to collect what you need. Don't forget applications, like web servers, that collect data. Accounting tools and security tools provide other possibilities. Tools like *ipfw*, *ipchains*, and *tcpwrappers* all support logging. (Log files are discussed in greater detail in Chapter 11.)

Host-monitoring tools can be essential in diagnosing problems related to host performance, but they give very little information about the performance of the network as a whole. Of course, if you have this information for every host, you'll have the data you need to construct a complete picture. Constructing that picture is another story.

Point-Monitoring Tools

A point-monitoring tool puts your network interface in promiscuous mode and allows you to collect information on all traffic seen at the computer's interface. The major limitation to point monitoring is it gives you only a local view of your network. If your focus is on host performance, this is probably all that you will need. Or, if you are on a shared media network such as a hub, you will see all of the local traffic. But, if you are on a switched network, you will normally be able to see only traffic to or from the host or broadcast traffic. And as more and more networks shift to switches for efficiency, this problem will worsen.

The quintessential point-monitoring tools are network sniffers. In Chapter 5, we saw several utilities that capture traffic and generate traffic summaries. These included *tcp-reduce*, *tcptrace*, and *xplot*. In general, sniffers are not really designed for traffic measurement—they are too difficult to use for this purpose, provide too much information, and provide information in a format ill-suited to this purpose. But if you really want to understand a problem, packet capture gives you the most complete picture, if you can wade through all the data.

ntop

ntop, the work of Luca Deri, is an excellent example of just how useful a point-monitoring tool can be. *ntop* is usually described as the network equivalent of the Unix utility *top*. Actually, it is a lot more.

ntop is based on the *libpcap* library that originated at the Lawrence Berkeley National Laboratory and on which *tcpdump* is based. It puts the network interface in promiscuous mode so that all traffic at the interface is captured. It will then begin to collect data, periodically creating summary statistics. (It will also use *lsof* and other plug-ins to collect data if available.)

ntop can be run in two modes: as a web-based utility using a built-in web server or in interactive mode, i.e., as a text-based application on a host. It closely resembles *top* when run in interactive mode. This was the default mode with earlier versions of *ntop* but is now provided by a separate command, *intop*. Normally, you will want to use a separate window when using interactive mode.

Interactive mode

Here is an example of the output with *intop*:

```
$<50>                   intop 0.0.1 (Sep 19 2000) listening on [eth0]
379 Pkts/56.2 Kb [IP 50.5 Kb/Other 5.7 Kb]         Thpt: 6.1 Kbps/24.9 Kbps
Host                   Act   -Rcv-Rcvd-    Sent   TC-TCP-       UDP    IC$
sloan                    B    69.0%   16.7%   38.8 Kb        0        0
lnx1a                    B    16.7%   69.4%    9.4 Kb        0        0
rip2-routers.mcast.net   R     3.7%    0.0%        0    2.1 Kb       0
172.16.3.1               B     2.1%    6.5%        0        0        0
Cisco CDPD/VTP [MAC]     I     4.7%    0.0%        0        0        0
172.16.3.3               B     2.2%    6.1%        0        0        0
```

Interpretation of the data is straightforward. The top two lines show the program name and version, date, interface, number of packets, total traffic, and throughput. The first column lists hosts by name or IP number. The second column reflects activity since the last update—Idle, Send, Receive, or Both. The next two columns are the amount of traffic sent and received, while the last two columns break traffic down as TCP, UPD, or ICMP traffic.

intop should be started with the *-i* option to specify which interface to use. For example:

```
lnx1# intop -i eth0
```

If your computer is multihomed, you can specify several interfaces on the command line, each with a separate *-i*. Once started, it prints an annoying 20 lines or so of general information about the program and then gives you a prompt. At this point, you can enter *?* to find out what services are available:

```
intop@eth0> ?
Commands enclosed in '<>' are not yet implemented.
Commands may be abbreviated. Commands are:

?               <warranty>      filter          swap            nbt
help            <copying>       sniff           top             <dump>
exit            history         uptime          lsdev           <last>
quit            open            <hash>          hosts           <nslookup>
prompt          <close>         info            arp
intop@eth0>
```

As you can see, a number of commands are planned but had not been implemented at the time this was written. Most are exactly what you would expect. You use the *top* command to get a display like the one just shown. The *info* command reports the interface and number of packets captured. With the *filter* command, you can set packet-capture filters. You use the same syntax as explained in Chapter 5 with *tcpdump*. (Filters can also be specified on the command line when *intop* is started.) The *lsdev* command lists interfaces. The *swap* command is used to jump between data collection on two different interfaces.

You can change how the data is displayed on-the-fly using your keyboard. For example, the *d* key will allow you to toggle between showing all hosts or only active hosts. The *l* key toggles between showing or not showing only local hosts. The *p* key can be used to show or suppress showing data as percentages. The *y* key is used to change the sorting order among the columns. The *n* key is used to toggle between hostnames and IP addresses. The *r* key can be used to reset or zero statistics. The *q* key is used to stop the program.

Web mode

Actually, you'll probably prefer web mode to interactive mode, as it provides considerably more information and a simpler interface. Since *ntop* uses a built-in web server, you won't need to have a separate web server running on your system. By default, *ntop* uses port 3000, so this shouldn't interfere with any existing web servers. If it does, or if you are paranoid about using default ports, you can use the *-w* option to select a different port. The only downside is that the built-in web server uses frames and displays data as tables, which still seems to confuse some browsers, particularly when printing.

There are a number of options, some of which are discussed next, but the defaults work well enough to get you started. Once you start *ntop*, point your browser to the machine and port it runs on. Figure 8-1 shows what the initial screen looks like.

As you can see, on startup *ntop* provides you with a brief description of the program in the larger frame to the right. The real area of interest is the menu on the left. By clicking on the triangles, each menu expands to give you a number of choices. This is shown to the left in Figure 8-2.

Figure 8-2 shows the All Protocols page, which groups traffic by protocol and host. This is available for both received and transmitted data. A number of statistics for other protocols—such as AppleTalk, OSPF, NetBIOS, and IGMP—have scrolled off the right of this window. You can click on the column header to sort the data based on that column. By default, this screen will be updated every two minutes, but this can be changed.

The IP option displays received or transmitted data grouped by individual IP protocols such as FTP, HTTP, DNS, and Telnet. The Throughput option gives a table organized by host and by throughput, average throughput, and peak throughput for both bits and packets.

Figure 8-1. ntop's home page

The Stats submenu offers a number of options. Multicast gives a table of multicast traffic. Traffic provides you with a number of tables and graphs showing how traffic breaks down. Figure 8-3 shows one of these graphs.

Figures and tables break down traffic by broadcast versus unicast versus multicast packets, by packet size categories, by IP versus non-IP traffic, by protocol category such as TCP versus UDP versus AppleTalk versus Other, and by application protocols such as FTP versus Telnet. Either bar graphs or pie charts are used to display the data. The tables give the data in both kilobytes and percentages. These graphs can save you a lot of work in analyzing data and discovering how your network is being used.

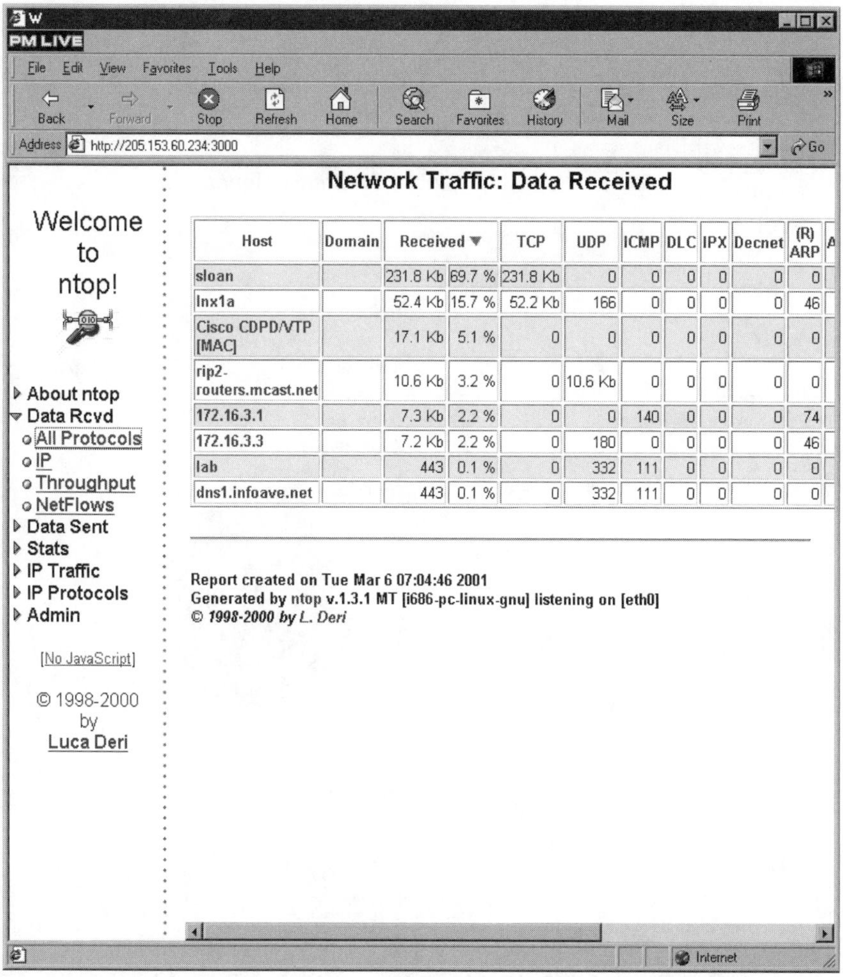

Host	Domain	Received ▼		TCP	UDP	ICMP	DLC	IPX	Decnet	(R) ARP	A
sloan		231.8 Kb	69.7 %	231.8 Kb	0	0	0	0	0	0	
lnx1a		52.4 Kb	15.7 %	52.2 Kb	166	0	0	0	0	46	
Cisco CDPD/VTP [MAC]		17.1 Kb	5.1 %	0	0	0	0	0	0	0	
rip2-routers.mcast.net		10.6 Kb	3.2 %	0	10.6 Kb	0	0	0	0	0	
172.16.3.1		7.3 Kb	2.2 %	0	0	140	0	0	0	74	
172.16.3.3		7.2 Kb	2.2 %	0	180	0	0	0	0	46	
lab		443	0.1 %	0	332	111	0	0	0	0	
dns1.infoave.net		443	0.1 %	0	332	111	0	0	0	0	

Report created on Tue Mar 6 07:04:46 2001
Generated by ntop v.1.3.1 MT [i686-pc-linux-gnu] listening on [eth0]
© 1998-2000 by L. Deri

Figure 8-2. ntop's All Protocols page

The Host option under Stats gives basic host information including hostnames, IP addresses, MAC addresses for local hosts, transmit bandwidth, and vendors for MAC addresses when known. By clicking on a hostname, additional data will be displayed as shown in Figure 8-4.

The host shown here is on a different subnet from the host running *ntop,* so less information is available. For example, there is no way for *ntop* to discover the remote host's MAC address or to track traffic to or from the remote host that doesn't cross the local network. Since this displays connections between hosts, its use has obvious privacy implications.

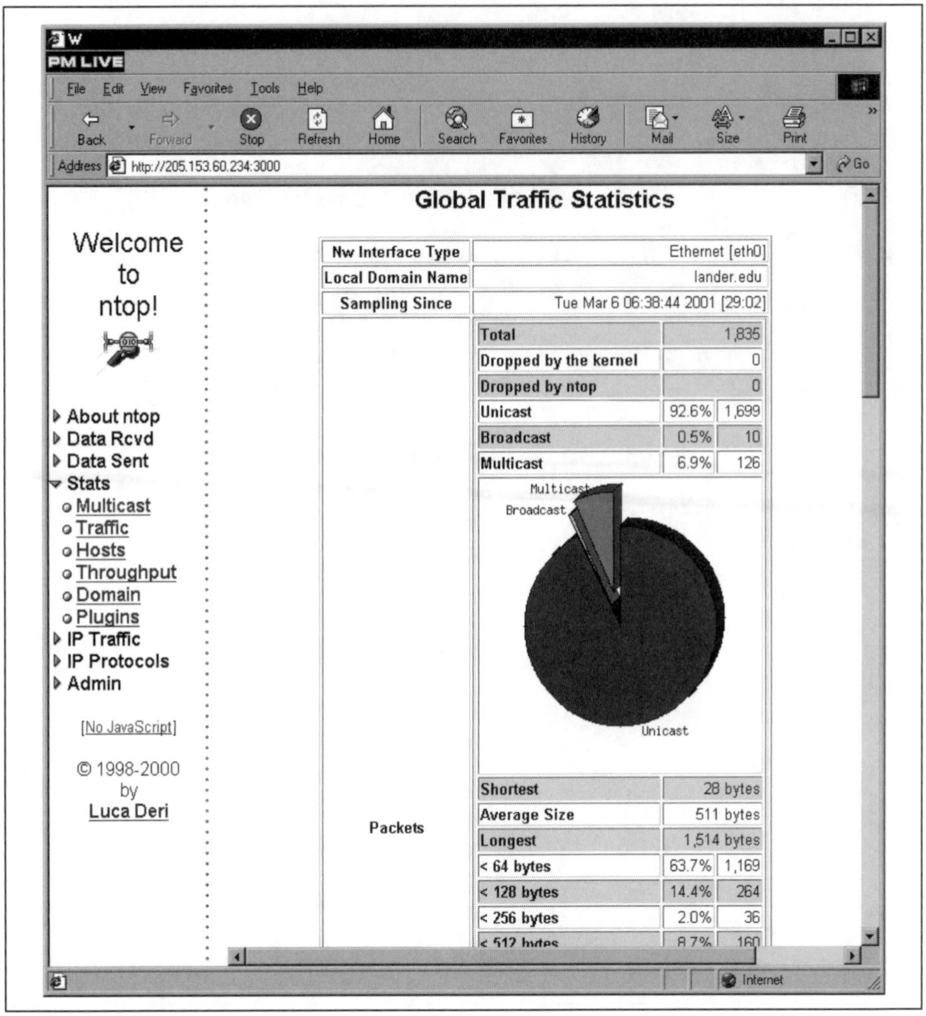

Figure 8-3. ntop's Traffic page under Stats

The Throughput option gives a graph of the average throughput over the last hour. Domain gives a table of traffic grouped by domain. Plug-ins provide a way to extend the functionality of *ntop* by adding other applications. Existing plug-ins provide support for such activities as tracking new ARP entries, NFS traffic, and WAP traffic and tracking and classifying ICMP traffic.

An important issue in capacity planning is what percentage of traffic is purely local and what percentage has a remote network for its source or destination (see the sidebar "Local Versus Remote Traffic"). The IP Traffic menu gives you options to collect this type of information. The Distribution option on the IP Protocols menu gives you plots and tables for local and remote IP traffic. For example, Figure 8-5

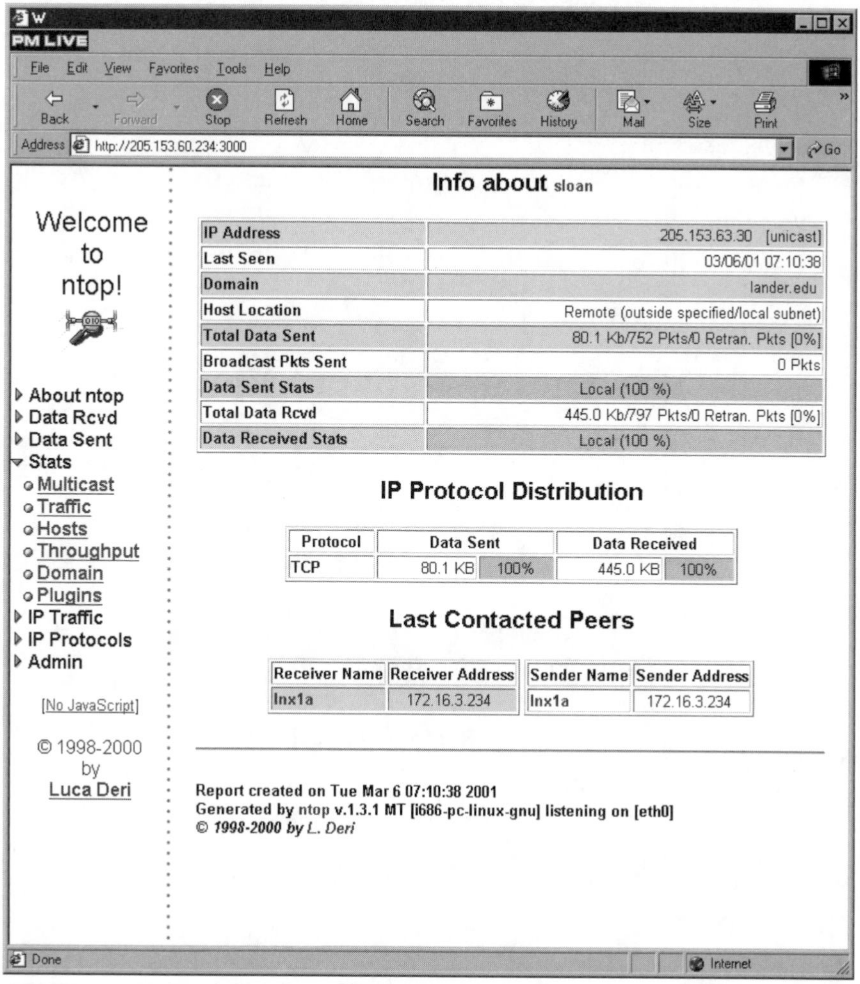

Figure 8-4. Host information

shows a graph and tables for local and remote-to-local traffic. There is a local-to-remote table that is not shown. The Usage option shows IP subnet usage by port. Sessions shows active TCP sessions, and Routers identifies routers on the local subnet.

The last menu, Admin, is used to control the operation of *ntop*. Switch NIC allows you to capture on a different interface, and Reset Stats zeros all cumulative statistics. Shutdown shuts down *ntop*. Users and URLs allow you to control access to *ntop*.

A number of command-line options allow you to control how *ntop* runs. These can be listed with the *-h* option. As noted previously, *-w* is used to change the port it listens to, and *-i* allows you to specify which interface to listen to. *-r* sets the delay

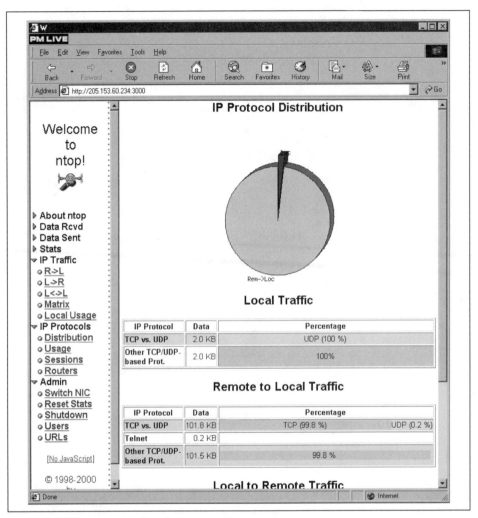

Figure 8-5. Measuring local and remote traffic

between screen updates in seconds. The *-n* option is used to specify numeric IP addresses rather than hostnames. Consult the documentation for other options.

ntop has other features not discussed here. It can be used as a lightweight intrusion detection system. It provides basic access control and can be used with secure HTTP. It also provides facilities to log data, including logging to a SQL database.

As previously noted, the real problem with point monitoring is that it doesn't really work well with segmented or switched networks. Unless you are mirroring all traffic to your test host, many of these numbers can be meaningless. If this is the case, you'll want to collect information from a number of sources.

Local Versus Remote Traffic

Before the Internet became popular, most network traffic stayed on the local network. This was often summarized as the 90-10 Rule (or sometimes the 80-20 Rule), a heuristic that says that roughly 90% of network traffic will stay on the local network. The Internet has turned the old 90-10 Rule on its head by providing a world of reasons to leave the local network; now most traffic does just that. Today the 90-10 Rule says that 90% of traffic on the local network will have a remote site as its source or destination.

Clearly, the 90-10 Rule is nothing more than a very general rule of thumb. It may be an entirely inappropriate generalization for your network. But knowing the percentage of local and remote traffic can be useful in understanding your network in a couple of ways. First, whatever the numbers, they really shouldn't be changing a lot over time unless something fundamental is changing in the way your network is being used. This is something you'll want to know about.

Second, local versus remote traffic provides a quick sanity check for network design. If 90% of your traffic is entering or leaving your network over a 1.544-Mbps T1 line, you should probably think very carefully about why you need to upgrade your backbone to gigabit speeds.

Network-Monitoring Tools

It should come as no surprise that SNMP can be used to collect performance information. We have already seen simple examples in Chapter 7. Using the raw statistics gathered with a tool like NET SNMP or even the stripcharts in *tkined* is alright if you need only a little data, but in practice you will want tools designed to deal specifically with performance data. Which tool you use will depend on what you want to do. One of your best choices from this family of tools is *mrtg*. (Although it is not discussed here, you also may want to look at *scion*. This is from Merit Networks, Inc., and will run under Windows as well as Unix.)

mrtg

mrtg (*Multirouter Traffic Grapher*) was originally developed by Tobias Oetiker with the support of numerous people, most notably Dave Rand. This tool uses SNMP to collect statistics from network equipment and creates web-accessible graphs of the statistics. It is designed to be run periodically to provide a picture of traffic over time. *mrtg* is ideally suited for identifying busy-hour traffic. All you need to do is scan the graph looking for the largest peaks.

mrtg is most commonly used to graph traffic through router interfaces but can be configured for other uses. For example, since NET SNMP can be used to collect disk usage data, *mrtg* could be used to retrieve and graph the amount of free space on the disk drive over time for a system running *snmpd*. Because the graphs are web-accessible, *mrtg* is well suited for remote measurement. *mrtg* uses SNMP's GET command to collect information. With the current implementation, collection is done by a Perl module supplied as part of *mrtg*. No separate installation of SNMP is needed.

mrtg is designed to be run regularly by *cron*, typically every five minutes. However, *mrtg* can be run as a standalone program, or the sampling interval can be changed. Configuration files, generally created with the *cfgmaker* utility, determine the general appearance of the web pages and what data is collected. *mrtg* generates graphs of traffic in GIF format and HTML pages to display these graphs. Typically, these will be made available by a web server running on the same computer as *mrtg*, but the files can be viewed with a web browser running on the same computer or the files can be moved to another computer for viewing. This could be helpful when debugging *mrtg* since the web server may considerably complicate the installation, particularly if you are not currently running a web server or are not comfortable with web server configuration.

Figure 8-6 shows a typical web page generated by *mrtg*. In this example, you can see some basic information about the router at the top of the page and, below it, two graphs. One shows traffic for the last 24 hours and the other shows traffic for the last two weeks, along with summary statistics for each. The monthly and yearly graphs have scrolled off the page. This is the output for a single interface. Input traffic is shown in green and output traffic is shown in blue, by default, on color displays.

It is possible to have *mrtg* generate a summary web page with a graph for each interface. Each graph is linked to the more complete traffic report such as the one shown in Figure 8-6. The *indexmaker* utility is used to generate this page once the configuration file has been created.

mrtg configuration file

To use *mrtg*, you will need a separate configuration file for each device. Each configuration file will describe all the interfaces within the device. Creating these files is the first step after installation. While a sample configuration file is supplied as part of the documentation, it is much easier to use the *cfgmaker* script. An SNMP community string and hostname or IP number must be supplied as parts to a compound argument:

```
bsd2# cfgmaker public@172.16.2.1 > mrtg.cfg
```

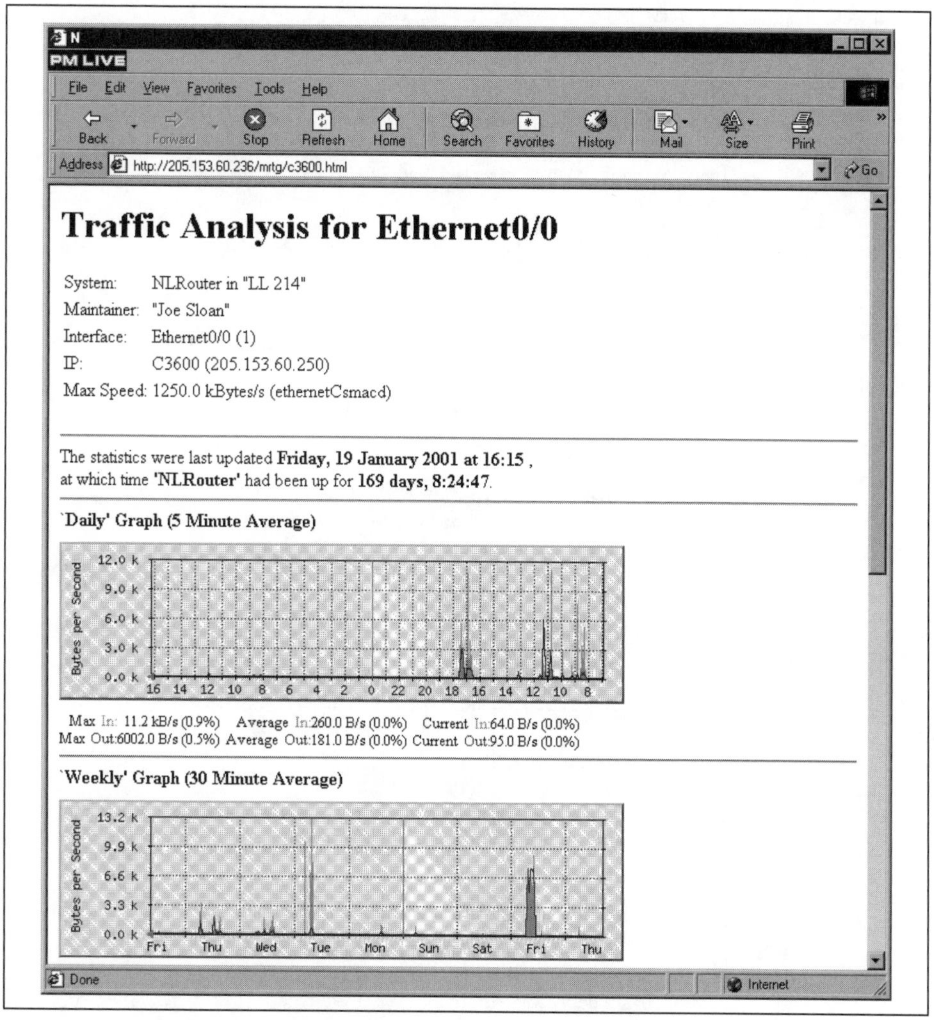

Figure 8-6. mrtg interface report

Since the script writes the configuration to standard output, you'll need to redirect your output to a file. If you want to measure traffic at multiple devices, then you simply need to create a different configuration file for each. Just give each a different (but meaningful) name.

Once you have a basic configuration file, you can further edit it as you see fit. As described next, this can be an involved process. Fortunately, *cfgmaker* does a reasonable job. In many cases, this will provide all you need, so further editing won't be necessary.

Here is the first part of a fairly typical configuration file. (You may want to compare this to the sample output shown in Figure 8-6.)

```
# Add a WorkDir: /some/path line to this file
WorkDir: /usr/local/share/doc/apache/mrtg

######################################################################
# Description: Cisco Internetwork Operating System Software IOS (tm) 3600
 Software (C3620-IO3-M), Version 12.0(7)T, RELEASE SOFTWARE (fc2) Copyright (c)
1986-1999 by cisco Systems, Inc. Compiled Wed 08-Dec-99 10:08 by phanguye
#      Contact: "Joe Sloan"
# System Name: NLRouter
#     Location: "LL 214"
#.......................................................................

Target[C3600]: 1:public@172.16.2.1
MaxBytes[C3600]: 1250000
Title[C3600]: NLRouter (C3600): Ethernet0/0
PageTop[C3600]: <H1>Traffic Analysis for Ethernet0/0
 </H1>
 <TABLE>
   <TR><TD>System:</TD><TD>NLRouter in "LL 214"</TD></TR>
   <TR><TD>Maintainer:</TD><TD>"Joe Sloan"</TD></TR>
   <TR><TD>Interface:</TD><TD>Ethernet0/0 (1)</TD></TR>
   <TR><TD>IP:</TD><TD>C3600 (205.153.60.250)</TD></TR>
   <TR><TD>Max Speed:</TD>
       <TD>1250.0 kBytes/s (ethernetCsmacd)</TD></TR>
 </TABLE>


#-----------------------------------------------------------------

Target[172.16.2.1.2]: 2:public@172.16.2.1
MaxBytes[172.16.2.1.2]: 1250000
Title[172.16.2.1.2]: NLRouter (No hostname defined for IP address): Ethernet0/1
PageTop[172.16.2.1.2]: <H1>Traffic Analysis for Ethernet0/1
 </H1>
 <TABLE>
   <TR><TD>System:</TD><TD>NLRouter in "LL 214"</TD></TR>
   <TR><TD>Maintainer:</TD><TD>"Joe Sloan"</TD></TR>
   <TR><TD>Interface:</TD><TD>Ethernet0/1 (2)</TD></TR>
   <TR><TD>IP:</TD><TD>No hostname defined for IP address (172.16.1.1)</TD></TR>
   <TR><TD>Max Speed:</TD>
       <TD>1250.0 kBytes/s (ethernetCsmacd)</TD></TR>
 </TABLE>


#-----------------------------------------------------------------
```

As you can see from the example, the general format of a directive is *Keyword[Label]: Arguments.* Directives always start in the first column of the configuration file. Their arguments may extend over multiple lines, provided the additional lines leave the first column blank. In the example, the argument to the first *PageTop* directive extends for 10 lines.

In this example, I've added the second line—specifying a directory where the working files will be stored. This is a mandatory change. It should be set to a directory that is accessible to the web server on the computer. It will contain log files, home pages, and graphs for the most recent day, week, month, and year for each interface. The interface label, explained shortly, is the first part of a filename. Filename extensions identify the function of each file.

Everything else, including the files just described, is automatically generated. As you can see, *cfgmaker* uses SNMP to collect some basic information from the device, e.g., *sysName*, *sysLocation*, and *sysContact*, for inclusion in the configuration file. This information has been used both in the initial comment (lines beginning with #) and in the HTML code under the *PageTop* directive. As you might guess, *PageTop* determines what is displayed at the top of the page in Figure 8-6.

cfgmaker also determines the type of interface by retrieving *ifType* and its maximum operating speed by retrieving *ifSpeed*, `ethernetCsmacd` and `125.0 kBytes/s` in this example. The interface type is used by the *PageTop* directive. The speed is used by both *PageTop* and the *MaxBytes* directive. The *MaxBytes* directive determines the maximum value that a measured variable is allowed to reach. If a larger number is retrieved, it is ignored. This is given in bytes per second, so if you think in bits per second, don't be misled.

cfgmaker collects information on each interface and creates a section in the configuration file for each. Only two interfaces are shown in this fragment, but the omitted sections are quite similar. Each section will begin with the *Target* directive. In this example, the first interface is identified with the directive `Target[C3600]: 1:public@172.16.2.1`. The interface was identified by the initial scan by *cfgmaker*. The label was obtained by doing name resolution on the IP address. In this case, it came from an entry in */etc/hosts*.* If name resolution fails, the IP and port numbers will be used as a label. The argument to *Target* is a combination of the port number, SNMP community string, and IP address of the interface. You should be aware that adding or removing an interface in a monitored device without updating the configuration file can lead to bogus results.

The only other directive in this example is *Title*, which determines the title displayed for the HTML page. These examples are quite adequate for a simple page, but *mrtg* provides both additional directives and additional arguments that provide a great deal of flexibility.

By default, *mrtg* collects the SNMP objects *ifInOctets* and *ifOutOctets* for each interface. This can be changed with the *Target* command. Here is an example of a small test file (the recommended way to test *mrtg*) that is used to collect the number of unicast and nonunicast packets at an interface.

---

* In this example, a different system name and hostname are used to show where each is used. This is not recommended.

```
bsd2# cat test.cfg
WorkDir: /usr/local/share/doc/apache/mrtg

Target[Testing]: ifInUcastPkts.1&ifInNUcastPkts.1:public@172.16.2.1
MaxBytes[Testing]: 1250000
Title[Testing]: NLRouter: Ethernet0/0
PageTop[Testing]: <H1>Traffic Analysis for Ethernet0/0
 </H1>
 <TABLE>
   <TR><TD>System:</TD><TD>NLRouter in "LL 214"</TD></TR>
   <TR><TD>Maintainer:</TD><TD>"Joe Sloan"</TD></TR>
   <TR><TD>Interface:</TD><TD>Ethernet0/0 (1)</TD></TR>
   <TR><TD>IP:</TD><TD>C3600 (205.153.60.250)</TD></TR>
   <TR><TD>Max Speed:</TD>
       <TD>1250.0 kBytes/s (ethernetCsmacd)</TD></TR>
 </TABLE>
```

mrtg knows a limited number of OIDs. These are described in the *mibhelp.txt* file that comes with *mrtg*. Fortunately, you can use dotted notation as well, so you aren't limited to objects with known identifiers. Nor do you have to worry about MIBs. You can also use an expression in the place of an identifier, e.g., the sum of two OIDs, or you can specify an external program if you wish to collect data not available through SNMP. There are a number of additional formats and options available with *Target*.

Other keywords are available that will allow you to customize *mrtg*'s behavior. For example, you can use the *Interval* directive to change the reported frequency of sampling. You'll also need to change your *crontab* file to match. If you don't want to use *cron*, you can use the *RunAsDaemon* directive, in conjunction with the *Interval* directive to set *mrtg* up to run as a standalone program. *Interval* takes an argument in minutes; for example, `Interval: 10` would sample every 10 minutes. To enable *mrtg* to run as a stand-alone program, the syntax is `RunAsDaemon: yes`.

Several directives are useful for controlling the appearance of your graphs. If you don't want all four graphs, you can suppress the display of selected graphs with the *Suppress* directive. For example, `Suppress[Testing]: my` will suppress the monthly and yearly graphs. Use *d* and *w* for daily and weekly graphs. You may use whatever combination you want.

One annoyance with *mrtg* is that it scales each graph to the largest value that has to be plotted. *mrtg* shouldn't be faulted for this; it is simply using what information it has. But the result can be graphs with some very unusual vertical scales and sets of graphs that you can't easily compare. This is something you'll definitely want to adjust.

You can work around this problem with several of the directives *mrtg* provides, but the approach you choose will depend, at least in part, on the behavior of the data you are collecting. The *Unscaled* directive suppresses automatic scaling of data. It uses the value from *MaxBytes* as maximum on the vertical scale. You can edit *MaxBytes* if you are willing to have data go off the top of the graph. If you change this, you should use *AbsMax* to set the largest value that you expect to see.

Other commands allow you to change the color, size, shape, and background of your graphs. You can also change the directions that graphs grow. Here is an example that changes the display of data to bits per second, has the display grow from left to right, displays only the daily and weekly graphs, and sets the vertical scale to 4000 bits per second:

```
Options[Testing]: growright,bits
Suppress[Testing]: my
MaxBytes[Testing]: 500
AbsMax[Testing]: 1250000
Unscaled[Testing]: dw
```

Notice that you still need to give *MaxBytes* and *AbsMax* in bytes.

Many more keywords are available. Only the most common have been described here, but these should be more than enough to meet your initial needs. See the *mrtg* sample configuration file and documentation for others.

Once you have the configuration file, use *indexmaker* to create a main page for all the interfaces on a device. In its simplest form, you merely give the configuration file and the destination file:

```
bsd2# indexmaker mrtg.cfg > /usr/local/www/data/mrtg/index.html
```

You may specify a router name and a regular expression that will match a subset of the interfaces if you want to limit what you are looking at. For example, if you have a switch with a large number of ports, you may want to monitor only the uplink ports.

You'll probably want to run *mrtg* manually a couple of times. Here is an example using the configuration file *test.cfg*:

```
bsd2# mrtg test.cfg
Rateup WARNING: .//rateup could not read the primary log file for testing
Rateup WARNING: .//rateup The backup log file for testing was invalid as well
Rateup WARNING: .//rateup Can't remove testing.old updating log file
Rateup WARNING: .//rateup Can't rename testing.log to testing.old updating log f
ile
```

The first couple of runs will generate warning messages about missing log files and the like. These should go away after a couple of runs and can be safely ignored.

Finally, you'll want to make an appropriate entry in your *contab* file. For example, this entry will run *mrtg* every five minutes on a FreeBSD system:

```
0,5,10,15,20,25,30,35,40,45,50,55 * * * * /usr/ports/net/mrtg/work/mrtg-2.8.12/r
un/mrtg /usr/ports/net/mrtg/work/mrtg-2.8.12/run/mrtg.cfg > /dev/null 2>&1
```

This should be all on a single line. The syntax is different on some systems, such as Linux, so be sure to check your local manpages.

rrd and the Future of mrtg

The original version of *mrtg* had two deficiencies, a lack of both scalability and portability. Originally, *mrtg* was able to support only about 20 routers or switches. It used external utilities to perform SNMP queries and create GIF images—*snmpget* from CMU SNMP and *pnmtogif* from the PBM package, respectively.

These issues were addressed by MRTG-2, the second and current version of *mrtg*. Performance was improved when Dave Rand contributed *rateup* to the project. Written in C, *rateup* improved both graph generation and handling of the log files.

The portability problem was addressed by two changes. First, Simon Leinen's Perl script for collecting SNMP is now used, eliminating the need for CMU SNMP. Second, Thomas Boutell's GD library is now used to directly generate graphics. At this point, *mrtg* is said to reasonably support querying 500 ports on a regular basis.

As an ongoing project, the next goal is to further improve performance and flexibility. Toward this goal, Tobias Oetiker has written *rrd (Round Robin Database)*, a program to further optimize the database and the graphing portion of *mrtg*. Although MRTG-3, the next version of *mrtg*, is not complete, *rrd* has been completed and is available as a standalone program. MRTG-3 will be built on top of *rrd*.

rrd is designed to store and display time-series data. It is written in C and is available under the GNU General Public License. *rrd* stores data in a round-robin fashion so that older data is condensed and eventually discarded. Consequently, the size of the database stabilizes and will not continue to grow over time.

cricket

A number of frontends are available for *rrd*, including Jeff Allen's *cricket*. Allen, working at WebTV, was using *mrtg* but found that it really wasn't adequate to support the 9000 targets he needed to manage. Rather than wait for MRTG-3, he developed *cricket*. At least superficially, *cricket* has basically the same uses as *mrtg*. But *cricket* has been designed to be much more scalable. *cricket* is organized around the concept of a configuration tree. The configuration files for devices are organized in a hierarchical manner so the general device properties can be defined once at a higher level and inherited, while exceptions can be simply defined at a lower level of the hierarchy. This makes *cricket* much more manageable for larger organizations with large numbers of devices. Since it is designed around *rrd*, *cricket* is also much more efficient.

cricket does a very nice job of organizing the pages that it displays. To access the pages, you will begin by executing the *grapher.cgi* script on the server. For example, if the server were at *172.16.2.236* and CGI scripts were in the *cgi-bin* directory, you would point your browser to the URL *http://172.16.2.236/cgi-bin/grapher.cgi*. This will present you with a page organized around types of devices, e.g., routers, router interfaces, switches, along with descriptions of each. From this you will select the type of device you want to monitor. Depending on your choice, you may be presented with a list of monitored devices items or with another subhierarchy such as that shown in Figure 8-7.

Figure 8-7. cricket router interfaces

You can quickly drill down to the traffic graph for the device of interest. Figure 8-8 shows an example of a traffic graph for a router interface on a router during a period of very low usage (but you get the idea, I hope).

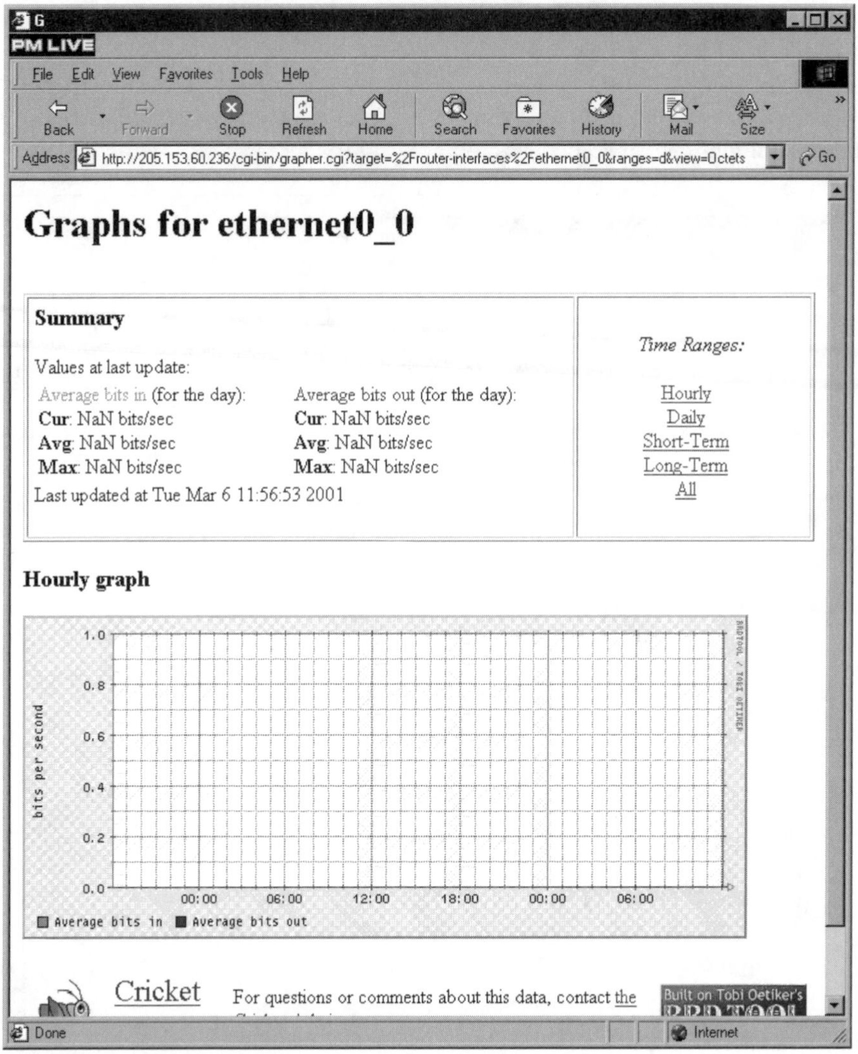

Figure 8-8. Traffic on a single interface

As you can see, this looks an awful lot like the graphs from *mrtg*. Unlike with *mrtg*, you have some control over which graphs are displayed from the web page. Short-Term displays both hourly and daily graphs, Long-Term displays both weekly and monthly graphs, and Hourly, Daily, and All are just what you would expect.[*]

Of course, you will need to configure each option for *mrtg* to work correctly. You will need to go through the hierarchy and identify the appropriate targets, set SNMP community strings, and add any descriptions that you want. Here is the *interfaces* file in the *router-interfaces* subdirectory of the *cricket-config* directory, the directory that contains the configuration tree. (This file corresponds to the output shown in Figure 8-8.)

```
target --default--
        router = NLCisco
        snmp-community=public

target Ethernet0_0
        interface-name  =       Ethernet0/0
        short-desc      =       "Gateway to Internet"

target Ethernet0_1
        interface-name  =       Ethernet0/1
        short-desc      =       "172.16.1.0/24 subnet"

target Ethernet0_2
        interface-name  =       Ethernet0/2
        short-desc      =       "172.16.2.0/24 subnet"

target Ethernet0_3
        interface-name  =       Ethernet0/3
        short-desc      =       "172.16.3.0/24 subnet"

target Null0
        interface-name  =       Null0
        short-desc      =       ""
```

While this may look simpler than an *mrtg* configuration file, you'll be dealing with a large number of these files. If you make a change to the configuration tree, you will need to recompile the configuration tree before you run *cricket*. As with *mrtg*, you will need to edit your *crontab* file to execute the *collector* script on a regular basis.

On the whole, *cricket* is considerably more difficult to learn and to configure than *mrtg*. One way that *cricket* gains efficiency is by using CGI scripts to generate web pages only when they are needed rather than after each update. The result is that the pages are not available unless you have a web server running on the same computer that *cricket* is running on. Probably the most difficult part of the *cricket* installation is setting up your web server and the *cricket* directory structure so that

---

[*] *mrtg* uses Daily to mean an hour-by-hour plot for 24 hours. *cricket* uses Hourly to mean the same thing. This shouldn't cause any problems.

the scripts can be executed by the web server without introducing any security holes. Setting up a web server and web security are beyond the scope of this book.

Unless you have such a large installation that *mrtg* doesn't meet your needs, my advice would be to start with *mrtg*. It's nice to know that *cricket* is out there. And if you really need it, it is a solid package worth learning. But *mrtg* is easier to get started with and will meet most people's needs.

RMON

As we saw in the last chapter, SNMP can be used to collect network traffic at an interface. Unfortunately, SNMP is not a very efficient mechanism in some circumstances. Frequent collection of data over an overused, low-bandwidth WAN link can create the very problems you are using SNMP to avoid. Even after you have the data, a significant amount of processing may still be needed before the data is in a useful form.

A better approach is to do some of the processing and data reduction remotely and retrieve data selectively. This is one of the ideas behind the *remote monitoring (RMON)* extensions to SNMP. RMON is basically a mechanism to collect and process data at the point of collection. RMON provides both continuous and offline data collection. Some implementation can even provide remote packet capture. The RMON mechanism may be implemented in software on an existing device, in dedicated hardware such as an add-on card for a device, or even as a separate device. Hardware implementations are usually called *RMON probes*.

Data is organized and retrieved in the same manner as SNMP data. Data organization is described in an RMON MIB, identified by OIDs, and retrieved with SNMP commands. To the users, RMON will seem to be little more than an expanded or super MIB. To implementers, there are significant differences between RMON and traditional SNMP objects, resulting from the need for continuous monitoring and remote data processing.

Originally, RMON data was organized in nine groups (RFCs 1271 and 1757) and later expanded to include a tenth group (RFC 1513) for token rings:

Statistics group
　　Offers low-level utilization and error statistics

History group
　　Provides trend analysis data based on the data from the statistics group

Alarm group

> Provides for the user to configure alarms

Event group

> Logs and generates traps for user-defined rising thresholds, falling thresholds, and matched packets

Host group

> Collects statistics based on MAC addresses

Top N Hosts group

> Collects host statistics for the busiest hosts

Packet Capture group

> Controls packet capture

Traffic Matrix group

> Collects and returns errors and utilization data based on pairs of addresses

Filter group

> Collects information based on definable filters

Token-ring group

> Collects low-level token-ring statistics

RMON implementations are often limited to a subset of these groups. This isn't unrealistic, but you should be aware of what you are getting when paying the premium prices often required for RMON support.

Provided you have the RMON MIB loaded, you can use *snmptranslate* to explore the structure of these groups. For example, here is the structure of the statistics group:

```
bsd2# snmptranslate -Tp rmon.statistics
+--statistics(1)
   |
   +--etherStatsTable(1)
      |
      +--etherStatsEntry(1)
         |
         +-- -R-- Integer    etherStatsIndex(1)
         |        Range: 1..65535
         +-- -RW- ObjID      etherStatsDataSource(2)
         +-- -R-- Counter    etherStatsDropEvents(3)
         +-- -R-- Counter    etherStatsOctets(4)
         +-- -R-- Counter    etherStatsPkts(5)
         +-- -R-- Counter    etherStatsBroadcastPkts(6)
         +-- -R-- Counter    etherStatsMulticastPkts(7)
         +-- -R-- Counter    etherStatsCRCAlignErrors(8)
         +-- -R-- Counter    etherStatsUndersizePkts(9)
         +-- -R-- Counter    etherStatsOversizePkts(10)
         +-- -R-- Counter    etherStatsFragments(11)
         +-- -R-- Counter    etherStatsJabbers(12)
```

```
+-- -R-- Counter    etherStatsCollisions(13)
+-- -R-- Counter    etherStatsPkts64Octets(14)
+-- -R-- Counter    etherStatsPkts65to127Octets(15)
+-- -R-- Counter    etherStatsPkts128to255Octets(16)
+-- -R-- Counter    etherStatsPkts256to511Octets(17)
+-- -R-- Counter    etherStatsPkts512to1023Octets(18)
+-- -R-- Counter    etherStatsPkts1024to1518Octets(19)
+-- -RW- String     etherStatsOwner(20)
|        Textual Convention: OwnerString
+-- -RW- EnumVal    etherStatsStatus(21)
         Textual Convention: EntryStatus
         Values: valid(1), createRequest(2), underCreation(3), invalid(
4)
```

You retrieve the number of Ethernet packets on each interface exactly as you might guess:

```
bsd2# snmpwalk 172.16.1.9 public rmon.1.1.1.5
rmon.statistics.etherStatsTable.etherStatsEntry.etherStatsPkts.1 = 36214
rmon.statistics.etherStatsTable.etherStatsEntry.etherStatsPkts.2 = 0
rmon.statistics.etherStatsTable.etherStatsEntry.etherStatsPkts.3 = 3994
rmon.statistics.etherStatsTable.etherStatsEntry.etherStatsPkts.4 = 242
rmon.statistics.etherStatsTable.etherStatsEntry.etherStatsPkts.5 = 284
rmon.statistics.etherStatsTable.etherStatsEntry.etherStatsPkts.6 = 292
rmon.statistics.etherStatsTable.etherStatsEntry.etherStatsPkts.7 = 314548
rmon.statistics.etherStatsTable.etherStatsEntry.etherStatsPkts.8 = 48074
rmon.statistics.etherStatsTable.etherStatsEntry.etherStatsPkts.9 = 36861
rmon.statistics.etherStatsTable.etherStatsEntry.etherStatsPkts.10 = 631831
rmon.statistics.etherStatsTable.etherStatsEntry.etherStatsPkts.11 = 104
rmon.statistics.etherStatsTable.etherStatsEntry.etherStatsPkts.12 = 457157
rmon.statistics.etherStatsTable.etherStatsEntry.etherStatsPkts.25 = 0
rmon.statistics.etherStatsTable.etherStatsEntry.etherStatsPkts.26 = 0
rmon.statistics.etherStatsTable.etherStatsEntry.etherStatsPkts.27 = 0
```

(This is data from a recently installed 12 port switch. The last three interfaces are currently unused uplink ports.)

The primary problem with RMON, as described, is that it is limited to link-level traffic. This issue is being addressed with RMON2 (RFC 2021), which adds another 10 groups. In order to collect network-level information, however, it is necessary to delve into packets. This is processing intensive, so it is unlikely that RMON2 will become common in the near future. For most purposes, the first few RMON groups should be adequate.

One final word of warning. While RMON may lessen network traffic, RMON can be CPU intensive. Make sure you aren't overloading your system when collecting RMON data. It is ironic that tools designed to analyze traffic to avoid poor performance can actually cause that performance. To make truly effective use of an RMON probe, you should consider using a commercial tool designed specifically for your equipment and goals.

Microsoft Windows

Apart from the basic text-based tools such as *netstat*, Microsoft doesn't really include many useful utilities with the consumer versions of Windows. But if you are using Windows NT or Windows 2000, you have more options. The *netmon* tool is included with the server versions. A brief description of how this tool can be used to capture traffic was included in Chapter 5. *netmon* can also be used to capture basic traffic information.

Figure 8-9 shows *netmon*'s basic capture screen. The upper-left pane shows five basic graphs for real-time traffic—network utilization, frames per second, bytes per second, broadcasts per second, and multicasts per second. The second pane on the left lists current connections between this and other hosts. The details of these connections are provided in the bottom pane. The pane on the right gives overall network statistics. To use *netmon* in this fashion, just start the program and select Capture → Start. In standalone mode, *netmon* functions as a point-monitoring tool, but as noted in Chapter 5, it can be used with agents to collect traffic throughout the network.

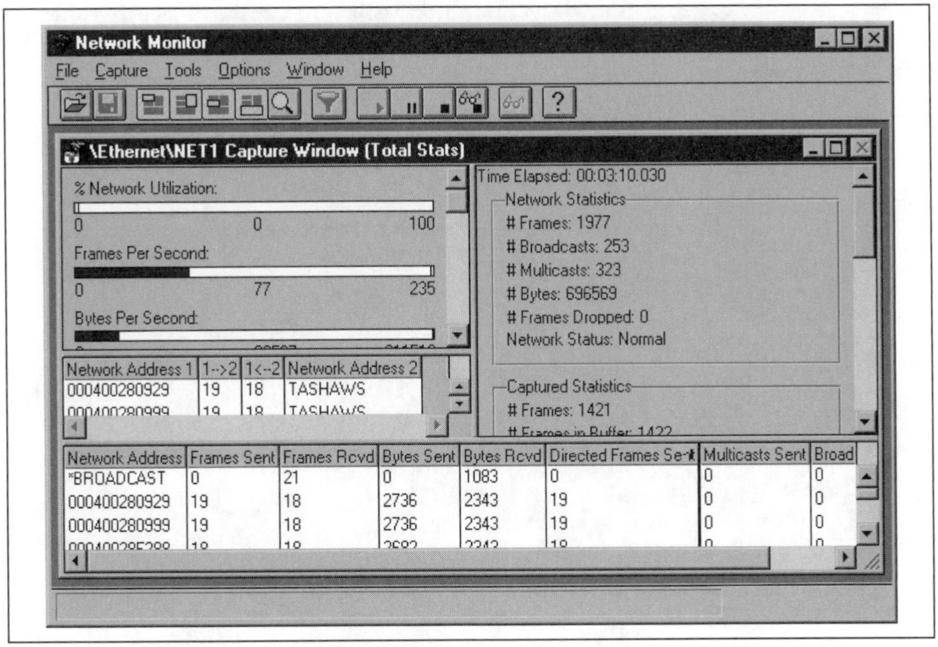

Figure 8-9. netmon traffic monitoring

For general systems monitoring, *perfmon* (Performance Monitor) is a better choice. It is also supplied with both the workstation and server versions. *perfmon* is a general performance-monitoring tool, not just a network-monitoring tool. You can use it to measure system performance (including CPU utilization) and I/O performance, as well as basic network performance. If appropriately configured, it will also monitor remote machines.

Data collected is organized by object type, e.g., groups of counters. For example, with the UDP object, there are counters for the number of datagrams sent per second, datagrams received per second, datagrams received errors, etc. For network monitoring, the most interesting objects include ICMP, IP, Network Interface, RAS Ports, RAS Total, TCP, and UDP.

perfmon provides four views—alert, chart, log, and report. With alert view you can set a threshold and be notified when a counter exceeds or drops below it. Chart view gives a real-time graph for selected counters. You can customize the sampling rate and scale. Log view logs all the counters for an object to a file periodically. Finally, report view displays numerical values in a window for selected counters. Each view is independent of the others. Figure 8-10 shows the process of adding a monitored object to the chart view for the Windows NT version.

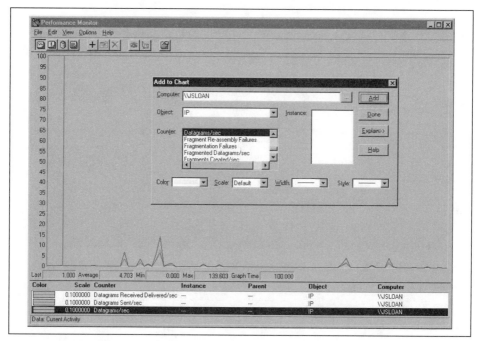

Figure 8-10. Windows NT perfmon

The Windows 2000 version has received a slight face-lift but seems to be the same basic program. *perfmon* can be particularly useful if you aren't sure whether you have a host problem or a network problem. Both *netmon* and *perfmon* are described in the Windows help files as well as several books described in Appendix B.

ntop, mrtg, and cricket on Windows

All three major packages described in this chapter—*ntop*, *mrtg*, and *cricket*—are available for Windows systems.

The developers of *ntop* have provided you with two choices. You can compile it yourself for free. Both the Unix and Windows versions share the same source tree. Or, if you can't easily compile it, you can buy a precompiled binary directly from them. Since *ntop* is basically a point-monitoring tool, you'll likely want to run it on multiple machines if you have a switched network or multiple subnetworks.

Since *mrtg* and *cricket* are primarily written in Perl, it is not surprising that they will run under Windows. You'll find *mrtg* fairly straightforward to set up. While *cricket* is said to work, at the time this was written there were no published directions on how to set it up, and the Unix directions don't generalize well.

Setting up *mrtg* for Windows is not that different from setting it up under Unix. To get *mrtg* running, you'll need to download a copy of *mrtg* with the binary for *rateup*. This was included with the copy of *mrtg* I downloaded, but the *mrtg* web page for NT has a separate link should you need it. You will need a copy of Perl along with anything else you may need to get Perl running. The *mrtg* site has links to the Active Perl site. Installing Active Perl requires an updated version of the Windows Installer, available at their site. You'll need to provide some mechanism for running *mrtg* on a regular basis. The file *fiveminute.zip* provided a program to add *mrtg* to the Windows NT scheduler. Finally, you'll want to provide some mechanism to view the output from *mrtg*. This could be a web server or, at a minimum, a web browser.

Once you have unpacked everything, you'll need to edit the *mrtg* script so that NT rather than Unix is the operating system. This amounts to commenting out the fourth line of the script and uncommenting the fifth:

```
#$main::OS = 'UNIX';
$main::OS = 'NT';
```

Also, make sure *rateup* is in the same directory as *mrtg*.

Creating the configuration file and running the script is basically the same as with the Unix version. You'll want to run *cfgmaker* and *indexmaker*. And, as with the Unix version, you'll need to edit the configuration file to set *WorkDir:*. You will need to invoke Perl explicitly and use explicit paths with these scripts. For example, here are the commands to run *indexmaker* and *mrtg* on my system:

```
D:\mrtg\run>perl d:\mrtg\run\indexmaker d:\mrtg\run\mrtg.cfg > d:\apache\htdocs\
mrtg
D:\mrtg\run>perl d:\mrtg\run\mrtg d:\mrtg\run\mrtg.cfg
```

On my system, *D:\mrtg\run* is the directory where *mrtg* is installed and *D:\apache\ htdocs\mrtg* is where the output is put so it can be accessed by the web server.

Finally, you'll need to make some provision to run *mrtg* periodically. As noted, you can use supplied code to add it to the scheduler. Alternately, you can edit the configuration file to have it run as a daemon. For example, you could add the following to your configuration file:

```
RunAsDaemon: yes
Interval: 5
```

You'll want to add *mrtg* to the startup group so that it will be run automatically each time the system is rebooted.

getif revisited

In Chapter 7, we introduced *getif* but did not discuss the graph tab. Basically, the graph tab provides for two types of graphs—graphs of ping round-trip delays and graphs of SNMP objects. The latter allows us to use *getif* as a traffic-monitoring tool.

Graphing SNMP objects is a three-step process. First, you'll need to go back to the Parameters tab and identify the remote system and set its SNMP community strings. Next, you'll need to visit the MBrowser tab and select the objects you want to graph. Locate the objects of interest by working your way down the MIB tree in the large pane on the upper left of the window. Visit the object by clicking the Walk button. The object and its value should be added to the large lower pane. Finally, select the item from the large pane and click on the Add to Graph button. (Both of these tabs were described in Chapter 7.)

You can now go to the Graph tab. Each of the selected variables should have been added to the legend to the right of the chart. You can begin collecting data by clicking on the Start button. Figure 8-11 shows one such graph.

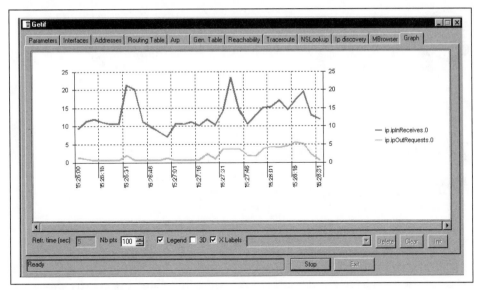

Figure 8-11. getif graph

The controls along the bottom of the page provide some control over the appearance of the chart and over the sampling rate.

9

Testing Connectivity Protocols

This chapter and the next describe tools used to investigate protocol-specific behavior. In this chapter, I describe tools used to explore connectivity protocols, protocols that work at the network and transport levels to provide connectivity. Chapter 10 focuses on tools used in testing protocols at the application level.

I begin with a description of packet generation tools. Custom packet generators, like *hping* and *nemesis*, will allow you to create custom packets to test protocols. Load generators, like *MGEN*, will let you flood your network with packets to see how your network responds to the additional traffic. We conclude with a brief discussion of network emulators and simulators.

Many of the tools described in this chapter and the next are not tools that you will need often, if ever. But should the need arise, you will want to know about them. Some of these tools are described quite briefly. My goal is to familiarize you with the tools rather than to provide a detailed introduction. Unless you have a specific need for one of these tools, you'll probably want to just skim these chapters initially. Should the need arise, you'll know the appropriate tool exists and can turn to the references for more information.

Packet Injection Tools

This first group of tools generates and injects packets into your network. Basically, there are two different purposes for generating packets, each with its own general approach and its own set of tools.

First, to test software configuration and protocols, it may be necessary to control the content of individual fields within packets. For example, customized packets can be essential to test whether a firewall is performing correctly. They can also be used to investigate problems with specific protocols or to collect information such as path MTU. They are wonderful learning tools, but using them can be a lot of work and will require a very detailed knowledge of the relevant protocols.

The second reason for generating packets is to test performance. For this purpose, you typically generate a large number of packets to see how your network or devices on the network respond to the increased load. We have already done some of this. In Chapter 4, we looked at tools that generated streams of packets to analyze link and path performance. Basically, any network benchmark will have a packet generator as a component. Typically, however, you won't have much control over this component. The tools described here give you much greater control over the number, size, and spacing of packets. Unlike custom packet generators, load generators typically won't provide much control over the contents of the packets.

These two uses are best thought of as extremes on a continuum rather than mutually exclusive categories. Some programs lie somewhere between these two extremes, providing a moderate degree of control over packet contents and the functionality to generate multiple packets. There is no one ideal tool, so you may want to become familiar with several, depending on your needs.

Custom Packets Generators

A number of different programs will construct custom packets for you. The utilities vary considerably in the amount of control you actually have. As all require a thorough understanding of the underlying protocols, none of these tools are particularly easy to use. All of the ones I am familiar with are command-line programs. This is really a plus since, if you find yourself using these programs heavily, you will want to call them from scripts.

Two programs, *hping* and *nemesis,* are briefly described here. A number of additional tools are cited at the end of this section in case these utilities don't provide the exact functionality you want or aren't easily ported to your system. Of the two, *hping* is probably the better known, but *nemesis* has features that recommend it. Neither is perfect.

Generally, once you have the idea of how to use one of these tools, learning another is simply a matter of identifying the options of interest. Most custom packet generators have a reasonable set of defaults that you can start with. Depending on what you want to do, you select the appropriate options to change just what is necessary—ideally as little as possible.

Custom packet tools have a mixed reputation. They are extremely powerful tools and, as such, can be abused. And some of their authors seem to take great pride in this potential. These are definitely tools that you should use with care. For some purposes, such as testing firewalls, they can be indispensable. Just make sure it is your firewall, and not someone else's, that you are testing.

hping

hping, or *hping2* as it is sometimes called, was written by Salvatore Sanfilippo. The documentation is a little rough at times and suggests uses that are inappropriate. Nonetheless, it is a powerful, versatile program.

When run with the default parameters, it looks a lot like *ping* and is useful for checking connectivity:

```
lnx1# hping 205.153.63.30
eth0 default routing interface selected (according to /proc)
HPING 205.153.63.30 (eth0 205.153.63.30): NO FLAGS are set, 40 headers + 0 data
bytes
46 bytes from 205.153.63.30: flags=RA seq=0 ttl=126 id=786 win=0 rtt=4.4 ms
46 bytes from 205.153.63.30: flags=RA seq=1 ttl=126 id=1554 win=0 rtt=4.5 ms
46 bytes from 205.153.63.30: flags=RA seq=2 ttl=126 id=2066 win=0 rtt=4.6 ms
46 bytes from 205.153.63.30: flags=RA seq=3 ttl=126 id=2578 win=0 rtt=5.5 ms
46 bytes from 205.153.63.30: flags=RA seq=4 ttl=126 id=3090 win=0 rtt=4.5 ms

--- 205.153.63.30 hping statistic ---
5 packets tramitted, 5 packets received, 0% packet loss
round-trip min/avg/max = 4.4/4.7/5.5 ms
```

At first glance, the output looks almost identical to *ping*'s. Actually, by default, *hping* does not send ICMP packets. It sends TCP packets to port 0. (You can change ports with the *-p* option.) Since this port is almost never used, most systems will reply with a RESET message. Consequently, *hping* will sometimes get responses from systems that block *ping*. On the other hand, it may trigger intrusion detection systems as well. If you want to mimic *ping*, you can use the *-1* argument, which specifies ICMP. Or, if you prefer, you can use *-2* to send UDP packets.

When using ICMP, this is what one of the replies from the output looks like:

```
46 bytes from 205.153.63.30: icmp_seq=0 ttl=126 id=53524 rtt=2.2 ms
```

Otherwise, the output will be almost identical to the default behavior.

If you want more information, you can use *-V* for verbose mode. Here is what a reply looks like with this option:

```
46 bytes from 172.16.2.236: flags=RA seq=0 ttl=63 id=12961 win=0 rtt=1.0 ms
          tos =         0 len =         40
          seq =         0 ack =  108515096
          sum =      a5bc urp =          0
```

There is also a debug mode if you are having problems with *hping*.

Other options that control the general behavior of *hping* include *-c* to set the number of packets to send, *-i* to set the time between packets, *-n* for numeric output (no name resolution), and *-q* for quiet output (just summary lines when done).

Another group of options allows you to control the contents of the packet header. For example, the *-a* option can be used to specify an arbitrary source address for a packet. Here is an example:

```
lnx1# hping2 -a 205.153.63.30 172.16.2.236
eth0 default routing interface selected (according to /proc)
HPING 172.16.2.236 (eth0 172.16.2.236): NO FLAGS are set, 40 headers + 0 data
bytes

--- 172.16.2.236 hping statistic ---
4 packets tramitted, 0 packets received, 100% packet loss
round-trip min/avg/max = 0.0/0.0/0.0 ms
```

In this case, the packet has been sent from a computer whose actual source address is *172.16.3.234*. The packet, however, will have *205.153.63.30* in its IP header as the source address. Of course, any reply from the destination will go back to the spoofed source address, not the actual source address. If this a valid address that belongs to someone else, they may not look kindly on your testing.

Spoofing source addresses can be useful when testing router and firewall setup, but you should do this in a controlled environment. All routers should be configured to drop any packets with invalid source addresses. That is, if a packet claims to have a source that is not on the local network or that is not from a device for which the local network should be forwarding a packet, then the source address is illegal and the packet should be dropped. By creating packets with illegal source addresses, you can test your routers to be sure they are, in fact, dropping these packets. Of course, you need to use a tool like *ethereal* or *tcpdump* to see what is getting through and what is blocked.[*]

The source port can be changed with the *-s* option. The TTL field can be set with the *-t* option. There are options to set the various TCP flags: *-A* for ACK, *-F* for FIN, *-P* for PUSH, *-R* for RST, *-S* for SYN, and *-U* for URG. Oddly, although you can set the urgent flag, there doesn't seem to be a way to set the urgent pointer. You can set the packet size with the *-d* option, set the TCP header length with the *-O* option, and read the packet's data from a file with the *-E* option. Here is an example of sending a DNS packet using data in the file *data.dns*:

```
bsd2# hping -2 -p 53 -E data.dns -d 31 205.153.63.30
```

hping generated an error on my system with this command, but the packet was sent correctly.

---

[*] If this is all you are testing, you may prefer to use a specialized tool like *egressor*.

Be warned, constructing a usable data file is nontrivial. Here is a crude C program that will construct the data needed for this DNS example:

```
#include <stdio.h>
main()
{
FILE *fp;

fp=fopen("data.dns", "w");
fprintf(fp, "%c%c%c%c", 0x00, 0x01, 0x01, 0x00);
fprintf(fp, "%c%c%c%c", 0x00, 0x01, 0x00, 0x00);
fprintf(fp, "%c%c%c%c", 0x00, 0x00, 0x00, 0x00);
fprintf(fp, "%c%s", 0x03, "www");
fprintf(fp, "%c%s", 0x05, "cisco");
fprintf(fp, "%c%s%c", 0x03, "com", 0x00);
fprintf(fp, "%c%c%c%c", 0x00, 0x01, 0x00, 0x01);
fclose(fp);
}
```

Even if you don't use C, it should be fairly clear how this works. The *fopen* command creates the file, and the *fprintf* commands write out the data. *%c* and *%s* are used to identify the datatype when formatting the output. The remaining arguments are the actual values for the data. (I'm sure there are cleaner ways to create this data, but this will work.)

Finally, *hping* can also be put in dump mode so that the contents of the reply packets are displayed in hex:

```
bsd2# hping -c 1 -j 172.16.2.230
HPING 172.16.2.230 (ep0 172.16.2.230): NO FLAGS are set, 40 headers + 0 data
bytes
46 bytes from 172.16.2.230: flags=RA seq=0 ttl=128 id=60017 win=0 rtt=2.1 ms
              0060 9706 2222 0060 088f 5f0e 0800 4500
              0028 ea71 0000 8006 f26b ac10 02e6 ac10
              02ec 0000 0a88 0000 0000 1f41 a761 5014
              0000 80b3 0000 0000 0000 0000


--- 172.16.2.230 hping statistic ---
1 packets transmitted, 1 packets received, 0% packet loss
round-trip min/avg/max = 2.1/2.1/2.1 ms
```

Numerous other options are described in *hping*'s documentation. You can get a very handy summary of options if you run *hping* with the *-h* option. I strongly recommend you print this to use while you are learning the program.

nemesis

nemesis, whose author is identified only as Obecian in the documentation, is actually a family of closely related command-line tools designed to generate packets. They are *nemesis-arp*, *nemesis-dns*, *nemesis-icmp*, *nemesis-igmp*, *nemesis-ospf*, *nemesis-rip*, *nemesis-tcp*, and *nemesis-udp*. Each, as you might guess, is designed to construct and send a particular type of packet. The inclusion of support for protocols like OSPF or IGMP really sets *nemesis* apart from similar tools.

Here is an example that sends a TCP packet:

```
bsd2# nemesis-tcp -v -D 205.153.63.30 -S 205.153.60.236

TCP Packet Injection -=- The NEMESIS Project 1.1
(c) 1999, 2000 obecian <obecian@celerity.bartoli.org>

205.153.63.30
[IP]   205.153.60.236 > [Ports] 42069 > 23
[Flags]
[TCP Urgent Pointer] 2048
[Window Size] 512
[IP ID] 0
[IP TTL] 254
[IP TOS] 0x18
[IP Frag] 0x4000
[IP Options]
Wrote 40 bytes

TCP Packet Injected
```

The *-v* option is for verbose mode. Without this option, the program sends the packet but displays nothing on the screen. Use this option to test your commands and then omit it when you embed the commands in scripts. The *-S* and *-D* options give the source and destination addresses. You can use the *-x* and *-y* to set source and destination ports. If you want to specify flags, you can use the *-f* option. For example, if you add *-fS -fA* to the command line, the SYN and ACK flags will be set. (Many firewalls will block packets with some combinations of SYN and ACK flags but will pass packets with different combinations. Being able to set the SYN and ACK flags can be useful in testing these firewalls.)

Here is an example setting the SYN and ACK flags and the destination port:

```
bsd2# nemesis-tcp -S 172.16.2.236 -D 205.153.63.30 -fS -fA -y 22
```

Notice the program performs silently without the *-v* option. A number of additional options are described in the Unix manpages.

The other programs in the *nemesis* suite work pretty much the same way. Here is an example for sending an ICMP ECHO REQUEST:

```
bsd2# nemesis-icmp -v -S 172.16.2.236 -D 205.153.63.30 -i 8

ICMP Packet Injection -=- The NEMESIS Project 1.1
(c) 1999, 2000 obecian <obecian@celerity.bartoli.org>

[IP]   172.16.2.236 > 205.153.63.30
[Type] ECHO REQUEST
[Sequence number] 0
```

```
[IP ID] 0
[IP TTL] 254
[IP TOS] 0x18
[IP Frag] 0x4000

Wrote 48 bytes

ICMP Packet Injected
```

The *-i* option specifies the type field in the ICMP header. In this case, the *8* is the code for an ECHO_REQUEST message. The destination should respond with an ECHO_REPLY.

The *-P* option can be used to read the data for the packet from a file. For example, here is the syntax to send a DNS query.

```
bsd2# nemesis-dns -v -S 172.16.2.236 -D 205.153.63.30 -q 1 -P data.dns

DNS Packet Injection -=- The NEMESIS Project 1.1
(c) 1999, 2000 obecian <obecian@celerity.bartoli.org>

[IP]   172.16.2.236 > 205.153.63.30
[Ports] 42069 > 53

[# Questions] 1
[# Answer RRs] 0
[# Authority RRs] 0
[# Additional RRs] 0


[IP ID] 420
[IP TTL] 254
[IP TOS] 0x18
[IP Frag] 0x4000
[IP Options]

00 01 01 00 00 01 00 00 00 00 00 00 03 77 77 .............ww
77 05 63 69 73 63 6F 03 63 6F 6D 00 00 01 00 w.cisco.com....
01                                           .

Wrote 40 bytes

DNS Packet Injected
```

Although it appears the data has been sent correctly, I have seen examples when the packets were not correctly sent despite appearances. So, be warned! It is always a good idea to check the output of a packet generator with a packet sniffer just to make sure you are getting what you expect.

Other tools

There are a number of other choices. *ipfilter* is a suite of programs for creating firewalls. Supplied with some operating systems, including FreeBSD, *ipfilter* has been ported to a number of other platforms. One of the tools *ipfilter* includes is *ipsend*. Designed for testing firewalls, *ipsend* is yet another tool to construct packets. Here is an example:

```
bsd2# ipsend -v -i ep0 -g 172.16.2.1 -d 205.153.63.30
Device:  ep0
Source:  172.16.2.236
Dest:    205.153.63.30
Gateway: 172.16.2.1
mtu:     1500
```

ipsend is not the most versatile of tools, but depending on what system you are using, you may already have it installed.

Yet another program worth considering is *sock*. *sock* is described in the first volume of Richard W. Stevens' *TCP/Illustrated* and is freely downloadable. While *sock* doesn't give the range of control some of these other programs give, it is a nice pedagogical tool for learning about TCP/IP. Beware, there are other totally unrelated programs called *sock*.

Finally, some sniffers and analyzers support the capture and retransmission of packets. Look at the documentation for the sniffer you are using, particularly if it is a commercial product. If you decide to use this feature, proceed with care. Retransmission of traffic, if used indiscriminately, can create some severe problems.

Load Generators

When compared to custom packet generators, load generators are at the opposite extreme of the continuum for packet injectors. These are programs that generate traffic to stress-test a network or devices on a network. These tools can help you judge the performance of your network or diagnose problems. They can also produce a considerable strain on your network. You should use these tools to test systems offline, perhaps in a testing laboratory prior to deployment or during scheduled downtime. Extreme care should be taken before using these tools on a production network. Unless you are absolutely convinced that what you are doing is safe and reasonable, don't use these tools on production networks.

Almost any application can be used to generate traffic. A few tools, such as *ping* and *ttcp*, are particularly easy to use for this purpose. For example, by starting multiple *ping* sessions in the background, by varying the period between packets with the *-i* option, and by varying the packet sizes with the *-s* option, you can easily generate a wide range of traffic loads. Unfortunately, this won't generate the type of traffic you may need for some types of tests. Two tools, *spray* and *mgen*, are described here. The better known of these is probably *spray*. (It was introduced in Chapter 4.) It is also frequently included with systems so you may already have a copy. *mgen* is one of the most versatile.

socket and netcat

While they don't fit cleanly into this or the next category, *netcat* (or *nc*) and Juergen Nickelsen's *socket* are worth mentioning. (The *netcat* documentation identifies only the author as Hobbit.) Both are programs that can be used to establish a connection between two machines. They are useful for debugging, moving files, and exploring and learning about TCP/IP. Both can be used from scripts.

You'll need to start one copy as a server (in listen mode) on one computer:

```
bsd1# nc -l -p 2000
```

Then start another as a client on a second computer:

```
bsd2# nc 172.16.2.231 2000
```

Here is the equivalent command for *socket* as a server:

```
bsd1# socket -s 2000
```

Here is the equivalent command for a client:

```
bsd2# socket 172.16.2.231 2000
```

In all examples 2000 is an arbitrarily selected port number.

Here is a simple example using *nc* to copy a file from one system to another. The server is opened with output redirected to a file:

```
bsd1# nc -l -p 2000 > tmp
```

Then the file is piped to the client:

```
bsd2# cat README | nc 172.16.2.231 2000
^C punt!
```

Finally, *nc* is terminated with a Ctrl-C. The contents of *README* on *bsd1* have been copied to the file *tmp* on *bsd2*. These programs can be cleaner than *telnet* in some testing situations since, unlike *telnet*, they don't attempt any session negotiations when started. Play with them, and you are sure to find a number of other uses.

spray

spray is useful in getting a rough idea of a computer's network performance, particularly its interface. *spray*, on the local computer, communicates with the *rpc. sprayd* daemon on the remote system being tested. (You'll need to make sure this is running on the remote system.) It effectively floods the remote system with a large number of fixed-length UDP packets. The remote daemon, generally started by *inetd*, receives and counts these packets. The local copy of *spray* queries the remote daemon to determine the number of packets that were successfully received. By comparing the number of packets sent to the number received, *spray* can calculate the number of packets lost.

Here is an example of *spray* using default values:

```
bsd2# spray sol1
sending 1162 packets of lnth 86 to 172.16.2.233 ...
        in 0.12 seconds elapsed time
        191 packets (16.44%) dropped
Sent:   9581 packets/sec, 804.7K bytes/sec
Rcvd:   8006 packets/sec, 672.4K bytes/sec
```

Command-line options allow you to set the number of packets sent (*-c*), the length of the packets sent (*-l*), and a delay between packets in microseconds (*-d*).

You should not be alarmed that packets are being dropped. The idea is to send packets as fast as possible so that the interface will be stressed and packets will be lost. *spray* is most useful in comparing the performance of two machines. For example, you might want to see if your server can keep up with your clients. To test this, you'll want to use *spray* to send packets from the client to the server. If the number of packets dropped is about the same, the machines are fairly evenly matched. If a client is able to overwhelm a server, then you may have a potential problem.

In the previous example, *spray* was run on *bsd2*, flooding *sol1*. Here are the results of running *spray* on *sol1*, flooding *bsd2*:

```
sol1# spray bsd2
sending 1162 packets of length 86 to 172.16.2.236 ...
        610 packets (52.496%) dropped by 172.16.2.236
        36 packets/sec, 3144 bytes/sec
```

Clearly, *sol1* is faster than *bsd2* since *bsd2* is dropping a much larger percentage of packets.

Unfortunately, while *spray* can alert you to a problem, it is unable to differentiate among the various reasons why a packet was lost—collision, slow interface, lack of buffer space, and so on. The obvious things to look at are the speed of the computer and its interfaces.

MGEN

The Multi-Generator Toolset or MGEN is actually a collection of tools for generating traffic, receiving traffic, and analyzing results. The work of Brian Adamson at the Naval Research Laboratory, this sophisticated set of tools will give you a high degree of control over the shape of the traffic you generate. However, you aren't given much control over the actual UDP packets the utility sends—that's not the intent of the tool. For its intended uses, however, you have all the control you are likely to need.

The traffic generation tool is *mgen*. It can be run in command-line mode or by using the *-g* option in graphical mode. At its simplest, it can be used with command-line options to generate traffic. Here is a simple example:

```
bsd2# mgen -i ep0 -b 205.153.63.30:2000 -r 10 -s 64 -d 5

MGEN: Version 3.1a3
MGEN: Loading event queue ...
MGEN: Seeding random number generator ...
MGEN: Beginning packet generation ...
      (Hit <CTRL-C> to stop)Trying to set IP_TOS = 0x0
MGEN: Packets Tx'd       :       50
MGEN: Transmission period:     5.018 seconds.
MGEN: Ave Tx pkt rate     :     9.964 pps.
MGEN: Interface Stats     :       ep0
              Frames Tx'd :       55
                Tx Errors :        0
               Collisions :        0
MGEN: Done.
```

In this case, 10 packets per second for 5 seconds yields 50 packets.

Other options for *mgen* include setting the interface (*-i*), the destination address and port (*-b*), the packet rate (*-r*), the packet size (*-s*), and the duration of the flow in seconds (*-d*). There are a number of other options described in the documentation, such as the type of service and TTL fields.

The real strength of *mgen* comes when you use it with a script. Here is a very simple example of a script called *demo*:

```
START NOW
00001 1 ON 205.153.63.30:5000 PERIODIC 5 64
05000 1 MOD 205.153.63.30:5000 POISSON 20 64
15000 1 OFF
```

The first line tells *mgen* to start generating traffic as soon as the program is started. (An absolute start time can also be specified.) The second line creates a flow with an ID of 1 that starts 1 millisecond into a run that has port 5000 on *205.153.63.30* as its destination. The traffic is 5 packets per second, and each packet is 64 bytes in length. The third line tells *mgen* to modify the flow with ID 1. 5000 milliseconds (or 5 seconds) into the flow, packet generation should switch to a Poission distribution with a rate of 20 packets per second. The last line terminates the flow at 15,000 milliseconds. While this script has only one flow, a script can contain many.

Here is an example of the invocation of *mgen* with a script:

```
bsd2# mgen -i ep0 demo

MGEN: Version 3.1a3
MGEN: Loading event queue ...
```

```
MGEN: Seeding random number generator ...
MGEN: Beginning packet generation ...
MGEN: Packets Tx'd       :      226
MGEN: Transmission period:    15.047 seconds.
MGEN: Ave Tx pkt rate     :    15.019 pps.
MGEN: Interface Stats     :       ep0
              Frames Tx'd :      234
                Tx Errors :        0
                Collisions :       0
MGEN: Done.
```

Since a Poisson distribution was used for part of the flow, we can't expect to see exactly 225 packets in exactly 15 seconds.

For many purposes, *mgen* is the only tool from the MGEN tool set that you will need. But for some purposes, you will need more. *drec* is a receiver program that can log received data. *mgen* and *drec* can be used with RSVP (with ISI's *rsvpd*). You will recall that with RSVP, the client must establish the session. *drec* has this capability. Like *mgen*, *drec* has an optional graphical interface. In addition to *mgen* and *drec*, the MGEN tool set includes a number of additional utilities that can be used to analyze the data collected by *drec*.

One last note on load generators—software load generators assume that the systems they run on are fast enough to generate enough traffic to adequately load the system being tested. In some circumstances, this will not be true. For some applications, dedicated hardware load generators must be used.

Network Emulators and Simulators

Basically, an emulator is a device that sits on a network and mimics the behavior of network devices or the behavior of part of a system, e.g., subnets. Actual traffic measurements are made on a network whose behavior is controlled, in part, by the emulator. Simulators are software systems that model with software the behavior of the system or networks. A simulator is a totally artificial or synthetic environment.

At best, network emulators and simulators are very unlikely troubleshooting tools. But for the extremely ambitious (or desperate), it is possible to investigate the behavior of a network using these tools. Neither of these approaches is for the fainthearted or novice. Generally an expensive and complex proposition, there are two projects that are making these approaches more accessible. If you are really interested in making the investment in time and effort needed to use emulators or simulators, read on.

There is a continuum of approaches to investigating the behavior of a network, ranging from direct measurement at one extreme through emulation to simulation at the opposite extreme. It's not unusual for emulators to provide limited simulation features or for simulators to have emulation features. This is certainly true for the two tools briefly described here.

We have already discussed measurement techniques. But while real measurements have an unquestionable authenticity, a number of problems are associated with real measurements. Lack of reproducibility is one problem. Scale problems, such as the cost of increasing the size of the test network, are another concern. If you are considering implementation issues, then direct measurement can only be done late in the development cycle, compounding the cost of mistakes. Emulation and simulation offer lower-cost alternatives.

Simulators have the advantages of being relatively cheap, providing highly reproducible results, scaling very well and inexpensively, and giving results quickly. It is generally very straightforward to customize the degree of detail in reports so you can focus on just what is of interest. Simulations vary in degree of abstraction. The greater the degree of abstraction, the easier it is to focus on what is of interest at the cost of lost realism. However, if a simulation is poorly designed, the results can have little basis in reality. Also, some simulators may be implemented primarily for one type of use and may not be appropriate for other uses. From a troubleshooting perspective, you might use a simulator to further investigate a hypothesis. Simulators would provide a way to closely examine behavior to confirm or refute the hypothesis without creating problems on a production network.

Emulators lie between simulators and live systems. They allow controlled experiments with a high degree of reproducibility. They make it much easier to create the type of traffic or events of interest. They also provide a mechanism to test real systems effectively. For example, an emulator might duplicate or approximate the behavior of an attached device or network. A router emulator might drop traffic or inject traffic into the actual test network. On the downside, some emulators tend to be very specialized and are usually platform specific. For troubleshooting, an emulator could be used to stress a network.

NISTNet

NIST Network Emulation Tool (*NISTNet*) is a general purpose tool that can be used to emulate the dynamics in an IP network. It was developed by the National Institute of Standards and Technology (NIST) and is implemented as an extension to the Linux operating system through a kernel module. Unlike many emulators, *NISTNet* supports a fairly heterogeneous approach to emulation. And since it will run on a fairly standard platform, it is remarkably inexpensive to set up and use.

NISTNet allows you to use a Linux system configured as a router, through an X Window interface, to model or emulate a number of different scenarios. For example, you can program both fixed and variable packet delays and random reordering of packets. Packets can be dropped either randomly (uniform distribution) or based on congestion.* Random duplication of packets, bandwidth limitations, or asymmetric bandwidth can all be programmed into *NISTNet*. You can also program in jitter and do basic quality-of-service measurements. *NISTNet* can be driven by traces from measurements from existing networks. User-defined packet handlers can be added to the system to add timestamps, do data collection, generate responses for emulated clients, and so forth.

ns and nam

If you want to consider simulations, you should first look into a pair of programs, *ns* and *nam*. *ns* is a network simulator, while *nam* is a network visualization tool. Both are under development by the Virtual InterNetwork Testbed (VINT) project, a DARPA-funded research project whose goal is to produce a simulator for studying scale and protocol interactions. VINT is a collaborative project that involves USC, Xerox PARC, LBNL, and UCB.

ns is derived from earlier simulation projects such as REAL and has gone through a couple of incarnations. The kernel is written in C++, while user scripts are written in MIT's Object Tool Command Language (OTCL), an object-oriented version of *Tcl*. With any simulation software, you should expect a steep learning curve, and *ns* is no exception. You'll need to learn how to use the product, and you will also need a broad knowledge of simulations in general. To use *ns*, you'll need to learn how to write scripts in OTCL.

Fortunately, the *ns* project provides a wealth of documentation. The Unix manpage is more than 30 pages and displays the typical unreadable terseness associated with Unix manual pages—great for looking up something you already know (arguably the intended use) but abysmal for learning something new. There is also a downloadable manual that runs more than 300 pages. However, the best place to start is with Marc Greis's tutorial. It is a more manageable 50 pages and introduces the scripting language in a series of readable examples.

One problem with simulations is that they can produce an overwhelming amount of information. Even worse, simulation results describe dynamic events that are difficult to interpret when viewed statically. *nam* is a visualization tool that animates network simulations. It is hard to convey the real flavor of *nam* from a single black-and-white snapshot, but Figure 9-1 should give you some idea of its value.

This is output from one of the sample scripts that comes with the program. The basic topology of the network should be obvious. Packets are drawn as colored rectangles. Different colors are used for different sources. As the animation is played,

---

* Gateway emulators that support this kind of behavior are sometimes less charitably called *flakeways*.

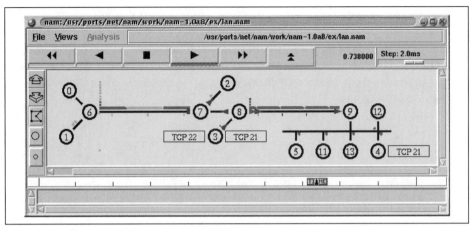

Figure 9-1. nam example

you see the packets generated, queued at devices, move across the network, and occasionally, dropped from the network. Node 6 in the figure shows a stack of packets that have been queued and one packet below the node that has been dropped. (Dropped packets fall to the bottom of the screen.) The control buttons at the top are used just as you would expect—to play, stop, or rewind the animation.

NISTNet, ns, and *nam* are all described as ongoing projects. But all three are more polished than many completed projects.

Microsoft Windows

Few of the tools described in this chapter are available for Windows. Those that are available include some of the more ambitious tools, however. In particular, *ns* and *nam* have downloadable binaries for Windows. According to the *mgen* documentation, a Windows "version may appear shortly." (*netcat* has also been ported to Windows.)

If you are interested in traffic generation for loading purposes, you might look to *ipload.* This is a very simple program that will flood a remote device with UDP packets. You can specify the destination address, destination port, packet rate, and packet payload. As the program runs, it will display a window with the elapsed time, the number of packets sent, the packet rate, and the number of bytes per second. *ipload* comes from BTT Software in the U.K. and requires no installation.

Several network-oriented benchmark programs available for Windows might also be of interest. In particular, you may want to look at *NetBench,* which can be downloaded from Ziff Davis's web site, *http://www.zdnet.com/etestinglabs/filters/benchmarks.* It is designed to test client/server performance. You'll need to download both client and server versions of the software.

10

Application-Level Tools

This chapter briefly surveys some additional tools that might be of interest. You will not need tools that are useful when setting up and debugging programs using application-level protocols. The chapter is organized around different application protocols. You will not need the tools described here often. The goal of this chapter is to make you aware of what is available should the need arise, and the approach described here may be more useful than the specific tools mentioned. Unless you have a specific problem, you'll probably want to just skim this chapter the first time through.

Application-Protocols Tools

Many network applications are built upon application-level protocols rather than being built directly upon network- or transport-level protocols. For example, email readers typically use SMTP to send email and POP2, POP3, or IMAP to receive email. For some applications, it is difficult to distinguish the application from the underlying protocol. NFS is a prime example. But when an implementation separates the application from its underlying protocol, a number of advantages can be realized. First, the separation helps to ensure interoperability. A client developed on one platform can communicate effectively with server software running on a different system. For example, your web browser can communicate with any web server because it uses a standardized protocol—HTTP. Tools based on the underlying protocol can be used to obtain basic information regardless of the specific application being used.

Most of the tools described in this chapter collect information at the protocol level. While it is unlikely that any of these tools will provide the detailed information you would want for a problem with a specific application, they should help you identify where the problem lies and will help if the problem is with the protocol. Most applications will have their own approaches to solving problems, e.g., debug modes, and log files. But you'll want to be sure the problem is with the application before you start with these. If the problem is with the application, you'll need to consult the specific documentation for the application.

If you are having trouble setting up a network application for the first time, you are probably better off rereading the documentation than investing time learning a new tool. But if you've read the directions three or four times in several different books or if you have used an application many times and it has suddenly stopped working, then it's probably time to look at tools. For many of the protocols, you'll have a number of choices. You won't need every tool, so pick the most appropriate, convenient tool and start there.

Providing a detailed description of all available tools is beyond the scope of any reasonable book. This would require both a detailed review of the protocol as well as a description of the tool. For example, Hal Stern's 400-page book, *Managing NFS and NIS*, has three chapters totaling about 125 pages on tools, debugging, and tuning NIS and NFS. What I'm trying to do here is provide you with enough information to get started and handle simple problems. If you need more information, you should consider looking at one of the many books, like Stern's, devoted to the specific protocol in question. A number of such books are described in Appendix B.

Generally, these applications are based on a client/server model. The approach you'll take in debugging a client may be different from that used to debug a server. The first step, in general, is to decide if the problem is with the client application, the server application, or the underlying protocols. If any client on any machine can connect to a server, the server and protocols are probably operating correctly. So when communications fail, the first thing you may want to try is a different client program or a similar client on a different computer. With many protocols, you don't even need a client program. Many protocols are based on the exchange of commands in NVT ASCII* over a TCP connection. You can interact with these servers using any program that can open a TCP connection using NVT ASCII. Examples include *telnet* and *netcat*.

Email

Email protocols such as SMTP, POP2, and POP3 are perfect examples of protocols where *telnet* is the optimal tool to begin with. Here is an example using *telnet* to

---

* Network Virtual Terminal (NVT) ASCII is a 7-bit U.S. variant of the common ASCII character code. It is used throughout the TCP/IP protocol. It uses 7 bits to encode a character that is transmitted as an 8-bit byte with the high-order bit set to 0.

send a brief message via SMTP. (Depending on your system, you may need to enable local echoing so that what you type will be visible.)

```
bsd2# telnet mail.lander.edu 25
Trying 205.153.62.5...
Connected to mail.lander.edu.
Escape character is '^]'.
220 mail.lander.edu ESMTP Sendmail 8.9.3/8.9.3; Wed, 22 Nov 2000 13:22:15 -0500
helo 205.153.60.236
250 mail.lander.edu Hello [205.153.60.236], pleased to meet you
mail from:<jsloan@205.153.60.236>
250 <jsloan@205.153.60.236>... Sender ok
rcpt to:<jsloan@lander.edu>
250 jsloan@lander.edu... Recipient ok
data
354 Enter mail, end with "." on a line by itself
This is the body of a message.
.
250 NAA28089 Message accepted for delivery
quit
221 mail.lander.edu closing connection
Connection closed by foreign host.
```

The process is very simple. *telnet* is used to connect to port 25, the SMTP port, on the email server in question. The next four lines were returned by the server. At this point, we can see that the server is up and that we are able to communicate with it. To send email, use the commands *helo* to identify yourself, *mail from:* to specify the email source, and *rcpt to:* to specify the destination. Use names, not IP addresses, to specify the destination. Notice that no password is required to send email. (The server is responding with the lines starting with numbers or codes.) The *data* command was used to signal the start of the body of the message. The body is one line long here but can be as long as you like. When you are done entering the body, it is terminated with a new line that has a single period on it. The session was terminated with the *quit* command. Clearly the server is up and can be reached in this example. Any problems you may be having must be with your email client.

As noted, you had a pretty good idea the server was working as soon as it replied and could have quit at this point. There are a couple of reasons for going through the process of sending a message. First, it gives a nice warm feeling seeing that everything is truly working. More important, it confirms that the recipient is known to the server. For example, consider the following:

```
rcpt to:<jsloane@lander.edu>
550 <jsloane@lander.edu>... User unknown
```

This reply lets us know that the user is unknown to the system. If you have doubts about a recipient, you can use the *vrfy* and *expand* commands. The *vrfy* command will confirm the recipient address is valid, as shown in the following example:

```
vrfy jsloan
250 Joseph Sloan <jsloan@mail.lander.edu>
vrfy freddy
550 freddy... User unknown
```

expn fully expands an alias, giving a list of all the recipients named in the alias. Be warned, *expn* and *vrfy* are often seen as security holes and may be disabled. (Prudence would dictate using *vrfy* and *expn* only on your own systems.) There are other commands, but these are enough to verify that the server is available.

Another reason for sending the email is that it gives you something to retrieve, the next step in testing your email connection. The process of retrieving email with *telnet* is similar, although the commands will vary with the specific protocol being used. Here is an example using a POP3 server:

```
bsd2# telnet mail.lander.edu 110
Trying 205.153.62.5...
Connected to mail.lander.edu.
Escape character is '^]'.
+OK POP3 mail.lander.edu v7.59 server ready
user jsloan
+OK User name accepted, password please
pass xyzzy
+OK Mailbox open, 1 messages
retr 1
+OK 347 octets
Return-Path: <jsloan@205.153.60.236>
Received: from 205.153.60.236 ([205.153.60.236])
        by mail.lander.edu (8.9.3/8.9.3) with SMTP id NAA28089;
        Wed, 22 Nov 2000 13:23:14 -0500
Date: Wed, 22 Nov 2000 13:23:14 -0500
From: jsloan@205.153.60.236
Message-Id: <200011221823.NAA28089@mail.lander.edu>
Status:

This is the body of a message.
.
dele 1
+OK Message deleted
quit
+OK Sayonara
Connection closed by foreign host.
```

As you can see, *telnet* is used to connect to port 110, the POP3 port. As soon as the first message comes back, you know the server is up and reachable. Next, you identify yourself using the *user* and *pass* commands. This is a quick way to make sure that the account exists and you have the right password. Often, email readers give cryptic error messages when you use a bad account or password. The system has informed us that there is one message waiting for this user. Next, retrieve that message with the *retr* command. The argument is the message number. This is the message we just sent. Delete the message and log off with the *dele* and *quit* commands, respectively. (As an aside, sometimes mail clients will hang with overlarge attachments. You can use the *dele* command to delete the offending message.)

Of course, this is how a system running POP3 or SMTP is supposed to work. If it works this way, any subsequent problems are probably with the client, and you need to turn to the client documentation. You can confirm this with packet capture software. If your system doesn't work properly, the problem could be with the server software or with communications. You might try logging onto the server and verifying that the appropriate software is listening, using *ps*, or, if it is started by *inetd*, using *netstat*. Or you might try using *telnet* to connect to the server directly from the server, i.e., `telnet localhost 25`. If this succeeds, you may have routing problems, name service problems, or firewall problems. If it fails, then look to the documentation for the software you are using on the server.

The commands used by most email protocols are described in the relevant RFCs. For SMTP, see RFC 821; for POP2, see RFC 937; for POP3, see REF 1939; and for IMAP, see RFC 1176.

HTTP

HTTP is another protocol that is based on commands in NVT ASCII sent over a TCP session. It can be fairly complicated to figure out the correct syntax, but even an error message will tell you that the server is running and the connection works. Try typing `HEAD / HTTP / 1.0` followed by two carriages returns. Here is an example:

```
bsd2# telnet localhost http
Trying 127.0.0.1...
Connected to localhost.lander.edu.
Escape character is '^]'.
HEAD / HTTP / 1.0

HTTP/1.1 200 OK
Date: Sun, 22 Apr 2001 13:27:32 GMT
Server: Apache/1.3.12 (Unix)
Content-Location: index.html.en
Vary: negotiate,accept-language,accept-charset
TCN: choice
Last-Modified: Tue, 29 Aug 2000 09:14:16 GMT
ETag: "a4cd3-55a-39ab7ee8;3a4a1b39"
Accept-Ranges: bytes
Content-Length: 1370
Connection: close
Content-Type: text/html
Content-Language: en
```

```
Expires: Sun, 22 Apr 2001 13:27:32 GMT
```

```
Connection closed by foreign host.
```

In this example, I've checked to see if the server is responding from the server itself. In general, however, using *telnet* is probably not worth the effort since it is usually very easy to find a working web browser that you can use somewhere on your network.

Most web problems, in my experience, stem from incorrectly configured security files or are performance problems. For security configuration problems, you'll need to consult the appropriate documentation for your software. For a quick performance profile of your server, you might visit Patrick Killelea's web site, *http://patrick.net*. If you have problems, you probably want to look at his book, *Web Performance Tuning*.

FTP and TFTP

FTP is another protocol that uses NVT ASCII and can be checked, to a very limited extent, with *telnet*. Here is a quick check to see if the server is up and can be reached:

```
lnx1# telnet bsd2 ftp
Trying 172.16.2.236...
Connected to bsd2.lander.edu.
Escape character is '^]'.
220 bsd2.lander.edu FTP server (Version 6.00LS) ready.
user jsloan
331 Password required for jsloan.
pass xyzzy
230 User jsloan logged in.
stat
211- bsd2.lander.edu FTP server status:
    Version 6.00LS
    Connected to 172.16.3.234
    Logged in as jsloan
    TYPE: ASCII, FORM: Nonprint; STRUcture: File; transfer MODE: Stream
    No data connection
211 End of status
quit
221 Goodbye.
Connection closed by foreign host.
```

Once you know the server is up, you'll want to switch over to a real FTP client. Because FTP opens a reverse connection when transferring information, you are limited with what you can do with *telnet*. Fortunately, this is enough to verify that the server is up, communication works, and you can successfully log on to the server.

Unlike FTP, TFTP is UDP based. Consequently, TCP-based tools like *telnet* are not appropriate. You'll want to use a TFTP client to test for connectivity. Fortunately, TFTP is a simple protocol and usually works well.

Name Services

Since name resolution is based primarily on UDP, you won't be able to debug it with *telnet.* Name resolution can be a real pain since problems are most likely to show up when you are using other programs or services. Name service applications are applications that you'll want to be sure are working on your system. For clients, it is one of the easiest protocols to test. For servers, however, ferreting out that last error can be a real chore. Fortunately, there are a number of readily available tools, particularly for DNS.

If you suspect name resolution is not working on a client, try using *ping,* alternating between hostnames and IP addresses. If you are consistently able to reach remote hosts with IP addresses but not with names, then you are having a problem with name resolution. If you have a problem with name resolution on the client side, start by reviewing the configuration files. It is probably easiest to start with */etc/hosts* and then look at DNS. Leave NIS until last.

nslookup and dig

There are several tools, such as *nslookup, dig, dnsquery,* and *host,* that are used to query DNS servers. These are most commonly used to retrieve basic domain information such as what name goes with what IP address, aliases, or how a domain is organized. With this information, you can map out a network, for example, at least to the extent the DNS entries reflect the structure of the network. When troubleshooting on the client side, it can be used to ensure the client can reach the appropriate DNS server. The real value for troubleshooting, however, is being able to examine the information returned by servers. This allows you to check this information for consistency, correctness, and completeness.

For most purposes, there is not much difference among these programs. Your choice will largely be a matter of personal preference. However, you should be aware that some other programs may be built on top of *dig,* so be sure to keep it around even if you prefer one of the other tools.

Of these, *nslookup,* written by Andrew Cherenson, is the most ubiquitous and the most likely to be installed by default. It is even available under Windows. It can be used either in command-line mode or interactively. In command-line mode, you use the name or IP address of interest as an argument:

```
sol1# nslookup 205.153.60.20
Server:  lab.lander.edu
```

```
Address:  205.153.60.5

Name:    ntp.lander.edu
Address:  205.153.60.20

bsd2# nslookup www.lander.edu
Server:  lab.lander.edu
Address:  205.153.60.5

Name:    web.lander.edu
Address:  205.153.60.15
Aliases:  www.lander.edu
```

As you can see, it returns both the name and IP address of the host in question, the identity of the server supplying the information, and, in the second example, that the queried name is an alias. You can specify the server you want to use as well as other options on the command line. You should be aware, however, that it is not unusual for reverse lookups to fail, usually because the DNS database is incomplete.

Earlier versions of *nslookup* required a special format for finding the names associated with IP addresses. For example, to look up the name associated with *205. 153.60.20*, you would have used the command `nslookup 20.60.153.205.in-addr.arpa`. Fortunately, unless you are using a very old version of *nslookup*, you won't need to bother with this.

While command-line mode is adequate for an occasional quick query, if you want more information, you'll probably want to use *nslookup* in interactive mode. If you know the right combination of options, you could use command-line options. But if you are not sure, it is easier to experiment step-by-step in interactive mode.

Interactive mode is started by typing `nslookup` without any arguments:

```
sol1# nslookup
Default Server:  lab.lander.edu
Address:  205.153.60.5

>
```

As you can see, *nslookup* responds with the name of the default server and a prompt. A *?* will return a list of available options. You can change the server you want to query with the *server* command. You can get a listing of all machines in a domain with the *ls* command. For example, *ls netlab.lander.edu* would list all the machines in the *netlab.lander.edu* domain. Use the *ls* command with caution—it can return a lot of information. You can use the *-t* option to specify a query type, i.e., a particular type of record. For example, *ls -t mx lander.edu* will return the mail entries from *lander.edu*. Query types can include *cname* to list canonical names for aliases, *hinfo* for host information, *ns* for name servers for named zones, *soa* for zone authority record, and so on. For more information, start with the manpage for *nslookup*.

One useful trick is to retrieve the *soa* record for local and authoritative servers. Here is part of one such record retrieved in interactive mode:

```
> ls -t soa lander.edu
[lab.lander.edu]
$ORIGIN lander.edu.
@                         1D IN SOA      lab root (
                                         960000090      ; serial
```

The entry labeled `serial` is a counter that should be incremented each time the DNS records are updated. If the serial number on your local server, when compared to the authoritative server, is off by more than 1 or 2, the local server is not updating its records in a timely manner. One possible cause is an old version of *bind*.

Many administrators prefer *dig* to *nslookup*. While not quite as ubiquitous as *nslookup*, it is included as a tool with *bind* and is also available as a separate tool. *dig* is a command-line tool that is quite easy to use. It seems to have a few more options and, since it is command line oriented, it is more suited for shell scripts. On the other hand, using *nslookup* interactively may be better if you are groping around and not really sure what you are looking for.

dig, short for Domain Internet Groper, was written by Steve Hotz. Here is an example of using *dig* to do a simple query:

```
bsd2# dig @lander.edu www.lander.edu

; <<>> DiG 8.3 <<>> @lander.edu www.lander.edu
; (1 server found)
;; res options: init recurs defnam dnsrch
;; got answer:
;; ->>HEADER<<- opcode: QUERY, status: NOERROR, id: 6
;; flags: qr aa rd ra; QUERY: 1, ANSWER: 2, AUTHORITY: 1, ADDITIONAL: 1
;; QUERY SECTION:
;;      www.lander.edu, type = A, class = IN

;; ANSWER SECTION:
www.lander.edu.         1D IN CNAME    web.lander.edu.
web.lander.edu.         1D IN A        205.153.60.15

;; AUTHORITY SECTION:
lander.edu.             1D IN NS       lander.edu.

;; ADDITIONAL SECTION:
lander.edu.             1D IN A        205.153.60.5

;; Total query time: 9 msec
;; FROM: bsd2.lander.edu to SERVER: lander.edu  205.153.60.5
```

```
;; WHEN: Tue Nov  7 10:26:42 2000
;; MSG SIZE  sent: 32  rcvd: 106
```

The first argument, in this case @lander.edu, is optional. It gives the name of the name server to be queried. The second argument is the name of the host you are looking up.

As you can see, a simple *dig* provides a lot more information, by default at least, than does *nslookup*. It begins with information about the name server and *resolver* flags used. (The flags are documented in the manpage for *bind*'s *resolver*.) Next come the header fields and flags followed by the query being answered. These are followed by the answer, authority records, and additional records. The format is the domain name, TTL field, type code for the record, and the data field. Finally, summary information about the exchange is included.

You can also use *dig* to get other types of information. For example, the *-x* option is used to do a reverse name lookup:

```
bsd2# dig -x 205.153.63.30

; <<>> DiG 8.3 <<>> -x
;; res options: init recurs defnam dnsrch
;; got answer:
;; ->>HEADER<<- opcode: QUERY, status: NOERROR, id: 4
;; flags: qr aa rd ra; QUERY: 1, ANSWER: 1, AUTHORITY: 1, ADDITIONAL: 1
;; QUERY SECTION:
;;      30.63.153.205.in-addr.arpa, type = ANY, class = IN

;; ANSWER SECTION:
30.63.153.205.in-addr.arpa.  1D IN PTR  sloan.lander.edu.

;; AUTHORITY SECTION:
63.153.205.in-addr.arpa.  1D IN NS  lander.edu.

;; ADDITIONAL SECTION:
lander.edu.              1D IN A       205.153.60.5

;; Total query time: 10 msec
;; FROM: bsd2.lander.edu to SERVER: default -- 205.153.60.5
;; WHEN: Mon Nov  6 10:54:17 2000
;; MSG SIZE  sent: 44  rcvd: 127
```

The *mx* option (no hyphen) will return mail records, the *soa* option will return zone authority records, and so on. See the manpage for details.

nslookup and *dig* are not unique. For example, *host* and *dnsquery* are other alternatives you may want to look at. *host* is said to be designed as a successor for *nslookup* and *dig*. But it does everything online and can generate a lot of traffic as a result. While very useful tools, all of them rely on your ability to go back and analyze the information returned. There are other tools that help to fill this gap.

doc, dnswalk, and lamers

doc is one such tool. It was originally written by Steve Hotz and Paul Mockapetris with later modifications by Brad Knowles. Built on top of *dig*, *doc* is a script that attempts to validate the consistency of information within a domain:

```
bsd2# doc lander.edu.
Doc-2.1.4: doc lander.edu.
Doc-2.1.4: Starting test of lander.edu.    parent is edu.
Doc-2.1.4: Test date - Mon Nov  6 11:55:07 EST 2000
;; res_nsend to server g.root-servers.net.  192.112.36.4: Operation timed out
DIGERR (UNKNOWN): dig @g.root-servers.net. for SOA of parent (edu.) failed
Summary:
    ERRORS found for lander.edu. (count: 3)
    WARNINGS issued for lander.edu. (count: 1)
Done testing lander.edu.  Mon Nov  6 11:55:40 EST 2000
```

The results are recorded in a log file; in this case *log.lander.edu.* is the filename. (Note its trailing period.)

dnswalk, written by David Barr, is a similar tool. It is a Perl script that does a zone transfer and checks the database for internal consistency. (Be aware that more and more systems are disabling zone transfers from unknown sites.)

```
bsd2# dnswalk lander.edu.
Checking lander.edu.
BAD: lander.edu. has only one authoritative nameserver
Getting zone transfer of lander.edu. from lander.edu...done.
SOA=lab.lander.edu       contact=root.lander.edu
WARN: bookworm.lander.edu A 205.153.62.205: no PTR record
WARN: library.lander.edu A 205.153.61.11: no PTR record
WARN: wamcmaha.lander.edu A 205.153.62.11: no PTR record
WARN: mrtg.lander.edu CNAME elmer.lander.edu: unknown host
0 failures, 4 warnings, 1 errors.
```

Be sure to include the period at the end of the domain name. This can produce a lot of output, so you may want to redirect output to a file. A number of options are available. Consult the manpage.

You'll want to take the output from these tools with a grain of salt. Even though these tools do a lot of work for you, you'll need a pretty good understanding of DNS to make sense of the error messages. And, as you can see, for the same domain, one found three errors and one warning while the other found one error and four warnings for a fully functional DNS domain. There is no question that this domain's database, which was being updated when this was run, has a few minor problems. But it does work. The moral is, don't panic when you see an error message.

Another program you might find useful is *lamers*. This was written by Bryan Beecher and requires both *doc* and *dig*. It is used to find lame delegations, i.e., a

name server that is listed as authoritative for a domain but is not actually performing that service for the listed domain. This problem most often arises when
name services are moved from one machine to another, but the parent domain is
not updated. *lamers* is a simple script that can be used to identify this problem.

Other tools

In addition to these debugging tools, there are a number of additional tools that
are useful in setting up DNS in the first place. Some, such as *make-zones, named-
bootconf,* and *named-xfer,* come with *bind.* Be sure to look over your port carefully. Others, often scripts or collections of scripts, are available from other
sources. Examples include *h2n* and *dnsutl.* There are a number of good tools out
there, so be sure to look around.

NIS and NIS+

NIS and its variants bring their own set of difficulties. If you are running both DNS
and NIS, the biggest problem may be deciding where the problem lies. Unfortunately, there is no easy way to do this that will work in every case. The original
implementation of *nslookup* completely bypasses NIS. If it failed, you could look
to DNS. If it succeeded, your problems were probably with NIS. Unfortunately, the
new, "improved" version of *nslookup* now queries NIS so this simple test is unreli-
able. (For other suggestions, see *Managing NFS and NIS* by Hal Stern or *DNS and
BIND* by Liu et al.)

If you are setting up NIS, your best strategy is to fully test DNS first. If you are
having problems with NIS, there are a number of simple utilities supplied with
NIS. *ypcat* lists an entire map, *ypmatch* matches a single key and prints an entry,
and *ypwhich* identifies client bindings. But if you have read the NIS documentation, you are already familiar with these.

Routing

If you are having routing problems, e.g., receiving error messages saying the host
or network is unreachable, then the first place to look is at the routing tables. On
the local machine, you'll use the *netstat -r* command as previously discussed. For
remote machines, you can use SNMP if you have SNMP access.

If you are using RIP, *rtquery* and *ripquery* are two tools that can be used to
retrieve routing tables from remote systems. *rtquery* is supplied as part of the
routed distribution, while *ripquery* comes with *gated.* The advantage of these tools
is that they use the RIP query and response mechanism to retrieve the route information. Thus, you can use either of these tools to confirm that the RIP exchange
mechanism is really working, as well as to retrieve the routing tables to check for
correctness.

It really doesn't matter which of these you use, as the output from the two is basi-cally the same. Here is the output from *ripquery*:

```
bsd2# ripquery 172.16.2.1
84 bytes from NLCisco.netlab.lander.edu(172.16.2.1) to 172.16.2.236 version 2:
            172.16.1.0/255.255.255.0    router 0.0.0.0        metric 1 tag
0000
            172.16.3.0/255.255.255.0    router 0.0.0.0        metric 1 tag
0000
            172.16.5.0/255.255.255.0    router 0.0.0.0        metric 2 tag
0000
            172.16.7.0/255.255.255.0    router 0.0.0.0        metric 2 tag
0000
```

Here is the output from *rtquery*:

```
bsd2# rtquery 172.16.2.1
NLCisco.netlab.lander.edu (172.16.2.1): RIPv2 84 bytes
   172.16.1.0/24     metric 1
   172.16.3.0/24     metric 1
   172.16.5.0/24     metric 2
   172.16.7.0/24     metric 2
```

You'll notice that these are not your usual routing tables. Rather, these are the tables used by RIP's distance vector algorithm. They give reachable networks and the associated costs. Of course, you could always capture a RIP update with *tcpdump* or *ethereal* or use SNMP, but the tools discussed here are a lot easier to use.

If you are using Open Shortest Path First (OSPF) (regretfully I don't at present), *gated* provides *ospf_monitor.* This interactive program provides a wealth of statis-tics, including I/O statistics and error logs in addition to OSPF routing tables. (For more information on routing protocols, you might consult *Routing in the Internet* by Christian Huitema or *Interconnections* by Radia Perlman.)

NFS

With time, Network File System (NFS) has become fairly straightforward to set up. At one time, there were a number of utilities for debugging NFS problems, but finding current ports has become difficult. At the risk of repeating myself, if you are having trouble setting up NFS, reread your documentation. Keep in mind that the various implementations of NFS all seem to be different, sometimes a lot dif-ferent. By itself, generic directions for NFS don't work—be sure to consult the spe-cific documentation for your operating system!

Unlike most other protocols where a single process is started, NFS relies on a number of different programs or daemons that vary from client to server and, to some extent, from system to system. If you are having problems with NFS, the first step is to consult your documentation to determine which daemons need to be

running on your system. Next, make sure they are running. Be warned, the daemons you need and the names they go by vary from operating system to operating system. For example, on most systems, *mountd* and *nfsd*, respectively,
mount filesystems and access files. On some systems they go by the names *rpc.
mountd* and *rpc.nfsd*. Since these rely on *portmap*, sometimes called *rpcbind*,
you'll need to make sure it is running as well. (NFS daemons are typically based
on RPC and use the *portmapper* daemon to provide access information.) The list of
daemons will be different for the client and the server. For example, *nfsiod* (or
biod) will typically be running on the client but not the server. Keep in mind,
however, that a computer may be both a client and a server.

There are a couple of ways to ensure the appropriate processes are available. You
could log on to both machines and use *ps* to discover what is running. This has
the advantage of showing you everything that is running. Another approach is to
use *rpcinfo* to do a *portmapper* dump. Here is an example of querying a server
from a client:

```
bsd2# rpcinfo -p bsd1
   program vers proto   port
    100000    2   tcp    111  portmapper
    100000    2   udp    111  portmapper
    100005    3   udp   1023  mountd
    100005    3   tcp   1023  mountd
    100005    1   udp   1023  mountd
    100005    1   tcp   1023  mountd
    100003    2   udp   2049  nfs
    100003    3   udp   2049  nfs
    100003    2   tcp   2049  nfs
    100003    3   tcp   2049  nfs
    100024    1   udp   1011  status
    100024    1   tcp   1022  status
```

This has the advantage of showing that these services are actually reachable across
the network.

Once you know that everything is running, you should check the access files, typically */etc/dfs/dfstab* or */etc/exports*, to make sure the client isn't being blocked. You
can't just edit these files and expect to see the results immediately. Consult your
documentation on how to inform your NFS implementation of the changes. Be
generous with privileges if you are having problems, but don't forget to tighten
security once everything is working.

Finally, check your syntax. Make sure the mount point exists and has appropriate
permissions. Mount the remote system manually and verify that it is mounted with
the *mount* command. You should see something recognizable. Here are mount
table entries returned, respectively, by FreeBSD, Linux, and Solaris:

```
bsd1:/ on /mnt/nfs type nfs (rw,addr=172.16.2.231,addr=172.16.2.231)
172.16.2.231:/ on /mnt/nfs (nfs)
/mnt/nfs on 172.16.2.231:/usr read/write/remote on Thu Nov 30 09:49:52 2000
```

While they are not too similar, you should see a recognizable change to the mount table before and after mounting a remote filesystem.

If you are having intermittent problems or if you suspect performance problems, you might want to use the *nfsstat* command. It provides a wealth of statistics about your NFS connection and its performance. You can use it to query the client, the server, or both. When called without any options, it queries both client and server. With the *-c* option, it queries the client. With the *-s* option, it queries the server. Here is an example of querying a client:

```
bsd2# nfsstat -c
Client Info:
Rpc Counts:
  Getattr   Setattr   Lookup  Readlink      Read    Write    Create   Remove
        0         0       33         2         0       21         4        0
   Rename      Link  Symlink     Mkdir     Rmdir  Readdir  RdirPlus   Access
        0         0        0         0         0        8         0       66
    Mknod    Fsstat   Fsinfo  PathConf    Commit   GLease    Vacate    Evict
        0        13        3         0         2        0         0        0
Rpc Info:
 TimedOut   Invalid X Replies   Retries  Requests
        0         0         0         0       152
Cache Info:
Attr Hits    Misses Lkup Hits    Misses BioR Hits    Misses BioW Hits   Misses
      232        36        74        33         0         0         0       21
BioRLHits    Misses BioD Hits    Misses DirE Hits    Misses
       13         2        18         8        13         0
```

Unfortunately, it seems that every operating system has its own implementation of *nfsstat* and each implementation returns a different set of statistics labeled in a different way. What you'll be most interested in is the number of problems in relation to the total number of requests. For example, a large number of timeouts is no cause for concern if it is a small percentage of a much larger number of total requests. If the timeouts are less than a couple of percent, they are probably not a cause for concern. But if the percent of timeouts is large, you need to investigate. You'll need to sort out the meaning of various numbers returned by your particular implementation of *nfsstat*. And, unfortunately, the labels aren't always intuitive.

Several other NFS tools were once popular but seem to have languished in recent years. You probably won't have much luck in finding these or getting them running. Two of the ones that were once more popular are *nhfsstone* and *nfswatch*. *nhfsstone* is a benchmark tool for NFS, which seems to have been superseded with the rather pricey SFS tool in SPEC. *nfswatch* is a tool that allows you to watch NFS traffic. *tcpdump* or *ethereal*, when used with the appropriate filters, provide a workable alternative to *nfswatch*.

Microsoft Windows

Many of the services described in this chapter are traditionally provided by Unix systems. While more and more are becoming available, there aren't a lot of tools that currently run under Windows. One exception is *nslookup*, which is nearly identical to its Unix counterpart. Of course, the *telnet*-based testing will work as shown. And you can always test a Windows server from a Unix client. If you want Windows-based tools, the best place to start looking is in the appropriate Windows Resource Kit from Microsoft.

11

Miscellaneous Tools

This chapter contains odds and ends that don't really fit any of the categories described in previous chapters. Most of the software presented here isn't really designed with network troubleshooting in mind, but it is, nonetheless, quite useful. These are tools that will make your life easier. With a few notable exceptions, you should already be familiar with most of the tools described here. Consequently, the descriptions of the tools are, for the most part, fairly brief. Feel free to jump around in this chapter as needed.

Communications Tools

If you are going to effectively administer remote systems, you will need to log on remotely. Even with small networks, it isn't reasonable to jump up and run to the remote system every time you need to do this. This section has three subsections. First, a quick review of techniques you can use to record or log your activities when using familiar tools like *telnet, rlogin,* and X Windows. Next comes a discussion of *vnc,* a tool that allows you to view a computer's graphical display remotely. Then I briefly discuss security concerns for these tools including a short description of *ssh.*

Automating Documentation

This book has assumed that you are familiar with tools like *telnet, rlogin,* and X Windows. To use these tools effectively, you'll want to be able to record or log your activities from time to time. Arguably, one reason documentation is so often flawed is that it is usually written after the fact. This is often done from memory or an incomplete set of notes several days after changes have been made. While the best time to write documentation is as you go, often this simply isn't possible.

When your network is down and management is calling every five minutes asking if it's fixed yet, you probably won't be pausing to write much down.

There are a few things you can do to help simplify writing documentation after the fact. First, get copious printouts at every stage, preferably with some kind of time and date stamp. When a production system is down, it is not the time to worry about the cost of paper. Several commands you are probably already familiar with may be easy to overlook with the stress of dealing with a dead system.

If you are using X Windows, you can use the *xwd* command to capture windows. To use this command, in an *xterm* window, type:

```
bsd1# xwd -out xwdfile
```

You can then click on the window you want to capture. In this example, the file *xwdfile* will be created in the current directory. The file can be examined later or printed using tools such as *xv* or *gimp*. Be sure to give these files meaningful names so that you can sort things out later.

If you are using a text-based interface and are interested in capturing the output of a single command, you may be able to use the *tee* command. This command allows you to send output from a command to both the screen and a file. For example, the following command will display the output of the command **arp -a** on the screen and write it to the file *outfile*:

```
bsd1# arp -a | tee outfile
```

The *tee* command may require special measures to work. For example, you must use the option *-l* with *tcpdump* if you want to use *tee*. An example was given in Chapter 5. As with *xwd*, you should be careful to use meaningful filenames, particularly if you are capturing windows on the fly.

An alternative to *tee* is *script*. It can be used to capture the output of a single command or a series of commands. To capture a series of commands, you start *script* and then issue the commands of interest. For example, the following command will create the file *scriptfile* and return to the system prompt:

```
bsd1# script scriptfile
Script started, output file is scriptfile
```

Everything that is displayed on your terminal will be logged to the file *scriptfile*. One advantage of logging a series of commands is that you can embed documentation into the file as you go. Simply type the comment character for your shell, and everything else you type on the line will be ignored. For example, with the Bourne shell, you might type something like:

```
bsd1# #Well, the foo program didn't work.  \
>Let's try the bar program.
```

The "\" character was used to continue the comment on a new line.

When you are done logging a session, type **exit** or press Ctrl+D as in:

```
bsd1# exit
```

```
Script done, output file is scriptfile
```

You can now print or edit the file as desired.

One option that is often overlooked is to include a command with the *script* command. For example:

```
bsd1# script scriptfile ifconfig -a
```

will run the program *ifconfig -a,* writing the output to the file *scriptfile* and displaying the output on the screen as well. This file will include two time and date stamps, one at the beginning and one at the end of the file.

You should be aware of a few problems with using *script.* First, the file can get very big very quickly. This shouldn't be much of a problem unless you are pressed for disk space, but it can be painful to read after the fact. Second, it is all too easy to lose the file. For example, if a system crashes or is halted, the file may be lost in the process. Third, commands that directly control the screen such as *vi* tend to fill the output file with garbage. Finally, since a new shell is started by *script,* environmental changes made while *script* is running may be lost.

If you are connecting to a remote system using a variant of *telnet,* you may be able to log the session or print the screen. This is particularly true for PC implementations of *telnet.* See the documentation for the version you are using.

vnc

vnc, short for *virtual network computing,* was developed by what is now the AT&T Laboratories at Cambridge. *vnc* is actually a pair of programs. One is a server, which generates and sends the local display's contents to another computer. The other is a viewer, which reconstructs the server's display. You use the computer running the viewer program to control the remote computer running the server program. An application, for example, would actually be running on the server's CPU but controlled by the station running the viewer.

The program's implementation is based on the concept of a *remote frame buffer* (i.e., remote video display memory). The server maintains the frame buffer, a picture of the server's display, and sends it to the viewer. The viewer recreates the display on the local host. The updates to the remote frame buffer may be the complete contents of the frame buffer or, to minimize the impact on bandwidth, just what has changed since the last update.

In a Unix environment, *vnc* provides a way to deliver an X Windows session to a host that may not support a native X Windows connection. On the surface, a *vnc* connection probably seems a lot like an X Windows connection. There are, however, some fundamental differences. *vnc* is designed so the viewer is a very thin client. Unlike an X Windows, almost no work is done at the viewer, and the client software is stateless. And *vnc* is freely available on some non-Unix systems where X Window isn't.

vnc can run in one of two modes. In *view only mode*, the screen is displayed, but the viewer is not given control of the server's mouse or keyboard. If view only mode is not selected, the viewer will share control of the mouse and keyboard. Please note, the mouse and keyboard will not necessarily be disabled at the server.

To use *vnc* in a Unix environment, *telnet* to the remote computer and start the *vnc* server with the *vncserver* command. The first time you run it, it will create a *.vnc* directory under your home directory and will query you for a connection password that will be used for all future sessions. (You can change this with the *vncpasswd* command.)

```
lnx1$ vncserver

You will require a password to access your desktops.

Password:
Verify:

New 'X' desktop is lnx1.lander.edu:1

Creating default startup script /home/jsloan/.vnc/xstartup
Starting applications specified in /home/jsloan/.vnc/xstartup
Log file is /home/jsloan/.vnc/lnx1.lander.edu:1.log
```

The command returns an address or hostname and a display number for the newly created display, in this instance `lnx1.lander.edu:1`. (Alternately, you could start the *vnc* server while seated at the machine and then go to the client. This will be necessary if you want to run the server on a Microsoft Windows platform.)

Next, connect a viewer to the display. To start the viewer on a Unix system, start an X Window session and then use the *vncviewer* command with the host and display number returned by the viewer program as an argument to the command. By default, *vncserver* uses the *twm* X Window manager, but this can be reconfigured.* If you are used to all the clutter that usually comes with *gnome* or something similar, the display may seem a little austere at first but will perform better. The basic

---

* To change the window manager, edit the file *xstartup* in the *.vnc* directory. For example, if you use *gnome*, you would change `twm` to `exec gnome-session`.

functionality you need will be there, and you will be able to run whichever X programs you need.

vnc starts a number of processes; you'll want to be sure that they are all stopped when you are done. You can stop *vnc* with the *-kill* option as shown here:

```
lnx1$ vncserver -kill :1
Killing Xvnc process ID 6171
```

Note that you need to specify only the display number, in this case :1. You should also be aware that this sometimes misses a process on some systems. You may need to do a little extra housekeeping now and then.

Once running, *vnc* supports sending special keystroke combinations such as Ctrl-Alt-Del. If both systems support it, you can cut and paste ASCII data between windows.

vnc also provides a reasonable level of security. Once the password has been set, it is not transmitted over the network. Rather, a challenge response system is used. In addition to the password, the Microsoft Windows version of *vncserver* can be configured to accept connections from only a specific list of hosts. It can also be configured to use a secure shell (SSH) session. The default port can be reassigned to simplify configuration with firewalls.

The viewer and server can be on the same or different machines or can even be used on different architectures. *vnc* will run on most platforms. In particular, the viewer will run on just about any Microsoft Windows machine including Windows CE. It will run under an X Window session, on Macintoshes, and as plug-ins for web browsers. *vnc* is available in Java, and the server contains a small web server that can be accessed by some Java-aware browsers. To do this, you simply add 5800 to the window number for the HTTP port number. In the previous example, the window was :1, so the HTTP port number would be :5801, and the URL would be *http://lnx1.lander.edu:5801*.

There is substantial documentation available at the AT&T Laboratories web site, *http://www.uk.research.att.com/vnc*.

ssh

One of the problems with *telnet, rlogin, rsh,* and the like is a lack of security. Passwords are sent in clear text and can be easily captured by any computer they happen to pass. And with the r-services, it can be very easy to mimic a trusted system. Attach a laptop to the network, set the IP address appropriately, and there is a good chance you can mimic a trusted host.

One alternative is *ssh*, written by Tatu Ylönen, a replacement for the r-services that uses encryption. While the original version is free, with Version 2 *ssh* has evolved into a commercial product, marketed by SSH Communications Security, Inc. However, Version 2 is freely available for academic and noncommercial use. Recently, the OpenSSH project, a spin-off of the OpenBSD project, released a free port that is compatible with both versions of *ssh* and is covered by the standard BSD license.

ssh is actually a set of programs that uses encryption to both authenticate users and provide encrypted sessions. It provides four levels of authentication, ranging from trusted users and systems, like *rsh* and *rlogin*, to RSA-based authentication. By doing host authentication as well as user authentication, DNS, IP, and route spoofing attacks can be circumvented.

On the downside, *ssh* provides minimal protection once your systems have been compromised. Version 1 of the SSH protocol has also been compromised by man-in-the-middle attacks when incorrectly configured. Also, some of its authentication methods can be relatively insecure. *ssh* is not trivial to configure correctly, but fortunately, there is a fair amount of documentation available for *ssh*, including two books devoted exclusively to *ssh*. If you need particularly robust security, pay close attention to how you configure it or consider Version 2.

The legality of *ssh* is yet another question. Since encryption is sometimes the subject of peculiar laws in some countries, using or exporting *ssh* may not be legal. The OpenBSD and OpenSSH projects avoid some of these problems by developing code outside of the United States. Consequently, the distribution of their code is not subject to the United States' peculiar munitions export laws since it can be obtained outside the United States.

Despite these concerns, *ssh* is something you should definitely consider if security is an issue.

Log Files and Auditing

A primary source of information on any system is its log files. Of course, log files are not unique to networking software. They are simply another aspect of general systems management that you must master.

Some applications manage their own log files. Web servers and accounting software are prime examples. Many of these applications have specific needs that aren't well matched to a more general approach. In dealing with these, you will have to consult the documentation and deal with each on a case-by-case basis. Fortunately, most Unix software is now designed to use a central logging service, *syslog*, which greatly simplifies management.

syslog

You are probably already familiar with *syslog*, a versatile logging tool written by Eric Allman. What is often overlooked is that *syslog* can be used across networks. You can log events from your Cisco router to your Unix server. There are even a number of Windows versions available. Here is a quick review of *syslog*.

An early and persistent criticism of Unix was that every application seemed to have its own set of log files hidden away in its own directories. *syslog* was designed to automate and standardize the process of maintaining system log files. The main program is the daemon *syslogd*, typically started as a separate process during system initialization. Messages can be sent to the daemon either through a set of library routines or by a user command, *logger*. *logger* is particularly useful for logging messages from scripts or for testing *syslog*, e.g., checking file permissions.

Configuring syslog

syslogd's behavior is initialized through a configuration file, which by default is */etc/syslog.conf*. An alternative file can be specified with the *-f* option when the daemon is started. If changes are made to the configuration file, *syslogd* must be restarted for the changes to take effect. The easiest way to do this is to send it a HUP signal using the *kill* command. For example:

```
bsd1# kill -HUP 127
```

where 127 is the PID for *syslogd*, found using the *ps* command. (Alternately, the PID is written to the file */var/run/syslogd.pid* on some systems.)

The configuration file is a text file with two fields separated by tabs, not spaces! Blank lines are ignored. Lines beginning with # in the first column are comments. The first field is a *selector*, and the second is an *action*. The selector identifies the program or facility sending the message. It is composed of both a facility name and a security level. The facility names must be selected from a short list of facilities defined for the kernel. You should consult the manpage for *syslogd* for a complete list and description of facilities, as these vary from implementation to implementation. The security level is also taken from a predefined list: *emerg*, *alert*, *crit*, *err*, *warning*, *notice*, *info*, or *debug*. Their meanings are just what you might guess. *emerg* is the most severe. You can also use * for all or *none* for nothing. Multiple facilities can be combined on a single line if you separate them with commas. Multiple selectors must be separated with semicolons.

The Action field tells where to send the messages. Messages can be sent to files, including device files such as the console or printers, logged-in users, or remote hosts. Pathnames must be absolute, and the file must exit with the appropriate permissions. You should be circumspect in sending too much to the console. Otherwise, you may be overwhelmed by messages when you are using the console, particularly when you need the console the most. If you want multiple actions, you will need multiple lines in the configuration file.

Here are a few lines from a *syslog.conf* file that should help to clarify this:

```
mail.info                          /var/log/maillog
cron.*                             /var/log/cron
security.*                         @loghost.netlab.lander.edu
*.notice;news.err                  root
*.err                              /dev/console
*.emerg                            *
```

The first line says that all informational messages from *sendmail* and other mail related programs should be appended to the file */var/log/maillog*. The second line says all messages from *cron*, regardless of severity, should be appended to the file */var/log/cron*. The next line says that all security messages should be sent to a remote system, *loghost.netlab.lander.edu*. Either a hostname or an IP address can be used. The fourth line says that all notice-level messages and any news error messages should be sent to root if root is logged on. The next to last line says that all error messages, including news error messages, should be displayed on the system console. Finally, the last line says emergency messages should be sent to all users. It is easy to get carried away with configuration files, so remember to keep yours simple.

One problem with *syslog* on some systems is that, by default, the log files are world readable. This is a potential security hole. For example, if you log mail transactions, any user can determine who is sending mail to whom—not necessarily something you want.

Remote logging

For anything but the smallest of networks, you really should consider remote logging for two reasons. First, there is simply the issue of managing and checking everything on a number of different systems. If all your log files are on a single system, this task is much easier. Second, should a system become compromised, one of the first things crackers alter are the log files. With remote logging, future entries to log files may be stopped, but you should still have the initial entries for the actual break-in.

To do remote logging, you will need to make appropriate entries in the configuration files for two systems. On the system generating the message, you'll need to specify the address of the remote logging machine. On the system receiving the message, you'll need to specify a file for the messages. Consider the case in which the source machine is *bsd1* and the destination is *bsd2*. In the configuration file for *bsd1*, you might have an entry like:

```
local7.*                           @bsd2.netlab.lander.edu
```

bsd2's configuration file might have an entry like:

```
local7.*                              /var/log/bsd1
```

Naming the file for the remote system makes it much easier to keep messages straight. Of course, you'll need to create the file and enable *bsd2* to receive remote messages from *bsd1*.

You can use the *logger* command to test your configuration. For example, you might use the following to generate a message:

```
bsd1# logger -p local7.debug "testing"
```

This is what the file looks like on *bsd2:*

```
bsd2# cat bsd1
Dec 26 14:22:08 bsd1 jsloan: testing
```

Notice that both a timestamp and the source of the message have been included in the file.

There are a number of problems with remote logging. You should be aware that *syslog* uses UDP. If the remote host is down, the messages will be lost. You will need to make sure that your firewalls pass appropriate *syslog* traffic. *syslog* messages are in clear text, so they can be captured and read. Also, it is very easy to forge a *syslog* message.

It is also possible to overwhelm a host with *syslog* messages. For this reason, some versions of *syslog* provide options to control whether information from a remote system is allowed. For example, with FreeBSD the *-s* option can be used to enter secure mode so logging requests are ignored. Alternately, the *-a* option can be used to control hosts from which messages are accepted. With some versions of Linux, the *-r* option is used to enable a system to receive messages over the network. While you will need to enable your central logging systems to receive messages, you should probably disable this on all other systems to avoid potential denial-of-service attacks. Be sure to consult the manpage for *syslogd* to find the particulars for your system.

Both Linux and FreeBSD have other enhancements that you may want to consider. If security is a major concern, you may want to investigate *secure syslog* (*ssyslog*) or *modular syslog* (*msyslog*). For greater functionality, you may also want to look at *syslog-ng*.

Log File Management

Even after you have the log files, whether created by *syslog* or some other program, you will face a number of problems. The first is keeping track of all the files so they don't fill your filesystem. It is easy to forget fast-growing files, so I recommend keeping a master list for each system. You'll want to develop a policy of what information to keep and how long to keep it. This usually comes down to some kind of log file rotation system in which older files are discarded or put on archival media. Be aware that what you save and for how long may have legal implications, depending on the nature of your organization.

Another issue is deciding how much information you want to record in the first place. Many authors argue, with some justification, that you should record anything and everything that you might want, no matter how remote the possibility. In other words, it is better to record too much than to discover, after the fact, that you don't have something you need. Of course, if you start with this approach, you can cut back as you gain experience.

The problem with this approach is that you are likely to be so overwhelmed with data that you won't be able to find what you need. *syslog* goes a long way toward addressing this problem with its support for different security levels—you can send important messages one place and everything else somewhere else. Several utilities are designed to further simplify and automate this process, each with its own set of strengths. These utilities may condense or display log files, often in real time. They can be particularly useful if you are managing a number of devices.

Todd Atkins' *swatch* (simple watcher) is one of the best known. Designed with security monitoring in mind, the program is really suitable to monitor general system activity. *swatch* can be run in three different ways—making a pass over a log file, monitoring messages as they are appended to a log file, or examining the output from a program. You might scan a log file initially to come up-to-date on your system, but the second usage is the most common.

swatch's actions include ignoring the line, echoing the line on the controlling terminal, ringing the bell, sending the message to someone by *write* or mail, or executing a command using the line as an argument. Behavior is determined based on a configuration file composed of up to four tab-separated fields. The first and second fields, the pattern expression and actions, are the most interesting. The pattern is a regular expression used to match messages. *swatch* is written in Perl, so the syntax used for the regular expressions is fairly straightforward.

While it is a powerful program, you are pretty much on your own in setting up the configuration files. Deciding what you will want to monitor is a nontrivial task that will depend on what you think is important. Since this could be almost anything— errors, full disks, security problems such as privilege violations—you'll have a lot of choices if you select *swatch*. The steps are to decide what is of interest, identify the appropriate files, and then design your filters.

swatch is not unique. *xlogmaster* is a GTK+ based program for monitoring log files, devices, and status-gathering programs. It was written by Georg Greve and is available under the GNU General Public License. It provides filtering and displays selected events with color and audio. Although *xlogmaster* is no longer being developed, it is a viable program that you should consider. Its successor is GNU AWACS. AWACS is new code, currently under development, that expands on the capabilities of *xlogmaster.*

Another program worth looking at is *logcheck.* This began as a shell script written by Craig Rowland. *logcheck* is now available under the GNU license from Psionic Software, Inc., a company founded by Rowland. *logcheck* can be run by *cron* rather than continuously.

You should be able to find a detailed discussion of log file management in any good book on Unix system administration. Be sure to consult Appendix B for more information.

Other Approaches to Logging

Unfortunately, many services traditionally don't do logging, either through the *syslog* facility or otherwise. If these services are started by *inetd*, you have a couple of alternatives.

Some implementations of *inetd* have options that will allow connection logging. That is, each time a connection is made to one of these services, the connection is logged. With *inetd* on Solaris, the *-t* option traces all connections. On FreeBSD, the *-l* option records all successful connections. The problem with this approach is that it is rather indiscriminate.

One alternative is to replace *inetd* with Panos Tsirigotis's *xinetd. xinetd* is an expanded version of *inetd* that greatly expands *inetd*'s functionality, particularly with respect to logging. Another program to consider is *tcpwrappers.*

tcpwrappers

The *tcpwrappers* program was developed to provide additional security, including logging. Written by Wietse Venema, a well-respected security expert, *tcpwrappers* is a small program that sits between *inetd* (or *inetd*-like programs) and the services started by *inetd*. When a service is requested, *inetd* calls the wrapper program, *tcpd*, which checks permission files, logs its actions, and then, if appropriate, starts the service. For example, if you want to control access to *telnet*, you might change the line in */etc/inetd.conf* that starts the *telnet* daemon from:

```
telnet stream  tcp    nowait  root    /usr/libexec/telnetd    telnetd
```

to:

```
telnet  stream  tcp    nowait  root    /usr/sbin/tcpd        telnetd
```

Now, the wrapper daemon *tcpd* is started initially instead of *telnetd*, the *telnet* daemon. You'll need to make similar changes for each service you want to control. If the service is not where *tcpd* expects it, you can give an absolute path as an argument to *tcpd* in the configuration file.

 Actually, there is an alternative way of configuring *tcpwrappers*. You can leave the *inetd* configuration file alone, move each service to a new location, and replace the service at its default location with *tcpd*. I strongly discourage this approach as it can create maintenance problems, particularly when you upgrade your system.

As noted, *tcpwrappers* is typically used for two functions—logging and access control.* Logging is done through *syslog*. The particular facility used will depend on how *tcpwrappers* is compiled. Typically, *mail* or *local2* is used. You will need to edit */etc/syslog.conf* and recompile *tcpwrappers* if you want to change how logging is recorded.

Access is typically controlled through the file */etc/hosts.allow*, though some systems may also have an */etc/hosts.deny* file. These files specify which systems can access which services. These are a few potential rules based on the example configuration:

```
ALL : localhost : allow
sendmail : nice.guy.example.com : allow
sendmail : .evil.cracker.example.com : deny
sendmail : ALL : allow
```

tcpwrappers uses a first match wins approach. The first rule allows all services from the local machine without further testing. The next three rules control the *sendmail* program. The first rule allows a specific host, *nice.guy.example.com*. All hosts on the domain *.evil.cracker.example.com* are blocked. (Note the leading dot.) Finally, all other hosts are permitted to use *sendmail*.

There are a number of other forms for rules that are permitted, but these are all pretty straightforward. The distribution comes with a very nice example file. But, should you have problems, *tcpwrappers* comes with two utilities for testing configuration files. *tcpdchk* looks for general syntax errors within the file. *tcpdmatch* can be used to check how *tcpd* will respond to a specific action. (Kudos to Venema for including these!)

The primary limitation to *tcpwrappers* is that, since it disappears after it starts the target service, its control is limited to the brief period while it is running. It provides no protection from attacks that begin after that point.

---

* *tcpwrappers* provides additional functionality not described here, such as login banners.

tcpwrappers is a ubiquitous program. In fact, it is installed by default on many Linux systems. Incidentally, some versions of *inetd* now have wrappers technology built-in. Be sure to review your documentation.

NTP

One problem with logging events over a network is that differences in system clocks can make correlating events on different systems very difficult. It is not unusual for the clock on a system to have drifted considerably. Thus, there may be discrepancies among timestamps for the same events listed in different log files. Fortunately, there is a protocol you can use to synchronize the clocks on your system.

Network Time Protocol (NTP) provides a mechanism so that one system can compare and adjust its clock to match another system's clock. Ideally, you should have access to a very accurate clock as your starting point. In practice, you will have three choices. The best choice is an authoritative reference clock. These devices range from atomic clocks to time servers that set their clocks based on time signals from radios or GPS satellites.

The next best source is from a system that gets its clock setting from one of these reference clocks. Such systems are referred to as stratum 1 servers. If you can't get your signal from a stratum 1 server, the next best choice is to get it from a system that does, a stratum 2 server. As you might guess, there is a whole hierarchy of servers with the stratum number incrementing with each step you take away from a reference clock. There are public time servers available on the Internet with fairly low stratum numbers that you can coordinate to occasionally, but courtesy dictates that you ask before using these systems.

Finally, if you are not attached to the Internet, you can elect to simply designate one of your systems as the master system and coordinate all your other systems to that system. Your clocks won't be very accurate, but they will be fairly consistent, and you will be able to compare system logs.

NTP works in one of several ways. You can set up a server to broadcast time messages periodically. Clients then listen for these broadcasts and adjust their clocks accordingly. Alternately, the server can be queried by the client. NTP uses UDP, typically port 123. Over the years, NTP has gone through several versions. Version 4 is the current one, but Version 3 is probably more commonly used at this point. There is also a lightweight time protocol, Simple Network Time Protocol (SNTP), used by clients that need less accuracy. SNTP is interoperable with NTP.

For Unix systems, the most common implementation is *ntpd*, formerly *xntpd*, which is described here. This is actually a collection of related programs including the daemon *ntpd* and support programs such as *ntpq, ntpdate,* and *ntptrace.* You'll want to start *ntpd* automatically each time you boot your system. *ntpd* uses a configuration file, */etc/ntp.conf,* to control its operation. This configuration file can get quite complicated depending on what you want to do, but a basic configuration file is fairly simple. Here is a simple three-line example:

```
server 205.153.60.20
logconfig =syncevents +peerevents +sysevents +allclock
driftfile /etc/ntp.drift
```

The first line identifies the server. This is the minimum you'll need. The second establishes which events will be logged. The last line identifies a drift file. This is used by *ntpd* to store information about how the clock on the system drifts. If *ntpd* is stopped and restarted, it can use the old drift information to help keep the clock aligned rather than waiting to calculate new drift information.

One minor warning about *ntpd* is in order. If your clock is too far off, *ntpd* will not reset it. (Among other things, this prevents failures from propagating throughout a network.) This is rarely a problem with computers, but it is not unusual to have a networking device whose clock has never been set. Just remember that you may need to manually set your clock to something reasonable before you run *ntpd.*

ntpdate can be used to do a onetime clock set:

```
bsd2# ntpdate 205.153.60.20
 4 Jan 10:07:36 ntpdate[13360]: step time server 205.153.60.20 offset 11.567081
sec
```

ntpdate cannot be used if *ntpd* is running, but there shouldn't be any need for it if that is the case.

ntpq can be used to query servers about their state:

```
bsd2# ntpq -p 172.16.2.1
     remote          refid       st t when poll reach   delay   offset  jitter
==============================================================================
*ntp.lander.edu  .GPS.           1 u   18   64  173   5.000   -1.049 375.210
 CHU_AUDIO(1)    CHU_AUDIO(1)    7 -   34   64  177   0.000    0.000 125.020
 172.16.3.3      0.0.0.0        16 -    -   64    0   0.000    0.000 16000.0
 172.16.2.2      0.0.0.0        16 u    -   64    0   0.000    0.000 16000.0
```

In this example, we have queried a system for a list of its peers.

ntptrace can be used to discover the chain of NTP servers, i.e., who gets their signal from whom:

```
bsd2# ntptrace 172.16.2.1
NLCisco.netlab.lander.edu: stratum 2, offset 0.009192, synch distance 0.00526
ntp.lander.edu: stratum 1, offset 0.007339, synch distance 0.00000, refid 'GPS '
```

Only two servers were involved in this example, but you should get the basic idea.

Each of these tools has other features that are documented in their manpages. NTP can be an involved protocol if used to its fullest. Fortunately, a lot of documentation is available. Whatever you want—information, software, a list of public NTP servers—the best place to start is at *http://www.eecis.udel.edu/~ntp*. The work of Dave Mills and others, this is a remarkable site.

Security Tools

A final group of tools that should not be overlooked is security tools. Security, of course, is an essential part of systems management. While this isn't a book on network security, security is so broad a topic that there is considerable overlap with it and the issues addressed in this book. Strictly speaking, a number of the tools described in this book (such as *portscan*, *nmap*, and *tcpwrappers*) are frequently described as security tools.

Basically, any tool that provides information about a network has both security implications and management potential. So don't overlook the tools in your security toolbox when addressing other networking problems. For example, security scanners like *satan*, *cops*, and *iss* can tell you a lot about how your system is configured.

One particularly useful group of tools is system integrity checkers. This class of programs tracks the state of your system and allows you to determine what is changing—such as files, permissions, timestamps. While the security implications should be obvious, management and troubleshooting implications should also be clear. Often described as tools to identify files that intruders have changed, they can be used to identify files that have been changed or corrupted for any reason. For example, they can be used to determine exactly what is changed when you install a new program.

The best known of these is *tripwire*. It is a considerable stretch to call *tripwire* a networking tool, but it is an administrative tool that can make managing a system, whether networked or not, much easier.

tripwire

tripwire was originally written by Eugene Spafford and Gene Kim. It is another product that has evolved into a commercial product. It is now marketed by Tripwire, Inc. The original free version is still available at the company's web site as the Academic Source Release. The current version, in a slightly modified form, is also available for free download for Linux. The current version is much easier to use, but the older version is usable if you are willing to take the time to learn it.

tripwire creates a database of information about files on the system including cryptographic checksums. A configuration file is used to determine what information is collected and for which files it is collected. If security is a concern, the collected information should be stored offline to prevent tampering.

As a security tool, *tripwire* is used to identify any changes that have been made to a compromised host. It doesn't prevent an attack, but it shows the scope to the attack and changes to the system. As a troubleshooting tool, it can be used to track any changes to a system, regardless of the cause—hacker, virus, or bit rot. It can also be used to verify the integrity of transferred files or the consistency of configurations for multiple installations.

If all you want is a checksum, you might consider just using the *siggen* program, which comes with *tripwire*. *siggen* will generate a number of checksums for a file. Here is an example:

```
bsd2# siggen siggen
sig0: nullsig  : 0
sig1: md5      : 0EpNJLBbf7JJgh1yUdAPgZ
sig2: snefru   : 25I3DS:thJ3N:16UchVdNR
sig3: crc32    : 0jeUpK
sig4: crc16    : 000560
sig5: md4      : 02x6dNiYw7GwjSssW7IeLW
sig6: md2      : 30s7ugrC1gLhk129Zo1BXW
sig7: sha      : EWed2qYLHGcK.i7P7bVDO2mtKvr
sig8: haval    : 1cqs7t9CwipMcuWPM3eRF1
sig9: nullsig  : 0
```

You can use an optional argument to limit which checksums you want. For example, the option *-13* will calculate just the first and third checksums, the MD5 digest and the 32-bit CRC checksum.

I certainly wouldn't recommend that you install *tripwire* just for troubleshooting. But if you have installed it as a security tool, something I would strongly recommend, then don't forget that you can use it for these other purposes. Incidentally, with some systems, such as OpenBSD, integrity checking is an integral part of the system.

Microsoft Windows

When documenting problems with Windows, the usual approach is to open a word processing file and copy and paste as needed. Unfortunately, some tools, such as Event Viewer, will not allow copying. If this is the case, you should look to see if there is a Save option. With Event Viewer, you can save the messages to a text file and then copy and paste as needed.

If this is not possible, you can always get a screen dump. Unfortunately, the way to do this seems to change with every version of Windows. Typically, if an individual window is selected, only that window is captured. If a window is not selected, the screen is copied. For Windows 95 and NT, Shift-PrintScreen (or Ctrl-PrintScreen) will capture the contents of the screen, while Alt-PrintScreen will capture just the current window. For Windows 98, use Alt-PrintScreen. The screen is copied on the system's clipboard. It can be viewed with ClipBook Viewer. While it is included with the basic Windows distribution, ClipBook Viewer may not be installed on all systems. You may need to go to your distribution disks to install it. With Windows NT, be sure to select Clipboard on the Windows menu. Unfortunately, this gives a bitmapped copy of the screen that is difficult to manipulate, but it is better than nothing.

As previously noted, *vnc* is available for Windows. The viewer is a very small program—an executable will fit on a floppy so it is very easy to take with you.

There are a number of implementations of *ssh* for Windows. You might look at Metro State College of Denver's *mssh*, Simon Tatham's *putty*, or Robert O'Callahan's *ttssh* extensions to Takashi Teranishi's *teraterm* communications program. If these don't meet your need, there are a number of similar programs available over the Web.

Although I have not used them, there are numerous commercial, shareware, and freeware versions of *syslog* for Windows. Your best bet is to search the Web for such tools. You might look at *http://www.loop-back.com/syslog.htm* or search for *kiwis_syslogd.exe*.

ntpd can be compiled for Windows NT. Binaries, however, don't seem to be generally available. If you just want to occasionally set your clock, you might also consider *cyberkit*. *cyberkit* was described in Chapter 6. Go to the Time tab, fill in the address of your time server, select the radio button SNTP, make sure the Synchronize Local Clock checkbox is selected, and click on the Go button. The output will look something like this:

```
Time - Thursday, December 28, 2000 09:02:59
Generated by CyberKit Version 2.5
Copyright © 1996-2000 by Luc Neijens

Time Server: ntp.netlab.lander.edu
Protocol: SNTP Protocol
Synchronize Local Clock: Yes

Leap Indicator 0, NTP Version 1, Mode 4
Stratum Level 1 (Primary reference, e.g. radio clock)
```

```
Poll Interval 6 (64 seconds), Precision -8 (3.90625 ms)
Root Delay 0.00 ms, Root Dispersion 0.00 ms
Reference Identifier GPS
Time server clock was last synchronized on Thursday, December 28, 2000 09:02:38

Server Date & Time: Thursday, December 28, 2000 09:02:38
Delta (Running slow): 1.590 ms
Round Trip Time 29 ms

Local clock synchronized with time server
```

The last line is the one of interest. It indicates that synchronization was successful. The help system includes directions for creating a shortcut that you can click on to automatically update your clock. Go to the index and look under tips and tricks for adding *cyberkit* to the startup menu and under command-line parameters for time client parameters.

A commercial version of *tripwire* is available for Windows NT.

12

Troubleshooting Strategies

While many of the tools described in this book are extremely powerful, no one tool does everything. If you have been downloading and installing these tools as you have read this book, you now have an extensive, versatile set of tools. When faced with a problem, you should be equipped to select the best tool or tools for the particular job, augmenting your selection with other tools as needed.

This chapter outlines several strategies that show how these tools can be used together. When troubleshooting, your approach should be to look first at the specific task and then select the most appropriate tool(s) based on the task. I do not describe the details of using the tools or show output in this chapter. You should already be familiar with these from the previous chapters. Rather, this chapter focuses on the selection of tools and the overall strategy you should take in using them. If you feel confident in your troubleshooting skills, you may want to skip this chapter.

Generic Troubleshooting

Any troubleshooting task is basically a series of steps. The actual steps you take will vary from problem to problem. Later steps in the process may depend on the results from earlier steps. Still, it is worth thinking about and mapping out the steps since doing this will help you remain focused and avoid needless steps. In watching others troubleshoot, I have been astonished at how often people perform tests with no goal in mind. Often the test has no relation to the problem at hand. It is just something easy to do. When your car won't start, what is the point of checking the air pressure of the tires?

For truly difficult problems, you will need to become formal and systematic. A somewhat general, standard series of steps you can go through follows, along with a running example. Keep in mind, this set of steps is only a starting point.

1. Document. Before you do anything else, start documenting what you are doing. This is a real test of willpower and self-discipline. It is extremely difficult to force yourself to sit down and write a problem description or take careful notes when your system is down or crackers are running rampant through your system.* This is not just you; everyone has this problem. But it is an essential step for several reasons.

   Depending on your circumstances, management may require a written report. Even if this isn't the usual practice, if an outage becomes prolonged or if there are other consequences, it might become necessary. This is particularly true if there are some legal consequences of the problem. An accurate log can be essential in such cases.

   If you have a complex problem, you are likely to forget at some point what you have actually done. This often means starting over. It can be particularly frustrating if you appear to have found a solution, but you can't remember exactly what you did. A seemingly insignificant step may prove to be a key element in a solution.

2. Collect information and identify symptoms. Actually, this step is two intertwined steps. But they are often so intertwined that you usually can't separate them. You must collect information while filtering that information for indications of anomalous behavior. These two steps will be repeated throughout the troubleshooting process. This is easiest when you have a clear sense of direction.

   As you identify symptoms, try to expand and clarify the problem. If the problem was reported by someone else, then you will want to try to recreate the problem so that you can observe the symptoms directly. Keep in mind, if you can't recognize normal behavior, you won't be able to recognize anomalous behavior. This has been a recurring theme in this book and a reason you should learn how to use these tools before you need them.

   As an example, the first indication of a problem might be a user complaining that she cannot *telnet* from host *bsd1* to host *lnx1*. To expand and clarify the problem, you might try different applications. Can you connect using *ftp*? You might look to see if *bsd1* and *lnx1* are on the same network or different net-

---

* Compromised hosts are a special problem requiring special responses. Documentation can be absolutely essential, particularly if you are contemplating legal action or have liability concerns. Documentation used in legal actions has special requirements. For more information you might look at Simson Garfinkel and Gene Spafford's *Practical UNIX & Internet Security* or visit *http://www.cert.org/nav/recovering.html*.

works. You might see if *lnx1* can reach *bsd1*. You might include other local and remote hosts to see the extent of the problem.

3. Define the problem. Once you have a clear idea, you can begin coming to terms with the problem. This is not the same as identifying the symptoms but is the process of combining the symptoms and making generalizations. You are looking for common elements that allow you to succinctly describe the anomalous behavior of a system.

Your problem definition may go through several refinements. Continuing with the previous problem, you might, over time, generate the following series of problem definitions:

- *bsd1* can't *telnet* to *lnx1*.

- *bsd1* can't connect to *lnx1*.

- *bsd1* can't connect to *lnx1*, but *lnx1* can connect to other hosts including *bsd1*.

- Hosts on the same network as *lnx1* can't connect to *lnx1*.

- Hosts on the same network as *lnx1* can't connect to *lnx1*, but hosts on remote networks can connect to *lnx1*.

(Yes, this was a real problem, and no, I didn't get that last one backward.)

It is natural to try to define the problem as quickly as possible, but you shouldn't be too tied to your definition. Try to keep an open mind and be willing to redefine your problem as your information changes.

4. Identify systems or subsystems involved. As you collect information, as seen in the previous example, you will define and refine not only the nature of the problem, but also the scope of the problem. This is the step in which we divide and hopefully conquer our problem.

In this example, we have worked outward from one system to include a number of systems. Usually troubleshooting tries to narrow the scope of the problem, but as seen from this example, in networking just the opposite may happen. You must discover the full scope of the problem before you can narrow your focus. In this running example, realizing that remote connections could connect was a key discovery.

5. Develop a testable hypothesis. Of course, what you can test will depend on what tools you have, the rationale for this book. But don't let tools drive your approach. With the definition of the problem and continual refinement comes the generation of the hypotheses as to the cause or nature of the problem. Such generalizations are relatively worthless unless they can be verified. (Remember those lectures on the scientific method in high school?) In this sense, developing a set of tests is more important than having an exact definition of a

problem. In many instances, if you know the source of the problem, you can correct it without fully understanding the problem. For example, if you know an Ethernet card is failing, you can replace it without ever worrying about which chip on the card malfunctioned. I'm not suggesting that you don't want to understand the problem, but that there are levels of understanding. Your hypotheses must be guided by what you can test. As in science, an untestable hypothesis is worthless.

In general, you want tests that will reduce the size of the search space (i.e., identify subsystem involved), that are easy to apply, that do not create further problems, and so on.

In our running example, a necessary first step in making a connection is doing address resolution. This suggests that there might be some problem with the ARP mechanism. Notice that this is not a full hypothesis, but rather a point of further investigation. Having expanded the scope of the problem, we are attempting to focus in on subsystems to reduce the problem. Also notice that I haven't used any fancy tools up to this point. Keep it simple as long as you can.

6. Select and apply tests. Not all tests are created equally. Some will be much easier to apply, while others will provide more information. Determining the optimal order for a set of tests is largely a judgment call. Clearly, the simple tests that answer questions decisively are the best.

   Returning to our example, there are several ways we could investigate whether the ARP mechanism is functioning correctly. One way would be to use *tcpdump* or *ethereal* to capture traffic on the network to see if the ARP requests and responses are present. A simpler test, however, is to use the *arp* command to see if the appropriate entries are in the ARP cache on the hosts that are trying to connect to *lnx1*. In this instance, it was observed that the entries were missing from all the hosts attempting to connect to *lnx1*. The exception was the router on the network that had a much longer cache timeout than did the local hosts. This also explained why remote hosts could connect but local hosts could not connect. The remote hosts always went through the router, which had cached the Ethernet address bypassing the ARP mechanism. Note that this was not a definitive test but was done first because it was much easier.

7. Assess results. As you perform tests, you will need to assess the results, refine your tests, and repeat the process. You will want new tests that confirm your results. This is clearly an iterative process.

   With our extended example, two additional tests were possible. One was to manually add the address of *lnx1* to *bsd1*'s ARP table using the *arp* command. When this was done, connectivity was restored. When the entry was deleted, connectivity was lost. A more revealing but largely unnecessary test using packet-capture software to watch the exchange of packets between the *bsd1* and *lnx1* revealed that *bsd1*'s ARP requests were being ignored by *lnx1*.

8. Develop and assess solutions. Once you have clearly identified the problem, you must develop and assess possible solutions. With many problems, there will be several possible solutions to consider. You should not hastily implement a solution until you have thought out the consequences. With *lnx1*, solutions ranged from rebooting the system to reinstalling software. I chose the simplest first and rebooted the system.

9. Implement and evaluate your solution. Once you have decided on a solution and have implemented it, you should confirm the proper operation of your system. Depending on the scope of the changes needed, this may mean extensive testing of the system and all related systems.

With our running problem, this was not necessary. Connectivity was fully restored when the system was rebooted. What caused the problem? That was never fully resolved, but since the problem never recurred, it really isn't an issue.

If restarting the system hadn't solved the problem, what would have been the next step? In this case, the likely problem was corrupted system software. If you are running an integrity checker like *tripwire*, you might try locating anything that has changed and do a selective reinstallation. Otherwise, you may be faced with reinstalling the operating system.

One last word of warning. It is often tempting to seize on an overly complex explanation and ignore simpler explanations. Frequently, problems really are complex, but not always. It is worth asking yourself if there is a simpler solution. Often, this will save a tremendous amount of time.

Task-Specific Troubleshooting

The guidelines just given are a general or generic overview of troubleshooting. Of course, each problem will be different, and you will need to vary your approach as appropriate. The remainder of this chapter consists of guidelines for a number of the more common troubleshooting tasks you might face. It is hoped that these will give you further insight into the process.

Installation Testing

Ironically, one of the best ways to save time and avoid troubleshooting is to take the time to do a thorough job of testing when you install software or hardware. You will be testing the system when you are most familiar with the installation process, and you will avoid disruptions to service that can happen when a problem isn't discovered until the software or hardware is in use.

This is a somewhat broad interpretation of troubleshooting, but in my experience, there is very little difference between the testing you will do when you install software and the testing you will do when you encounter a problem. Overwhelmingly the only difference for most people is the scope of the testing done. Most people will test until they believe that a system is working correctly and then stop. Failures, particularly multiple failures, may leave you skeptical, while some people tend to be overly optimistic when installing new software.

Firewall testing

Because of the complexities, firewall testing is an excellent example of the problems that installation testing may present. Troubleshooting a firewall is a demanding task for several reasons. First, to avoid disruptions in service, initial firewall testing should be done in an isolated environment before moving on to a production environment.

Second, you need to be very careful to develop an appropriate set of tests so that you don't leave gaping holes in your security. You'll need to go through a firewall rule by rule. You won't be able to check every possibility, but you should be able to test each general type of traffic. For example, consider a rule that passes HTTP traffic to your web server. You will want to pass traffic to port 80 on that server. If you are taking the approach of denying all traffic that is not explicitly permitted, potentially, you will want to block traffic to that host at all other ports. You will also want to block traffic to port 80 on other hosts.[*] Thus, you should develop a set of three tests for this one action. Although there will be some duplicated tests, you'll want to take the same approach for each rule. Developing an explicit set of tests is the key step in this type of testing.

The first step in testing a firewall is to test the environment in which the firewall will function without the firewall. It can be extraordinarily frustrating to try to debug anomalous firewall behavior only to discover that you had a routing problem before you began. Thus, the first thing you will want to do is turn off any filtering and test your routing. You could use tools like *ripquery* to retrieve routing tables and examine entries, but it is probably much simpler to use *ping* to check connectivity, assuming ICMP ECHO_REQUEST packets aren't being blocked. (If this is the case, you might try tools like *nmap* or *hping.*)

You'll also what to verify that all concomitant software is working. This will include all intrusion detection software, accounting and logging software, and

---

[*] If you doubt the need for this last test, read RFC 3093, a slightly tongue-in-cheek description of how to use port 80 to bypass a firewall.

testing software. For example, you'll probably use packet capture software like *tcpdump* or *ethereal* to verify the operation of your firewall and will want to make sure the firewall is working properly. I hate to admit it, but I've started packet capture software on a host that I forgot was attached to a switch and banged my head wondering why I wasn't seeing anything. Clearly, if I had used this setup to make sure packets were blocked without first testing it, I could have been severely misled.

Test the firewall in isolation. If you are adding filtering to a production router, admittedly this is going to be a problem. The easiest way to test in isolation is to connect each interface to an isolated host that can both generate and capture packets. You might use *hping, nemesis*, or any of the other custom packet generation software discussed in Chapter 9. Work through each of your tests for each rule with the rule disabled and enabled. Be sure you explicitly document all your tests, particularly the syntax.

Once you are convinced that the firewall is working, it is time to move it online. If you can schedule offline testing, that is the best approach. Work through your tests again with and without the filters enabled. If offline testing isn't possible, you can still go through your tests with the filters enabled.

Finally, don't forget to come back and go through these tests periodically. In particular, you'll want to reevaluate the firewall every time you change rules.

Performance Analysis and Monitoring

If a system simply isn't working, then you know troubleshooting is needed. But in many cases, it may not be clear that you even have a problem. Performance analysis is often the first step to getting a handle on whether your system is functioning properly. And it is often the case that careful performance analysis will identify the problem so that no further troubleshooting is needed.

Performance analysis is another management task that hinges on collecting information. It is a task that you will never complete, and it is important at every stage in the system's life cycle. The most successful network administrator will take a proactive approach, addressing issues before they become problems. Chapter 7 and Chapter 8 discussed the use of specific tools in greater detail.

For planning, performance analysis is used to compare systems, establish system requirements, and do capacity planning and forecasting. For management, it provides guidance in configuring and tuning the system. In particular, the identification of bottlenecks can be essential for management, planning, and troubleshooting.

There are three general approaches to performance analysis—*analytical modeling, simulations,* and *measurement.* Analytical models are mathematical models usually based on queuing theory. Simulations are computer models that attempt to mimic the behavior of the system through computer programs. Measurement is, of course, the collection of data from an existing network. This book has focused primarily on measurement (although simulation tools were mentioned in Chapter 9).

Each approach has its role. In practice, there can be a considerable overlap in using these approaches. Analytical models can serve as the basis for simulations, or direct measurements may be needed to supply parameters used with analytical models or simulations.

Measurement has its limitations. Obviously, the system must exist before measurements can be made so it may not be a viable tool for planning. Measurements tend to produce the most variable results. And many things can go wrong with measurements. On the positive side, measurement carries a great deal of authority with most people. When you say you have measured something, this is treated as irrefutable evidence by many, often unjustifiably.

General steps

Measuring performance is something of an art. It is much more difficult to decide what to measure and how to make the actual measurements than it might appear at first glance. And there are many ways to waste time collecting data that will not be useful for your purposes.

What follows is a fairly informal description of the steps involved in performance analysis. As I said before, listing the steps can be very helpful in focusing attention on some parts of the process that might otherwise be ignored.* Of course, every situation is different, so these steps are only an approximation. Designing performance analysis tests is an iterative process. You should go back through these steps as you proceed, refining each step as needed.

1. State your goal. This is the question you want to answer. At this point, it may be fairly vague, but you will refine it as you progress. You need a sense of direction to get started. A common mistake is to allow a poorly defined goal to remain vague throughout the process, so be sure to revisit this step often. Also, try to avoid goals that bias your approach. For instance, set out to compare systems rather than show that one system is better than another.

   As an example, a network administrator might ask if the network backbone is adequate to support current levels of traffic. While an extremely important

---

* If you would like a more complete discussion of the steps in performance analysis, you should get Raj Jain's exceptional book, *The Art of Computer Systems Performance Analysis.* Jain's book considers performance analysis from a broader perspective than this book.

question, it is quite vague at this point. But stating the goal allows you to start focusing on the problem. For example, formally stating this problem may lead you to ask what *adequate* really means. Or you might go on to consider what the relevant time frame is, i.e., what *current* means.

2. Define your system. The definition of your system will vary with your goal. You will need to decide what parts of the system to include and in what detail. You may want to exclude those parts outside your control. If you are interested in server performance, you will undoubtedly want to consider the various subsystems of the server separately—such as disks, memory, CPU, and network interfaces.

   With the backbone example, what exactly is the backbone? Certainly it will include equipment such as routers and switches, but does it include servers? If you do include servers, you will want to view the server as a single entity, a source or sink for network traffic perhaps, but not component by component.

3. Identify possible outcomes. This step consists of identifying possible answers to the question you want to answer. This is a refinement of Step 1 but should be addressed after the parts of the system are identified. Identifying outcomes establishes the level of your interest, how much detail you might need, and how much work you are going to have to do. You are determining the granularity of your measurements with this step.

   For example, possible outcomes for the question of backbone performance might be that performance is adequate, that the system suffers minor congestion during the periods of heaviest load, or that the system is usually suffering serious congestion with heavy packet loss. For many purposes, just selecting one of these three answers might be adequate. However, in some cases, you may want a much more descriptive answer. For example, you may want some estimation of the average utilization, maximum utilization, percent of time at maximum utilization, or number of lost packets. Ultimately, the degree of detail required by the answer will determine the scope of the project. You need to make this decision early, or you may have to repeat the project to gather additional information.

4. Identify and select what you will measure. Metrics are those system characteristics that can be quantitatively measured. The choice of a metric will depend on the services you are examining. Be careful in your selection. It is often tempting to go with metrics based on how easy the data is to collect rather than on how relevant the data is to the goal. For a network backbone, this might include throughput, delay, utilization, number of packets sent, number of packets discarded, or average packet size.

5. If appropriate, identify test parameters and factors.* Parameters and factors are characteristics of the system that affect performance that can be changed. You'll change these to see what effect they have on the system. Parameters include both system and load (or traffic) parameters. Try to be as systematic as possible in identifying and evaluating parameters to avoid arbitrary decisions. It is very easy to overlook relevant parameters or include irrelevant ones.

For a network backbone, system parameters may include interface speeds and link speeds or the use of load sharing. For traffic, you might use a tool like *mgen* to add an additional load. But for simple performance measurement, you may elect to change nothing.

6. Select tools. Once you have a clear picture of what you want to do, it is time to select the tools of interest. It is all too easy to do this too soon. Don't let the tools you have determine what you are going to do. Tools for backbone performance might include using *ntop* on a link or SNMP-based tools.

7. Establish measurement constraints. On a production network, establishing constraints usually means deciding when and where to make your measurements. You will also need to decide on the frequency and duration of your measurements. This is often more a matter of intuition than engineering. This is something that you will have to do iteratively, adjusting your approach based on the results you get. Unless you have a very compelling reason, measurements should be taken under representative conditions.

For backbone performance, for example, router interfaces are the obvious places to look. Server interfaces are another reasonable choice. You may also need to look at individual links as well, particularly in a switched network. You will also need to sample at different times, including in particular those times when the load is heaviest. (Use *mrtg* or *cricket* to determine this.) You will need to ensure that your measurements have the appropriate level of detail. If you have isochronous applications, such as video conferencing, that are extremely sensitive to delay, five-minute averages will not provide adequate information.

8. Review your experimental design. Once you have decided what you want to measure and how, you should look back over the process before you begin. Are there any optimizations you can make to minimize the amount of work you will have to do? Will the measurements you make really answer your questions? It is wise to review these questions before you invest large amounts of time.

---

* Further distinctions between parameters and factors are sometimes made but don't seem relevant when considered solely from the perspective of measurements.

9. Collect data. The single most important consideration in collecting data is that you adequately document what you are doing. It is an all too common experience to discover that you have a wonderful collection of data, but you don't fully know or remember the circumstances surrounding its collection. Consequently, you don't know how to interpret it. If this happens, the only thing you can do is discard the data and start over. Remember, collecting data is an iterative process. You must examine your results and make adjustments as needed. It is too easy to continue collecting worthless data when even a cursory examination of your data would have revealed you were on the wrong track.

10. Analyze data. Once the data is collected, you must analyze, interpret, and act upon your results. This analysis will, of course, depend heavily on the context and goals of the investigation. But an essential element is to condense the data and extract the needed information, presenting it in a concise form. It is often the case that measurements will create massive amounts of data that are meaningless until carefully analyzed.

Don't get too carried away. Often the simplest analyses are of greater value than overly complex analyses. Simple analyses can often be more easily understood. But whatever you conclude, you'll need to do it all again. System performance analysis is a never-ending task.

Bottleneck analysis

Since networks are composed of a number of pieces, if the pieces are not well matched, poor performance may depend on the behavior of a single component. Bottleneck analysis is the process of identifying this component.

When looking at performance, you'll need to be sure you get a complete picture. Generally, one bottleneck will dominate performance statistics. Many systems, however, will have multiple bottlenecks. It's just that one bottleneck is a little worse than the others. Correcting one bottleneck will simply shift the problem—the bottleneck will move from one component to another. When doing performance monitoring, your goal should be to discover as many bottlenecks as possible.

Often identifying a bottleneck is easy. Once you have a clear picture of your network's architecture, topology, and uses, bottlenecks will be obvious. For example, if 90% of your network traffic is to the Internet and you have a gigabit backbone and a 56-Kbps WAN connection, you won't need a careful analysis to identify your bottleneck.

Identifying bottlenecks is process dependent. What may be a bottleneck for one process may not be a problem for another. For example, if you are moving small files, the delay in making a connection will be the primary bottleneck. If you are moving large files, the speed of the link may be more important.

Bottleneck analysis is essential in planning because it will tell you what improvements will provide the greatest benefit to your network. The only real way to escape bottlenecks is to grossly overengineer your network, not something you'll normally want to do. Thus, your goal should not be to completely eliminate bottlenecks but to minimize their impact to the point that they don't cause any real problems. Upgrading the network in a way that doesn't address bottlenecks will provide very little benefit to the network. If the bottlenecks on your network are a slow WAN connection and slow servers, upgrading from Fast Ethernet to Gigabit Ethernet will be a foolish waste of money. The key consideration here is utilization. If you are seeing 25% utilization with Fast Ethernet, don't be surprised to see utilization drop below 3% with Gigabit Ethernet. But you should be aware that even if the utilization is low, increasing the capacity of a line will shorten download times for large files. Whether this is worthwhile will depend on your organization's mission and priorities.

Here is a rough outline of the steps you might go through to identify a bottleneck:

1. Map your network. The first step is to develop a clear picture of your network's topology. To do this, you can use the tools described in Chapter 6. *tkined* might be a good choice. Often potential bottlenecks are obvious once you have a clear picture of your network. At the very least, you may be able to distinguish the parts of the network that are likely to have bottlenecks from parts that don't need to be examined, reducing the work you will have to do.

2. Identify time-dependent behavior. The problems bottlenecks cause, unless they are really severe, tend to come and go. The next logical step is to locate the most heavily used devices and the times when they are in greatest use. You'll want to use a tool like *mrtg* or *cricket* to identify time-dependent behavior. (Understanding time-dependent behavior can also be helpful in identifying when you can work on the problem with the least impact on users.)

3. Pinpoint the problems. At this point, you should have narrowed your focus to a few key parts of the network and a few key times. Now you will want to drill down on specific devices and links. *ntop* is a likely choice at this point, but any SNMP-based tool may be useful.

4. Select the tool. How you will proceed from here will depend on what you have discovered. It is likely that you will be able to classify the problem as stemming from an edge device, such as a server or a path between devices. Doing so will simplify the decision of what to do next.

   If you believe the problem lies with a path, you can use the tools described in Chapter 4 to drill down to a specific device or single link. You'll probably want to get an idea of the nature of the traffic over the link. *ntop* is one choice, or you could use a tool like *tcpdump, ethereal,* or one of the tools that analyzes *tcpdump* traffic.

For a link device like a router or switch, you'll need to look at basic performance. SNMP-based tools are the best choice here.

For end devices, you need to look at the performance of the device at each level of the communications architecture. You could use *spray* to examine the interface performance. For the stack, you might compare the time between SYN and ACK packets with the time between application packets. (Use *ethereal* or *tcpdump* to collect this information.) The setup times should be independent of the application, depending only on the stack. If the stack responds quickly and the application doesn't, you'll need to focus on the application.

5. Fix the problem. Once you have an idea of the source of the problem, you can then decide how to deal with it. For poor link performance, you have several choices. You can upgrade the link bandwidth or alter the network topology to change the load on the link. Adding interfaces to a server is one very simple solution. Attaching a server to multiple subnets is a quick way to decrease traffic between those subnets. Policy-based routing is yet another approach. You can use routing priorities to ensure that important traffic is handled preferentially.

   For an edge device such as an attached server, you'll want to distinguish among hardware problems, operating system problems, and application problems, then upgrade accordingly.

Bottleneck analysis is something you should do on an ongoing basis. The urgency will depend on user perceptions. If users are complaining, it doesn't matter what the numbers say, you have a problem. If users aren't complaining, your analysis is less pressing but should still be done.

Capacity planning

Capacity planning is an extremely important task. Done correctly, it is also an extremely complex and difficult task, both to learn and to do. But this shouldn't keep you from attempting it. The description here can best be described as a crude, first-order approximation of capacity planning. But it will give you a place to start while you are learning.

Capacity planning is really an umbrella that describes several closely related activities. *Capacity management* is the process of allocating resources in a cost-efficient way. It is concerned with the resources that you currently have. (As you might guess, this is closely related to bottleneck analysis.) *Trend analysis* is the process of looking at system performance over time, trying to identify how it has changed in the past with the goal of predicting future changes. *Capacity planning* attempts to combine capacity management and trend analysis. The goal is to predict future needs to provide for effective planning.

The basic steps are fairly straightforward to describe, just difficult to carry out. First, decide what you need to measure. That means looking at your system in much the same way you did with bottleneck analysis but augmenting your analysis with anything you know about the future growth of your system. You'll need to think about your system in context to do this.

Next, select appropriate tools to collect the information you'll need. (*mrtg* and *cricket* are the most obvious tools among those described in this book, but there are a number of other viable tools if you are willing to do the work to archive the data.) With the tools in place, begin monitoring your system, recording and archiving appropriate data. Deciding what to keep and how to organize it is a tremendously difficult problem. Every situation is different. Each situation is largely a question of balancing the amount of work involved in keeping the data in an organized and accessible manner with the likelihood that you will actually use it. This can come only from experience.

Once you have the measurements, you will need to analyze them. In general, focus on areas that show the greatest change. Collecting and analyzing data will be an iterative process. If little is different from one measurement to the next, then collect data less frequently. When there is high variability, collect more often.

Finally, you'll make your predictions and adjust your system accordingly.

There are a number of difficulties in capacity planning. Perhaps the greatest difficulty comes with unanticipated, fundamental changes in the way your network is used. If you will be offering new services, predictions based on trends that predate these services will not adequately predict new needs. For example, if you are introducing new technologies such as Internet telephony or video, trend analysis before the fact will be of limited value. There is a saying that you can't predict how many people will use a bridge by counting how many people are currently swimming across the river. If this is the case, about the best you can do is look to others who have built similar bridges over similar rivers.

Another closely related problem is differential growth. If your network, like most, provides a variety of different services, then they are probably growing at different rates. This makes it very difficult to predict aggregate performance or need if you haven't adequately collected data to analyze individual trends.

Yet another difficulty is motivation. The key to trend analysis is keeping adequate records, i.e., measuring and recording information in a way that makes it accessible and usable. This is difficult for many people since the records won't have much immediate utility. Their worth comes from being able to look back at them over time for trends. It is difficult to invest the time needed to collect and maintain this data when there will be no immediate return on the effort and when fundamental changes can destroy the utility of the data.

You should be aware of these difficulties, but you should not let them discourage you. The cost of not doing capacity planning is much greater.

A

Software Sources

This appendix begins with a brief discussion of retrieving and installing software tools. It then provides a list of potential sources for the software. First I describe several excellent general sources for tools, then I list specific sources.

Much of this software requires root privileges and could contain dangerous code. Be sure you get your code from reliable sources. Considerable effort has been made to provide canonical sources, but no guarantee can be made for the trustworthiness of the code or the sources listed here. Most of these programs are available as FreeBSD ports or Linux packages. I have used them, when available, for testing for this book.

Installing Software

I have not tried to describe how to install individual tools in this book. First, in my experience, a set of directions that is accurate for one version of the software may not be accurate for the next version. Even more likely, directions for one operating system may fail miserably for another. This is frequently true even for different versions of the same operating system. Consequently, trying to develop a reasonable set of directions for each tool for a variety of operating systems was considered unfeasible. In general, the best source of information, i.e., the only information that is likely to be reliable, is the information that comes with the software itself. Read the directions!

Having said this, I have tried to give some generic directions for installing software. At best, these are meant to augment the existing directions. They may help clarify matters when the included directions are a little too brief. These instructions are not meant as replacements.

Installing software has gotten much easier in the last few years, thanks in part to several developments. First, GNU configure and build tools have had a tremendous impact in erasing the differences created by different operating systems. Second, there have been improvements in file transfer and compression tools as well as increased standardization of the tools used. Finally, several operating systems now include mechanisms to automate the process. If you can use these, your life will be much simpler. I have briefly described three here—the Solaris package system, the Red Hat package manager, and the FreeBSD port system. Please consult the appropriate documentation for the details for each.

Generic Installs

Here is a quick review of basic steps you will go through in installing a program. Not every step will be needed in every case. If you have specific directions for a product, use those directions, not these! (Although slightly dated, a very comprehensive discussion can be found in *Porting Unix Software* by Greg Lehey.)

1. Locate a reliable, trustworthy source for both the software and directions. Usually, the best sources are listed on a web page managed by the author or her organization.

2. If you can locate directions before you begin, read them first. Typically, basic directions can be found at the software's home page. Frequently, however, the most complete directions are included with the software distribution, so you may need to retrieve and unpack the software to get at these.

3. Download the tool using FTP. You may be able to do this with your web browser. Be certain you use a binary transfer if you are doing this manually.

4. Uncompress the software if needed. If the filename ends with *.tgz* or *.gz*, use *gunzip*. These are the two most common formats, but there are other possibilities. Lehey's book contains a detailed list of possibilities and appropriate tools.

5. Use *tar* to unpack the software if needed, i.e., if the filename ends with *.tar*. Typically, I use the *-xvf* options.

6. Read any additional documentation that was included with the distribution.

7. If the file is a precompiled binary, you need only move it to the correct location. In general, it is safer to download the source code and compile it yourself. It is much harder to hide Trojan horses in source code (but not impossible).

8. If you have a very simple utility, you may need to compile it directly. This means calling the compiler with the appropriate options. But for all but the

simplest programs, a makefile should be provided. If you see a file named *Makefile*, you will use the *make* command to build the program. It may be necessary to customize the *Makefile* before you can proceed. If you are lucky, the distribution will include a *configure* script, a file that, when executed, will automatically make any needed changes to the *Makefile*. Look for this script first. If you don't find it, look back over your directions for any needed changes. If you don't find anything, examine the makefile for embedded directions. If all else fails, you can try running *make* without making any changes.

9. Finally, you may also need to run *make* with one or more arguments to finish the installation, e.g., *make install* to move the files to the appropriate directories or *make clean* to remove unused files such as object modules after linking. Look at your directions, or look for comments embedded in the makefile.

Hopefully each of these steps will be explained in detail in the documentation with the software.

Solaris Packages

In Solaris, packages are directories of the files needed to build or run a program. This is the mechanism Sun Microsystems uses to distribute software. If you are installing from a CD-ROM, the files will typically be laid out just the way you need them. You will only need to mount the CD-ROM so you can get to them. If you are downloading packages, you will typically need to unpack them first, usually with the *tar* command. You may want to do this under the default directory */var/spool/pkg*, but you can override this location with command options when installing the package.

Once you have the appropriate package on your system, you can use one of several closely related commands to manage it. To install a package, use the *pkgadd* command. Without any arguments, *pkgadd* will list the packages on your system and give you the opportunity to select the package of interest. Alternately, you can name the package you want to install. You can use the *-d* option to specify a different directory.

Other commands include the *pkgrm* command to remove a package, the *pkginfo* command to display information on which packages are already installed on your system, and *pkgchk* to check the integrity of the package.

For other software in package format, you might begin by looking at *http:// sunfreeware.com* or searching the Web for Sun's university alliance software repositories. Use the string "sunsite" in your search.

Red Hat Package Manager

Different versions of Linux have taken the idea of packages and expanded on it. Several different package formats are available, but the Red Hat format is probably the most common. There are several programs for the installation of software in the RPM format. Of these, the Red Hat Package Manager (*rpm*) is what I generally use. Two other package management tools that provide GUIs include *glint* and *gnorpm*.

First, download the package in question. Then, to install a package, call *rpm* with the options *-ivh* and the name of the package. If all goes well, that is all there is to it. You can use the *-e* option to remove a package.

A variety of packages come with many Linux distributions. Numerous sites on the Web offer extensive collections of Linux software in RPM format. If you are using Red Hat Linux, try *http://www.redhat.com*. Many of the repositories will provide you with a list of dependencies, which you'll need to install first.

FreeBSD Ports

Another approach to automating software installation is the port collection approach used by FreeBSD. This, by far, is the easiest approach to use and has been adapted to other systems including OpenBSD and Debian Linux. The FreeBSD port collection is basically a set of directions for installing software. Literally thousands of programs are available.

Software is grouped by category in subdirectories in the */usr/ports* directory. You change to the appropriate directory for the program of interest and type *make install*. At that point, you sit back and watch the magic. The port system will attempt to locate the appropriate file in the */usr/ports/distfiles* directory. If the file is not there, it will then try downloading the file from an appropriate site via FTP. Usually the port system knows about several sites so, if it can't reach one, it will try another. Once it has the file, it will calculate and verify a checksum for the file. It next applies appropriate patches and checks dependencies. It will automatically install other ports as needed. Once everything is in place, it will compile the software. Finally, it installs the software and documentation. When it works, which is almost always, it is simply extraordinary. The port collection is an installation option with FreeBSD. Alternately, you can visit *http://www.freebsd.org*. The process is described in the *FreeBSD Handbook*.

When evaluating a new piece of software, I have the luxury of testing the software on several different platforms. In general, I find the FreeBSD port system the easiest approach to use. If I have trouble with a FreeBSD port, I'll look for a Linux package next. If that fails, I generally go to a generic source install. In my experience, Solaris packages tend to be hard to find.

Generic Sources

The Cooperative Association for Internet Data Analysis (CAIDA) maintains an extensive listing of measurement tools on the Web. The page at *http://www.caida. org/tools/measurement* has a number of tables grouping tools by function. Brief descriptions of each tool, including links to relevant sites, follow the tables. This listing includes both free and commercial tools and seems to be updated on a regular basis. Another CAIDA page, *http://www.caida.org/tools/taxonomy/,* provides a listing of tools by taxonomy.

Another web site maintaining a list of network-monitoring tools is *http://www.slac. stanford.edu/xorg/nmtf/nmtf-tools.html.* In general, there are several collaborative Internet measurement projects that regularly introduce or discuss measurement tools. These include CAIDA and the Stanford Linear Accelerator Center (SLAC), among others.

Other sites that you might want to look at include those that develop tools, such as *http://moat.nlanr.net,* *http://www-nrg.ee.lbl.gov/,* and *http://www.merit.edu.* Don't forget special purpose sites. Security sites like *http://www.cert.org* and *http:// www.ciac.org/ciac/* may have links to useful tools. Keep your eyes open.

Finally, several RFCs discuss tools. The most comprehensive is RFC 1470. Unfortunately, it is quite dated. RFC 1713, also somewhat dated, deals with DNS tools, and RFC 2398 deals with tools for testing TCP implementation.

Licenses

Although some commercial software has been mentioned, this book has overwhelmingly focused on freely available software. But "freely available" is a very vague expression that covers a lot of ground.

At one extreme is software that is released without any restrictions whatsoever. You can use it as you see fit, modify it, and, in some cases, even try to sell your enhanced versions. Most of the software described here, however, comes with some limitations on what you can do with it, particularly with respect to reselling it.

Some of this software is freely available to some classes of users but not to others. For example, some software distinguishes between commercial and noncommercial users or between commercial and academic users. For some of the tools, binaries are available, but source code is either not available or requires a license. Some of the software exists in multiple forms. For example, there may be both free and commercial versions of a tool. Other tools restrict what you do with them. For example, you may be free to use the tool, but you may be expected to share any improvements you make.

You should also be aware that licensing may change over time. It is not uncommon for a tool to move from the free category to the commercial category, particularly as new, improved versions are released. This seems to be a fairly common business model.

I have not attempted to describe the licensing for individual tools. I am not a lawyer and do not fully understand all the subtleties of license agreements. Different licenses will apply to different organizations in different ways. In some cases, such as when encryption is involved, different countries have laws that impact licenses in unusual ways. Finally, license agreements change so frequently, anything I write could be inaccurate by the time you read this.

The bottom line, then, is that you should be sure to check appropriate licensing agreements whenever you retrieve any software. Ultimately, it is your responsibility to ensure that your use of these tools is permissible.

Sources for Tools

This section gives basic information on each tool discussed in this book. I have not included built-in tools like *ps*. The tools are listed alphabetically. I have tried to make a note of which tools are specific to Windows, but I did not list Windows tools separately, since many tools are available for both Unix and Windows.

A few tools discussed in the book, particularly older tools, seem to have no real home but may be available in some archives. This is generally an indication that the tool is fading into oblivion and should be used as a last alternative. (Some of these tools, however, are alive and well as Linux packages or FreeBSD ports.) While I was writing this book, a number of home pages for tools changed. Also, several of the sites seem to be down more than they are up. I have supplied the most recent information I have, but many of the tools will have moved.

These URLs are nothing more than starting points. If you can't find the tool at the URL given here, consider doing an Internet search. In fact, I really recommend doing your own search over using this list. I find that I have the most luck with searches if I do a compound search with the tool's name and the author's last name.

That one version of a tool is safe, stable, and useful doesn't mean the next version won't have severe problems. New programs are introduced on an almost daily basis. So keep your eyes open.

Analyzer—Piero Viano

This is a protocol analyzer for Windows. (Directions are available only in Italian.) *http://netgroup-serv.polito.it/analyzer/*

argus—Carter Bullard

This is a generic IP network transaction auditing tool. *ftp://ftp.sei.cmu.edu/pub/argus-1.5*

arping—marvin@nss.nu

This *ping*-like program uses ARP requests to check reachability. *http://synscan.nss.nu/programs.php*

arpwatch—Lawrence Berkeley National Laboratory

This tool watches for new or changed MAC addresses. *ftp://ftp.ee.lbl.gov/arpwatch.tar.Z*

AWACS—Georg Greve

This is log management software currently under development. *http://www.gnu.org/software/awacs/awacs.html*

bb—BB4 Technologies, Inc.

This is web-based monitoring software. *http://www.bb4.com/*

bind—University of California at Berkeley and the Internet Software Consortium

This is the Berkeley Internet Name Daemon, i.e., domain name server software. It includes a number of testing tools. *http://www.isc.org/products/BIND/*

bing—Pierre Beyssac

This tool measures point-to-point bandwidth. *http://www.freenix.fr/freenix/logiciels/bing.html*

bluebird—Shane O'Donnell et al.

This is a general network management applications framework. *http://www.opennms.org/*

bprobe and cprobe

These tools measure the bandwidth at the slowest link on a path. *ftp://cs-www.bu.edu/carter/probes.tar.Z*

cheops—Mark Spencer

This is a Linux-based network management platform. *http://www.marko.net/cheops/*

Chesapeake port scanner—Mentor Technologies

This is a simple port scanner for Windows. *http://www.mentortech.com/learn/tools/pscan.shtml*

clink—Allen Downey

This is another *pathchar* variant, a tool for measuring the bandwidth of links on a path. *http://www.cs.colby.edu/~downey/clink/*

CMU SNMP—Carnegie Mellon University

> This set of SNMP tools has largely been superseded by NET SNMP. They are still commonly available for Linux. *http://www.gaertner.de/snmp/*

cpm—CERT at Carnegie Mellon University

> This tool checks to see if any interfaces are in promiscuous mode. *ftp://info. cert.org/pub/tools/cpm.tar.Z*

cricket—Jeff Allen

> This tool queries devices, collecting information over time, typically router traffic, and graphs the collected information. *http://cricket.sourceforge.net/*

cyberkit—Luc Neijens

> This multipurpose Windows-based tool includes *ping, traceroute,* scanning, and SNMP. It is postcardware. *http://www.cyberkit.net*

dig

> Part of the *bind* distribution. This tool retrieves domain name information from a server.

dnsquery

> Part of the *bind* distribution. This tool retrieves domain name information from a server.

dnsutl—Peter Miller

> This is a tool to simplify DNS configuration. *http://www.pcug.org.au/~millerp/ dnsutl/dnsutl.html*

dnswalk—David Barr

> This tool retrieves and analyzes domain name information from a server. *http:// www.cis.ohio-state.edu/~barr/dnswalk/*

doc—Steve Hotz, Paul Mockapetris, and Brad Knowles

> This tool retrieves and analyzes domain name information from a server.

dsniff—Dug Song

> This is a set of utilities that can be used to test or breach the security on your system. *http://naughty.monkey.org/~dugsong/dsniff/*

echoping—Stéphane Bortzmeyer

> This is an alternative to *ping* that uses protocols other than ICMP. *ftp://ftp. internatif.org/pub/unix/echoping/*

egressor—Mitre

> This tool set verifies that your router will not forward packets with spoofed addresses. *http://www.packetfactory.net/Projects/Egressor/*

ethereal—Gerald Combs et al.

> This is a protocol analyzer that runs under X Window and Windows. It requires GTK+, which in turn requires GLIB. *http://www.ethereal.com*

fping—Roland J. Schemers

This is a *ping* variant that can check multiple systems in parallel. *http://www.fping.com*

fressh—FreSSH Organization

This is another alternative to *ssh*. *http://www.fressh.org/*

getif—Philippe Simonet

This is a multipurpose Windows tool that uses SNMP. *http://www.geocities.com/SiliconValley/Hills/8260/*

gimp

This is an image manipulation program. It is also available for Windows. *http://www.gimp.org/*

GTK+—Peter Mattis, Spencer Kimball, and Josh MacDonald

This is a GUI development toolkit. Its libraries may be needed by other tools. *http://www.gtk.org/*

gtkportscan—Rafael Barrero

This is a port scanner that is written in *GTK+*. The last reported site was *http://armageddon.splorg.org/gtkportscan/*.

GxSNMP

This is a network management applications framework. *http://www.gxsnmp.org/*

h2n

This Perl tool translates a host table to name server file format. *ftp://ftp.uu.net/published/oreilly/nutshell/dnsbind/dns.tar.Z*

host

Part of the *bind* distribution. This tool retrieves domain name information from a server.

hping

Salvatore Sanfilippo. This tool sends custom packets and displays responses. *http://www.kyuzz.org/antirez/software.html*

iperf—Mark Gates and Alex Warshavsky

This is a tool for measuring TCP and UDP bandwidth. *http://dast.nlanr.net/Projects/Iperf/*

ipfilter—Darren Reed

This is a set of programs to filter TCP/IP packets. It includes *ipsend*, a tool to send custom packets. *http://coombs.anu.edu.au/~avalon/ip-filter.html*

ipload—BTT Software

This is a load generator for Windows. *http://www.bttsoftware.co.uk/ipload.html*

ipsend—Darren Reed

This tool is part of the *ipfilter* package. *http://coombs.anu.edu.au/~avalon/ip-filter.html*

lamers—Bryan Beecher

This tool checks for lame delegations in a DNS database. Its current official location is unknown. The last reported official site: *ftp://terminator.cc.umich.edu/dns/lame-delegations*. I found links to copies at *http://www.dns.net/dnsrd/tools.html*.

logcheck—Craig Rowland

This log management tool is suitable for use with *syslog* files. *http://www.psionic.com/abacus/logcheck/*

lsof—Victor Abell

This tool lists open files on a Unix system. *ftp://vic.cc.purdue.edu/pub/tools/unix/lsof/*

MGEN—Brian Adamson and Naval Research Laboratory

This tool set generates and receives traffic. It is used primarily for load testing. *http://manimac.itd.nrl.navy.mil/MGEN/*

mon—Jim Trocki

This is a general purpose resource-monitoring system for host and service availability. *http://www.kernel.org/software/mon/*

mrtg—Tobias Oetiker and Dave Rand

This tool queries devices, collects information over time (typically router traffic) and graphs collected information. *http://ee-staff.ethz.ch/~oetiker/webtools/mrtg/*

mssh—Metro State College of Denver

This is a version of *ssh* for Windows. *http://cs.mscd.edu/MSSH/index.html*

msyslog—Core SDI

This is *modular syslog*, a replacement for *secure syslog*. *http://www.core-sdi.com/english/freesoft.html*

nam—Steven McCanne and VINT

This is a *Tcl/Tk*-based network visualization and animation tool. *http://www.isi.edu/nsnam/nam/*

nemesis—obecian@celerity.bartoli.org

This tool generates a wide variety of custom IP packets. *http://www.packetninja.net/nemesis/*

nessus—Jordan Hrycij and Renaud Deraison

This is a security scanning and auditing tool. *http://www.nessus.org/*

NET SNMP—Wes Hardaker

This is an updated version of CMU SNMP. It is postcardware. *http://net-snmp. sourceforge.net/*

netcat—hobbit@avian.org

This simple utility reads and writes data across network connections. It is available for both Unix and Windows. *http://www.canonware.com/canonware/* and *http://www.l0pht.com/~weld/netcat/*

netmon

Supplied with Microsoft NT Server. This is network-monitoring software. A basic, stripped-down version of the netmon.exe program is supplied with Microsoft NT Server. The full version is part of Microsoft's System Management Server.

netperf—Hewlett-Packard

This is network benchmarking and performance measurement software. *http:// www.netperf.org/netperf/NetperfPage.html*

nfswatch—Dave Curry and Jeff Mogul

This is a tool for watching NFS traffic. The last known site was *ftp://ftp.cerias/ purdue.edu/pub/tools/unix/netutils/nfswatch/*.

nhfsstone—Legato Systems

This is a tool for benchmarking NFS traffic. Current availability is unknown, but it was originally from *www.legato.com.*

NIST Net—National Institute of Standards and Technology

This is a network emulation package that runs on Linux. *http://is2.antd.nist. gov/itg/nistnet/*

nmap—fyodor@dhp.com

This is a general scanning and probing tool with lots of functionality including OS fingerprinting. *http://www.insecure.org/nmap*

nocol—Netplex Technologies, Inc.

This is system- and network-monitoring software. *http://www.netplex-tech.com/ software/nocol/*

ns—Steven McCanne, Sally Floyd, and VINT

This is a network simulator for protocol performance and scaling. *http://www. isi.edu/nsnam/ns/*

nslookup

Part of the *bind* distribution. This tool retrieves domain name information from a server.

ntop—Luca Deri

This is a versatile tool for monitoring network usage. *http://www.ntop.org/ntop.html*

ntpd—David Mills

This is a collection of tools to set and coordinate system clocks using NTP. *http://www.eecis.udel.edu/~ntp/*

openssh

This is another version of *ssh*. *http://www.openssh.com/*

p0f—Michal Zalewski

This is a passive stack fingerprinting system. *http://lcamtuf.hack.pl/p0f-1.7.tgz*

pathchar—Van Jacobson

This program measures the bandwidth of the links along a network path. *ftp://ftp.ee.lbl.gov/* or *http://ee.lbl.gov/*

pchar—Bruce Mah

This tool is a reimplementation of *pathchar*. *http://www.employees.org/~bmah/Software/pchar/*

portscan—Tennessee Carmel-Veilleux

This is a simple port scanner. *http://www.ameth.org/~veilleux/portscan.html*

putty—Simon Tatham

This is a Windows implementation of *ssh*. *http://www.chiark.greenend.org.uk/~sgtatham/putty/*

Qcheck—Ganymede

This is a Windows network benchmarking tool. *http://www.qcheck.net*

queso—savage@apostols.org

This is an OS fingerprinting tool. *http://savage.apostols.org/projects.html*

ripquery

Part of the *gated* distribution. This tool retrieves the routing table from a system running RIP. *http://www.gated.org/*

rrd—Tobias Oetiker

This is a round-robin database system useful for collecting and archiving data over time. *http://ee-staff.ethz.ch/~oetiker/webtools/rrdtool/*

rtquery

Part of the *routed* distribution. This is a tool for retrieving the routing table from a system running RIP.

samspade—Steve Atkins

This is a multipurpose Windows tool with a wide range of features. *http://samspade.org/ssw/*

Sanitize—Vern Paxson

This is a set of Bourne scripts that use the standard Unix utilities *sed* and *awk*. It is used to clean up *tcpdump* traces to ensure privacy. *http://ita.ee.lbl.gov/html/contrib/sanitize.html*

scion—Merit Networks, Inc.

This is network statistics collection and reporting software (also called *NetSCARF.*) It is also available for Windows. *http://www.merit.edu/internet/net-research/netscarf/*

scotty—Jürgen Schönwälder

This provides network management extension to the *Tcl/Tk* language. *http://wwwhome.cs.utwente.nl/~schoenw/scotty/*

SFS—SPEC

This is a commercial (but nonprofit) NFS benchmark. *http://www.spec.org*

siphon—Subterrain Security Group

This is a passive OS fingerprinter. The last known site was *http://www.subterrain.net/projects/siphon/.*

sl4nt—Franz Krainer

This is a Windows replacement for *syslogd*. *http://www.netal.com/SL4NT03.htm*

SNMP for Perl 5—Simon Leinen

This is a package of Perl 5 modules providing SNMP support. *http://www.switch.ch/misc/leinen/snmp/perl/*

sock—W. Richard Stevens

This is a tool for generating traffic. It is a companion tool for Steven's book, *TCP/IP Illustrated,* vol. 1, *The Protocols. ftp://ftp.uu.net/published/books/stevens.tcpipiv1.tar.Z*

socket—Juergen Nickelsen

This program creates a TCP socket connected to *stdin* and *stdout*. *http://home.snafu.de/jn/socket/*

spidermap—H. D. Moore

This is a set of Perl scripts for network scanning. *http://www.secureaustin.com*

spray

This tool sends a burst of packets for load testing typically included with many systems.

ssh—Tatu Ylönen

This is a secure replacement for r-services. *http://www.ssh.com/*

ssyslog—Core SDI

This is a secure replacement for *syslog*. It has been replaced by *modular syslog. http://www.core-sdi.com/english/freesoft.html*

strobe—Julian Assange

This program locates all listening TCP ports on a remote machine. The last known official site was *ftp://suburbia.net/pub/strobe.tgz*.

swatch—Todd Atkins

This log management tool is suitable for use with *syslog* files. *http://www. stanford.edu/~atkins/swatch/*

syslog-ng—BalaBit IT Ltd.

This is an enhanced *syslog* that features filtering and sorting logs to different destinations. *http://www.balabit.hu/en/products/syslog-ng/*

Tcl/Tk—John Ousterhout

This is a general scripting language that has been extended to support many network management tasks. *http://dev.scriptics.com*

tcpdpriv—Greg Minshall

This program sanitizes *tcpdump* trace files. *http://ita.ee.lbl.gov/html/contrib/ tcpdpriv.html*

tcpdump—Van Jacobson, Craig Leres, and Steven McCanne

This is command-line–based packet capture program. *http://ee.lbl.gov/, http:// www.tcpdump.org,* or *ftp://ftp.ee.lbl.gov/tcpdump.tar.Z*

tcpflow—Jeremy Elson

This is a capture program that separates traffic into individual flows. *http:// www.circlemud.org/~jelson/software/tcpflow*

tcp-reduce—Vern Paxson

The program *tcp-reduce* and its companion program *tcp-summary* are Bourne shell scripts used to selectively extract information from *tcpdump* trace files. *http://ita.ee.lbl.gov/html/contrib/tcp-reduce.html*

tcpshow—Mike Ryan

This program reads and decodes *tcpdump* files. The official home for this is unknown, but it is available in several archives such as *http://www.cerias. purdue.edu/coast/archive/*.

tcpslice—Vern Paxson

This tool is used to create subsets of *tcpdump* trace files. *ftp://ftp.ee.lbl.gov/ tcpslice.tar.Z* or *http://www.tcpdump.org/related.html*

tcp-summary—Vern Paxson

The program *tcp-reduce* and its companion program *tcp-reduce* are Bourne shell scripts used to selectively extract information from *tcpdump* trace files. *http://ita.ee.lbl.gov/html/contrib/tcp-reduce.html*

tcptrace—Shawn Ostermann

This is a *tcpdump* trace analysis program. *http://www.tcptrace.org*

tcpwrappers—Wietse Venema

This daemon sits between user and services to log and manage connections. *ftp://ftp.porcupine.org/pub/security/index.html*

teraterm—T. Teranishi

This is a Windows telnet client that can be extended to support SSH. (See also *TTSSH.*) *http://hp.vector.co.jp/authors/VA002416/teraterm.html*

tjping—Top Jimmy

This is a *ping* and *traceroute* program for Windows. *http://www.topjimmy.net/tjs/*

tkined—Jürgen Schönwälder

This provides a network management program based on *scotty* and *Tcl/Tk*. *http://wwwhome.cs.utwente.nl/~schoenw/scotty/*

tmetric—Michael Bacarella

This tool finds available bandwidth. *http://netgraft.com/downloads/tmetric/*

top—William LeFebvre

This displays the most active processes on a system. *http://www.groupsys.com/top/about.html*

traceroute—Van Jacobson

This reconstructs the route taken by packets over a network. It is probably supplied with your system. *ftp://ftp.ee.lbl.gov/* or *http://ee.lbl.gov/*

trafshow—Vladimir Vorobyev

This full screen traffic capture program gives a continuous update on network traffic. Its last reported site was *http://www.rinetsoft.nsk.su/trafshow/index_en.html*.

trayping—Mike Gleason

This is a Windows tool that monitors connectivity using *ping*. *http://www.ncftpd.com/winstuff/trayping/*

treno—Matt Mathis

This is a tool to measure the bulk transfer capacity. *ftp://ftp.psc.edu/pub/net_tools/*

tripwire—Eugene Spafford and Gene Kim

This is a system integrity checker. *http://www.tripwire.com* or *http://www.tripwire.org*

ttcp—Mike Muuss

This is a load testing program for TCP. *ftp://ftp.arl.mil/pub/ttcp/ttcp.c*

TTSSH

This is a set of SSH extensions for Windows telnet program, *teraterm*. *http://www.zip.com.au/~roca/ttssh.html*

vnc—AT&T Laboratories, Cambridge

>   This tool displays X Window and Windows desktops on remote systems. *http://www.uk.research.att.com/vnc/*

WinDump and WinDump95—Loris Degioanni, Piero Viano, and Fulvio Risso

>   These are ports of *tcpdump* to Windows NT and Windows 95/98. *http://netgroup-serv.polito.it/windump/*

winping—Rich Morgan

>   This is another *ping* utility for Windows. *http://www.cheap-price.com/winping/*

xinetd—Panos Tsirigotis

>   This is a secure replacement for the *inetd* utility. *http://www.synack.net/xinetd/*

xlogmaster—Georg Greve

>   This is Greve's older log management software. You may want to check on the status of *AWACS* before using it. *http://www.gnu.org/software/xlogmaster/*

xplot—David Clark

>   A tool for graphing data in an X Window environment. There are several programs with this name, so be sure you have the right one. *ftp://mercury.lcs.mit.edu/pub/shep/*

xv—John Bradley

>   This is a modestly priced shareware program for the interactive display of images from an X Window system. You should probably try *gimp* first. *ftp://ftp.cis.upenn.edu/pub/xv*

B

Resources and References

A good network administrator is part librarian. Anyone who thinks he can learn everything he needs in this profession from a single book, or even a couple of dozen books, is lost in a fantasy world. This appendix is designed to get you up to speed quickly, but professional growth is a never-ending task. I am not attempting to be exhaustive or definitive here. I'm just trying to give some starting places that have worked for me. This is a personal overview of my favorites.

Sources of Information

While this appendix is devoted primarily to books, there is a variety of other obvious resources. You should already be familiar with most, but the following checklist may be useful in jogging your memory. It is in no particular order.

User groups

These seem less popular than they once were, but they still exist. For system administrators, USENIX at *http://www.usenix.org* and SAGE at *http://www.sage. org* are two good places to start.

Mailing lists

There are thousands of these. Finding ones that are helpful can be painful. Be prepared to subscribe, lurk, and then unsubscribe to a number of different lists (or visit their archives). Follow a list for a while before you start posting to the list.

Newsgroups

Keep in mind that you may find an answer in related groups. Your Solaris problem may be answered in a Linux newsgroup posting. A quick search of *Deja News* can sometimes be helpful.

Vendor web sites

> In networking and telecommunication, a vendor that doesn't maintain a reasonable web site probably should be avoided. This is the most obvious way to disseminate information about their products. Some vendors have excellent problem resolution sites, such as Microsoft's TechNet. Other sites, like Cisco's, contain such a staggering amount of information that whatever you want is there, but it can take forever to find it. Be prepared to spend a lot of time searching wherever you go.

Software web sites

> Don't forget the home pages for software, particularly operating systems. It is easy to forget about sites like *http://www.linux.org* and *http://www.freebsd.org*. And even minor tools may have a site devoted exclusively to them.

Chatrooms

> Frankly, I don't have time for chatrooms, but some people find them useful, particularly those devoted to specific pieces of software.

FAQ list

> This is often an excellent starting point, particularly when you are installing new software. Keep in mind these may change frequently, so make sure you are looking at a current list.

README files

> In the rush to get things running, many people skip these. If everything appears to work, they never go back. Don't forget to look at these even if you don't have a problem.

Comments in makefiles and source code

> This is a long shot, but if you are using open source software, there is an off chance you can find something of value.

Service contracts

> For some reason, some timid people seem reluctant to use their service contracts. If you have paid for a service contract, you should not be intimidated from placing reasonable calls.

> I always try to get an idea of what resources the technicians are using to answer my questions. I've had technicians send me some truly remarkable "internal" documents. Before I hang up, I always try to ask how I could have resolved the question without calling them. Most technicians seem delighted to answer that question.

Formal training

> This could be from the vendor or from a third party. This is a big business, particularly with the recent trend toward certification. Short courses can be very focused-providing exactly what you need. Beware, these courses can be

quite expensive and what you learn can become dated very quickly. Some companies, e.g., Microsoft and Novell, now cancel certification if you don't recertify within an established time limit.

Formal courses at colleges and universities tend to be more general and, consequently, often remain relevant for a much longer period of time. I would recommend a formal degree over certification any day, but I'm biased. Some potential employers may have different biases.

Printed and online vendor documentation

The undeniable trend is toward putting as much online as possible. This reduces costs and allows the user to search the material. With Unix, online manpages accessible through the *man* command are universally available. Recently, there has been a movement toward alternatives such as *info* pages, HOWTOs, AnswerBooks, and web-based documentation. Use whatever is appropriate to your system, but consider buying printed copies. I kill a lot of trees printing online documentation. I want something I can read in comfort and something I can write on. And then when I can't find what I've printed, I print it again, and again, and . . . .

Diagnostic software

This is often provided by the vendor with the initial purchase of their software or equipment or as downloads from their web site. It can supply the answer to your question. However, diagnostic software is often limited in what it can test. A clean bill of health from diagnostic software does not necessarily mean that there isn't a problem with the vendor's product.

Helpdesks

Keep in mind that many people use these in place of reading the documentation. The first person you talk to probably won't be very helpful (unless you didn't read the documentation). With perseverance, it is usually possible to get your call escalated a couple of times so that you end up talking to someone who is helpful. Be prepared to be on the phone for a while. And be polite!

Magazines and journals

For me, these are most useful for tutorials on new topics and for product reviews. I read *NetworkWorld* for general news and *NetworkMagazine* and *IEEE Computer* for articles with a little more depth. Cisco's *Internet Protocol Journal* is also a favorite. I also enjoy *Wired*. (Just don't believe everything you read in it.) Don't overlook business magazines. Knowing what company is about to fold can save you from making a costly mistake. Both the ACM and IEEE have online searches for registered users. For less technical information, *Computer Select* is an excellent (but expensive) source of information.

e-magazines and magazine web sites

There are a number of magazines or similar sites published online that you should not forget. These include *http://www.bsdtoday.com, http://www. linuxgazette.com,* and *http://www.oreillynet.com/meerkat/* among others. Also, many print magazines have web sites with back issues online. These sites, since the content has been edited and reviewed, are my first choice when searching the Web. Try *http://sw.expert.com, http://www.sunworld.com, http:// www.networkworld.com,* and *http://www.networkmagazine.com* for starters. Microsoft Windows users might try *http://www.zdnet.com/pcmag/.* There are many, many more.

Trade shows

While the first person you're likely to talk to will be a sales rep, there is probably a technical person lurking somewhere in the background to help out when the rep discovers she is out of her depth. This may be your only real chance to meet face-to-face with someone technically involved in a product.

Friends, colleagues, and teachers

Ask yourself who you know who might be able to help. But remember this is a two-way street, so be prepared to help others in the future. Always remember, even the best expert will sometimes provide poor advice.

Other network managers and administrators

People at similar institutions are often willing to share information. It's better, of course, to build a network of contacts before you need them. In particular, your predecessor, if he left on good terms, can be an ideal contact.

While these might be obvious resources, it is not uncommon to overlook one or more of them when trying to solve some hairy problem. You may want to highlight this list and add to it in the margin. Many of these sources have standards of etiquette that should be observed. Don't abuse them! Even if you are paying for the call and your contact can't answer your question, try to remain pleasant. Save your hostilities for calls from telemarketers.

References by Topic

This section describes books grouped by topic. Full bibliographical citations follow. Online sites like *http://www.amazon.com* and *http://www.bn.com* have replaced *Books in Print* for me. They make it easy to find out what is available for whatever topic I'm interested in. Bookstores and libraries are the best ways to see if a book is really useful. Even well-intentioned advertisements and reviews can be very misleading.

Often there is a lot of consistency, for better or worse, among books from the same publisher, so you may want to visit their web sites as well. For example, the majority of the books mentioned here are O'Reilly books because O'Reilly & Associates has specialized in Unix tool books longer than anyone else. Addison Wesley Longman does a very good job with some of the more theoretical treatments of protocols. Prentice Hall is a reliable source for textbooks on network related topics.

System Management

This book assumes that you understand the basics of system administration. If this isn't the case, you should consider several books. My top choices are *Unix System Administration Handbook* by Nemeth et al. and *Essential System Administration* by Frisch. Both provide extensive overviews of the tasks system administrators face. For general tools, you may want to look at *Unix Power Tools* by Peek, et al.

TCP/IP

You aren't going to get very far dealing with TCP/IP without a thorough understanding of the protocols. There are actually several approaches you can take, depending on your goal. The definitive treatments are in the relevant RFCs. These are probably too terse for most readers. They are certainly not where you will want to start if you are new to TCP/IP. (If you do use them, be sure to check the RFC-INDEX so that you are using the current version.)

If your goal is TCP/IP administration, then there are two paths you can take. *TCP/IP Network Administration* by Craig Hunt is an excellent general introduction. (PC users should look at *Networking Personal Computers with TCP/IP* by Hunt.) Alternatively, you might want to go to vendor-specific documentation for the operating system you are dealing with. These won't teach you the theory, but they will tell you enough to get something done.

If you want a general introduction to the TCP/IP protocol, there are several reasonable books. One good choice is Eric Hall's *Internet Core Protocols: The Definitive Guide*. This will give you a fairly complete picture that should meet your needs for quite a while. The book comes with Shomiti's Surveyor Lite on a CD-ROM in the back. This is a good place to start for most network administrators.

If you want a treatment with all the details of the protocols, and you are willing to put out the effort needed, there are two sets of books you should consider. *Internetworking with TCP/IP* by Douglas Comer et al. and *TCP/IP Illustrated* by W. Richard Stevens et al. Both are multi-volume sets running about 2000 pages per set. You'll get a pretty complete picture if you just read the first volume of either. Comer is somewhat more descriptive of general behavior and gives a better sense of history. His book is also a little more current. Stevens takes a hands-on, experimental approach, looking closely at the behavior of the protocols. You'll see more of the details in his book. Because of the sheer size of these, you'll need a high degree of commitment to make it through either.

Finally, if you want a good overview of routing algorithms, take a look at Perlman's *Interconnections* or Huitema's *Routing in the Internet*. Both are considerably more theoretical than most of the books listed here, but quite worthwhile.

Specific Protocols

When it comes to specific protocols, there are a number of books on each and every protocol. Here a few suggestions to get you started:

DNS

> For name services, *DNS and BIND* by Liu et al. is the standard.

Ethernet

> For a complete overview of Ethernet, the place to start is Spurgeon's *Ethernet: The Definitive Guide*. For Fast Ethernet and Gigabit Ethernet, you may want to add *Gigabit Etherenet* by Kadambi et al. to your collection.

Email

> Basic administration is discussed in the books listed under system administration and will probably meet your needs. The most commonly cited book on *sendmail* is *sendmail* by Costales et al. For IMAP, you might consider *Managing IMAP* by Mullet and Mullet.

NFS

> For NFS, you have a couple of choices. If you want to understand the inner working, consider Callaghan's *NFS Illustrated*. If you want to get NFS working, consider Stern's *Managing NFS and NIS*.*

PPP

> *PPP Design and Debugging* by Carlson is the best book on the internals. Sun's *Using & Managing PPP* is the place to turn to get PPP up and running.

SNMP

> There are a number of books on SNMP, none perfect. I think Held's *LAN Management with SNMP and RMON* and *Network Management: A Practical Perspective* by Leinwand and Conroy are readable introductions. Udupa's *Network Management Systems Essentials* does a very nice job of describing the standard MIB objects but is awfully dry reading. You may also want to visit *http://www.simple-times.org/*, an online magazine devoted to SNMP. If you are using Windows, you'll want to consider Murry's *Windows NT SNMP*.

---

* At the time this was written, the current version of Stern's book was quite dated but a second edition was in the works and is probably now available.

SSH

Get Barrett and Silverman's *SSH, the Secure Shell: The Definitive Guide.*

Web protocols

For an overview of a number of web services, consider getting *Managing Internet Information Services* by Liu et al.

There are a lot of other books out there, so keep your eyes open.

Performance

Performance is a difficult area to master and requires a lot of practical experience. Jain's *The Art of Computer Systems Performance Analysis* is a truly outstanding introduction to the theory and practice of performance analysis. But it won't supply you with much information on the tools you'll need. As a network administrator, you'll need to know the basics of system administration. For a practical introduction, you'll want to get Loukides' *System Performance Tuning*. This is primarily oriented to system administrators rather than network administrators, but it is a good place to start.

Troubleshooting

The definitive book on troubleshooting has yet to be written. I doubt it ever will be considering the breadth of the subject. One of the goals of this book is to introduce you to tools you can use in troubleshooting. But this is only one aspect of troubleshooting. There are other tool books, most notably Maxwell's *Unix Network Management Tools*. There is considerable overlap between this book and Maxwell's. This book covers considerably more tools, but Maxwell's provides greater depth and a different perspective on some of the tools. Both are worth having.

There are several other worthwhile books. Haugdahl's *Network Analysis and Troubleshooting* is a good overview, but more details would have been nice. Miller has several useful books. Two you might want to consider are *LAN Troubleshooting Handbook* and *Troubleshooting TCP/IP*.

Wiring

While this is a little off topic for this book, you won't get very far without good wiring. For a general introduction, look at *LAN Wiring: An Illustrated Guide to Network Cabling* by Trulove or, my personal favorite, *Cabling: The Complete Guide to Network Wiring* by Groth and McBee. For a more formal treatment, the TIA/EIA standards for cabling are available from Global Engineering Documents (*http://www.global.ihs.com/*). The two that are most useful are *TIA/EIA–606,* which discusses labeling and *TIA/EIA–568–A,* which discusses infrastructure. These standards are not easy reading. Visit your local library before you buy, as they are quite expensive.

Security

For general Unix security, nothing even comes close to *Practical UNIX & Internet Security* by Garfinkel and Spafford. This is a must-have for any Unix system administrator. For firewalls, you have several excellent choices. For general treatments, consider *Firewalls and Internet Security* by Cheswick and Bellovin or *Building Internet Firewalls* by Zwicky et al. If you are using Linux or OpenBSD, you might consider *Building Linux and OpenBSD Firewalls* by Sonnenreich and Yates. Don't forget security organizations like CERT at *http://www.cert.org* or CIAC at *http://www.ciac.org/ciac/.*

Scripting

Quite a few scripting languages are available for Unix. Apart from standard shell scripts, I use only Tcl and Perl, so I can't comment on the others. For Perl, I began with Schwartz's *Learning Perl* and now use *Programming Perl* by Wall et al. as a reference. For more detailed guidance with system administration tasks, you might also consider *Perl for System Administration* by Blank-Edelman.

For Tcl, Ousterhout's *Tcl and the Tk Toolkit,* while not necessarily the best, is the standard introduction. He did invent the language. For network applications, you might consider *Building Networking Management Tools with Tcl/Tk* by Zeltserman and Puoplo. If you just want a quick overview of Perl or Tcl, there are a number of tutorials on the Web.

Microsoft Windows

For Windows, you might begin by looking at Frisch's *Essential Windows NT System Administration* or the appropriate Windows Resource Kit from Microsoft. Frisch is more readable and doesn't always follow the Microsoft party line. The Microsoft documentation can be quite comprehensive. There are different versions for each flavor of Windows.

References

Barrett, Daniel, and Richard Silverman. *SSH, the Secure Shell: The Definitive Guide.* Sebastopol, CA: O'Reilly & Associates, Inc., 1999.

Blank-Edelman, David. *Perl for System Administration.* Sebastopol, CA: O'Reilly & Associates, Inc., 1999.

Callaghan, Brent. *NFS Illustrated.* Reading, MA: Addison Wesley Longman, 1998.

Carasik, Anne. *Unix Secure Shell.* New York, NY: McGraw-Hill, 1999.

Carlson, James. *PPP Design and Debugging.* Reading, MA: Addison Wesley Longman, 1998.

Cheswick, William, and Steven Bellovin. *Firewalls and Internet Security.* Reading, MA: Addison Wesley Longman, 1994.

Comer, Douglas. *Internetworking with TCP/IP: Principles, Protocols, and Architectures,* vol. 1, 4th ed. Upper Saddle River, NJ: Prentice Hall, 2000.

Costales, Bryan et al. *sendmail,* 2d ed. Sebastopol, CA: O'Reilly & Associates, Inc., 1997.

Frisch, Æleen. *Essential System Administration.* Sebastopol, CA: O'Reilly & Associates, Inc., 1991.

————. *Essential Windows NT System Administration.* Sebastopol, CA: O'Reilly & Associates, Inc., 1998.

Garfinkel, Simson, and Gene Spafford. *Practical UNIX & Internet Security.* Sebastopol, CA: O'Reilly & Associates, Inc., 1990.

Groth, David, and Jim McBee. *Cabling: The Complete Guide to Network Wiring.* Alameda, CA: Sybex, 2000.

Hall, Eric A. *Internet Core Protocols: The Definitive Guide.* Sebastopol, CA: O'Reilly & Associates, Inc., 2000.

Haugdahl, J. Scott. *Network Analysis and Troubleshooting.* Reading, MA: Addison Wesley Longman, 2000.

Held, Gilbert. *LAN Management with SNMP and RMON.* New York, NY: John Wiley & Sons, 1996.

Huitema, Christian. *Routing in the Internet,* 2d ed. Upper Saddle River, NJ: Prentice Hall, 2000.

Hunt, Craig. *Networking Personal Computers with TCP/IP,* 2d ed. Sebastopol, CA: O'Reilly & Associates, Inc., 1995.

————. *TCP/IP Network Administration,* 2d ed. Sebastopol, CA: O'Reilly & Associates, Inc., 1998.

Jain, Raj. *The Art of Computer Systems Performance Analysis.* New York, NY: John Wiley & Sons, 1991.

Kadambi, Jayant, Ian Crayford, and Mohan Kalkunte. *Gigabit Ethernet: Migrating to High-Bandwidth LANs.* Upper Saddle River, NJ: Prentice Hall, 1998.

Killelea, Patrick. *Web Performance Tuning.* Sebastopol, CA: O'Reilly & Associates, Inc., 1998.

Kurtzweil, Ray. *The Age of Spiritual Machines: When Computers Exceed Human Intelligence.* New York, NY: Viking Penguin, 1999.

Lehey, Greg. *Porting Unix Software.* Sebastopol, CA: O'Reilly & Associates, Inc., 1995.

Leinwand, Allan, and Karen Conroy. *Network Management: A Practical Perspective,* 2d ed. Reading, MA: Addison Wesley Longman, 1996.

Liu, Cricket et al. *Managing Internet Information Services.* Sebastopol, CA: O'Reilly & Associates, Inc., 1994.

Liu, Cricket, Paul Albitz, and Mike Loukides. *DNS and BIND,* 4th ed. Sebastopol, CA: O'Reilly & Associates, Inc., 1998.

Loukides, Mike. *System Performance Tuning.* Sebastopol, CA: O'Reilly & Associates, Inc., 1990.

Maxwell, Steve. *Unix Network Management Tools.* New York, NY: McGraw-Hill, 1999.

Miller, Mark. *LAN Troubleshooting Handbook,* 2d ed. New York, NY: M&T Books, 1993.

————. *Troubleshooting TCP/IP,* 2d ed. New York, NY: M&T Books, 1996.

Mullet, Dianna, and Kevin Mullet. *Managing IMAP.* Sebastopol, CA: O'Reilly & Associates, Inc., 2000.

Murry, James. *Windows NT SNMP.* Sebastopol, CA: O'Reilly & Associates, Inc., CA, 1998.

Nemeth, Evi et al. *Unix System Administration Handbook,* 3d ed. Upper Saddle River, NJ: Prentice Hall, 2001.

Ousterhout, John K. *Tcl and the Tk Toolkit.* Reading, MA: Addison Wesley Longman, 1994.

Peek, Jerry, Tim O'Reilly, and Mike Loukides. *Unix Power Tools,* 2d ed. Sebastopol, CA: O'Reilly & Associates, Inc., 1998.

Perlman, Radia. *Interconnections,* 2d ed. Reading, MA: Addison Wesley Longman, 2000.

Peter, Laurence, and Raymond Hull. *The Peter Principle.* New York, NY: W. Morrow, 1969.

Robichaux, Paul. *Managing the Windows 2000 Registry.* Sebastopol, CA: O'Reilly & Associates, Inc., 2000.

Schwartz, Randal. *Learning Perl.* Sebastopol, CA: O'Reilly & Associates, Inc., 1993.

Sonnernreich, Wes, and Tom Yates. *Building Linux and OpenBSD Firewalls.* New York, NY: John Wiley & Sons, 2000.

Spurgeon, Charles. *Ethernet: The Definitive Guide*. Sebastopol, CA: O'Reilly & Associates, Inc., 2000.

Stern, Hal. *Managing NFS and NIS*. Sebastopol, CA: O'Reilly & Associates, Inc., 1991.

Stevens, W. Richard. *TCP/IP Illustrated,* vol. 1, *The Protocols*. Reading, MA: Addison Wesley Longman, 1994.

Sun, Andrew. *Using & Managing PPP*. Sebastopol, CA: O'Reilly & Associates, Inc., 1999.

Thomas, Steven. *Windows NT 4.0 Registry: A Professional Reference*. New York, NY: McGraw-Hill, 1998.

TIA/EIA. *Administration Standard for the Telecommunications Infrastructure of Commercial Buildings (TIA/EIA–606)*. Englewood, CO: Global Engineering Documents, 1993.

————. *Commercial Building Telecommunications Cabling Standard (TIA/EIA–568–A)*. Englewood, CO: Global Engineering Documents, 1995.

Trulove, James. *LAN Wiring: An Illustrated Guide to Network Cabling*. New York, NY: McGraw-Hill, 1997.

Udupa, Divakara. *Network Management Systems Essentials*. New York, NY: McGraw-Hill, 1996.

Wall, Larry, Tom Christiansen, and Randal Schwartz. *Programming Perl*, 3d ed. Sebastopol, CA: O'Reilly & Associates, Inc., 2000.

Zeltserman, Dave, and Gerard Puoplo. *Building Networking Management Tools with Tcl/Tk*. Upper Saddle River, NJ: Prentice Hall, 1998.

Zwicky, Elizabeth, Simon Cooper, and D. Brent Chapman. *Building Internet Firewalls*, 2d ed. Sebastopol, CA: O'Reilly & Associates, Inc., 2000.

Index

We'd like to hear your suggestions for improving our indexes. Send email to *index@oreilly.com.*

About the Author

Joseph D. Sloan has been working with computers since the mid-1970s. He began using Unix as a graduate student in 1981, first as an applications programmer and later as a system programmer and system administrator. Since 1988 he has taught mathematics and computer science at Lander University. He also manages the networking computer laboratory at Lander, where he can usually be found testing and using the software tools described in this book.

Colophon

Our look is the result of reader comments, our own experimentation, and feedback from distribution channels. Distinctive covers complement our distinctive approach to technical topics, breathing personality and life into potentially dry subjects.

The animal on the cover of *Network Troubleshooting Tools* is a basilisk, a lizard belonging to the iguana family. Its name comes from the mythological basilisk (also known as a cockatrice), a reptile with a deadly gaze and breath, said to have been hatched from a rooster's egg by a serpent.

Though the two crests along their backs may make them look ferocious, basilisk lizards aren't deadly to anyone but the bugs and occasional worms and small animals they eat. They grow to about two or two and a half feet long, with most of that length in their tail. The banded basilisk is brown with a yellow stripe along each side of its body, and other basilisk species are green or brown.

Unlike their mythological counterparts, real basilisks are hatched from basilisk eggs. The female basilisk digs a shallow hole in moist dirt, lays up to 18 eggs in the hole, and covers them with dirt. Then she goes back to her swinging single basilisk life, leaving the eggs and later the young lizards to fend for themselves. They do this quite well, taking up residence in trees and finding their own food soon after hatching.

The talent that basilisks are most known for is their ability to do something that looks remarkably like walking on water. In reality, their webbed hind feet trap a bubble of air beneath them as they run, buoying them up so that their feet don't sink more than an inch or so below the water. A small basilisk can run like this for up to 60 feet without sinking.

Catherine Morris was the production editor and proofreader, and Norma Emory was the copyeditor for *Network Troubleshooting Tools*. Sarah Jane Shangraw, Emily Quill, and Claire Cloutier provided quality control. Jan Wright wrote the index.

Emma Colby designed the cover of this book, based on a series design by Edie Freedman. The cover image is a 19th-century engraving from the Dover Pictorial Archive. Emma Colby produced the cover layout with QuarkXPress 4.1 using Adobe's ITC Garamond font.

Melanie Wang designed the interior layout based on a series design by Nancy Priest. Anne-Marie Vaduva converted the files from Microsoft Word to FrameMaker 5.5.6 using tools created by Mike Sierra. The text and heading fonts are ITC Garamond Light and Garamond Book; the code font is Constant Willison. The illustrations that appear in the book were produced by Robert Romano and Jessamyn Read using Macromedia FreeHand 9 and Adobe Photoshop 6. This colophon was written by Leanne Soylemez.

Whenever possible, our books use a durable and flexible lay-flat binding. If the page count exceeds this binding's limit, perfect binding is used.

 # More Titles from O'Reilly

Unix System Administration

Essential System Administration, 2nd Edition

By AEleen Frisch
2nd Edition September 1995
788 pages, ISBN 1-56592-127-5

Covering all major versions of Unix, this second edition of *Essential System Administration* provides a compact, manageable introduction to the tasks faced by everyone responsible for a Unix system. Whether you use a standalone Unix system, routinely provide administrative support for a larger shared system, or just want an understanding of basic administrative functions, this book is for you. Offers extensive sections on networking, electronic mail, security, and kernel configuration.

Managing NFS and NIS, 2nd Edition

By Hal Stern, Mike Eisler & Ricardo Labiaga
2nd Edition July 2001
510 pages, 1-56592-510-6

This long-awaited new edition of a classic, now updated for NFS Version 3 and based on Solaris 8, shows how to set up and manage a network filesystem installation. *Managing NFS and NIS* is the only practical book devoted entirely to NFS and the distributed database NIS; it's a "must-have" for anyone interested in Unix networking.

The Perl CD Bookshelf, Version 2.0

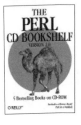

By O'Reilly & Associates, Inc.
May 2001
672 pages, Features CD-ROM
ISBN 0-596-00164-9

We've updated the *Perl CD Bookshelf* with the third edition of *Programming Perl* and our new *Perl for System Administration*. Our Perl powerhouse of O'Reilly guides also includes *Perl in a Nutshell*, *Perl Cookbook*, and *Advanced Perl Programming*, all unabridged and searchable.

Volume 8: X Window System Administrator's Guide

By Linda Mui & Eric Pearce
1st Edition October 1992
372 pages, ISBN 0-937175-83-8

This book focuses on issues of system administration for X and X-based networks—not just for Unix system administrators, but for anyone faced with the job of administering X (including those running X on standalone workstations).

Unix Backup & Recovery

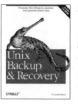

By W. Curtis Preston
1st Edition November 1999
734 pages, Includes CD-ROM
ISBN 1-56592-642-0

This guide provides a complete overview of all facets of Unix backup and recovery and offers practical, affordable backup and recovery solutions for environments of all sizes and budgets. It explains everything from freely available backup systems to large-scale commercial utilities.

Using Samba

By Bob Eckstein, David Collier-Brown & Peter Kelly
1st Edition November 1999
416 pages, Includes CD-ROM
ISBN 1-56592-449-5

Samba turns a Unix or Linux system into a file and print server for Microsoft Windows network clients. This complete guide to Samba administration covers basic 2.0 configuration, security, logging, and troubleshooting. Whether you're playing on one note or a full three-octave range, this book will help you maintain an efficient and secure server. Includes a CD-ROM of sources and ready-to-install binaries.

O'REILLY®

TO ORDER: **800-998-9938** • **order@oreilly.com** • **www.oreilly.com**
ONLINE EDITIONS OF MOST O'REILLY TITLES ARE AVAILABLE BY SUBSCRIPTION AT **safari.oreilly.com**
ALSO AVAILABLE AT MOST RETAIL AND ONLINE BOOKSTORES

Unix System Administration

Using & Managing PPP

By Andrew Sun
1st Edition March 1999
444 pages, ISBN 1-56592-321-9

This book is for network administrators and others who have to set up computer systems to use PPP. It covers all aspects of the protocol, including how to set up dial-in servers, authentication, debugging, and PPP options. In addition, it contains overviews of related areas, like serial communications, DNS setup, and routing.

UNIX Power Tools, 2nd Edition

By Jerry Peek, Tim O'Reilly & Mike Loukides
2nd Edition August 1997
1120 pages, Includes CD-ROM
ISBN 1-56592-260-3

Loaded with practical advice about almost every aspect of Unix, this second edition of UNIX Power Tools addresses the technology that Unix users face today. You'll find thorough coverage of POSIX utilities, including GNU versions, detailed bash and tcsh shell coverage, a strong emphasis on Perl, and a CD-ROM that contains the best freeware available.

The UNIX CD Bookshelf, 2nd Edition

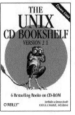

By O'Reilly & Associates, Inc.
2nd Edition February 2000
624 pages, Features CD-ROM
ISBN 0-596-00000-6

The second edition of The UNIX CD Bookshelf contains six books from O'Reilly, plus the software from UNIX Power Tools—all on a convenient CD-ROM. Buyers also get a bonus hard-copy book, UNIX in a Nutshell, 3rd Edition. The CD-ROM contains UNIX in a Nutshell, 3rd Edition; UNIX Power Tools, 2nd Edition (with software); Learning the UNIX Operating System, 4th Edition; Learning the vi Editor, 6th Edition; sed & awk, 2nd Edition; and Learning the Korn Shell.

How to stay in touch with O'Reilly

1. Visit Our Award-Winning Web Site

http://www.oreilly.com/

★ "Top 100 Sites on the Web" —PC Magazine
★ "Top 5% Web sites" —Point Communications
★ "3-Star site" —The McKinley Group

Our web site contains a library of comprehensive product information (including book excerpts and tables of contents), downloadable software, background articles, interviews with technology leaders, links to relevant sites, book cover art, and more. File us in your Bookmarks or Hotlist!

2. Join Our Email Mailing Lists

New Product Releases
To receive automatic email with brief descriptions of all new O'Reilly products as they are released, send email to:
ora-news-subscribe@lists.oreilly.com
Put the following information in the first line of your message (not in the Subject field):
subscribe ora-news

O'Reilly Events
If you'd also like us to send information about trade show events, special promotions, and other O'Reilly events, send email to:
ora-news-subscribe@lists.oreilly.com
Put the following information in the first line of your message (not in the Subject field):
subscribe ora-events

3. Get Examples from Our Books via FTP

There are two ways to access an archive of example files from our books:

Regular FTP
• ftp to:
  ftp.oreilly.com
  (login: anonymous
  password: your email address)
• Point your web browser to:
  ftp://ftp.oreilly.com/

FTPMAIL
• Send an email message to:
  ftpmail@online.oreilly.com
  (Write "help" in the message body)

4. Contact Us via Email

order@oreilly.com
To place a book or software order online. Good for North American and international customers.

subscriptions@oreilly.com
To place an order for any of our newsletters or periodicals.

books@oreilly.com
General questions about any of our books.

cs@oreilly.com
For answers to problems regarding your order or our products.

booktech@oreilly.com
For book content technical questions or corrections.

proposals@oreilly.com
To submit new book or software proposals to our editors and product managers.

international@oreilly.com
For information about our international distributors or translation queries. For a list of our distributors outside of North America check out:
http://www.oreilly.com/distributors.html

5. Work with Us

Check out our website for current employment opportunites:
http://jobs.oreilly.com/

O'Reilly & Associates, Inc.
1005 Gravenstein Hwy North
Sebastopol, CA 95472 USA
TEL   707-829-0515 or 800-998-9938
      (6am to 5pm PST)
FAX   707-829-0104

O'REILLY®

TO ORDER: **800-998-9938** • **order@oreilly.com** • **www.oreilly.com**
ONLINE EDITIONS OF MOST O'REILLY TITLES ARE AVAILABLE BY SUBSCRIPTION AT **safari.oreilly.com**
ALSO AVAILABLE AT MOST RETAIL AND ONLINE BOOKSTORES

International Distributors

http://international.oreilly.com/distributors.html • international@oreilly.com

UK, Europe, Middle East, and Africa (EXCEPT FRANCE, GERMANY, AUSTRIA, SWITZERLAND, LUXEMBOURG, AND LIECHTENSTEIN)

INQUIRIES
O'Reilly UK Limited
4 Castle Street
Farnham
Surrey, GU9 7HS
United Kingdom
Telephone: 44-1252-711776
Fax: 44-1252-734211
Email: information@oreilly.co.uk

ORDERS
Wiley Distribution Services Ltd.
1 Oldlands Way
Bognor Regis
West Sussex PO22 9SA
United Kingdom
Telephone: 44-1243-843294
UK Freephone: 0800-243207
Fax: 44-1243-843302 (Europe/EU orders)
or 44-1243-843274 (Middle East/Africa)
Email: cs-books@wiley.co.uk

France

INQUIRIES & ORDERS
Éditions O'Reilly
18 rue Séguier
75006 Paris, France
Tel: 33-1-40-51-71-89
Fax: 33-1-40-51-72-26
Email: france@oreilly.fr

Germany, Switzerland, Austria, Luxembourg, and Liechtenstein

INQUIRIES & ORDERS
O'Reilly Verlag
Balthasarstr. 81
D-50670 Köln, Germany
Telephone: 49-221-973160-91
Fax: 49-221-973160-8
Email: anfragen@oreilly.de (inquiries)
Email: order@oreilly.de (orders)

Canada

(FRENCH LANGUAGE BOOKS)
Les Éditions Flammarion ltée
375, Avenue Laurier Ouest
Montréal (Québec) H2V 2K3
Tel: 1-514-277-8807
Fax: 1-514-278-2085
Email: info@flammarion.qc.ca

Hong Kong

City Discount Subscription Service, Ltd.
Unit A, 6th Floor, Yan's Tower
27 Wong Chuk Hang Road
Aberdeen, Hong Kong
Tel: 852-2580-3539
Fax: 852-2580-6463
Email: citydis@ppn.com.hk

Korea

Hanbit Media, Inc.
Chungmu Bldg. 210
Yonnam-dong 568-33
Mapo-gu
Seoul, Korea
Tel: 822-325-0397
Fax: 822-325-9697
Email: hant93@chollian.dacom.co.kr

Philippines

Global Publishing
G/F Benavides Garden
1186 Benavides Street
Manila, Philippines
Tel: 632-254-8949/632-252-2582
Fax: 632-734-5060/632-252-2733
Email: globalp@pacific.net.ph

Taiwan

O'Reilly Taiwan
1st Floor, No. 21, Lane 295
Section 1, Fu-Shing South Road
Taipei, 106 Taiwan
Tel: 886-2-27099669
Fax: 886-2-27038802
Email: mori@oreilly.com

India

Shroff Publishers & Distributors Pvt. Ltd.
12, "Roseland", 2nd Floor
180, Waterfield Road, Bandra (West)
Mumbai 400 050
Tel: 91-22-641-1800/643-9910
Fax: 91-22-643-2422
Email: spd@vsnl.com

China

O'Reilly Beijing
SIGMA Building, Suite B809
No. 49 Zhichun Road
Haidian District
Beijing, China PR 100080
Tel: 86-10-8809-7475
Fax: 86-10-8809-7463
Email: beijing@oreilly.com

Japan

O'Reilly Japan, Inc.
Yotsuya Y's Building
7 Banch 6, Honshio-cho
Shinjuku-ku
Tokyo 160-0003 Japan
Tel: 81-3-3356-5227
Fax: 81-3-3356-5261
Email: japan@oreilly.com

Singapore, Indonesia, Malaysia, and Thailand

TransQuest Publishers Pte Ltd
30 Old Toh Tuck Road #05-02
Sembawang Kimtrans Logistics Centre
Singapore 597654
Tel: 65-4623112
Fax: 65-4625761
Email: wendiw@transquest.com.sg

Australia

Woodslane Pty., Ltd.
7/5 Vuko Place
Warriewood NSW 2102
Australia
Tel: 61-2-9970-5111
Fax: 61-2-9970-5002
Email: info@woodslane.com.au

New Zealand

Woodslane New Zealand, Ltd.
21 Cooks Street (P.O. Box 575)
Waganui, New Zealand
Tel: 64-6-347-6543
Fax: 64-6-345-4840
Email: info@woodslane.com.au

Argentina

Distribuidora Cuspide
Suipacha 764
1008 Buenos Aires
Argentina
Phone: 54-11-4322-8868
Fax: 54-11-4322-3456
Email: libros@cuspide.com

All Other Countries

O'Reilly & Associates, Inc.
1005 Gravenstein Hwy North
Sebastopol, CA 95472 USA
Tel: 707-829-0515
Fax: 707-829-0104
Email: order@oreilly.com

O'REILLY®

TO ORDER: **800-998-9938** • order@oreilly.com • www.oreilly.com
ONLINE EDITIONS OF MOST O'REILLY TITLES ARE AVAILABLE BY SUBSCRIPTION AT safari.oreilly.com
ALSO AVAILABLE AT MOST RETAIL AND ONLINE BOOKSTORES